SAP PRESS e-books

Print or e-book, Kindle or iPad, workplace or airplane: Choose where and how to read your SAP PRESS books! You can now get all our titles as e-books, too:

- ▶ By download and online access
- ▶ For all popular devices
- ▶ And, of course, DRM-free

Convinced? Then go to **www.sap-press.com** and get your e-book today.

Sales and Distribution in SAP® ERP—Practical Guide

SAP PRESS

SAP PRESS is a joint initiative of SAP and Galileo Press. The know-how offered by SAP specialists combined with the expertise of the Galileo Press publishing house offers the reader expert books in the field. SAP PRESS features first-hand information and expert advice, and provides useful skills for professional decision-making.

SAP PRESS offers a variety of books on technical and business-related topics for the SAP user. For further information, please visit our website: *www.sap-press.com*.

Matt Chudy, Luis Castedo
Procurement with SAP MM—Practical Guide
2014, 496 pp., hardcover
ISBN 978-1-59229-840-2

Matt Chudy, Luis Castedo
100 Things You Should Know About Sales and Distribution with SAP
2012, 363 pp., paperback
ISBN 978-1-59229-405-3

Janet Salmon
Controlling with SAP—Practical Guide (2nd edition)
2014, 700 pp., hardcover
ISBN 978-1-4932-1012-1

Ashish Mohapatra
Sales and Distribution in SAP: Functionality and Configuration
2010, 517 pp., hardcover
ISBN 978-1-59229-329-2

Matt Chudy, Luis Castedo, Ricardo Lopez

Sales and Distribution in SAP® ERP—
Practical Guide

Galileo Press

Bonn • Boston

Galileo Press is named after the Italian physicist, mathematician, and philosopher Galileo Galilei (1564–1642). He is known as one of the founders of modern science and an advocate of our contemporary, heliocentric worldview. His words *Eppur si muove* (And yet it moves) have become legendary. The Galileo Press logo depicts Jupiter orbited by the four Galilean moons, which were discovered by Galileo in 1610.

Editor Laura Korslund
Acquisitions Editor Emily Nicholls
Copyeditor Pamela Siska
Cover Design Graham Geary
Photo Credit Shutterstock.com: 72178102/© NAN728, 145915421/© bloomua, 179463953/© TTstudio
Layout Design Vera Brauner
Production Graham Geary
Typesetting SatzPro, Krefeld (Germany)
Printed and bound in the United States of America, on paper from sustainable sources

ISBN 978-1-4932-1054-1
© 2015 by Galileo Press Inc., Boston (MA)
2nd edition 2015

Library of Congress Cataloging-in-Publication Data
Chudy, Matt.
[Practical guide to sales and distribution in SAP ERP]
Sales and distribution in SAP ERP : practical guide / Matt Chudy, Luis Castedo, Richardo Lopez. -- 2nd edition.
pages cm
Includes index.
ISBN 978-1-4932-1054-1 (print : alk. paper) -- ISBN 1-4932-1054-8 (print : alk. paper) -- ISBN 978-1-4932-1055-8 (ebook) -- ISBN 978-1-4932-1056-5 (print and ebook : alk. paper) 1. Sales management--Computer programs. 2. Inventories, Retail--Data processing. 3. Inventory control--Data processing. 4. SAP ERP. I. Castedo, Luis. II. Lopez, Richardo. III. Title.
HF5438.35.C48 2014
658.8'10028553--dc23
2014039971

Contents at a Glance

Dear Reader,

The concepts of sales and distribution seem quite simple. But combine that with computer functionality, and you might find yourself with another animal altogether. This book is here to help you tame the beast: it's here to break sales and distribution processes in SAP down for you, and give you the steps you need to do your job, and do your job *well*.

Breaking down complex topics into digestible steps is a skill that's rarer than you might think. The authors of this book—Matt, Luis, and Ricardo—deserve the most thanks for taking their years of knowledge about SD and deconstructing it. I'm confident that their combined expertise will help you with the ins and outs of working with the SD component in SAP ERP.

What did you think about *Sales and Distribution in SAP ERP—Practical Guide*? Your comments and suggestions are the most useful tools to help us make our books the best they can be, and we encourage you to visit our website at *www.sap-press.com* and share your feedback.

Thank you for purchasing a book from SAP PRESS!

Laura Korslund
Editor, SAP PRESS

Galileo Press
Boston, MA

laura.korslund@galileo-press.com
www.sap-press.com

Contents

Preface

In today's competitive environment, the ability to handle business processes cost-effectively is critical. Sales and Distribution in SAP ERP (which, in this book, we'll refer to as SD) offers such a set of tools. As one of the most important and most often implemented SAP logistics functionalities, SD makes information more manageable and accessible.

With several books on the market covering details of SAP implementation from blueprinting to go-live and focusing mostly on members of the implementation teams, we came to the conclusion that the end user community doesn't really have anything readily available to help out in day-to-day operations. So, the target group for this book includes members of the end-user SD community who are executing sales and distribution transactions as part of their primary job function, "super-users" and system support members helping others solve issues, and all people trying to polish and master new functionality to better fit in the corporate positions, such as the following:

▶ Sales analysts

▶ Sales managers

▶ Shipping and transportation planners/managers

▶ Customer service representatives

What This Book Covers

This book provides you with a detailed, comprehensive guide to the day-to-day use of the key SD functions. Its objective is to give you an easy-to-use resource for learning how to perform all of the key functions of the system, how to trouble-shoot minor problems and system issues, how to explore advanced functions and reports, and how to get the most out of the system.

This publication serves both as a tutorial and reference for all key processes in sales and distribution.

The book starts out with a general introduction to SAP logistics processes and Sales and Distribution, and quickly moves on to the main processes: pre-sales, sales order processing, availability check, pricing, delivery, picking, transportation, and billing. **Chapter 1** will walk you through the basics of SAP ERP and will shed some light on enterprise structure building blocks mandatory for Sales and Distribution (SD) in SAP ERP to function. **Chapter 2** introduces you to some of the most important master data objects influencing your SD processes, and **Chapter 3** will describe some of the most important SD functions and transactions starting with inquiries, quotations, and contracts finishing with returns processes. **Chapter 4** will focus on the logistics aspects, including delivery processing, picking and packing, and transportation planning. **Chapter 5** will describe the billing process for you and integration points with Financial Accounting. **Chapter 6** will introduce some of the commonly used SD reports used to simply access and analyze data. In this second edition, we've added a few more chapters to cover updates to the SAP software, and provide insight on new skills that you can add to your arsenal. **Chapter 7** introduces you to some of the functions you can find if your business also runs SAP Customer Relationship Management; these functions will give you additional tools and also enhance existing SD functionality. We'll finish this book with **Chapter 8**, which explains some of the steps you'll need to know to work with Financial Supply Chain Management.

You'll also come across a few **appendices** in the back of the book. These will help you understand the basic navigation in an SAP system, and provide further insight into a few niche topics.

> **Note**
>
> Bonus downloads on SAP HANA and enhancement packages are available at *www.sap-press.com/3672*.

Our goal is to present detailed information in a compact format that includes enough material to fulfill the "80/20" principle—most of the focus will be on the top 20% of functions used by 80% of end users.

We hope you'll use the book as a reference to quickly search for and use practical information by topic and function.

There was a time in enterprise software when each area in a company used a different technology, a different vendor, and a different system, creating a corporate Babel Tower. SAP changed all that.

1   Introduction

It was 1972 when a group of five IBM engineers from Manheim, Germany— Dietmar Hopp, Hans-Werner Hector, Hasso Plattner, Klaus Tschira, and Claus Wellenreuther—decided to create the next big thing in systems history: the first enterprise resource planning (ERP) system.

At that time, the software industry was formed by a multitude of vendors; each had developed its own technologies, developed systems for functional business areas, and created software systems for accounting, inventory control, purchasing, order processing, and more. Each of these computer systems was designed differently and used different file systems, different programming languages, and often even different hardware platforms. To exchange information, different areas had to print out reports, and, many times, the information contained in the reports had to be captured in the other system.

Software has come a long way since 1972. In this chapter, we'll quickly overview today's SAP Business Suite, how an enterprise structure is set up in SAP software, and then focus our attention more specifically on executing logistics and explaining the Sales and Distribution component in SAP ERP.

1.1   The SAP Business Suite

Today, the SAP software catalog is vast and complex, including the enterprise resource planning application now known as SAP ERP (replacing R/3), which takes care of the day-to-day operations of a company. It also includes SAP Supply Chain Management (SAP SCM) for complex operations planning and SAP Business Warehouse (SAP BW) for complex decision making. In the following sections, we'll review the other tools within the SAP Business Suite.

1.1.1 SAP ERP

SAP ERP is used to execute the everyday operations of a company. A company can plan and execute the whole collection of steps involved in its supply chain, from the sales forecasts, master production scheduling, production planning, production scheduling, purchasing, inventory management, and warehousing to the logistics chain that's involved in shipping, transportation planning, and yard management.

At the heart of SAP ERP is the General Ledger (GL); like a hub and spokes, it touches every other component and functionality. Every time you sell, buy, pay, collect, or manufacture, the accounting system is updated. Values are posted to an account in the ledger to show a customer's balance, changes in inventory value, the payables needed to cover the vendors, and so on.

SAP ERP is divided into functional pieces called *components, modules,* or *functionalities*. Each functional area of a company might use one or more component or functionality, but many times a person's work won't involve more than one.

The following is a list of the components that are included in SAP ERP (we'll cover these in more detail in Section 1.3):

- ▶ Financial Accounting
- ▶ Controlling
- ▶ Project System
- ▶ Sales and Distribution
- ▶ Materials Management
- ▶ Logistics Execution
- ▶ Quality Management
- ▶ Plant Maintenance
- ▶ Production Planning and Control
- ▶ Human Resources or Human Capital Management

1.1.2 SAP PLM

SAP Product Lifecycle Management (SAP PLM) is a completely separate application that performs the activities involved in creating, developing, prototyping, and moving a new product into the manufacturing process. Some of the functions covered include the following:

► Portfolio planning (planning and tracking, budgeting)
► Development and manufacturing (product data management, engineering change management, variant configuration, recipe management, digital manufacturing)
► Service (maintenance of service manuals, product documentation, process definition for claim and warranty management, management of physical assets)

1.1.3 SAP CRM

SAP Customer Relationship Management (SAP CRM) is another separate application that helps companies with sales lifecycle management. It supports the following functions within the sales and marketing processes:

► Marketing (campaign management, branding, loyalty management, segmentation, e-marketing)
► Sales (e-commerce, interaction center, channel management, offer management)
► Service (interaction center, business communication, channel management, e-service)
► Contact Center (interaction center, business communication, marketing, sales, service, offer management)
► E-Commerce (e-marketing, e-commerce, e-service, web channel analytics)

1.1.4 SAP SRM

SAP Supplier Relationship Management (SAP SRM) was designed to automate, simplify, and accelerate procure-to-pay processes for goods and services with a very important focus on web-based operations and e-commerce. Some of the functions included in this application are listed here:

► E-sourcing (spend analysis, category and project management, requests for proposal, information and quotation, forward and reverse auctions, contract generation and management, supplier management)
► On-demand e-sourcing
► Contract lifecycle management
► SAP Spend Performance Management

1.1.5 SAP SCM

The SAP Supply Chain Management (SAP SCM) application is probably the most complex of all of the applications built around the original SAP ERP. It helps integrate complex supply chains into a single planning, execution, and monitoring system.

SAP SCM is capable of rapidly sharing information with your company's supply chain partners and enhancing the collaboration capabilities. SAP SCM evolved from SAP Advanced Planning & Optimization (SAP APO). Integration of the new collaboration and execution components made it a very powerful tool. Now it helps you deal with multi-plant capacity planning and scheduling, Global ATP management, distribution planning, and other complex functions that in many cases used to be executed outside of the ERP systems. The latest release of SAP SCM includes SAP Event Management and a completely redesigned SAP Extended Warehouse Management (SAP EWM) application designed to compete with the best of breed.

The following are some of the functions supported by SAP SCM:

- Planning (demand planning and forecasting, safety stock planning, supply network planning, distribution planning, strategic supply chain design)
- Execution (order fulfillment, procurement, transportation, warehousing, manufacturing)
- Supplier collaboration (access to supply chain information for demand and supply synchronization)
- Customer collaboration (replenishment management, vendor managed inventory)
- Contract manufacturer collaboration (extends the visibility of the manufacturing process)

Important Note

All of the preceding applications use SAP NetWeaver to communicate among themselves and with other non-SAP applications. The interfaces are known as *connectors* and serve as the highway through which the information runs from one application to another.

1.1.6 Financial Supply Chain Management

Financial Supply Chain Management is commonly known as FSCM or Financial Supply. It got its name from leveraging the advantages of successful models such as SCM (Supply Chain Management) that for several years have shown benefits. FSCM is a component of SAP ERP Financials suites and manages the cash-to-cash cycle. Financial Supply Chain Management integrates the supply chain of the cash flow to provide you with an incorporated module, improving visibility and cash control. In simple terms, FSCM effectively manages the demand and supply of cash and cash equivalents of a company, lowering the associated operational cost and even increasing customer satisfaction.

You will find that by using SAP FSCM, you have greater visibility and more control over the cash-related processes of a company. This is because FSCM integrates sales and logistics, finance and company operations to a more effective cash flow. Additionally, you'll discover that FSCM interconnected events of the working capital, product inventory, payment terms, credits and pricing and even the employee's behavior will give you a more harmonized view, including sales tendencies, usually impacted by the employee's bonuses or time of the year, as some examples.

Initially, the module was launched with five basic submodules such as Credit Management, Collection Management, Dispute Management, and Biller Direct, but now it's offered with additional functionality such as In-house Cash, Treasure and Risk Management, Cash and Liquidity Management, and more recently, Bank Relationship Management and Billing Consolidation.

In Chapter 8, we'll provide a deeper analysis of the FSCM functionality and submodules, including common transactions and how each subcomponent integrates with Sales and Distribution and your daily tasks.

1.1.7 SAP Enhancement Packages and Shipping Strategy

In 2006, SAP introduced a way to deliver new functionality without having companies spend time and effort to bring the latest features and technology. The objective was to alleviate the effort that you or any other SAP customer spends adopting, managing and implementing new software functionality on top of SAP ERP 6.0. Typically, when SAP had a new release or functionality available, it was delivered under a full software release or version such as version 3.1c, 3.1d, or

4.0. On more than one occasion, SAP clients decided to scrap their current ERP version to be able to better upgrade to the next one. Does this sound familiar to you? That strategy was not only risky to the overall well-being of the companies, but also allocated significant time, resources, and budget.

SAP has released enhancement package 7 as an optional package that customers can selectively install in their ERP systems. In the next couple of chapters, we will go into detail about the areas in which is SAP offering modified functionality or added features.

However, how can you understand what an SAP enhancement package (EHP) is? Moreover, what's the difference between an SAP enhancement package and an SAP Support Package?

Those two concepts are bound tightly together and certainly may cause you a lot of confusion, the same as any SAP end user. Everybody needs to understand the basics of these concepts and how they impact your daily activities. We describe the details and definitions on enhancement packages, SAP Notes, and Support Packages in the next section.

Enhancement Package Concept

Optional in nature, the EHP delivers SAP software innovations, which typically are described in three major categories: innovations for user interface (UI) simplifications, functional enhancements to any functionality, and Enterprise services. As we mentioned, EHPs are also cumulative and there is a major distinction between EHPs and Support Packages, discussed in detail later.

Figure 1.1 shows how the current strategy is designed to eliminate the expensive upgrades involved in traditional delivery by offering enhancement in smoother and shorter increments, while the business requirements are also in smaller increments.

SAP delivered EHP with the following main objectives:

▶ **Less disruption**
The EHPs are installed but activated only selectively and based upon the current needs of each client. They also can be selected as add-ons to any existing deployment or simply as a separate side-by side project or deployment.

▶ **Continuity**

The EHPs are cumulative and each contains previous EHPs. They also package consolidated functionality to be delivered on a continuous basis; more importantly, this saves clients time and money.

▶ **Ease**

Each EHP is provided as part of configuration and customization, which lowers the implementation effort. SAP has also provided a Software Update Manager (SUM), a tool to facilitate the process.

▶ **Functionality**

EHPs are redesigned to accumulate functionality that's delivered in Support Packages and In-Advance Shipments together, so you don't have to install each application individually.

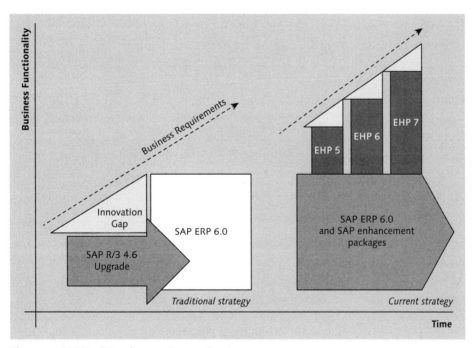

Figure 1.1 SAP Traditional versus Current Strategy

Since their introduction, EHPs have been based on a proven strategy and proven concept; therefore, SAP intends to keep the same as long as SAP ERP 6.0 is on the market. No major revisions of the SAP ERP 6.0 release are scheduled until several years in the future (2020). This is why you or any user should understand and manage EHPs not only as a concept, but also as way to increase productivity and as evolution to the current functionality.

SAP follows synchronized numbering for enhancement package delivery, starting with EHP 1 for ERP released in 2006 until 2013, when EHP 7 was released. EHP 7 includes SAP ERP (EHP 7), SAP CRM (EHP 3), SAP SCM (EHP 3), and SAP SRM (EHP 3). You can find more information about enhancement packages in the online download at *www.sap-press.com/3672*.

The screenshots in this book are based off of EHP 7.

SAP Notes

There are several classifications of SAP Notes, but in general they can be explained as a way to achieve continuous shipping support and corrections. In general, SAP allows you to communicate via Notes to report program errors or even make suggestions to SAP. In turn, SAP provides warranty support via program corrections or additions and even delivers certain functionality using SAP Notes delivered to customers. SAP Notes contain detailed instructions about known errors in SAP programs or routines. On other occasions, the SAP Notes could include workarounds or could provide correction instructions, with detailed steps on how to correct ABAP repository objects. In an SAP Note, you could also find the Support Package number where the note is included.

Support Packages

Support Packages (SP) are, in plain terms, accumulations of SAP Notes that are delivered at one time (corrections). Legal improvements, continuous improvements, and even interfaces are included in Support Packages. The SPs delivered functionality can be also implemented optionally and selectively.

In-Advance Shipments

In-Advance Shipments were created by SAP to make innovation available upfront to selected customers. They are also used by early adaptors in new technology or new functionality (one example is SAP HANA, which was optionally delivered to selected SAP customers in EHP 6 as an early adoption). Thereafter, In-Advance Shipments are incorporated into EHPs.

As shown in Figure 1.2, the SAP shipping elements together contain In-Advance Shipment, SAP Notes, and Support Package, constituting the continuous Shipment Strategy of SAP improvements delivered to you. SAP also claims that their SPs have no "side-effects;" they're easy to deploy and represent a minimum impact to your business.

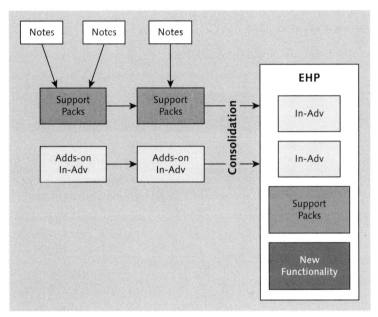

Figure 1.2 Elements of the SAP Shipping Strategy

Let's now discuss concepts on how the enterprise is represented in SAP software via the enterprise structure.

1.2 Enterprise Structure in SAP

Because it's a process-oriented application, SAP needs to reflect the company's structure. To do that, it has its own enterprise structure. This structure consists of several levels across various areas: a finance structure, logistics structure, manufacturing structure, sales structure, and so on. For our purposes, we need to get acquainted with the finance, logistics, and sales structures. See Figure 1.3 for an overview of the enterprise components. We'll discuss the SD structure in more detail later in this chapter.

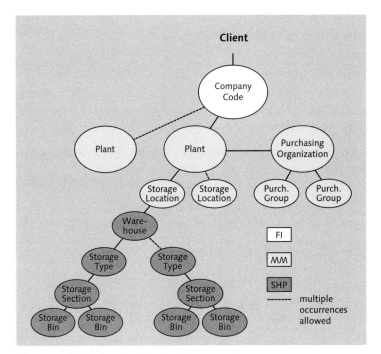

Figure 1.3 SAP Enterprise Structure Components

1.2.1 Client

The highest level in the SAP structure is a general level called the *client number*. The client number is the SAP instance in which we'll be working. You have to enter this number in the logon screen along with your user ID and password.

1.2.2 Company Code

Next is the *company code*, which is the first functional level, and it belongs to Financial Accounting. The company code reflects a company's legal entity. If your company is a conglomerate of companies, then your SAP instance probably has more than one company code. Each company code has a General Ledger.

The finance and controlling structure also consists of the following levels that provide reporting and consolidation capabilities:

▸ **Business area**
One company code can be divided into multiple business areas, and a business area can belong to more than one company code.

▶ **Company**

The company is hierarchically above the company code, and it's the smallest unit for which you can have a chart of accounts in the SAP system.

▶ **Credit control area**

This is the level at which all of the accounts receivables from a customer are totaled. This level can be defined across several company codes.

▶ **Funds management area**

The funds management area is the level at which you plan the expenditures of one or several company codes. It controls the budget management.

▶ **Dunning area**

The dunning area manages the communications with customers to ensure the collection of accounts receivables. In the SAP system, it groups together the different sets of procedures to communicate with customers under different circumstances.

▶ **Chart of accounts**

This contains the General Ledger accounts. A company code can only have one chart of accounts.

▶ **Controlling area**

Controlling areas put together information that has to be provided to external parties. A controlling area can group together several company codes.

1.2.3   Plant

The logistics structure reflects the operational structure of a company; at the top of the pyramid stands the *plant*. The plant is the element where a company's operations are executed (i.e., purchasing, production, inventory, and sales).

The plant should be an SAP element that reflects a physical location within the company structure. In other words, it's the SAP tool to reflect a manufacturing plant or a distribution center. In some cases, when the operations within a facility are too different from one another, you can also reflect two separate plants in the SAP system. For example, if you have a manufacturing plant that assembles radios in one wing and TV sets in another, then you might want to split it into two separate plants within SAP. Below the plant, there are several levels from different functional areas.

1.2.4 Storage Location

These are places where stock is kept. In the SAP system, the storage locations keep the quantity and value of every material a company uses. Every time a material is received from a vendor, used in a production order, or sold to a customer, the storage location reflects these changes in the stock levels and at the same time it updates the accounting General Ledger.

1.2.5 Warehouse

The warehouse number represents the physical warehouse complex, including all of the racks, cages, and crates that are used to store the product. While the storage location tells you how many units of a certain product you have and how much they are worth, the warehouse number tells you where in the warehouse to find them. It is built from a number of storage types, storage sections and finally storage bins. Basically, it's a system of coordinates to pinpoint a product location.

▸ **Storage type**
These definable logical and physical locations allow you to reflect either the physical layout of the facility or the logical division of zones based on the picking or putaway techniques. Storage type consists of one or more storage sections.

▸ **Storage section**
This structure gives you the ability to subdivide your storage type and you must have at least one section per storage type for the warehouse structure to function. Sections allow you to group together storage bins with similar features or uses.

▸ **Storage bin**
Storage type and storage section can contain one or several storage bins — for example, rack spaces or slots. This is the smallest available unit of space in a warehouse. The storage bin provides the information on location of the goods in the warehouse structure.

1.2.6 Purchasing Organization

This represents the different purchasing groups in your company. For example, if there is a group in charge of buying raw materials for manufacturing, another in charge of buying computer equipment, another one for capital assets, and so on, each of them could be set up in the SAP system as a different purchasing organization.

1.2.7 Purchasing Group

The purchasing groups represent the people in charge of procurement—simply put, the people responsible for buying things you need. Each purchasing group can have a name, telephone number, fax number, and email address. All this information is added to a purchase order when it's printed or sent to the vendor so users have a way of contacting the buyer.

1.3 SAP ERP Logistics: Components and Integration

Logistics in SAP ERP is built on a collection of applications, components, and functionalities that crisscross themselves, automating and recording materials and services requirements, external procurement, production, storage, quality management, foreign trade, and so on. It's been expanding release after release, bringing some of the former add-ons to a standard core set of functionalities. The current version of SAP ERP 6.0 includes many new functionalities that add new features, such as global trade management, compensation management, and agency business, but the core has not changed much throughout the years. Some companies may also be implementing components such as SAP Project System and SAP Environmental, Health, and Safety Management (SAP EHS Management). Common features used by almost all logistics subcomponents may also include handling unit management, batch management, engineering change management, and variant configuration.

Let's review some of the most important logistics components in a little bit more detail.

1.3.1 Materials Management

The Materials Management functionality in SAP ERP is one of the oldest functionalities and serves as a foundation for the logistics functions of the entire company. The key components of Materials Management include consumption-based planning, purchasing, inventory management, logistics invoice verification, and physical inventory. It houses key master data objects that are shared with other functionalities and includes the material master, service master, batch records, and vendor master.

Outside of integrated master data objects, such as the material master, which is shared by almost all of the ERP components and functionalities, there are also component-specific master data objects, such as purchasing info records, source lists, and quota arrangements. These are very important while executing the different system transactions, because the system will determine the correct data based on these master data records.

1.3.2 Sales and Distribution

Sales and Distribution covers the entire chain of processes (order-to-cash) from customer inquiry and sales orders to the delivery of products to the customer destination of choice through billing and payment collection. The components of logistics execution are also heavily integrated and include picking, packing, and shipping. We'll talk about SD functions later in this chapter in detail.

1.3.3 Logistics Execution

The Logistics Execution functionality of SAP ERP covers all product movements for your company—starting with goods receipts via inbound delivery, where goods are following the standard of pick, pack, and putaway. This is accomplished using the Warehouse Management (LE-WM) functions via transfer order processing. Then the goods can be moved internally within the plant between storage locations, using inventory management functions or using shipping functions via outbound delivery to execute cross-plant or cross-company movements. It can also involve the SAP Transportation Management (LE-TRA) functionality that allows grouping deliveries into a shipment or chain of shipments. The same process also applies to customer orders, where it's integrated into the sales order fulfillment part. If the WM functionality is implemented, a very granular process is available where transfer orders help in executing picking and packing, and where tasks and resources are managed efficiently with the use of RF (radio frequency) devices. Also, the yard management (LE-YM) functionality is available to streamline the dock and trailer yard operations. We'll touch base on the Logistics Execution processes throughout this book.

1.3.4   Production Planning and Control

The Production Planning functionality in SAP ERP helps you manage your company's production process. The production process starts with the analysis of your requirements and includes input from long-term or short-term forecasts, Sales and Operations planning, external planning tools such as SAP APO (Advanced Planning & Optimization), and material master settings.

The basic planning procedures are defined in different material requirements planning (MRP) types. Using consumption-based planning, the system looks at past consumption values and forecast or statistical calculations to determine future requirements.

The MRP procedure takes current and future sales figures as its base point to determine future requirements for the entire BOM structure, which produces better planning results than consumption-based planning.

Production Planning has its own master data objects, including work centers, routings, BOMs, and recipes, and allows you to execute capacity planning, master production scheduling (MPS), execute MRP, and perform and capture shop floor operations.

1.3.5   Plant Maintenance

The Plant Maintenance functionality is used to maintain the equipment and other technical infrastructure used by your company and your customers. It allows you to plan, schedule, and execute inspections, preventive maintenance, repairs, and refurbishment, as well as manage external services. Plant Maintenance has its own enterprise structure components, including maintenance plant, locations and plant sections, and master data applicable exclusively to Plant Maintenance, such as functional locations, work centers, equipments, and BOMs.

1.3.6   Customer Service

The Customer Service functionality helps companies service customers with warranty repairs and servicing of products where materials can either be sent back to you or your affiliates for repair or be maintained on site. If you manufacture and sell products with warranties, this functionality in SAP ERP will help your company maximize the efficiency of your service and repair operations. Customer

Service is frequently implemented in tandem with Quality Management, which helps resolve product quality issues.

1.3.7 Quality Management

The Quality Management functionality is fully integrated with other SAP functionalities and components, and it is configured to fit your company-specific requirements. Settings could be specific to industry sectors and geared to support FDA or GMP regulations.

The standard Quality Management functionality supports the classic quality management tasks such as quality planning, quality inspection, and quality control, as well as supplementary functions such as integration with Engineering Change Management (ECM). It's also fully integrated with other logistics components such as Materials Management, Production Planning, Sales and Distribution, Project Systems, Plant Maintenance, and Customer Service.

1.3.8 SAP Global Trade Management

SAP Global Trade Management (GTM) is part of the family of modules from the SAP ERP Business Suite. It was designed by SAP, taking into consideration those companies oriented to Global Operations with large scale trading contracts or partners around the world and involving multiple trading countries. The GTM application is delivered by SAP as an add-on, which means that you need to activate it to make it available for configuration and usage in SAP ERP.

You can activate GTM via the Configuration menu (SPRO) Logistics • General • Global Trade Management • Activate Components. During activation, you will find that GTM can be activated generally or specifically one functionality at a time based on your company needs.

GTM is particularly useful when purchasing and sales orders are involved in a transaction, even when they're triggered in parallel. General traders or commodity traders, wholesales, and importers or exporters are some typical SAP clients who use GTM as part of their ERP System. One of the main objectives of GTM is to keep and improve the effectiveness of the supply chain, primarily by integrating all elements of the logistics, accounting, and settlements to buyers as well as sellers.

GTM Processes

At first instance, you can say that domestic sales, domestic sales with receipt to warehouse, and foreign sales constitute the main processes covered by SAP GTM. Each begins with an inquiry followed by the draft contract, which in turn gets confirmation as a final contract. You can find an overview of the GTM components in Table 1.1.

GTM Component	Description
Trading Contract	Allows both sales and purchase orders to be maintained within a single transaction. You have control of both in one place. Based on the type of scenario you are running, a Trading Contract also is the integration between sales and purchase documents in ERP, such as in import trading contracts or export trading contracts.
Trading Execution Workbench (TEW)	TEW is a central tool or cockpit that helps you process trading contracts and subsequent components such as sales and purchase orders.
Position Management	GTM delivers a subcomponent to help you reduce inventory risks and loss of sales via two main functionalities: Portfolio Management and Association Management.
Trading Expenses	Trading incurred costs and commissions are controlled via Trading Expenses in GTM, including your freights, storage and loading costs, insurances, commissions and customs duties, among others.
Archiving Data in SAP Global Trade Management	This tool provided by GTM is very useful to keep reduced data to a minimum. Archiving data helps your system perform faster and is easy to maintain.
Differential Invoices	Differential Invoices enables business functions using Contract-to Cash for Commodities and Procure-to Pay for Commodities, to establish the differentials in Purchasing, Inventory Management, and Logistics.
Invoice Forecasting (IFW)	IFW is primarily a tool that enables current outstanding contracts to be invoiced. IFW is a real-time tool. It provides you with real-time prices of commodities, market prices, prices on the contract, average pricing, FX under consider periods, among others.

Table 1.1 Global Trade Management Components in SAP ERP 6.0

Sales and Distribution Integration

Global trading and trading business starts with a sales order for customers or a purchase order for vendors. The implementation and configuration of both Sales and Distribution and Material Management (MM) components and settings are mandatory. The customer and vendor master data should be configured to allow the GTM application to coexist and integrate properly (see Figure 1.4).

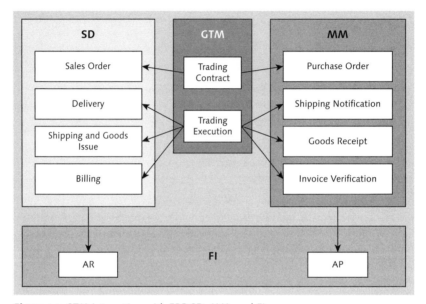

Figure 1.4 GTM Integration with ERP SD, MM, and FI

Additional SD elements such as pricing conditions and sales transactions are also required. Enabling purchasing transactions in the MM side is also essential to the well operation of the GTM application. Trading Contract interacts with sales orders as well as purchase orders, while Trading Execution interacts with Delivery, Shipping, and Billing on the SD side, as well as Shipping, Goods Receipts, and Invoice Verification on the MM side. AR and AP postings are placed throughout the supply chain cycle.

1.4   Sales and Distribution

The Sales and Distribution functionality in SAP ERP (which throughout this book we'll simply refer to as Sales and Distribution or SD), with the help of integration with other functionalities such as Materials Management and Logistics Execution, covers the entire order-to-cash process of your company. This is also one of the oldest applications, which was part of the SAP R/2 version.

SD has evolved to be a very robust and flexible functionality of the core SAP ERP solution that today is very well complemented by the SAP Business Suite packages such as SAP Customer Relationship Management (SAP CRM) covering the frontend of business activities and customer interaction, and by SAP Supply Chain Management (SAP SCM) covering the distribution and delivery end.

In this section, we'll describe the enterprise structure components (see Figure 1.5 for an overview of all structures that are used in SD), talk about the sales area, and define the main activities that we'll be covering in later chapters. Let's start with pre-sales, credit management, order processing, picking, shipping, transportation, and billing.

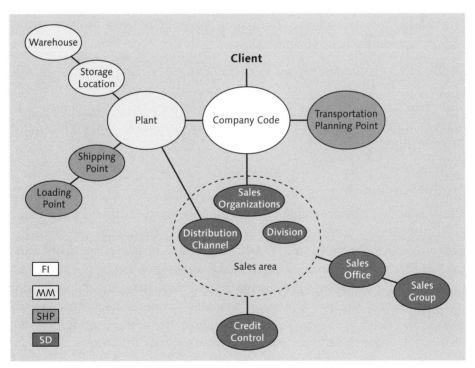

Figure 1.5 Enterprise Structure Overview and Integration in SAP ERP

1.4.1 Organizational Structure in Sales and Distribution

The SAP system allows complex multitudes of business units to be defined and to represent the functional and legal structure of your company. As described in previous sections, every business activity in the SAP system is transparent and may be recorded by multiple functionalities or components that use different enterprise structures supporting them in an integrated fashion. SD is integrated as well and joined with Financial Accounting, Materials Management, and Logistics Execution components such as Shipping & Transportation.

Sales Organization

The sales organization has an enterprise structure in logistics that's defined for distributing goods and services. This structure can mirror the business presence of your sales organization and mimic regional structure or international layout. The SAP system requires at least one sales organization to be defined for the SD functionality to work. A sales organization has to be assigned to the company code for accounting to be integrated.

Bear in mind that more than one sales organization can be assigned to a single company code. All activities within this structure are reported at the sales organization level as a summation level. The sales organization has its own address, currency, and calendar that can be different and unique to each sales organization you've defined.

Distribution Channel

The distribution channel identifies a unique way for your customers to obtain goods and services from your company, such as wholesale, retail, Internet sales, and so on. By design, to use the SD functions, you need at least one distribution channel. A distribution channel doesn't have addresses, calendars, or currencies to maintain. They're defined in the parent object: the sales organization. Each distribution channel can span across one, some, or all of your sales organizations. You can also assign one or more plants to a combination of sales organization and distribution channel, but you need at least one for SD to function. After you define the distribution channel, you'll be able to do the following:

▶ Define materials and services master data.

▶ Create and maintain your customer master data.

- Allow for complex pricing strategies.
- Define determination of sales document types.
- Use the channel in sales statistics.

Division

This SAP enterprise structure is usually based on a wide group of products or services. Just like a distribution channel, a single division can be assigned to multiple sales organizations, and you need exactly one division for SD to function. Your material and customer master data has parts that are specific to the division, therefore allowing you to maintain business activity limited to a narrow group of goods and services.

> **Note**
>
> A material master record can belong to only one division and is maintained on the master data tab SALES: SALES ORG. DATA 1.

You can make customer-specific agreements, set pricing, set terms of payment, and perform statistical reporting that limits the data selection to a specific division.

> **Note**
>
> Customer master data is specific to a division and is one of the key structures used in master data maintenance.

Sales Office

In the SAP system, the sales office is optional. You can use SD without creating sales offices. If your organization needs this granularity of data, you should know the following:

- A sales office can be assigned to one or more sales areas.
- A sales office can consist of sales groups, usually representing a salesperson or a group of salespeople.
- You can maintain an address for the sales office.
- The sales office acts as a selection criterion for sales document maintenance.
- You can use a sales office to determine the output for your sales documents.

Sales Group

In the standard SAP system, the definition of sales groups is optional and usually represents the salesperson or a group of salespeople. You can use the SD functionality without creating any sales groups. However, if you're using this in your system, it allows you to do the following:

- Assign a salesperson to the code representing a sales group.
- Assign a sales group to one or more sales offices.
- Select the sales group as a criterion for sales documents.
- Use this structure to influence printer determination for your sales documents output.

Sales Area

The main component required for SD to function is the sales area. A sales area is built from a combination of sales organization, distribution channel, and division described earlier. Basically, the sales area defines the distribution channel that a specific sales organization can use to sell products or services of a particular division. See Figure 1.6 for a layout showing the basic sales area.

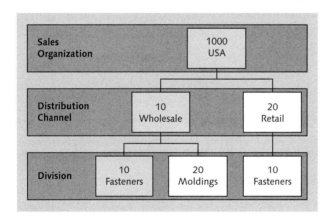

Figure 1.6 Basic Sales Area Structure

In this figure, you should identify three sales areas:

- **Sales Area 1:**
  - Sales Organization: 1000

- ▶ Distribution Channel: 10
- ▶ Division: 10
- ▶ **Sales Area 2:**
  - ▶ Sales Organization: 1000
  - ▶ Distribution Channel: 10
  - ▶ Division: 20
- ▶ **Sales Area 3:**
  - ▶ Sales Organization: 1000
  - ▶ Distribution Channel: 20
  - ▶ Division: 10

Credit Control Area

The credit control area is a Financial Accounting organizational unit that maintains and monitors credit limits for customers. A credit control area can be assigned to one or more company codes. It isn't possible, however to assign a company code to multiple control areas. Multi-currency credit limits aren't supported within single credit control areas.

Plant, Storage Location, and Warehouse

To procure, store, and distribute goods and services, you need a Materials Management structure called a plant, which we discussed earlier in this chapter. The plant is linked to the company code, which is defined in SAP ERP Financials Financial Accounting. It's also linked to the Sales Organization and Distribution Channel, integrating all three together—Materials Management (material inventory) and Financial Accounting (where all transactions are recorded on the company books).

To inventory your products, you also need a storage location or multiple storage locations representing your warehouses, including at least one for SD to function and fulfill the deliveries.

To get down to the bin level management of your goods, you also create a warehouse structure that can be assigned to one or more storage locations.

Shipping Point

The enterprise structure component responsible for the distribution activities is a shipping point. This logical definition can mirror your physical shipping dock, mail depot, or a group of people responsible for distribution activities. You can have multiple shipping points per plant, but you need at least one for the shipping functionality to be available. More than one plant can also be assigned to a shipping point, although this is recommended only for plants that are close to each other. A shipping point has its own address and calendar, influencing the scheduling and processing of deliveries to customers, as well as your own replenishment deliveries. The shipping point also influences the pick storage location determination together with plant and shipping condition. The organizational assignment of the shipping point is carried out at plant level.

> **Note**
>
> Single sales orders or stock transport orders can have multiple lines and multiple deliveries. A single delivery can be processed only by one shipping point.

Loading Point

Shipping points can have loading points, representing structures such as loading docks, and can be assigned during delivery processing. You can also assign the name of the person responsible for the loading dock location. Loading points are optional and aren't required for the shipping functionality to work.

Transportation Planning Point

The transportation planning point is assigned to the company code and allows for planning and execution of shipments (documents that group one or more deliveries). Transportation planning points can represent a physical transportation department responsible for type of shipment, geographical territory responsibility, and have its own address. You need at least one for transportation functionality to be available. You can have one or more transportation planning points for a company code, but you can't share the transportation planning points among multiple company codes.

1.4.2 Processes in Sales and Distribution

The SAP software package is designed to capture almost any business activity, and if the standard functionality isn't available, it allows you to create custom solutions to close the gap between the pre-packaged application and the desired state. Out-of-the-box SD functionality covers most of the standard business functions that are universal for most industries. See Figure 1.7 for a quick process overview.

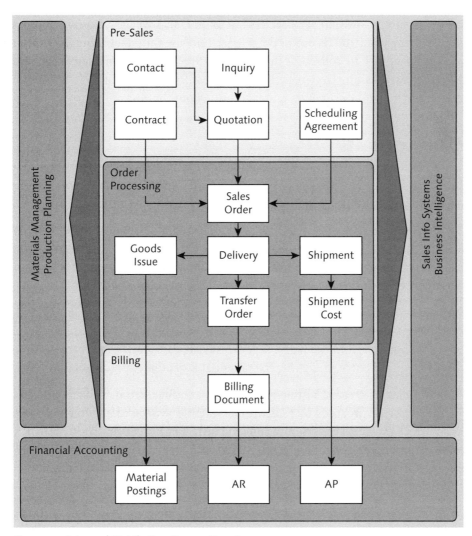

Figure 1.7 Sales and Distribution Process Overview

Pre-Sale Activities

In real-life scenarios, before the sale takes place, your business needs to collect basic data and create master records in the system for either existing or potential customers. You'll create data for contact people, sales prospects, and existing customers, and you'll also maintain data about your competitors. After this foundation is established, the actual contact with the sales prospects is made and can be recorded as an SD document in the form of inquiry or quotation. These documents can help you determine important sales-related data that can be accessed for reporting purposes, to evaluate sales activities, and finally to convert to sales orders, giving you a full record of the sales activities from establishing the contact with the customer to collecting the payment. Storage of the pre-sales data also helps with establishing large contracts and scheduling agreements. We'll cover all of the activities and documents in detail throughout the rest of this book.

Order Processing

Order processing is built on myriad activities and usually starts with recording the actual sales order, then procurement steps if goods or services aren't available, followed by delivery picking, packing, and shipping to the final destination.

The sales order document stores the data of customer's firmed request for your goods or services. The system uses master data you've maintained and established to fulfill this request. Sales orders are recorded either by your own sales force or directly by customer via web front, EDI, or XML interface messages.

The sales order contains customer information, partner data (sold-to, ship-to, bill-to), material, quantity, pricing, delivery date, and shipping and transportation information required for delivery. A goods availability check is performed at the time of the order entry, triggering the potential procurement requests as needed.

The requirements created by the sales order can be filled from available on-hand stock inventories, procured by replenishment that is processed by internal source such as stock transport orders or production orders or by external sources such as purchase orders replenishing your in-house stock levels, or via third-party delivery—performed by external supplier shipping goods directly to your customer on your behalf.

On the shipping due date, the delivery documents are created, and the route is determined if you are using the SAP Transportation Management software. You can then start the process of picking, packing, staging, and loading, if you're using all of these steps in your business process. If you are using SAP WM functionality (lean warehouse management or standard Warehouse Management in SAP ERP), you're using transfer orders to initiate picking. The transfer order includes data copied from the delivery document. Standard SAP functionality provides some complicated picking methods such as grouped deliveries, wave picking, and two-step. Transfer orders can be processed as printed pick tickets or in electronic form using RF devices on the warehouse floor. The confirmation of the transfer order completes the picking activities. If you use the transportation functionality, you can also start collaborating with freight service providers, start the tendering process, and finish up by creating the shipment cost document, which captures the payable activities related to the delivery of goods to your customers. Delivery packing list and bill of lading output are usually triggered at the completion of these steps.

The posting of the goods issue completes the process and results in stock movement or a confirmation of service that changes your on-hand inventory balance, reducing it and updating the balance sheet accounts in Financial Accounting.

Billing

The last step before collecting your customer's payment is creating a billing document or invoice that is sent to the customer's bill-to party for payment request. Just as with the delivery document, data is copied from either the sales document or the delivery document and other billing documents, creating credit or debit memos. When you create the billing document, account determination is performed, and appropriate GL account postings are executed that debit the customer's receivables and credit the revenue account.

Financial Accounting

As we touched on earlier in this chapter, the integrated philosophy of SAP is showing you how all activities, in one form or another, end up recorded in the balance sheet accounts in Financial Accounting.

The material documents recorded when the goods issue was posted, and a subsequent accounting document stored the stock movement data. The transportation service provider purchase order ended up as an entry for accounts payable, and the incoming payment from the customer was also posted against the invoice (billing document) submitted in the earlier steps.

Additional activities may also be performed when differences are reconciled and potentially resolved with either credit or debit memos.

All activities in the SD process end up reflected in the system as documents, master data, and pricing records, and they are used as a foundation for the sales info system (SIS) or SAP Business Warehouse for reporting.

1.4.3 SAP HANA Overview and SD Application

In this section, we explain in simple terms what SAP HANA has to offer, how your daily job will be impacted by this technology, and also what SAP HANA is and how it impacts the Sales and Distribution component.

Let's begin by saying that SAP HANA is a piece of technology that allows you to process massive analysis of real-time data in the memory of the servers. This means no more delays or long hours spent on a Friday night running that report required by Monday. Without being too technical, SAP HANA is becoming the platform for current and future SAP analytics and applications. This is the reason why it's important to understand the basics of SAP HANA to manage the coming changes better.

> **Note**
>
> SAP HANA stands for *high-performance analytic appliance* and relates to an in-memory, relational database management system developed by SAP.

SAP HANA for the Cloud, Mobile, and Social Media

SAP now supports cloud computing. In October 2012, HANA One was announced as a variation of the original SAP HANA technology, which uses a smaller amount of memory via Amazon Web Services. In 2013, SAP HANA also began offering the HANA Cloud Platform (hosting services and cloud environment), and SAP HANA enterprise cloud (enterprise solutions for SAP Business Suites and Business Warehouse as Service). Mobile and social networks are supported by a real-time data platform in SAP to allow you uniformity and a faster data analysis.

SAP HANA functions are delivered to SAP ERP via Services Packages (SP) rather than the regular software versioning (see Section 1.1.7).

SAP HANA Impact on Sales and Distribution (SD)

As of EHP 6 with SAP HANA, only SAP HANA-Optimized is delivered with functionality for SD. SAP HANA also provides you with a platform to develop applications and is expected in a near SP to have more SD applications based on this new technology. SAP HANA significantly expedites the time spent running Sales and Distributions reports. Do you remember having to stay longer at work running the billing list or the shipping list? Or having to trigger them via a nightly batch process just to find out the next day they weren't finished yet? SAP HANA-Optimized could be the solution.

SAP HANA-Optimized and How It Can Help You in Sales and Distribution

SAP HANA-Optimized is part of business intelligence (BI) that uses HANA technology. SAP HANA-Optimized BI content uses DataSources and BEx queries to expedite analysis of SD reports such as sales overviews, delivery, pricing conditions, service levels, and even SD backorders. SAP delivers BEx queries using MultiProvider, which enables you to run reports at a more granular level without the loading of data into an InfoCube (real-time data). In contrast to the current InfoCube in BI, data upload is required.

> **MultiProvider**
>
> InfoProviders and MultiProviders are the objects or views that are relevant for reporting. A MultiProvider is a type of object that combines data from a number of InfoProviders for reporting purposes.

SAP delivers the following SD BEx queries that run on MultiProviders applicable to Sales and Distribution. They'll be discussed in detail in the online download (refer to *www.sap-press.com/3672*).

- Sales Overview (/IMO/SD_M10),
- SD-DLV: Service Level (/IMO/SD_M50)
- Delivery (/IMO/SD_M20)
- Delivery Overview (/IMO/SD_M20_Q0001)

- Billing SD-DLV: Backorders (/IMO/SD_D51):
- Billing SD-DLV (/IMO/SD_D30):
- Pricing Conditions (/IMO/SD_M40)

1.5 Summary

In this chapter, we provided a lot of information as briefly and simply as possible, including a history of SAP, a discussion of enterprise structure, and an overview of key SD processes. You should now understand all enterprise structure components of SAP ERP. You should also be able to recognize SD-specific enterprise structure components and understand the core integration points with other functionalities. Understanding these components provides a great foundation to continue with the next chapters, where we'll discuss master data and sales processes in detail.

Master data might very well be the one piece in an SAP ERP implementation that can make the difference between getting the expected results or not.

2   Master Data

What is master data? In SAP terms, master data refers to the collections of the products you sell, the materials you use to manufacture them, the bills of materials (BOMs) with the components for each product, and the list of your company's customers and vendors. It also refers to the rules governing the relationship with your business partners (e.g., customers and vendors, detailing prices, discounts, and terms).

SAP transactions take the information contained in the master data and use it to produce a result. This result may be a sales order, purchase order, production order, or bill, to mention just some of the different documents that SAP works with.

In this chapter, we'll take a look at the most influential master data objects for Sales and Distribution.

2.1   Importance of Master Data

Master data in the SAP system and specifically in Sales and Distribution (SD) is the foundation on which transactions are executed. When you create a sales order in the SAP system, for example, you have to enter the customer number for the party you are selling to and the material number of the product you are selling.

Based on this information, the system will determine the price and discounts that you can offer this client, shipping address, place where you are shipping the materials from, shipping conditions, and shipping methods. It will also determine what kind of information will need to be passed on to the warehouse so that they can start picking the product and be able to pack and ship it.

As you see, when you create transactional data, the system makes determinations for the execution of that business process. All of these determinations have to be based on business rules, and on the master data that is involved in that transaction.

So, if you want to obtain accurate results, you need your master data to be accurate. The more time that's invested in making sure that the master data is correct and complete, the better your transactional results will be, and you'll be able to substantially reduce the time you need to invest in correcting or completing incomplete or incorrect transactions. In the end, this will result in higher customer satisfaction.

If you make sure that the material master data for SD has been created for all of the relevant sales organizations and channels your clients belong to, then you are off to a good start. You can also double-check that your customers have complete sales and shipping data so that the product can be delivered to them. You can do that by running Transaction XD03 (Display Customer Master) or by following the menu path LOGISTICS • SALES AND DISTRIBUTION • MASTER DATA • BUSINESS PARTNER • CUSTOMER • CHANGE • COMPLETE. On the initial screen, enter the account and select the CUSTOMERS SALES AREAS button. You'll see a list of sales areas activated for your customer. We'll talk about customer master data maintenance in detail later in this chapter.

Pricing is another important element. You need to make sure that the relevant pricing condition records and price lists have been created. This will help you avoid errors in the value of the sales orders. Pricing will be discussed in detail in later chapters.

Records are also kept in the system to calculate freight charges, and you need to be sure to maintain them regularly because prices vary depending on the freight company, the distance, the mode of transportation, and even the season of the year.

Important

Master data isn't static, and it's important to maintain master data constantly and accurately. If you understand and apply this message, your SAP experience will be much more productive and much less stressful.

2.2   Business Partners

To initiate any transaction in the system, such as creating a sales order or purchase order, you must have master data objects defined. This includes your business partners. In SAP ERP, you can clearly divide these business partners as
follows:

▶ **Customers**
A business partner to whom you are providing goods or services. Customers
can be external or internal, and if that customer is also providing you with
goods and services, you can link the customer master record to a vendor master. Individual customer master records can be defined for specific partner
functions and can be linked together.

▶ **Vendors**
A business partner who provides your company, affiliates, or external customers directly with goods and services. Vendors can also be both internal and
external, such as your distribution warehouses or other affiliates procuring
goods within your organization. Also, if your vendor is buying goods and services from your organization, you can link the vendor master record to the customer master.

▶ **Other partners**
Includes a mix of things such as site data, contact person, sales personnel, and
competitors. Some of these objects can also be linked to other business partner
master records.

2.2.1   Account Group and Number Ranges

Before you can create a customer master record for a business partner, you have
to assign an account group. Depending on the configuration setting, you may
need to specify the account number using an external number range, or let the
system assign the internal number range for you. The selected account group will
determine the following for you:

▶ Display screens, their sequence, and fields that are mandatory for entering data

▶ Partner functions valid for the account group and partner function combinations

2.2.2 Partner Functions

In real-life scenarios, if the customer who places an order is the same customer who receives the delivery of goods and pays the invoice, you'll have one customer master record assigned to all mandatory partner functions. If, on the other hand, your customer-affiliated company places an order and its headquarters pay the invoice, you'll have a separate customer master record with set of accounts responsible for different functions, in which the sold-to party who placed the order, the ship-to party who received the delivery, and the invoiced party are all different.

You can define partner function relations using the customer organizational structure. You can create links between the partner functions in the customer master record of the sold-to party, as shown in Figure 2.1.

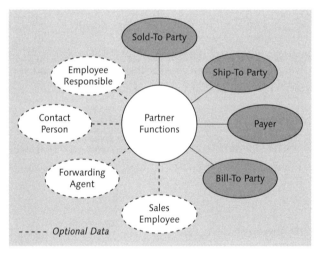

Figure 2.1 Partner Function Sample Structure

In a real business scenario, you have to replicate the customer hierarchy to some degree. You are probably getting orders from multiple business units, shipping your goods to a number of customer warehouses, and billing a corporate office, for example. The SAP system provides you with some of the most common business partner codes, as well as gives you the flexibility to co-create new ones. The following are some of the partner functions available in SAP ERP:

▶ **Sold-to party**
   This is a person or company that places an order for your goods or services. It

also stores data on sales, such as the assignment to a sales office or a pricing procedure. It's coded as SP in the standard SAP predelivered version.

▸ **Ship-to party**
This receives the goods provided by your company or a third-party supplier. The ship-to partner record also stores data such as unloading points and receiving hours.

▸ **Bill-to party**
This receives the billing document or invoice list for the goods provided by your company. This partner record houses the address, printing-related data, and electronic communication information.

▸ **Payer**
This sends the payment for your invoices and stores bank data and billing schedule information.

> **Note**
>
> Define your partner functions as simply as possible. It makes your master data maintenance straightforward and clean, especially if you're dealing with multiple systems and multitudes of legacy applications.

2.2.3 Customer Master Data Structure

Customer master records group information based on the level of detail, from the most general to very specific. Customer master data stores the information that is relevant for the different SAP functionalities. The customer master is broken down into general data, company code, and SD data. Go to Transaction XD03 (Customer Master Display) or use the menu path LOGISTICS • SALES AND DISTRIBUTION • MASTER DATA • BUSINESS PARTNER • CUSTOMER • CHANGE • COMPLETE. Several different data tabs are available. The following sections explain each data group.

General Data

General data applies globally to one, unique business partner for all your defined business organizational structures. As you can see in Figure 2.2, the standard screen shows the address information on the GENERAL DATA tab screen. This section includes the following tabs:

► ADDRESS

This is where you store the name of the customer, search terms for fast entry, physical address, and, if needed, the PO box information and communication information such as phone numbers, fax, and email address.

► CONTROL DATA

This is where you can link your customer with the vendor master records, and add reference data further defining the industry, location, transportation zone, tax, and VAT information.

► PAYMENT TRANSACTIONS

This tab stores the customer's bank information and alternative payer data.

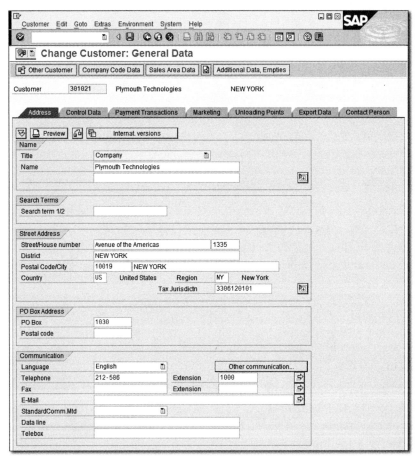

Figure 2.2 Customer Master – General Data Section

- MARKETING

   This tab stores classification data, including Nielsen ID and industry-specific information about your customer, including key figures such as annual sales, number of employees, and so on.

- UNLOADING POINTS

   This is where you can maintain the detailed information about the destination of your shipments by specifying the unloading points, departments, and hours of operations.

- EXPORT DATA

   Here you can maintain the boycott and embargo dates, preventing restricted customers from receiving any of your goods if needed, and you can set the usage to military or civilian and maintain classifications.

- CONTACT PERSON

   This tab holds the miscellaneous master data object that allows you to create a detailed contact list of people that you're communicating with. You can keep records of their home address, personal data, and visiting hours.

> **Note**
>
> If you maintain a customer master record without specifying a sales area or a company code, the system will display general data screens only.

Company Code

The company code data is the next segment of the customer master and applies to one unique company code, storing information relevant to Financial Accounting. If you had multiple company codes, you would have multiple records created. This section includes the following tabs:

- ACCOUNT MANAGEMENT

   This tab stores accounting data such as reconciliation accounts, interest calculations, and reference data, including the previous account number, personnel number, and buying group.

- PAYMENT TRANSACTIONS

   This tab records the terms of payment and tolerance group, and allows you to enable payment the history recording. Here you can also set the time for the deposited checks to clear for monitoring purposes. You can also maintain information for automatic payment transactions.

▶ CORRESPONDENCE
In this tab, you can maintain data related to dunning procedures and accounting clerk data responsible for communication with the customer, and set payment notices to be sent to your customer after the payments clear.

▶ INSURANCE
This tab records the insurance policy number, provider, and amount insured, as well as the validity dates of the export credit insurance.

▶ WITHHOLDING TAX
In this tab, you can maintain the tax withholding data by selecting the tax types, tax codes, and validity periods applicable to them.

Sales and Distribution Data

Data maintained in the SALES AND DISTRIBUTION DATA section influences the order-to-cash functions. SD data is specific to the sales area that the customer master is extended to and can be different for each sales area in scope. The information is grouped by functional influence of the order-to-cash processes and includes the following:

▶ SALES
This is where you can store the sales office, sales group information, and order currency, and you can maintain the pricing data that influences the procedure determination during order processing.

▶ SHIPPING
The data set here will help you during outbound delivery processing, where you can maintain delivery priority, shipping conditions, order combination, your preferred delivery plant that will ship the goods, and partial delivery settings and tolerance levels.

▶ BILLING DOCUMENTS
Here you can maintain data relevant to subsequent invoice processing, set rebates and price determination for customer hierarchy nodes, set valid calendars for invoice and invoicing lists dates, maintain incoterms for your deliveries, set terms of payment, assign the credit control area, set account assignment group that the system uses as one of the criteria during the determination of

revenue accounts, and set taxes relevant for the destination country and valid tax conditions.

▶ PARTNER FUNCTIONS

As you saw in previous sections, you can maintain the partner functions data by assigning the mandatory partners and their account numbers as needed. These partner functions are used in partner determination procedures to specify mandatory functions for processing a particular order/document type.

2.2.4 Customer Hierarchies

Customer hierarchies allow you to create flexible objects to reflect the organizational structure of your customers. For example, if your customer has a very complex purchasing department, or multiple distribution centers or retail stores, you can build hierarchies to reflect these structures. Figure 2.3 shows a sample customer hierarchy displayed in the maintenance transaction (VDH1N).

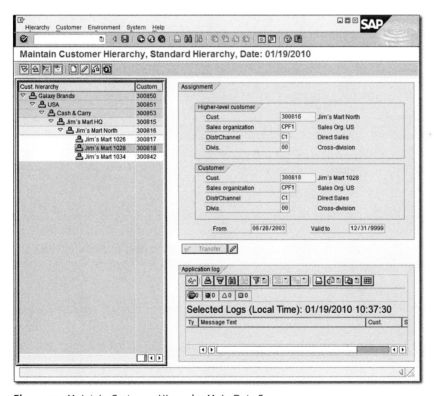

Figure 2.3 Maintain Customer Hierarchy Main Data Screen

You can use customer hierarchies in sales order and billing document processing for both partner and pricing determination (including rebate determination) and for statistical reporting in profitability analysis (CO-PA) and in the Sales Information System (SIS). You can also use customer hierarchies to assign price conditions and rebate agreements to one of the customer's subordinate hierarchy levels, making it valid for all subordinate levels.

> **Note**
>
> For each hierarchy node marked as relevant for pricing, you can create a pricing condition record. If one or more nodes in a hierarchy contain pricing data, it's automatically used during order processing.

2.2.5   Processing Customer Master Data

As we discussed in the previous sections, there are multiple data objects that you can maintain for your business partners. Figure 2.4 identifies the location of the maintenance transactions on the standard SAP menu path (SAP Menu • Logistics • Sales and Distribution • Master Data • Business Partner).

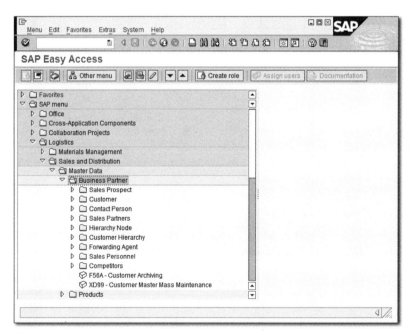

Figure 2.4 Business Partner Data Maintenance Menu Path

You can create, change, and display master data records for all of the partner functions. There are several ways to do this, depending on your company's security policy. You should be able to create the complete customer master record or partial records, restricted to GENERAL and SALES DATA sections. You can access the business partner maintenance using transaction codes that follow the SAP rule of 3sm where the numbers in Transaction *xx01* stands for create, *xx02* for change, and *xx03* for display functions. Or you can navigate to the transactions using the SAP Easy Access menu paths. To maintain general data for your customer master, all you need is the customer account number. To maintain the company code and related accounting data, you also need the company code number. Finally, to maintain sales data, you have to specify the sales area. Table 2.1 lists the transactions available to maintain the customer master.

Transaction Code	Menu Path
XD01 – Create Complete	LOGISTICS • SALES AND DISTRIBUTION • MASTER DATA • BUSINESS PARTNER • CUSTOMER • CREATE • COMPLETE
XD02 – Change Complete	LOGISTICS • SALES AND DISTRIBUTION • MASTER DATA • BUSINESS PARTNER • CUSTOMER • CHANGE • COMPLETE
XD03 – Display Complete	LOGISTICS • SALES AND DISTRIBUTION • MASTER DATA • BUSINESS PARTNER • CUSTOMER • CHANGE • COMPLETE
VD01 – Create Sales and Distribution	LOGISTICS • SALES AND DISTRIBUTION • MASTER DATA • BUSINESS PARTNER • CUSTOMER • CREATE • SALES AND DISTRIBUTION
VD02 – Change Sales and Distribution	LOGISTICS • SALES AND DISTRIBUTION • MASTER DATA • BUSINESS PARTNER • CUSTOMER • CHANGE • SALES AND DISTRIBUTION
VD03 – Display Sales and Distribution	LOGISTICS • SALES AND DISTRIBUTION • MASTER DATA • BUSINESS PARTNER • CUSTOMER • CHANGE • SALES AND DISTRIBUTION

Table 2.1 Customer Master Transaction Codes

Although most of the business partner types can be maintained from the same group of transactions, some partner details may be restricted because of your security access settings. To create a complete record, you're better off using the transactions created especially to maintain these records, which are listed in Table 2.2.

Transaction	Menu Path
Sales Prospect	
V+21 – Create	LOGISTICS • SALES AND DISTRIBUTION • MASTER DATA • BUSINESS PARTNER • SALES PROSPECT • CREATE
Contact Person	
VAP1 – Create	LOGISTICS • SALES AND DISTRIBUTION • MASTER DATA • BUSINESS PARTNER • CONTACT PERSON • CREATE
VAP2 – Change	LOGISTICS • SALES AND DISTRIBUTION • MASTER DATA • BUSINESS PARTNER • CONTACT PERSON • CHANGE
VAP3 – Display	LOGISTICS • SALES AND DISTRIBUTION • MASTER DATA • BUSINESS PARTNER • CONTACT PERSON • DISPLAY
Sales Partners	
V+23 – Create	LOGISTICS • SALES AND DISTRIBUTION • MASTER DATA • BUSINESS PARTNER • SALES PARTNERS • CREATE
Hierarchy Node	
V-12 – Create	LOGISTICS • SALES AND DISTRIBUTION • MASTER DATA • BUSINESS PARTNER • HIERARCHY NODE • CREATE
Customer Hierarchy	
VDH2N – Display	LOGISTICS • SALES AND DISTRIBUTION • MASTER DATA • BUSINESS PARTNER • CUSTOMER HIERARCHY • DISPLAY
VDH1N – Edit	LOGISTICS • SALES AND DISTRIBUTION • MASTER DATA • BUSINESS PARTNER • CUSTOMER HIERARCHY • EDIT

Table 2.2 Business Partner Maintenance Transactions

Whenever a customer master record is created, there is another record that your company will discontinue, block, or archive. Also, customer hierarchies are maintained the same way, requiring you to update validity, and add or remove nodes or customers.

Master data groups within your organization will also monitor and make mass changes to your business partner master records. There are additional transactions to perform these functions as well, as you can see in Table 2.3 for commonly used functions.

Block/Unblock	
XD05 – Block/Unblock	ACCOUNTING • FINANCIAL ACCOUNTING • ACCOUNTS RECEIVABLE • MASTER RECORDS • MAINTAIN CENTRALLY • BLOCK/UNBLOCK
VD05 – Block	LOGISTICS • SALES AND DISTRIBUTION • MASTER DATA • BUSINESS PARTNER • CUSTOMER • BLOCK
Flag for Deletion	
XD06 – Set Deletion Indicator	ACCOUNTING • FINANCIAL ACCOUNTING • ACCOUNTS RECEIVABLE • MASTER RECORDS • MAINTAIN CENTRALLY • SET DELETION INDICATOR
VD06 – Flag for Deletion	LOGISTICS • SALES AND DISTRIBUTION • MASTER DATA • BUSINESS PARTNER • CUSTOMER • FLAG FOR DELETION
Display Changes	
XD04 – Complete	LOGISTICS • SALES AND DISTRIBUTION • MASTER DATA • BUSINESS PARTNER • CUSTOMER • DISPLAY CHANGES • COMPLETE
VD04 – Sales and Distribution	LOGISTICS • SALES AND DISTRIBUTION • MASTER DATA • BUSINESS PARTNER • CUSTOMER • DISPLAY CHANGES • SALES AND DISTRIBUTION
OV51 – Several Customers	LOGISTICS • SALES AND DISTRIBUTION • MASTER DATA • BUSINESS PARTNER • CUSTOMER • DISPLAY CHANGES • SEVERAL CUSTOMERS
Other Transactions	
OV50 – Master Data Comparison	LOGISTICS • SALES AND DISTRIBUTION • MASTER DATA • BUSINESS PARTNER • CUSTOMER •MASTER DATA COMPARISON
F56A – Customer Archiving	LOGISTICS • SALES AND DISTRIBUTION • MASTER DATA • BUSINESS PARTNER • CUSTOMER ARCHIVING
XD99 – Customer Master Mass Maintenance	LOGISTICS • SALES AND DISTRIBUTION • MASTER DATA • BUSINESS PARTNER • CUSTOMER MASTER MASS MAINTENANCE
XD07 – Change Account Group	LOGISTICS • SALES AND DISTRIBUTION • MASTER DATA • BUSINESS PARTNER • CUSTOMER • CHANGE ACCOUNT GROUP

Table 2.3 Business Partner Maintenance Transactions

2.3 Products

The products functionality in SAP ERP includes the information related to the products and services your company sells and also gives you the flexibility to group them in frequently used lists to speed up order processing.

2.3.1 Material

Most of the information about products resides in what is called the material master. The material master is a collection of data about everything your company sells, buys, or transforms.

There are several types of products a company can sell, which are under the MATERIAL menu:

▶ **Trading goods**
In standard SAP, defined as material type HAWA. These are products that your company buys and then resells without any transformation. This could be the case of a wholesaler such as D&H selling IT products (software, hardware, and licenses) or a sales company that acquires manufactured goods from companies such as HP, IBM, and Microsoft, and then sells them to retailers or end customers.

▶ **Non-stock materials**
Delivered as material type NLAG. These are materials that you don't actually keep in a warehouse. A good example is software that is downloaded from a "digital warehouse" instead of a tangible CD shipped from a warehouse.

▶ **Services**
In standard SAP, defined as DIEN. If your company is in the service industry, then all of the different services you provide to your customers must be created as such in the material master.

▶ **Packaging materials**
Identified as material type VERP. These are the materials that will contain or wrap your products when shipped from the warehouse. Examples of packaging materials are boxes, crates, containers, and so on.

▶ **Competitive products**
Defined in SAP as WETT. Some companies decide to keep material master records for products of their competitors to keep track of the product characteristics and also how they compare to their own products.

▶ **Other materials**
In some cases, companies sell raw materials, sometimes because they have excessive inventory or because other business partners use them as parts for repairing your finished products. In these cases, you also need to maintain sales data for those raw materials so you can process them in sales documents.

In the material master, you keep generic information such as the SKU number, a brief description of the item, dimensions, weight, and unit of measure. You can also classify the item by assigning it a material group and a place in the product hierarchy. This is also where you can assign an EAN code.

Specific information is also grouped in views. In the material master, there are basic and sales views.

Basic Views

As we've mentioned, the basic view contains information that all departments in a company use. The following is a list of some of the most important basic views fields:

▶ Material Number
This is the number that *uniquely* identifies the SKU item in the system. In the SAP system, the number can be assigned automatically by the system using internal number ranges or can be assigned by the user using external number ranges. In your company, you'll have internally or externally assigned numbers, depending on your own needs and business definitions.

▶ Cross Plant Material Status
This field communicates the stage in the product's lifecycle. These statuses are maintained during the configuration of the system and tell you that the material is, for example, in development, released for sales, blocked, or discontinued. This field doesn't just provide information—it drives specific functionality based on the configuration of the system, allowing or blocking certain business functions, such as buying or selling.

▶ Base Unit of Measure
Every material is handled differently. For example, if you work in the chemical industry, you might be selling your products by either weight or volume. So your materials' unit of measure may be kilograms, pounds, liters, or fluid ounces. This allows you to know how much stock is available for sale in the

warehouse and how much of your product is ordered by your customer. In the consumer product industry, you most likely sell your products by the piece, so *piece* would be the base unit of measure.

▶ Net Weight, Gross Weight, and Volume
These fields are very important for shipping and transportation activities. If these values are inaccurate, your company may be overpaying postage on shipments, or overloading trucks, which in both cases will result in stopped shipments and unsatisfied customers.

▶ Product Hierarchy and Material Group
These two fields help you classify your products. If your company, for example, sells sporting goods, then you might have a materials group that segregates golf products from clothing, from baseball products, and so on. The material group uses nine characters, and it's mostly used by Materials Management. The hierarchy does a similar classification but it can be more granular. You could have several levels that would allow you to build a product family tree. Product hierarchy having 18 characters available is mostly defined for sales functionality. Other important features of the material group and product hierarchy are that they are used by SAP ERP Financials to derive special postings and profitability analysis. They are also used for special pricing, such as promotions and offers. As you can see in Figure 2.5, an aluminum bat would be assigned a hierarchy value of 10203040, showing that it belongs to the Bat family under the Baseball Products family that also belongs to the Sporting Goods family.

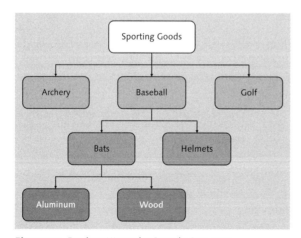

Figure 2.5 Product Hierarchy Sample Structure

▶ DIVISION

This is another field that helps you classify your company's products. Division, such as most fields in the material master, determines functionality behavior. In this case, the division determines sales and business areas. This field, in conjunction with the customer master data, helps you determine whether a product can be sold to a customer or not.

Sales Views

This set of material master views is very important for SD functions, driving things such as pricing, taxes, item category determination, and more. Figure 2.6 shows a sample sales view of a material master.

▶ SALES UNIT OF MEASURE

There are some cases in which you sell materials using a different unit than the SKU. Sales unit of measure is related to base unit of measure by maintaining a conversion factor in alternative unit of measure section on material master. This can be further explained with a simple example: The material base unit of measure is defined as 1 piece; however, when you sell it, you are using a sales unit—a box containing 24 pieces—if you sell them in bulk only. The maintained conversion in the material master will be set to alternative unit of measure: 1 box = 24 pieces.

▶ X-DISTR.CHAINSTATUS

Like the X-Plant Status, this field helps the system identify part numbers that might not be sellable because of the part's development status.

▶ DELIVERING PLANT

This field directs the system's shipping and inventory functions to the plant they should use in a sales document to withdraw the material from.

▶ TAX DATA

This section of the sales views indicates the tax relevance for this item in the different regions where it's sold, including the country, tax category, and whether the material is relevant for this taxation.

▶ MINIMUM ORDER QUANTITY

This field sets the minimum quantity that can be sold to a customer. Depending on the configuration, it can send an error when creating a sales order or just give a warning message.

Figure 2.6 Sales General View of a Material Master

▶ MINIMUM DELIVERY QUANTITY

This field limits the minimum quantity, which can be a partial quantity of the *minimum sales quantity*. You can still create the deliveries though despite the system issues warning message.

▶ GENERAL ITEM CATEGORY GROUP and ITEM CATEGORY GROUP

These two fields direct the system into determining the item types or groups that will be used in a sales document to determine item categories and corresponding schedule lines.

Although there are several other fields in the sales views, and in general in the material master, these fields tend to be the most problematic and need to be set properly or they'll cause the most problems during sales document processing. There are other views in the material master that influence how functionalities integrate with SD, including accounting, costing, and plant views, but we aren't going to cover the entire material master plethora of fields. For this conversation, we need to focus on the sales-specific data directly impacting sales documents. Table 2.4 provides a list of transactions for material master maintenance.

Transaction	Menu Path
MMH1 – Create Trading Goods	LOGISTICS • SALES AND DISTRIBUTION • MASTER DATA • PRODUCTS • MATERIAL • TRADING GOODS • CREATE
MMN1 – Create Non-Stock	LOGISTICS • SALES AND DISTRIBUTION • MASTER DATA • PRODUCTS • MATERIAL • NON-STOCK • CREATE
MMS1 – Services	LOGISTICS • SALES AND DISTRIBUTION • MASTER DATA • PRODUCTS • MATERIAL • SERVICES • CREATE
MMV1 – Create Packaging Materials	LOGISTICS • SALES AND DISTRIBUTION • MASTER DATA • PRODUCTS • MATERIAL • PACKAGING MATERIAL • CREATE
MMH1 – Competitive Product	LOGISTICS • SALES AND DISTRIBUTION • MASTER DATA • PRODUCTS • MATERIAL • COMPETITIVE PRODUCT • CREATE
MM01 – Other (or any of the above)	LOGISTICS • SALES AND DISTRIBUTION • MASTER DATA • PRODUCTS • MATERIAL • OTHER MATERIAL • CREATE
MM02 – Change (any material type)	LOGISTICS • SALES AND DISTRIBUTION • MASTER DATA • OTHER MATERIAL • CHANGE
MM03 – Display (any material type)	LOGISTICS • SALES AND DISTRIBUTION • MASTER DATA • OTHER MATERIAL • CHANGE

Table 2.4 Material Master Maintenance Transactions

2.3.2   Item Proposal

The item proposal functionality gives you the ability to create lists of materials that are regularly bought by one customer. Depending on the configuration of your sales orders, and also in combination with data in the customer master, it can automatically suggest items while creating sales orders.

You can maintain the product proposal for a sales area that your materials and customers are extended to. After the record is created, you have to assign your product proposal record to the customer master.

Let's create an item proposal with the following procedure.

1. Use Transaction VA51 or follow the menu path LOGISTICS • SALES AND DISTRIBUTION • MASTER DATA • PRODUCTS • ITEM PROPOSAL • CREATE.

2. On the initial screen, enter "Proposal Type – MS" and your sales organization data information, as you can see in Figure 2.7.

Figure 2.7 Create Item Proposal Initial Screen

3. Enter a description of the proposal and the materials and quantities to complete it, as shown in Figure 2.8.

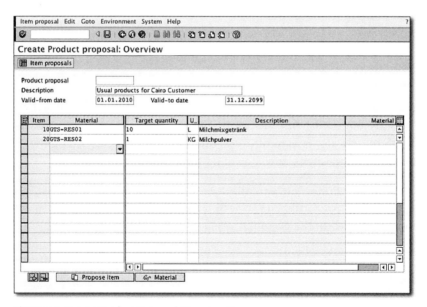

Figure 2.8 Create Product Proposal Overview Screen

4. Save your proposal and note the number.

Now that you have successfully created an item proposal, you can link it to the customers that may order the item by following these steps:

1. Follow the menu to edit customer information by using Transaction XD02 or VD02 (see Figure 2.9), or follow the menu path Logistics • Sales and Distribution • Master Data • Business Partner • Customer • Change • Complete.

Figure 2.9 Customer Master Record Change Transaction Initial Screen

Transaction	Menu Path
VA51 – Create Item Proposal	Logistics • Sales and Distribution • Master Data • Products • Item Proposal • Create
VA52 – Change Item Proposal	Logistics • Sales and Distribution • Master Data • Products • Item Proposal • Change
VA53 – Display Item Proposal	Logistics • Sales and Distribution • Master Data • Products • Item Proposal • Display
VA55 – List Item Proposals by Material	Logistics • Sales and Distribution • Master Data • Products • Item Proposal • List by Material

Table 2.5 Item Proposal Maintenance Transactions

2. In the Sales area, select the Sales tab, enter the item proposal number in the Sales Order section, and save your data, as shown in Figure 2.10.

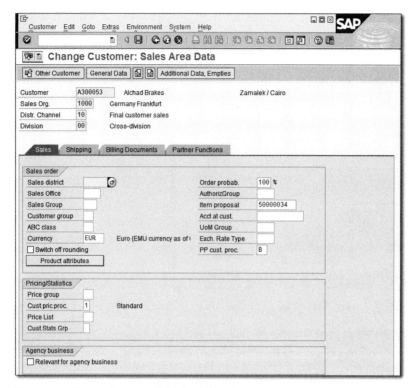

Figure 2.10 Change Customer Sales Area Data Screen

2.3.3 Material Determination

Material determination is probably one of the most useful tools available to help you enter your customer orders in the SAP system. It's basically a cross-reference table in which you can maintain a couple of important data objects such as a list of your customer material numbers and references to your company's material numbers. Another example is a list of discontinued materials that you can reference into the new materials that replace them.

In either case, you can enter material identifications that are linked in these records when you process your sales documents instead of the SAP material master numbers.

This simple transaction allows you to create sales orders by entering material identifications. Then, the SAP system will automatically substitute them with the appropriate material number.

Here is an example of how the material determination functionality works:

1. Start with Transaction VB11 (Create Material Determination) or follow menu path Logistics • Sales and Distribution • Master Data • Products • Material Determination • Create.

2. On the initial screen, choose the determination type by selecting A001 Material Entered (Figure 2.11). After selecting the material determination type, press ⌐Enter⌐ to continue to the next screen.

Figure 2.11 Create Material Determination Initial Screen

3. Enter the validity period for the equivalence you're creating, the text for your customer's material in the MatEntered column, and the SAP material number in the Material column. You can also enter a reason for the substitution in the Description field (see Figure 2.12). If the reason applies to all of the materials in the list, then you can use the field at the top and the reason will be copied to the whole list.

Figure 2.12 Create Material Determination Fast Entry Screen

4. After entering the SAP material number, press ⌈Enter⌉. SAP retrieves the material description. Save and you're done.

Transaction	Menu Path
VB11 – Create Material Determination	LOGISTICS • SALES AND DISTRIBUTION • MASTER DATA • PRODUCTS • MATERIAL DETERMINATION • CREATE
VB14 – Create Material Determination using Template	LOGISTICS • SALES AND DISTRIBUTION • MASTER DATA • PRODUCTS • MATERIAL DETERMINATION • CREATE WITH TEMPLATE
VB12 – Change Material Determination	LOGISTICS • SALES AND DISTRIBUTION • MASTER DATA • PRODUCTS • MATERIAL DETERMINATION • CHANGE
VB13 – Display Material Determination	LOGISTICS • SALES AND DISTRIBUTION • MASTER DATA • PRODUCTS • MATERIAL DETERMINATION • DISPLAY

Table 2.6 Material Determination Maintenance Transactions

2.3.4 Cross Selling

Cross selling allows you to market products together. Using an example from the fast food industry, cross selling allows you to ask "Would you like fries with your order?"

Like other master data, you need to create the list of materials that you think your customer service representatives should propose to your customers every time they buy a specific product. In the following example, a customer is buying motorcycles and the system will propose that the client also buy motorcycle helmets.

1. Start by running Transaction VB41 (Create Cross Selling) or by going to LOGISTICS • SALES AND DISTRIBUTION • MASTER DATA • PRODUCTS • CROSS SELLING • CREATE.

2. On the initial screen, select condition type C001 (CTyp) (Figure 2.13). You should note, however, that this is in the standard system. It may vary in your system. Press ⌈Enter⌉.

3. Enter the validity period for this data, and then, in the first column, enter the main material number for the "hook" product, which is the motorcycle in this example. In the second column, enter the material(s) that you want to "suggest" to your customer. See Figure 2.14 for reference.

Figure 2.13 Create Cross Selling Initial Screen

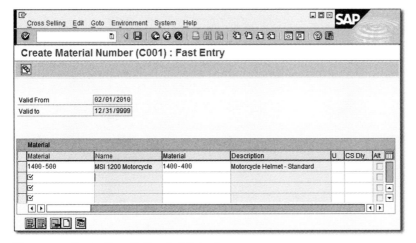

Figure 2.14 Create Cross Selling Fast Entry Screen

4. Save your record.

Transaction	Menu Path
VB41 – Create Cross Selling	LOGISTICS • SALES AND DISTRIBUTION • MASTER DATA • PRODUCTS • CROSS SELLING • CREATE
VB44 – Create Cross Selling using Template	LOGISTICS • SALES AND DISTRIBUTION • MASTER DATA • PRODUCTS • CROSS SELLING • CREATE WITH TEMPLATE

Table 2.7 Cross Selling Maintenance Transactions

Transaction	Menu Path
VB42 – Change Cross Selling	LOGISTICS • SALES AND DISTRIBUTION • MASTER DATA • PRODUCTS • CROSS SELLING • CHANGE
VB43 – Display Cross Selling	LOGISTICS • SALES AND DISTRIBUTION • MASTER DATA • PRODUCTS • CROSS SELLING • DISPLAY

Table 2.7 Cross Selling Maintenance Transactions (Cont.)

2.3.5 Listings and Exclusions

At times, you may need to block certain materials from being sold to certain customers. This could be because they were specially developed for a group of customers or because your company's products can't be exported to their country. See Table 2.8 for a list of helpful transactions that you'll use for this activity.

Transaction	Menu Path
VB01 – Create Listings and Exclusions Maintenance Transactions	LOGISTICS • SALES AND DISTRIBUTION • MASTER DATA • PRODUCTS • LISTINGS AND EXCLUSIONS • CREATE
VB02 – Change Listings and Exclusions	LOGISTICS • SALES AND DISTRIBUTION • MASTER DATA • PRODUCTS • LISTINGS AND EXCLUSIONS • CHANGE
VB03 – Display Listings and Exclusions	LOGISTICS • SALES AND DISTRIBUTION • MASTER DATA • PRODUCTS • LISTINGS AND EXCLUSIONS • DISPLAY

Table 2.8 Listings and Exclusions Maintenance Transactions

To do this, you need to set up an exclusion record by following these steps:

1. Run Transaction VB01 (Create) or follow the menu path LOGISTICS • SALES AND DISTRIBUTION • MASTER DATA • PRODUCTS • LISTINGS AND EXCLUSIONS • CREATE.

2. On the initial screen, select condition type B001 for exclusions, as shown in Figure 2.15.

3. On the detailed screen, enter the customer number, validity period, and the list of materials you want to prevent this customer from buying, as shown in Figure 2.16.

4. Save your exclusion record.

With the last step you performed, the system created you exclusion record.

Figure 2.15 Create Listing/Exclusion Initial Screen

Figure 2.16 Create Exclusion Fast Entry Screen

2.4 Pricing and Conditions

This section provides you with a quick overview of pricing conditions, what they are, how they are used by your business, and how you maintain them.

Pricing consists of conditions that include prices, discounts, freight, taxes, surcharges, and costs—generally, things that can be automatically determined when you execute a business transaction. These conditions store the data in the form of condition records, but if your pricing policies allow changing prices manually, you may be able to enter or change certain prices or discounts within a validity range. In other words, pricing represents the calculation of prices and costs using conditions.

Conditions represent a set of variable criteria that are filled when a price is calculated during document processing. For example, if your customer orders a quantity of a certain product, the defined variables are the following:

▶ Your customer's account number

▶ The product

▶ The quantity

▶ The order date

These are all used to determine the final price by accessing stored pricing information in the system. Information about each of these factors can be stored as master data, in the form of condition records. Figure 2.17 provides an overview of the pricing procedure and condition types in determination of the item pricing.

Figure 2.17 Pricing Procedure and Components

2.4.1   Condition Record

A condition record allows you to store and retrieve your pricing data for a condition type and its variables stored in condition tables that are used in pricing procedure calculations. These records include rates, scales, units of measure, and validity periods. Figure 2.18 shows a standard condition record maintenance screen.

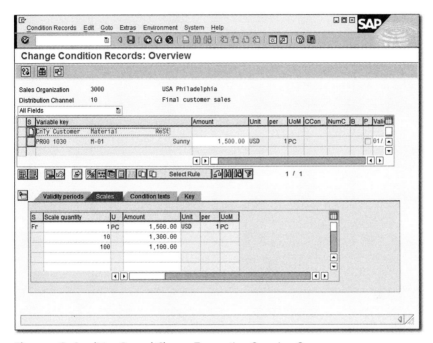

Figure 2.18 Condition Record Change Transaction Overview Screen

Condition records are usually managed at the sales organization and distribution channel level, and you typically have to specify the organizational level when maintaining them. These criteria are usually set in the condition table used to access the records.

2.4.2   Condition Table

Condition tables store the actual variables (fields that are defined as qualifiers you'll use to access the condition records). Condition tables are also used by many functions of SAP ERP, not just SD. The condition technique is a common method of providing access to complex data retrieval and storage logic delivered.

These tables can reflect criteria as simple as material or a material and customer combination, or as elaborate as combinations of several fields pulled together from a definable catalog of fields. Figure 2.19 provides a preview of a condition table definition. This figure shows you the configuration Transaction V/05 (Display Condition Table). Although your implementation team normally does this, it's important for you to understand all of the components.

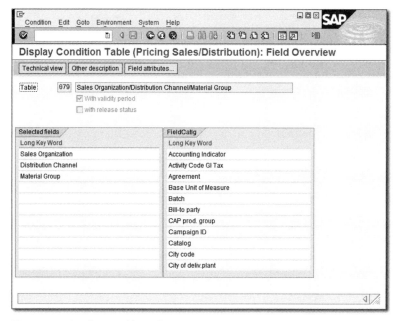

Figure 2.19 Condition Table Definition

Several condition tables are already preset for you in the predelivered SAP system, but you can also set your own tables in SAP Customizing. To maintain your own tables, use Transaction V/05.

2.4.3 Access Sequence

An access sequence is an object that stores the accesses or names of condition tables that you want to access in defined sequence. It allows you to retrieve the most specific condition records and instantly connect your condition tables (accesses) with condition types used during price determination. Basically, it determines the sequence in which the system searches for valid pricing condition records.

The defined name of the access sequence usually matches the name of the condition type it will be attached to. It consists of one or more accesses or condition tables. See Figure 2.20 for a sample definition of access sequence. This is also another example of components defined in configuration yet playing a very important role in pricing setup and maintenance.

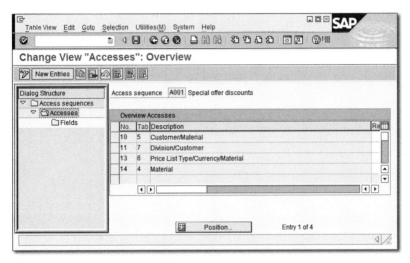

Figure 2.20 Access Sequence Definition

The sequence of the accesses establishes which condition records have priority over the others. Not all condition types require automatic price determination, which results in no access assignment (e.g., in header discounts). Usually you also control the sequence of accesses and define them starting with the most specific (e.g., sales org/customer/material) to more generic (e.g., material) tables to fetch the most appropriate price.

2.4.4 Condition Type

A condition type is like a template for a part of a price calculation. You can use an access sequence and corresponding variables of the condition tables to retrieve a condition record, or you can populate it manually. Basically, condition types are price elements such as prices, discounts, and taxes used in the pricing procedure that can automatically retrieve data records or wait for a manual entry.

You define the condition types and all corresponding control parameters, such as condition class, calculation type, condition category, links to access sequences, and pricing procedures in SAP Customizing. See Figure 2.21 for an example of condition type definition. Your implementation team also maintains condition types, but we want to make sure you understand why your condition behaves in certain way.

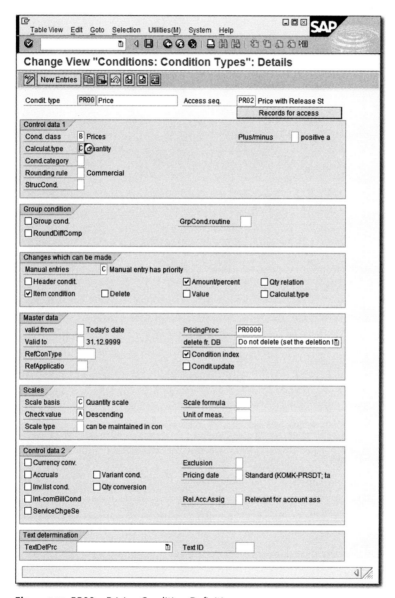

Figure 2.21 PR00 – Pricing Condition Definition

Table 2.9 lists the standard SAP condition types that you can use in your pricing procedures.

Condition Type	Description
JS02	Sales Promotion
K004	Material
K005	Customer/Material
KA00	Sales Promotion
KF00	Freight
RA00	% Discount from Net
RA01	% Discount from Gross
RC00	Quantity Discount
RD00	Weight Discount
RF00	Discount Formula
SKTO	Cash Discount
PB00	Price (Gross)
PI01	Intercompany Price
PR00	Price
UTX1	State Sales Tax
UTX2	County Sales Tax
UTX3	City Sales Tax
VKP0	Sales Price
VPRS	Cost

Table 2.9 Standard Condition Types

2.4.5 Pricing Procedure

Pricing procedure is determined when you create or update the sales order for a customer. Your settings stored in SAP Customizing for document pricing procedure and customer pricing procedures are checked, and the final pricing procedure is determined. Organizational structures such as sales organization, distribution channel, and division are also part of the determination criteria. Figure 2.22 depicts the configuration of a pricing procedure determination. Again, the implementation team takes care of this, and it's maintained in the SAP IMG.

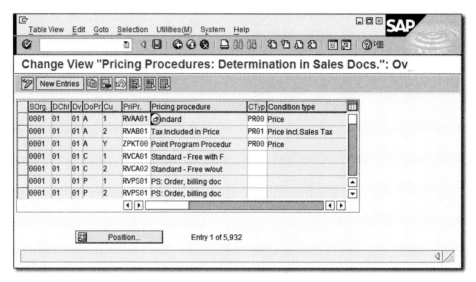

Figure 2.22 Pricing Procedure Determination Table in Customizing

The primary job of a pricing procedure is to define a group of condition types in a particular sequence. See Figure 2.23 for a definition of a standard pricing procedure. The pricing procedure also determines the following:

► Subtotals that appear during pricing

► Whether manual pricing can be processed

► How the system calculates discounts and surcharges

► Which condition type requirements must be fulfilled before the system takes the condition into account

► Accounting postings by use of the accrual keys so the system can post amounts to certain types of accruals accounts, and by use of account keys, which allow you to automatically post condition values/amounts to certain types of revenue accounts

Figure 2.23 Pricing Procedure Control Data Screen

2.4.6 Condition Maintenance

Several transactions allow you to maintain condition records. Some are older than others and are less intuitive, and others—shown in Table 2.10—are modified to make your maintenance more efficient.

The transactions interface allows you to perform mass maintenance of conditions and meet specific criteria defined in condition tables, such as sales area and customer, or material number. Figure 2.24 shows the screen layout. You can get to this screen by using Transaction VK32 or by using menu path LOGISTICS • SALES AND DISTRIBUTION • MASTER DATA • CONDITIONS • CHANGE. Table 2.10 lists the condition maintenance transactions for your reference.

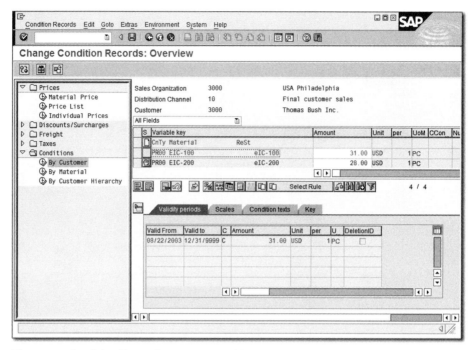

Figure 2.24 Condition Change Transaction – VK32

Transaction	Menu Path
VK31 – Create	LOGISTICS • SALES AND DISTRIBUTION • MASTER DATA • CONDITIONS • CREATE
VK34 – Create with Template	LOGISTICS • SALES AND DISTRIBUTION • MASTER DATA • CONDITIONS • CREATE WITH TEMPLATE
VK32 – Change	LOGISTICS • SALES AND DISTRIBUTION • MASTER DATA • CONDITIONS • CHANGE
VK33 – Display	LOGISTICS • SALES AND DISTRIBUTION • MASTER DATA • CONDITIONS • DISPLAY

Table 2.10 Condition Maintenance New Transactions

By using this interface, you can maintain all material prices for a specific customer and maintain all related discounts or surcharges during the same session, within the same transaction. Condition records can also be maintained per individual condition type and condition table selection criteria. You can do this using either the new or the old transactions. There are also pricing reports, price lists, and archiving transactions, as you can see in Table 2.11.

Transaction	Menu Path
VK11 – Create	LOGISTICS • SALES AND DISTRIBUTION • MASTER DATA • CONDITIONS • SELECT USING CONDITION TYPE • CREATE
VK14 – Create with Template	LOGISTICS • SALES AND DISTRIBUTION • MASTER DATA • CONDITIONS • SELECT USING CONDITION TYPE • CREATE WITH TEMPLATE
VK12 – Change	LOGISTICS • SALES AND DISTRIBUTION • MASTER DATA • CONDITIONS • SELECT USING CONDITION TYPE • CHANGE
VK13 – Display	LOGISTICS • SALES AND DISTRIBUTION • MASTER DATA • CONDITIONS • SELECT USING CONDITION TYPE • DISPLAY
V/LD – Pricing Report	LOGISTICS • SALES AND DISTRIBUTION • MASTER DATA • CONDITIONS • LIST • PRICING REPORT
V/LD – Net Price List	LOGISTICS • SALES AND DISTRIBUTION • MASTER DATA • CONDITIONS • LIST • NET PRICE LIST

Table 2.11 Other Condition Maintenance Transactions

2.5 Output

SAP ERP is capable of producing different messages to either customers or other SAP users. The formats depend on the sales document that you're working with; each company has different formats (printed or electronic) to send out to their customers. To produce each of these output messages, the system has to be configured with output types. Each output type represents all of the instructions for the system on how to produce the printed or electronic communication.

To know "when" to produce a message, the output types work together with another very important piece of the SAP system called conditions, which we discussed previously. In SAP ERP, you have to create conditions for each output type you want the system to produce. These conditions will indicate, for example, for which customer of which sales organization or shipping point you want the output to be produced.

Conditions records are also master data objects that have to be maintained; without them, the system can't print or send any communication to your customers or peers in other departments of your company.

> **Note**
>
> If your company deals with dangerous goods, then the SAP system probably also contains all of the health and safety information about these goods. In that case, both the delivery note and the packing list will contain the substance number, the substance name, and the fire safety information.

In its standard configuration, SAP ERP produces some outputs for each document type per function, which you'll see in the examples in the following sections.

Sales Documents

Let's take a look at some of the available standard output conditions used for sales documents. All of the sales documents—starting with presales activities—are capable of producing output, whether it's a printed form, EDI, fax, or email. Of course, they also require maintenance (see Table 2.12 for a list of maintenance transactions). Let's get you familiar with some of the sales document output types:

▶ **Output type AN00 – Quotation**
When a customer requests a formal quote for any of your company's products, you can produce an output message directly from the SD quotation. This message is also called a quotation, and it contains all of the items the customer requested along with prices and approximate delivery date.

▶ **Output type BA00 – Order confirmation**
Confirmation to the customer that the order has been entered and confirmed in the SAP system.

▶ **Output type KRML – Credit Processing**
Message sent to the credit representative when a credit block is generated for a sales order.

▶ **Output type ZWWW – Mail Internet Order**
If customers place orders over the Internet, the system can automatically send back a confirmation email to the customer as soon as the order has been placed and confirmed.

- **Output type BA01 – EDI Order Response**
  Another type of order confirmation that SAP ERP can send for orders received through EDI. EDI messages follow a very strict structure and content, so they can only be used in an EDI environment.

- **Output type ESYM – Internal Warnings and Info**
  Message used only when the sales orders are being entered into the system by an interface method called *batch input*. Batch inputs are programmatic "robots" that enter information into the SAP system by mimicking all of the keystrokes a human user would enter. Because this procedure for data entry happens in the background, we use this message to communicate any information messages that would have otherwise popped up during data entry.

Transaction	Menu Path
VV11 – Create	LOGISTICS • SALES AND DISTRIBUTION • MASTER DATA • OUTPUT • SALES DOCUMENT • CREATE
VV12 – Change	LOGISTICS • SALES AND DISTRIBUTION • MASTER DATA • OUTPUT • SALES DOCUMENT • CHANGE
VV13 – Display	LOGISTICS • SALES AND DISTRIBUTION • MASTER DATA • OUTPUT • SALES DOCUMENT • DISPLAY

Table 2.12 Sales Documents Output Maintenance

Shipping Documents

Just as with sales documents, your shipping department is also required to produce output, including pick lists, pack list, manifests, and so on. Just like all of the others, shipping documents need to be maintained (see Table 2.13 for the maintenance transactions list.

- **Output Type LALE – Advanced Shipping Notification**
  Message to customers telling them that the product has been shipped. This communication can be sent either by standard EDI, email, or printout. The information includes when the product left your warehouse, the shipping method, and the estimated delivery date.

- **Output Type LD00 – Delivery Note**
  In addition to the information sent to the customer, you also need to print out the shipping information for your truck drivers or freight forwarders. The

delivery note output contains all of the information related to the customer's ship-to destination. It also gives a summary of the goods shipped along with the total freight weight and volume.

▶ **Output Type PL00 – Packing List**
The detailed information of the goods shipped to the customer, including the detailed model, quantity, weight, and volume for each of the items shipped.

Transaction	Menu Path
VV21 – Create	LOGISTICS • SALES AND DISTRIBUTION • MASTER DATA • OUTPUT • SHIPPING • CREATE
VV22 – Change	LOGISTICS • SALES AND DISTRIBUTION • MASTER DATA • OUTPUT • SHIPPING • CHANGE
VV23 – Display	LOGISTICS • SALES AND DISTRIBUTION • MASTER DATA • OUTPUT • SHIPPING • DISPLAY

Table 2.13 Shipping Output Maintenance

Billing Document

The sales process ends with billing, where you also produce output for invoices and invoice lists. You also have to maintain the conditions (see Table 2.14 for the maintenance transactions list).

▶ **Output Type RD00 – Invoice**
The document officially presented to your customer that details the items with unit prices, shipping costs, and all of the pricing elements that show the total amount the customer owes.

▶ **Output Type FUPI – Proforma Invoice US**
The proforma invoice document used mostly in foreign trade transactions presented to your customer that details the items with unit prices, shipping costs, and all of the pricing elements that show the total amount your customer owes. This is not an obligation to pay; it's for declaration purposes only.

▶ **Output Type FUCO – Certificate of Origin US**
This output lists the countries of origin for the goods.

Transaction	Menu Path
VV31 – Create	LOGISTICS • SALES AND DISTRIBUTION • MASTER DATA • OUTPUT • BILLING DOCUMENT • CREATE
VV32 – Change	LOGISTICS • SALES AND DISTRIBUTION • MASTER DATA • OUTPUT • BILLING DOCUMENT • CHANGE
VV33 – Display	LOGISTICS • SALES AND DISTRIBUTION • MASTER DATA • OUTPUT • BILLING DOCUMENT • DISPLAY

Table 2.14 Billing Output Maintenance

We covered the most commonly used output conditions defined by SAP and available for your use. Normally you always modify these condition details to a degree because your forms are different, and print programs could have been modified. The standards available should provide you with a solid base for your output needs.

2.6   Agreements

Following the standard SAP Easy Access menu, we've finally reached the AGREE-MENTS section of your SD master data. Agreements can be defined in multiple ways, but, in a nutshell, they represent pieces of master data or documents storing information related to future business transactions. They may include customer material info records, contracts, rebate agreements, promotions and sales deals, and all related validity dates, terms, and conditions. Most of these objects, except for customer material info records, are basically pricing agreements that allow you to create condition records so that they'll be available during pricing and when processing your sales orders.

2.6.1   Customer Material Info Records

Customer material info records store your customers' material data using their naming convention—specific to their material master—and link it to your material master. The info records include the following:

► Customer-specific material number
► Customer material description
► Customer shipping data requirements and delivery tolerances

During order entry, you can enter material data by keying the material master number or using the customer-specific material number. The shipping data maintained on the customer material info record can also be checked and transferred to the sales order. You can also store text in the customer material information record, which is then copied to the relevant document items during the sales order text determination. This feature is used relatively frequently and helps avoid order entry mistakes.

Table 2.15 provides a list of customer material info record maintenance transactions.

Transaction	Menu Path
VD51 – Create	LOGISTICS • SALES AND DISTRIBUTION • MASTER DATA • AGREEMENTS • CUSTOMER MATERIAL INFORMATION • CREATE
VD52 – Change	LOGISTICS • SALES AND DISTRIBUTION • MASTER DATA • AGREEMENTS • CUSTOMER MATERIAL INFORMATION • CHANGE
VD53 – Display	LOGISTICS • SALES AND DISTRIBUTION • MASTER DATA • AGREEMENTS • CUSTOMER MATERIAL INFORMATION • DISPLAY
VD54 – Display for Material	LOGISTICS • SALES AND DISTRIBUTION • MASTER DATA • AGREEMENTS • CUSTOMER MATERIAL INFORMATION • DISPLAY FOR MATERIAL

Table 2.15 Customer Material Information Maintenance Transactions

2.6.2   Contracts

Customer contracts can be used in a variety of ways. You can use any of the pre-delivered contracts or outline customer agreements in the SAP system, or you can create your own to satisfy your company needs. The standard version of the SAP system delivers the following types of contracts:

▶ **Master contract**
The master contract is a master document where you can group lower level contracts together. This makes all of the data maintained for the master contract default for all lower-level documents. This data includes your sales area data, general contract terms and validity, shipping default information, incoterms, billing and billing plan schedules, accounting, and partner data.

▶ **Quantity contract**

A quantity contract represents an agreement in which your customer orders a certain quantity of product to be delivered within specified a validity period. This type of contract allows you to store basic quantity and price; however, it doesn't specify delivery dates (scheduling).

▶ **Value contract**

A valuc contract is an agreement with a customer that contains the materials and/or services that the customer may receive within a validity period and up to a specified target value. A value contract can be specific to individual materials or groups of materials represented by a product hierarchy or assortment module.

▶ **Service contract**

A service contract represents an agreement that defines the conditions for delivery of services to your customer. Like all other contract types, the service contract also contains validity dates, conditions, and pricing agreements.

Contract maintenance isn't mandatory for the SD functionality to work, and it isn't required for all subsequent functions to be executed. If your company doesn't have long- or short-term sales contracts defined, you can start your process flow with a customer inquiry or order directly. Table 2.16 shows where you can find the list of contract maintenance transactions for your reference.

Transaction	Menu Path
VA41 – Create	LOGISTICS • SALES AND DISTRIBUTION • MASTER DATA • AGREEMENTS • CONTRACTS • CREATE
VA42 – Change	LOGISTICS • SALES AND DISTRIBUTION • MASTER DATA • AGREEMENTS • CONTRACTS • CHANGE
VA43 – Display	LOGISTICS • SALES AND DISTRIBUTION • MASTER DATA • AGREEMENTS • CONTRACTS • DISPLAY

Table 2.16 Contract Maintenance Transactions

2.6.3　Rebate Agreements

A rebate represents a discount paid retroactively to a customer, based on a predefined sales volume within a certain validity period. Your rebate agreements are created in the SAP system to store all of the details related to the rebate process.

Table 2.17 lists the maintenance transactions, which help you to determine the following:

▸ Rebate criteria by selecting rebate agreement type. See Figure 2.25 for a list of standard agreement types.

▸ Customer who will receive the rebate payment.

▸ Condition values defining the amount of the rebate to be accrued.

Transaction	Menu Path
VB01 – Create	LOGISTICS • SALES AND DISTRIBUTION • MASTER DATA • AGREEMENTS • REBATE AGREEMENTS • CREATE
VB02 – Change	LOGISTICS • SALES AND DISTRIBUTION • MASTER DATA • AGREEMENTS • REBATE AGREEMENTS • CHANGE
VB03 – Display	LOGISTICS • SALES AND DISTRIBUTION • MASTER DATA • AGREEMENTS • REBATE AGREEMENTS • DISPLAY
VB(D – Extend	LOGISTICS • SALES AND DISTRIBUTION • MASTER DATA • AGREEMENTS • REBATE AGREEMENTS • DISPLAY

Table 2.17 Rebate Agreement Maintenance Transactions

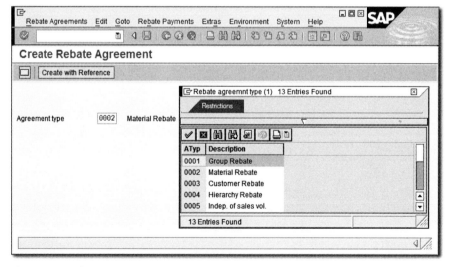

Figure 2.25 Rebate Agreement Types

Rebates differ from other discounts because they are based on the customer's sales volume within a specific time period and are paid retroactively, unlike most discounts, which are included in the sales order and processed immediately by the subsequent billing document. Your rebates, however, use the same pricing elements as other kinds of SAP pricing elements. This means that your rebate data is saved in condition records, and you control its behavior in much the same way as described earlier in Section 2.4, by using condition types, pricing procedures, and access sequences.

As mentioned earlier, rebates are paid at the end of the validity period of the rebate agreement, so your system keeps track of all billing documents relevant for rebate processing and then automatically posts rebate accruals. This gives accounting an overview of the cumulated value of the rebate. A rebate agreement is finally settled when you issue a credit memo to the customer for the accumulated rebate total. In Chapter 6, we'll cover the accruing, payments, and settlement portions of the rebate processing as part of billing in detail.

2.6.4 Promotions and Sales Deals

It's common practice to use promotions or sales deals as marketing programs. Your company probably sets special conditions for a set period of time and for individual products or product groups to boost revenue or speed up replacement of old inventory with new models. The SAP system provides standard agreement types, such as promotions and sales deals.

Promotion

A promotion typically represents a high-level marketing program for your particular products or product lines, and you can include a number of different sales deals representing each of these products.

For example, if your promotion covers a range of different product lines, you can create separate sales deals for each product line. This is like a header level document where sales deals are line items. Figure 2.26 shows an overview of a promotion screen. You can reach this screen using Transaction VB32 or following the menu path LOGISTICS • SALES AND DISTRIBUTION • MASTER DATA • AGREEMENTS • PROMOTION • CHANGE. Table 2.18 lists the promotion transactions.

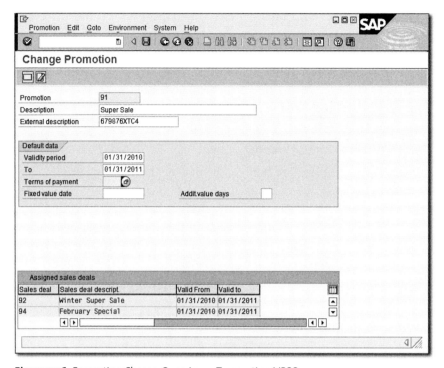

Figure 2.26 Promotion Change Overview – Transaction VB32

Transaction	Menu Path
VB31 – Create	LOGISTICS • SALES AND DISTRIBUTION • MASTER DATA • AGREE-MENTS • PROMOTION • CREATE
VB32 – Change	LOGISTICS • SALES AND DISTRIBUTION • MASTER DATA • AGREE-MENTS • PROMOTION • CHANGE
VB33 – Display	LOGISTICS • SALES AND DISTRIBUTION • MASTER DATA • AGREE-MENTS • PROMOTION • DISPLAY

Table 2.18 Promotion Transactions

Sales Deal

The sales deal provides detailed level data for your promotional activities. Here, you can maintain specific condition records that are linked to the sales deal or you can assign existing condition records. If the sales deal is linked to a promotion, the condition record will also contain the number of the promotion, which makes it possible later on to list all of the condition records that refer to a particular promotion and analyze its successes and failures. Subsequently, the promotion and sales deal numbers are passed to the sales order and billing document. Again, the same principles and pricing elements apply in case of sales deal conditions. You can maintain the rules in Customizing to expand what the standard SAP version has to offer. Table 2.19 list sales deal maintenance transactions.

Transaction	Menu Path
VB21 – Create	LOGISTICS • SALES AND DISTRIBUTION • MASTER DATA • AGREEMENTS • SALES DEAL • CREATE
VB22 – Change	LOGISTICS • SALES AND DISTRIBUTION • MASTER DATA • AGREEMENTS • SALES DEAL • CHANGE
VB23 – Display	LOGISTICS • SALES AND DISTRIBUTION • MASTER DATA • AGREEMENTS • SALES DEAL • DISPLAY
VB25 – List of Sales Deals	LOGISTICS • SALES AND DISTRIBUTION • MASTER DATA • INFORMATION SYSTEM • AGREEMENTS • LIST OF SALES DEALS

Table 2.19 Sales Deal Maintenance Transactions

2.7 Others

So far, we've discussed the types of master data used most often, which will guarantee that when you try to create a document, it will be created flawlessly. In the following subsections, we'll discuss other useful master data elements that mostly are maintained by your IT department, but we'll discuss them here so that you are familiar with what they do and how they affect your work.

2.7.1 Routes

If you use the transportation components of the Logistics Execution functionality, you'll maintain routes as one of the master data objects. A *route* defines the path that products will take after they leave your company's warehouse and until they arrive at your customer's unloading point.

A route can be as simple or as complex as your transportation processes require and can have one or more stages between connection points. In general, if you can maintain routes as target areas, you'll be looking at generic routes that give you enough of an idea about getting goods delivered to a customer without any elaborate transportation-relevant details determined upfront or if you only perform a limited number of shipments, the data available suffices. If your transportation requirements include more finite planning and actual data collection, and you interact with multiple modes of transport and load/unload scenarios, your configuration should look at routes based on connection points. If you process multi-stage shipments, you should maintain stages as well. Figure 2.27 shows the route stages maintenance screen. You can get there by using Transaction 0VTC (Change View Routes Overview), or you can follow the menu path LOGISTICS • LOGISTICS EXECUTION • MASTER DATA • TRANSPORTATION • DEFINE ROUTES • DEFINE ROUTES AND STAGES.

Figure 2.27 Route and Stage Maintenance – Transaction 0VTC

The SAP system can propose a route automatically, based on your configuration settings made in Customizing, but you can change the route assignment manually as well. The route determines the means of transport and the legs, or stages, involved. You can also determine the duration and distances for your shipment based on the data maintained for stages. This data is taken into account during the availability check and material requirements planning (MRP) if you are processing inbound shipments or shipments for stock transport orders between your own plants or subsidiaries.

Route Determination

Route determination is performed at the line item level of your sales documents. You can also redetermine the routes every time you make changes to key data elements used during the route determination and at a different stage of your process.

Sales Order Route Determination

Routes are determined for every sales order item. The following is taken into account:

- Departure country and transportation zone of the shipping point, taken from the address of the shipping point, maintained in configuration
- Shipping condition copied from the sales order, which is copied for the customer master SALES AREA data section on the SHIPPING tab
- Transportation group from the material master record (SALES GENERAL/PLANT DATA section of material master)
- Destination country and transportation zone of the ship-to party (GENERAL SECTION control tab in the customer master)

If you change the ship-to party partner data in the sales order, the route will be redetermined. In SAP Customizing, you also maintain settings for each delivery type, whether the transportation route determination will be executed again when delivery processing starts. Figure 2.28 shows how route determination is performed according to the steps just mentioned.

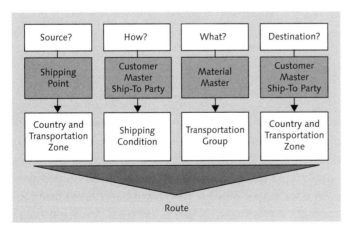

Figure 2.28 Sales Order Route Determination

Delivery Route Determination

As mentioned in the previous section, the setting for delivery type determines if the route needs to be redetermined when the exact weight of the delivery has been finally estimated at the time of delivery document creation. Unlike the sales order, where a route can be set for an individual order line item, the route for the delivery applies at the header level and includes all items in the delivery document. It allows you to monitor the over-delivery and under-delivery situations and gives you an alternative route in result. Figure 2.29 shows the factors taken into account during delivery route determination with weight groups.

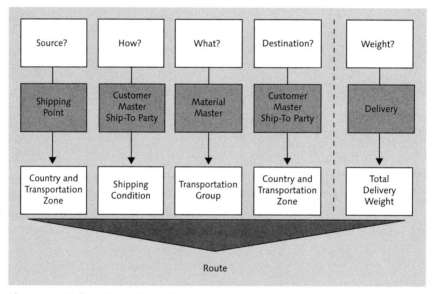

Figure 2.29 Delivery Route Determination with Weight Groups

Table 2.20 lists the most commonly used route maintenance transactions.

Transaction	Menu Path
0VTC – Define Routes and Stages	LOGISTICS • LOGISTICS EXECUTION • MASTER DATA • TRANSPORTATION • DEFINE ROUTES • DEFINE ROUTES AND STAGES
0VRF – Maintain Route Determination	LOGISTICS • LOGISTICS EXECUTION • MASTER DATA • TRANSPORTATION • ROUTE DETERMINATION • 0VRF – MAINTAIN ROUTE DETERMINATION

Table 2.20 Route Maintenance Transactions

2.7.2   Packing Instructions and Packing Instruction Determination

Another couple of pieces of master data that are frequently set up with reference to customer's requirements are the packing instructions and packing instruction determination. You probably often get approached by your customers to pack your materials in a specific way, restricting the packaging materials you can use and specifying allowed pallet dimensions (tie-high). This is all done to speed up receiving, avoid re-packing, and enable your customers to move your products faster through their supply network. You can also pass these requirements to your suppliers and require them to comply with your standards as well.

Packing Instructions

Packing instructions work hand-in-hand with handling units. (We'll discuss handling unit functionality in the later chapters.) Packing instructions are defined as a template for handling units that will be proposed during packing functions, and you can consistently reproduce and enforce the customer's specific packaging requirements every time you pick/pack the customer's orders.

Figure 2.30 shows the packing instruction Transaction POP2 screen. Let's take a look at the components of packing instructions:

▶ **Materials**
SAP packing instructions use materials that are defined by categories, depending on their use. So you have materials you are packing, packaging materials that your goods are packed into or onto, and reference materials that use the same packing instructions as your main item.

▶ **Subordinate packing instructions**
Multi-level packing instructions are the second type of instructions in which you define several packing levels (nesting) of handling units. You have to define master data for each of the levels you are trying to use and then enter them as subordinate packing instructions into the multi-level instruction definition screen.

▶ **Texts**
To store simple text notes or instructions, texts are available and can be entered as items in the packing instruction record.

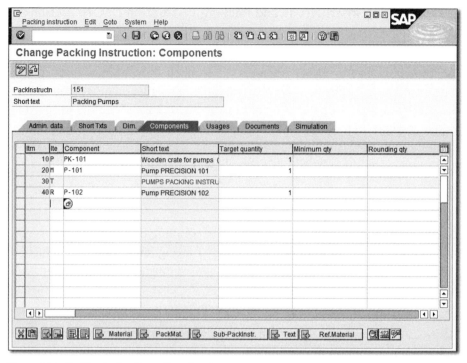

Figure 2.30 Packing Instructions Overview Screen

▶ **Documents**

You can also link documents stored in the SAP Document Management System (DMS) to your packing instructions to provide you own packing personnel or third-party service providers with a detailed description of the packing procedures, schematics, drawings, pictures, and so on.

▶ **Dimensions**

The system copies the dimensions from the material master record and uses these values to calculate the weight and volume for the proposed handling unit in the packing instruction. There is a PACKAGING CLOSED check box, which is set to indicate that the container (e.g., a box) is closed. The volume is determined by the tare volume of the load carrier, and a packaging material master data record is used for calculations. If this indicator isn't set, the system assumes you are using an open load carrier such as a pallet, and the volume is calculated automatically by adding load carrier volume to the packed material volume.

Sometimes, however, your dimensions for unpacked materials are different from materials that are packed, wrapped, or placed in the carton box that multiple quantities of the materials in it. You can maintain dimensions, weight, and volume of the handling unit manually on the packing instruction DIMENSIONS tab. This data is then copied into the handling unit during packing instead. Figure 2.31 shows the details of the dimension maintenance.

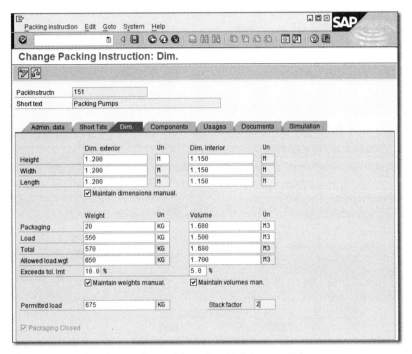

Figure 2.31 Packing Instructions – Dimension Maintenance Tab

Table 2.21 provides some of the most commonly used packing instruction maintenance transactions.

Transaction	Menu Path
POP1 – Create	LOGISTICS • SALES AND DISTRIBUTION • MASTER DATA • AGREEMENTS • PACK • PACKING INSTRUCTIONS • CREATE
POP2 – Change	LOGISTICS • SALES AND DISTRIBUTION • MASTER DATA • AGREEMENTS • PACK • PACKING INSTRUCTIONS • CHANGE

Table 2.21 Packing Instruction Maintenance Transactions

Transaction	Menu Path
POP3 – Display	LOGISTICS • SALES AND DISTRIBUTION • MASTER DATA • AGREE-MENTS • PACK • PACKING INSTRUCTIONS • DISPLAY
POP4 – Remove Deletion Indicator	LOGISTICS • SALES AND DISTRIBUTION • MASTER DATA • AGREE-MENTS • PACK • PACKING INSTRUCTIONS • REMOVE DELETION INDICATOR

Table 2.21 Packing Instruction Maintenance Transactions (Cont.)

Packing Instruction Determination

You can automate access to packing instructions during packing by maintaining determination records using a condition technique and by maintaining condition records. Just as with pricing, you can either use the SAP predefined conditions and access sequences or configure your own logic that refers to specific characteristics, such as material/reference material and ship-to party (see Figure 2.32). Table 2.22 lists the transactions that allow you to maintain the determination records.

Figure 2.32 Determination Records Maintenance

Transaction	Menu Path
POF1 – Create	LOGISTICS • SALES AND DISTRIBUTION • MASTER DATA • AGREE-MENTS • PACK • DETERMINATION RECORDS • CREATE
POF2 – Change	LOGISTICS • SALES AND DISTRIBUTION • MASTER DATA • AGREE-MENTS • PACK • DETERMINATION RECORDS • CHANGE
POF3 – Display	LOGISTICS • SALES AND DISTRIBUTION • MASTER DATA • AGREE-MENTS • PACK • DETERMINATION RECORDS • DISPLAY

Table 2.22 Determination Record Maintenance Transactions

Whenever you initiate the packing function during delivery processing, you'll see the HANDLING UNIT PACKING screen. To initiate automatic packing that starts the search for packaging instructions, you have to specify the quantity of the material to be packed and click the AUTOMATIC PACKING button. The system will perform a search for packing instructions based on the condition setup, and, once found, it will propose all of the necessary handling units for you—all you need to do is accept it to proceed. This functionality is very helpful in controlling the delivery of customer-specific packing requirements that may be linked to penalties and returns.

2.7.3   Terms of Payment

The terms of payment are the conditions under which your customers will be paying for the products they are buying. These terms are normally negotiated with the customer upon their initial account setup and must be approved by your credit department. Figure 2.33 shows an overview of terms of payment by using Transaction OBB8 (Terms of Payment), or by going to LOGISTICS • SALES AND DIS-TRIBUTION • MASTER DATA • OTHERS • TERMS OF PAYMENT.

The terms of payment are maintained in the customer master, and they describe when the payment must occur related to the sales billing. They also contain any cash or early payment discounts they might be eligible for. Figure 2.34 shows the assignment of payment terms to a customer master record.

Figure 2.33 Terms of Payment Overview

Figure 2.34 Payment Terms in Customer Master Sales Area Data

2.7.4 Incoterms

Incoterms refer to the international standards that apply to most of the commercial transactions. Incoterms are international rules used for interpretation of the trade terms. They are globally recognized as standards, and when you use them in your sales contracts, they reduce the risk of misidentification. See Figure 2.35 for the screenshot of incoterms, which you can get to using Transaction OVSG or the menu path LOGISTICS • SALES AND DISTRIBUTION • MASTER DATA • OTHERS • INCOTERMS.

Figure 2.35 Overview of Customer Incoterms

The incoterms are also maintained in the material master and apply as the default for all transactions with that customer, but they can be changed in sales documents, as shown in Figure 2.36.

Using the configuration records, as shown in Figure 2.35, most incoterms consist of two parts:

▸ **Incoterms key**
  This is the acronym that represents the delivery conditions and both seller and buyer obligations.

▶ **Location mandatory**

This indicates whether you must enter a place name in the second INCOTERMS field. If, for example, you enter FOB (Free on board) in the first INCOTERMS field, you must enter the name of the port of departure in the second INCOTERMS field (e.g., FOB New York). It's basically the place where the goods change ownership.

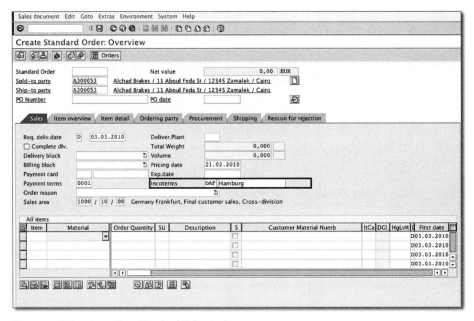

Figure 2.36 Incoterms in a Standard Sales Order

2.8 Summary

In this chapter, we covered a variety of different master data objects that you'll be using in SD transactions. We identified influencing master data objects such as business partners, material master, pricing and rebate agreements, contracts, routes, and packing instructions. Depending on your business needs, you may use all or just a few of them, but after reading this chapter, you should be able to identify, maintain, and describe the relationship of those data objects to your sales process with ease.

Based on the information we've covered, you can tell now that there is a lot of master data to maintain, which is why it's very important to maintain it and keep it clean.

Now, together with the information from Chapter 1 that introduced you to the enterprise structure of your company and armed you with a wealth of information about master data, we're ready to move on to Chapter 3, where we'll detail standard SD transactions that are used during the sales process.

Sales is the core activity involved in providing your customers with products or services in return for payment. In this chapter, we'll walk through the entire process, from inquiry to order creation.

3   Sales

Sales is the process that enables you to deliver goods or services to your customers so you can collect payment or replace a faulty product, and be able to measure the effectiveness of your order fulfillment. In this chapter, we won't discuss how to excel in sales techniques; instead, you'll learn about how you can better use the sales functionality in the SAP system. We'll walk through the entire sales process from inquiry to order creation or customer returns. We'll also cover credit management, some basic foreign trade, and back order processing functions that interact with your standard sales activities on a transactional basis. First, however, we'll start our discussion about sales by defining the organizational structures in which sales transactions occur, and how different topics and items are grouped.

3.1   Sales Document Components

As mentioned before, all of your sales transactions occur within the organizational structures that you defined in configuration; will use pieces of master data you've maintained, as described in the previous chapter; and will finally come together in a business transaction recorded in the system as sales documents. These documents can be grouped into four distinct categories, and then within each category there are several document types (see Table 3.1) for details:

- ► Presales documents (inquiries and quotations)
- ► Sales orders
- ► Outline agreements (contracts and scheduling agreements)
- ► Customer complaints (free-of-charge orders and credit memos)

Document Category	Description	Sales Document Type
Presales Documents	Inquiry	IN
	Quotation	QT
Sales Orders	Standard Sales Order	OR
	Cash Sale	BV
	Rush Order	SO
Outline Agreements	Quantity Contract	CQ
	Maintenance Contract	WV
	Rental Contract	MV
	Scheduling Agreement	DS
Complaints	Credit Memo Request	CR
	Debit Memo Request	DR
	Returns	RE

Table 3.1 Sample of Standard Sales Document Types

3.1.1 Sales Document Structure

Before we start the detailed review of each of the document categories, we'll define the functions of the document types and item categories, and describe how they interact with each other as they store the history in the document flow.

▶ **Document flow**

The entire processing chain of sales documents, the history of your transactions—from the inquiry, quotation, sales order, delivery, and then invoice—creates a document flow stored in the database. This history is linked to all documents, which creates a visual hierarchy displayed in each of the documents in the chain. This allows you to navigate from one document into another seamlessly to help track history and resolution should issues arise.

▶ **Document type**

Document types represent a set of controls that enable you to define an individual behavior that mimics your business process at the document level. Your document type controls how some of the functions are performed when you start processing business transactions, such as order entry. You can find a variety of these predefined sales document types, or you can set your own in Customizing. Figure 3.1 shows some of the predelivered order types in SAP ERP.

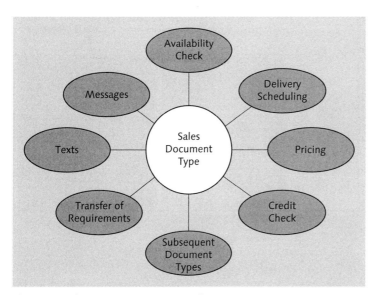

Figure 3.1 Sales Document Type Control Functions

For example, you can define your document type to perform delivery scheduling to predetermine the shipment start dates, and run the availability check to confirm promised quantities. You can automate the pricing and tax determination or leave some for manual input. You can set up your document to auto-determine texts you want to include when printing documents. All of these functions control not just the sales document itself but also the follow-on documents and their behavior. Figure 3.1 provides an overview of controls and most important influencing elements defined in Customizing for sales document types.

3.1.2 Customizing Settings of a Sales Document

We aren't going to cover Customizing transactions and details on setting up your document types, but you need to understand the influence of its components during sales processing.

Each document type has different attributes, and these attributes are set in customizing. Some of the most relevant settings are:

▶ **General Data**

▶ CHECK DIVISION: This controls whether the division value used in the sales document will be taken from the material master record for all items or whether the alternative division specified in the header will take precedence.

▶ REFERENCE MANDATORY: This means the preceding document is required. For example, you would need to require an inquiry before a quotation is created.

▶ CHECK CREDIT LIMIT: This means that your customer credit check will be performed.

▶ ITEM DIVISION: This controls whether the value for the division comes from the material master record of the item. If the field is blank, the division in the document header applies to all items.

▶ READ INFO RECORD: This means the system will search for customer material info records during order entry.

▶ SCREEN SEQUENCE: This controls which screens and in what sequence you see them during document processing.

▶ INCOMPLETION PROCEDURE: This controls the assignment of the incompletion procedure that checks your order for fields that are defined as mandatory before further processing can take place.

▶ INCOMPLETION MESSAGES: This means that you control whether the incomplete document can be saved.

▶ DOCUMENT PRICING PROCEDURE: This setting determines how the system carries out pricing for the sales document.

▶ LEAD TIME IN DAYS: This defines the number of days from the current day added to the calculations for the proposed delivery date.

▶ DATE TYPE: This is where you can set up whether your schedule lines will use day, week, or month as a base time unit.

▶ PROPOSAL FOR PRICING DATE: This is where you can control whether the pricing will use the proposed delivery date or a date of the order creation.

▶ PROPOSE DELIVERY DATE: If this is set, the system uses the current date as your delivery date.

▶ PROPOSE PO DATE: If this is set, the system automatically proposes the current date as the purchase order date.

▶ **Shipping Data**

▶ DELIVERY TYPE: This determines which delivery type will be created as a subsequent document type.

▶ DELIVERY BLOCK: This is where you can define whether the delivery block should be set automatically, or whether someone in your organization needs to check the delivery details before shipping takes place.

▶ SHIPPING CONDITION: When creating sales documents, this setting is normally copied from the customer master record, but if this value is maintained in configuration for the document type, it will take priority over the customer master data and will be set as a default value for your sales document.

▶ SHIPMENT COST INFO PROFILE: If you maintain this entry, the selected profile will be used to carry out options for shipment cost determination.

▶ IMMEDIATE DELIVERY: If this is set, your subsequent delivery can be created as soon as the order is saved.

▶ **Billing Data**

▶ DELIVERY RELEVANT BILLING TYPE: This defines which billing document type will be the default for the sales document.

▶ ORDER RELEVANT BILLING TYPE: Here you control which billing document type will be applied for sales document items that aren't relevant for delivery but are relevant for billing.

▶ INTERCOMPANY BILLING: This specifies a default billing document type for intercompany transactions.

▶ BILLING BLOCK: You can define this as a default, which would automatically assign a billing block value in configuration and force you to check the document before billing can be executed.

▶ CONDITION TYPE LINE ITEMS: You can define the condition type used to transfer the cost of line items. If defined, the same pricing condition will be used for all line items of your document.

3.1.3   Item Categories

SAP item categories are defined to arm you with additional controls during sales document processing. Basically, the same material can behave differently when processed by different order types. Just like with the document types, item category settings can give you completely different end results, depending on your business scenarios.

For example, the behavior of your normal standard order item can be totally different for returns order or cash sales. In real life, you may create the quotation for your customer's inquiry. The item category on the quotation isn't subject to delivery or billing. Then you create a subsequent sales order with reference to your quotation, so the item is deliverable by a third party. During your order creation, Customizing settings were accessed, and the destination order type and item categories were determined. Of course, you can create your own item categories by making the settings in Customizing to fine-tune controls and to match your needs. Table 3.2 lists some of the available standard delivered item categories.

Item Category	Description
AFN	Inquiry item
AGN	Standard item in a quotation
AGX	Quotation item
REN	Standard Return item
REQ	Full product returns
RLN	Returns order
TAC	Variant configuration
TAD	Service
TAG	Generic article
TAK	Make-to-order product
TAM	Assembly item
TAN	Standard sales item
TANN	Free of charge item
TAS	Third-party item
TAK	Make-to-order item

Table 3.2 Sample of Available Standard Item Categories

Also, you maintain the assignment of the item categories to your document types in Customizing by defining which item categories can be used with certain document types. Then you set up copy controls that allow subsequent documents to be generated with reference, where allowed combinations of source and target document types and item categories are maintained. You control what is getting copied for you from inquiry to sales order, and creating shipping and billing documents.

Important Functions

The following are some of the most important functions controlled by item category Customizing:

▶ **General Data**

　▷ ITEM TYPE: You can define whether the item is to be a material or a text item; for example, by changing how the system will perform certain functions such as tax determination.

　▷ SPECIAL STOCK: If you need to process special stocks in a different way, you have to select stock in scope.

　▷ PRICING: You can define whether set pricing for the item will be carried out.

　▷ BUSINESS ITEM: You can select all item data to deviate from those at the header level of the document.

　▷ SCHEDULE LINE ALLOWED: You can define whether schedule lines will be allowed for the item.

　▷ RETURNS: You can determine whether the item is a return item

　▷ CREDIT ACTIVE: You can specify whether the item will be subject to credit management controls and updates.

　▷ BOM AND CONFIGURATION: You can define controls around variant configurable materials.

▶ **Shipping Data**

　▷ ITEM RELEVANT FOR DELIVERY: If you set this flag, the item category is subject for delivery.

　▷ WEIGHT/VOLUME RELEVANT: You can determine the weight and volume of an item.

▸ **Billing Data**

- ▸ BILLING RELEVANCE: You can define whether the item is relevant for billing.

- ▸ DETERMINE COST: If you select this, the system will determine the cost.

- ▸ BILLING BLOCK: You can assign an automatic billing block for documents that have to be reviewed before billing.

- ▸ STATISTICAL VALUE: You can define whether the system will add the statistical item value to the total value of the order. If this is set, the customer isn't charged for the item.

Item Category and Order Type Interaction

Finally, we have all of the pieces of this puzzle together, and we can draft a picture, as shown in Figure 3.2, of how order types and item categories come together during order processing.

▸ **Determining the item category**

The item category in the sales document is determined based on the combination of the sales document type and material master item category group.

For example, you have a material master defined with item category group NORM. During quotation entry—sales document type Q —your item category determination will select the default value, which is AGN Standard Item. In another example, if you're using the same material, you enter the standard sales order—sales document type OR—and the determination will look for a default value finding TAN – Standard Item Category.

▸ **Schedule line categories**

We started analysis of sales document control elements from document type, adding a line item layer represented by item categories, and finally we're down to the most granular level represented by schedule line category. The schedule line is required for any sales order to create the subsequent delivery document. Also, the assignment of schedule lines to item categories and MRP types makes a connection between your sales activities and materials planning where MRP type is also assigned in the material master. You can have up to three manual schedule line categories assigned to a single item category/MRP type combination.

Standard predelivered schedule line categories' key characters represent the schedule line usage, as shown in Table 3.3.

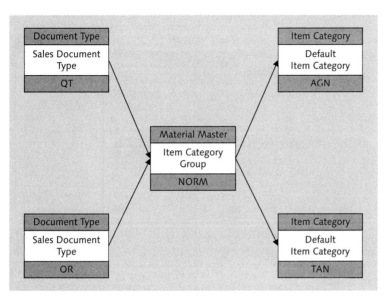

Figure 3.2 Item Category Determination Example

First Character	Usage
A	Inquiry
B	Quotation
C	Sales order
D	Returns
Second Character	**Usage**
T	No inventory management
X	No inventory management with goods issue
N	No planning
P	MRP
V	Consumption-based planning

Table 3.3 Schedule Line Usage Definition

The schedule line allows you to control the following data types.

▶ **General Data**

    ▶ MOVEMENT TYPE: This is where you assign the movement type that will be used during goods issue—posting quantity and value changes to inventory and accounting. This shouldn't be set up for inquiry, quotations, and sales orders in SAP environments without integration with Inventory Management. Movement type is also to be specified for return delivery but not for return items.

    ▶ REQUIREMENTS: You have to set this flag to recognize the requests for materials that are assigned to your line item schedule line by MRP, transfer of requirements will also be carried out.

    ▶ AVAILABILITY: Here you control availability check relevancy. This is the lowest level of the availability check control.

    ▶ PURCHASE ORDER/PURCHASE REQUISITION: If you select this checkbox, purchase requisition can be automatically generated where default data for the purchase order type, item category, and account assignment category comes from values you maintain here.

    ▶ INCOMPLETION PROCEDURE: This is where you can control the assignment to incompletion procedure that determines which fields must be completed before the document can be processed further.

▶ **Shipping Data**

    ▶ ITEM RELEVANT FOR DELIVERY: You can set this checkbox if the schedule lines for your order items are relevant for physical delivery of goods.

    ▶ DELIVERY BLOCK: You can use this feature if you decide to automatically block your orders schedule lines from being delivered. Just like with order types and item categories, it allows certain orders to be reviewed before further processing takes place.

Now that you have a good understanding of the core fundamental structure of sales documents, let's move on to discuss the actual documents in the works starting with the presales documents: inquiry and quotation.

3.2   Inquiry and Quotation

As we briefly described in Chapter 1, the SAP system provides you with tools to capture all sales-related activities from the very first contact with your potential prospects to establishing long-term contractual agreements that capture all of your sales and marketing employees.

Armed with the information about current and prospective customers and contacts, you can now start recording your initial sales activities in the form of an inquiry and follow up with a quotation document that will be created as a response to the customer's inquiry. During the course of negotiations, you may be changing delivery dates, partners to whom the goods are to be shipped, or payment terms. You may have to adjust item categories and schedule lines if the negotiations require it. Standard predelivered document types and the combination of item categories and schedule lines are listed in Table 3.4.

Document Type	Item Category	Schedule Line
IN – Inquiry	▸ AFN – Inquiry Item	▸ AT – Inquiry Schedule Line
QT – Quotation	▸ AGN – Standard Item ▸ AGNN – Free-of-Charge Item	▸ BV – Consumption MRP ▸ BN – No MRP ▸ BP – Deterministic MRP

Table 3.4 Inquiry and Quotation Components Structure

You can also leverage the alternative items function to offer your customers substitute materials just in case the item requested isn't available. If your customer decides to accept one of the alternative materials, you can copy it from the quotation when you create the sales order.

When you create the quotation document with reference to an inquiry with alternative items or when you create a sales order with reference to a quotation with alternative items, the system automatically copies only the main items. If you want, you can copy an alternative item instead. To do so, on the initial screen of the document creation, open the LIST options, and choose the alternative items instead of the main items.

In the following sections, we'll go into the processes you'll need to follow to work with both inquiries and quotations.

3.2.1 Inquiry

You may receive inquiries from your customers asking for a specific product, price, and availability. Your customer may also give you the required delivery dates with a quotation submittal deadline. When you start recording the inquiry, you must specify the sales area. Remember: the sales area will be responsible for further processing of this inquiry.

Table 3.5 provides a list of inquiry transactions. When you start using these transactions, you'll notice that all standard sales document functions apply, if configured, and you can use the full capability of pricing, partner determination, and most of the other master data components described in earlier chapters.

Transaction	Menu Path
VA11 – Create	LOGISTICS • SALES AND DISTRIBUTION • SALES • INQUIRY • CREATE
VA12 – Change	LOGISTICS • SALES AND DISTRIBUTION • SALES • INQUIRY • CHANGE
VA13 – Display	LOGISTICS • SALES AND DISTRIBUTION • SALES • INQUIRY • DISPLAY
VA15 – Inquiries List	LOGISTICS • SALES AND DISTRIBUTION • SALES • INFORMATION SYSTEM •INQUIRIES • INQUIRIES LIST
V.03 – Incomplete Inquiries	LOGISTICS • SALES AND DISTRIBUTION • SALES • INFORMATION SYSTEM •INQUIRIES • INCOMPLETE INQUIRIES

Table 3.5 Inquiry Transaction List

The processing screens have the same controls throughout all transactions, so whether you make initial contact with your prospects or create sales orders, you should be able to navigate easily through all of these familiar screens. See Figure 3.3 for an overview of the CHANGE INQUIRY transaction screen.

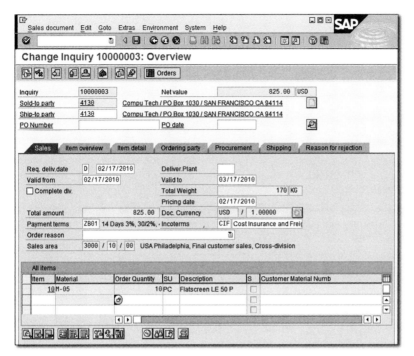

Figure 3.3 Inquiry Change Transaction Sales Screen

Create an Inquiry

Let's walk through the example of creating an inquiry. Start by running Transaction VA11 (Create Inquiry), or follow the menu path LOGISTICS • SALES AND -DISTRIBUTION • SALES • INQUIRY • CREATE.

1. On the CREATE INQUIRY: INITIAL SCREEN, enter the inquiry type and necessary organizational data, and then press ⌈Enter⌋ (see Figure 3.4).

2. On the CREATE INQUIRY: OVERVIEW screen shown in Figure 3.5, enter the following data:

   ▷ Customer number of the sold-to party and ship-to party if it's different

   ▷ Inquiry validity dates (start and end date)

   ▷ Material numbers or text in the DESCRIPTION field if no material number exists

   ▷ Order quantity

   ▷ Note item categories

Figure 3.4 Create Inquiry – Initial Screen

Figure 3.5 Create Inquiry – Overview Screen

Offer Alternative Material

If you want to offer your customer optional alternative material, follow these steps:

1. Start with the customer's first choice, and enter it in your inquiry.

2. Enter your alternative item directly under the main item to be replaced, and specify the material number.

3. Find the alternative item column (ALTITM), and enter the line item number (in our example, it is 10) of the material for which this item is defined as an alternative (the material you entered in the previous step—line item 10).

4. If you offer more than one alternative for an item, repeat the steps and enter the main item number as before (i.e., 10) (see Figure 3.6 for example).

Figure 3.6 Create Inquiry – Overview Entry of Alternative Item

After each entry you make, press ⌈Enter⌋ to continue, and click on SAVE when you're ready to close and store your document.

3.2.2 Quotation

The next presales transaction, the quotation, can be initiated as a subsequent transaction for the inquiry. Table 3.6 provides a list of quotation transactions for your reference.

Transaction	Menu Path
VA21 – Create	LOGISTICS • SALES AND DISTRIBUTION • SALES • QUOTATION • CREATE
VA22 – Change	LOGISTICS • SALES AND DISTRIBUTION • SALES • QUOTATION • CHANGE
VA23 – Display	LOGISTICS • SALES AND DISTRIBUTION • SALES • QUOTATION • DISPLAY
VA25 – Quotations List	LOGISTICS • SALES AND DISTRIBUTION • SALES • INFORMATION SYSTEM • QUOTATIONS • QUOTATIONS LIST
V.03 – Incomplete Quotations	LOGISTICS • SALES AND DISTRIBUTION • SALES • INFORMATION SYSTEM • QUOTATIONS • INCOMPLETE QUOTATIONS

Table 3.6 Quotation Transactions List

You can also create the quotation without a reference if you can immediately assist your customer and if you have all of the data needed to do so. This is a legally binding document that specifies the sold-to and ship-to partners and confirms a delivery of products or services based on conditions that you detail in this document, such as pricing, delivery schedule, incoterms, and so on. The quotation also has a validity period after which this offer expires. As with the inquiry, the look and feel is pretty much the same as that of the other sales document transactions you use when creating sales orders or inquiries.

Let's walk through a scenario of a quotation being created with reference to an inquiry. Start by running Transaction VA21 (Create Quotation), or follow the menu path LOGISTICS • SALES AND DISTRIBUTION • SALES • QUOTATION • CREATE.

Here, you're creating a quotation with a reference to an inquiry:

1. On the CREATE QUOTATION: INITIAL SCREEN, enter the quotation document type and then click the CREATE WITH REFERENCE button, as shown in Figure 3.7.

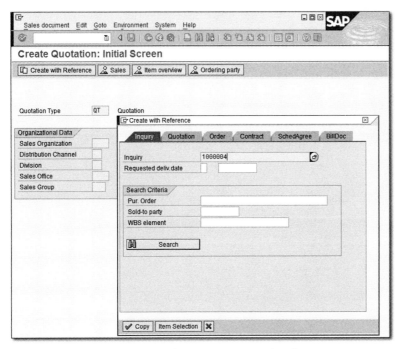

Figure 3.7 Create Quotation: Initial Screen – Create with Reference

2. Within the pop-up window, you have to specify the source inquiry document number. If you used the alternative items in your inquiry, click on the ITEM SELECTION button to check which item(s) you'll be quoting in your document. In no selection is made, the system will select main items from the inquiry, including alternative items. If you don't plan on making any item selections, simply click on COPY to continue.

3. On the main CREATE QUOTATION: OVERVIEW screen (Figure 3.8), enter the quotation validity dates (start and end date), and validate the following data:

   ▶ Material numbers or text in the DESCRIPTION field if no material number exists

   ▶ Quantities

   ▶ Note item categories determined

4. If you need to make changes to pricing, which is usually the data object maintained the most during this presales activity, you can select the line item and use the ITEM CONDITION icon or the drop-down menus by choosing GOTO • ITEM • CONDITION, as shown in the item condition screen in Figure 3.9.

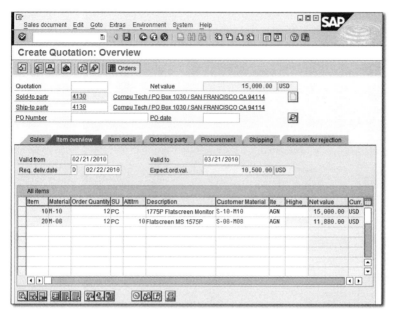

Figure 3.8 Create Quotation: Overview Screen

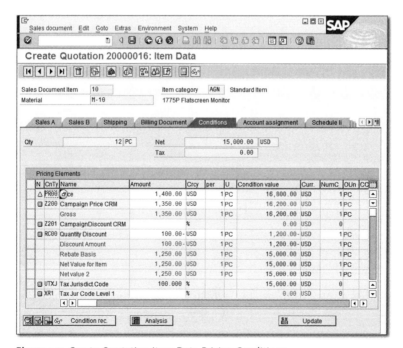

Figure 3.9 Create Quotation Item Data Pricing Conditions

After all of your entries are complete, click on the SAVE button when you're ready to close and store your document. The subsequent output condition can issue a printed or electronic version of your quotation ready to be submitted to your customer.

> **Note**
>
> If you're starting the quotation without a reference, you have to specify the document type and sales area data just as you do for an inquiry.

3.3 Sales Order

In the previous section, we covered your presales activities. Now, after you've sent the final, revised quotation to your customers, their own purchasing departments will decide if they are ready to purchase the quoted products or services and communicating to you their purchase order. After you get the go ahead from your customers, you can start creating the sale order with reference to the quotation used in the presales steps.

If your process isn't using any of the presales activities and documents, you can start creating your sales order directly without a reference. Your standard order will then follow the process flow discussed in Chapter 1, when we discussed the Sales and Distribution processes. You'll create the delivery document, finish your picking and transportation activities, send the goods on their way to your customer, and finish up with the billing run. Refer to Figure 1.7 in Chapter 1 for a quick process review and reminder.

Some of the standard SAP documents don't have these prerequisites, such as cash, catalog, or rush sales orders. Regardless of whether you're creating an order with or without a reference, you'll start with the same transaction. Table 3.7 provides a list of sales order transactions for your reference.

Transaction	Menu Path
VA01 – Create	LOGISTICS • SALES AND DISTRIBUTION • SALES • ORDERS • CREATE
VA02 – Change	LOGISTICS • SALES AND DISTRIBUTION • SALES • ORDERS • CHANGE

Table 3.7 Sales Order Maintenance Transactions

Transaction	Menu Path
VA03 – Display	LOGISTICS • SALES AND DISTRIBUTION • SALES • ORDERS • DISPLAY
VA05 – List of Sales Orders	LOGISTICS • SALES AND DISTRIBUTION • SALES • INFORMATION SYSTEM • ORDERS • LIST OF SALES ORDERS
V.02 – Incomplete Orders	LOGISTICS • SALES AND DISTRIBUTION • SALES • INFORMATION SYSTEM • ORDERS • INCOMPLETE ORDERS

Table 3.7 Sales Order Maintenance Transactions (Cont.)

For a sales order to be created, you must have either a predecessor document that you'll be using as a reference, or you must provide at the minimum some of the following information that comes from the master data objects covered in detail in Chapter 2, such as the following:

▶ Customer sold-to account number

▶ Material or service number sold to the customer

▶ Quantities ordered (if the item proposal is maintained or if the sale is being created with reference to a quotation, then the quantities will be copied, otherwise, they need to be entered manually)

▶ Pricing condition(s) for your materials or services

▶ Required delivery dates

▶ Shipping data, such as incoterms

▶ Billing data required for processing of payment

Also during order processing, you'll be using some of the functions we covered already or will cover in the next chapters. These include the following:

▶ Pricing

▶ Availability check

▶ Transferring requirements to MRP (material requirements planning)

▶ Delivery scheduling

▶ Shipping point and route determination

▶ Checking credit limits

In the next sections, we'll discuss some of the most important variations of sales order processes. Depending on your business scenarios and configuration, you should be able to find a few that will satisfy your business requirements.

Table 3.8 provides a list of a few of the standard predelivered document types you can use.

Document Type	Item Category
BV – Cash Sale	BVN – Cash Sales
	BVNN – Cash Sales Free of Charge
CR – Credit Memo Request	G2N – Request
	G2S – Statistical Request
	G2W – Request
	GFN – Request Billing Plan
	LFN – Request Billing Plan
DR – Debit Memo Request	L2N – Request
	L2S – Statistical Request
	L2W – Request
	GFN – Request Billing Plan
	LFN – Request Billing Plan
FD – Deliv.Free of Charge	KLN – Free of Charge Item
	KLS – F.O.C Non-Stock Item
	KLX – Free-of-Charge Item
KA – Consignment Pick-up	KAN – Consignment Pick-up
KB – Consignment Fill-up	KBN – Consignment Fill-up
KE – Consignment Issue	KEN – Consignment Issue
OR – Standard Order	TAB – Indiv. Purchase Order
	TAC – Config.at Mat.Level
	TAD – Service

Table 3.8 Sales Order Structure

Document Type	Item Category
	TAN – Standard Item
	TANN – Free-of-Charge Item
	TAS – Third-Party Item
	TAX – Non-Stock Item
	TAZ – Empties (Linked)
SO – Rush Order	TAN – Standard Item
	TANN – Free-of-Charge Item
TAM – Delivery Order	TAMA – Delivery Order Item

Table 3.8 Sales Order Structure (Cont.)

You can see now that most of the order behavior and follow-on functions will be dependent on the order type and item category definitions. With that in mind, we'll walk through some of the most commonly used document type examples and refer to some of the master data objects discussed in Chapter 2.

3.3.1 Creating a Standard Order

Let's walk through a scenario of a sales order being created with reference to a quotation. Start by running Transaction VA01 (Create Sales Order), or follow the menu path LOGISTICS • SALES AND DISTRIBUTION • SALES • ORDERS • CREATE.

> **Note**
>
> If starting your order without a reference, you have to specify the document type and sales area data just as you did while working on the inquiry and quotation.

1. On the CREATE SALES ORDER: INITIAL SCREEN, enter the sales order document type you'll be creating and then click the CREATE WITH REFERENCE button.

2. On the pop-up window, you have to specify the source quotation document number (see Figure 3.10). If you used alternative items (for example, in your source quotation), we suggest you click the ITEM SELECTION button to check which item(s) you'll be using in your sales order. If you don't plan on making any item selections, simply click the COPY button to continue.

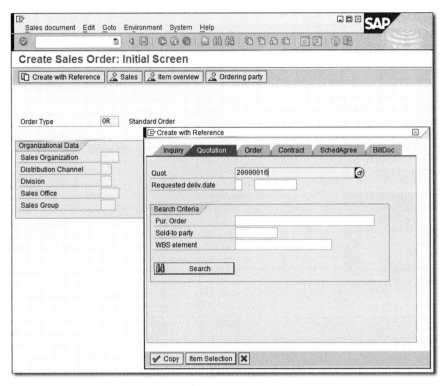

Figure 3.10 Create Sale Order with Reference Initial Screen

The SAP system will reference a main item from the quotation without the alternative items. If you choose to provide your customer with the alternative items, you must select the correct item on the SELECTION LIST FOR REFERENCE DOCUMENT screen (Figure 3.11).

3. On the main STANDARD ORDER: OVERVIEW screen, verify the data that was copied from your source quotation, including the following:

   ▸ Material numbers or text in the DESCRIPTION FIELD if no material number exists

   ▸ Quantities

   ▸ Note item categories determined

4. If you need to make changes to pricing, just as with quotations, you can select the line item and use the ITEM CONDITION icon or use the pull-down menu GOTO • ITEM • CONDITION.

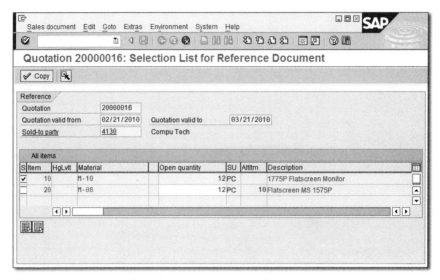

Figure 3.11 Selection List for Reference Document – Alternative Item

5. When you're ready to complete the process, click the SAVE button, the subsequent output condition can be issued, and a printed or electronic version of your order confirmation will be ready for your customer.

3.3.2 Using an Item Proposal in Sales Orders

In Chapter 2, we covered the master data definition procedure for an item proposal. Now you should be able to use your item proposal functionality in the sales order. Let's create a sales order without a reference, so you can see how it works. Let's start with running Transaction VA01 (Create Order), or you can follow the menu path LOGISTICS • SALES AND DISTRIBUTION • SALES • ORDERS • CREATE.

1. On the CREATE SALES ORDER: INITIAL SCREEN, enter the sales order document type (i.e., OR – Standard Order), fill in your sales organization data, and press Enter. See Figure 3.12 for an example.

   Refer to Chapter 2 to revisit the example on how to create an item proposal.

2. Enter the number for the customer sold-to that you've maintained in your item proposal, as shown in Figure 3.13, and press Enter to determine other partners.

Figure 3.12 Create Sales Order: Initial Screen – Item Proposal Sample

Figure 3.13 Create Standard Order – Overview Screen

3. To initiate the item proposal function, go to Edit • Additional Functions • Propose Items, as shown in Figure 3.14.

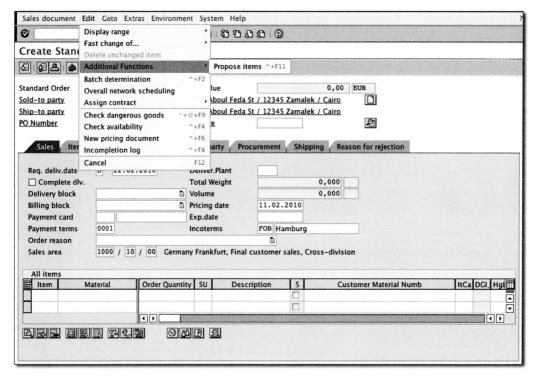

Figure 3.14 Create Standard Order: Overview Screen – Item Proposal Menu

4. Finally, you'll be prompted to confirm the proposal number. Here, you can select between proposing items with or without quantity. For this example, select the DEFAULT WITH QUANTITY button, as shown in Figure 3.15.

Figure 3.15 Propose Item Selection Window

The result is that the items you included in the item proposal are brought over to the sales order, as you can see in Figure 3.16 (both items came from the example that we set up in Chapter 2).

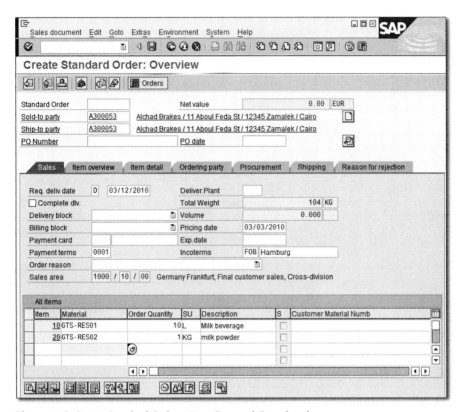

Figure 3.16 Create Standard Order – Item Proposal Completed

3.3.3 Material Determination in Sales Orders

Another piece of master data we've covered in Chapter 2 was material determination, and now you should be able to use it during sales order creation. To see how this works, let's create a sales order by using Transaction VA01 (Create Order) or by following the menu path LOGISTICS • SALES AND DISTRIBUTION • SALES • ORDERS • CREATE. Then follow these steps:

1. On the CREATE SALES ORDER: INITIAL SCREEN, enter the sales order document type (e.g., OR – Standard Order), fill in your sales organization data, and press Enter .

2. Enter the number for the customer sold-to that you've maintained in your material determination master data, as you can see in Figure 3.17, and press ⌈Enter⌋ to determine the other partners.

3. In the line item MATERIAL column, type the material determination record name text. Figure 3.17 provides an example of how we use this record (for more details on material determination records, revisit Chapter 2). The system will determine the pricing for the item.

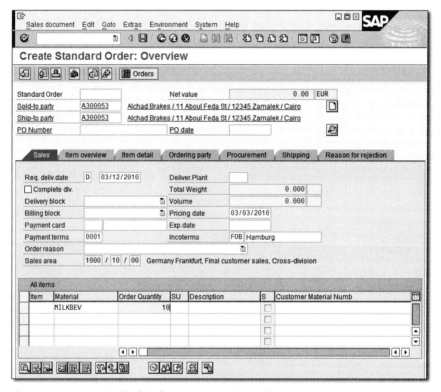

Figure 3.17 Create Standard Order Overview – Material Determination Entry

4. Press ⌈Enter⌋ to continue. It's important to note that the material determination will substitute the description text you've entered with the valid SAP material number, as you can see in Figure 3.18.

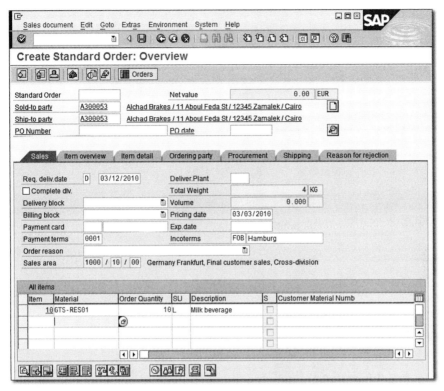

Figure 3.18 Create Standard Order – Material Determination Completion

3.3.4 Cross Selling in Sales

Cross selling, which we discussed in Chapter 2, can now be demonstrated during the sales order creation. To see how it comes together, create a sales order starting again with Transaction VA01 (Create Order) or by following the menu path LOGISTICS • SALES AND DISTRIBUTION • SALES • ORDERS • CREATE. Follow these steps:

1. On the CREATE SALES ORDER: INITIAL SCREEN, enter the sales order document type, such as OR – Standard Order, fill in your sales organization data, and press ⌷Enter⌷.

2. Enter the number for the customer sold-to that you've maintained in your item proposal, as shown earlier in Figure 3.13, and press ⌷Enter⌷ to determine the other partners.

3. Enter the material number for the main product, and then click on the CROSS SALES icon at the bottom right of the screen, as highlighted in Figure 3.19.

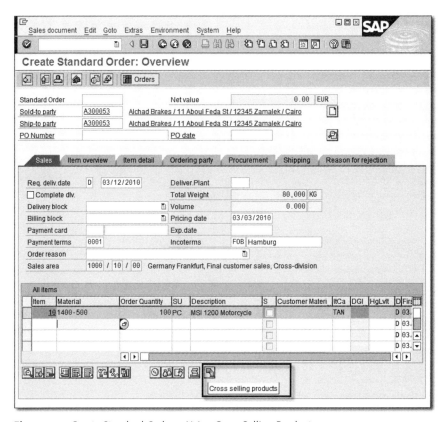

Figure 3.19 Create Standard Order – Using Cross Selling Products

4. You'll now see the CROSS SALES pop-up window (Figure 3.20), which lists all of the materials that can be sold with the main material. If the customer wants them, you have to enter the quantity and click on the COPY button.

The copy function transfers the suggested cross-selling material to your sales order and adds a new line item with the quantities you've entered in the CROSS SELLING MATERIALS OVERVIEW screen, as shown in Figure 3.21.

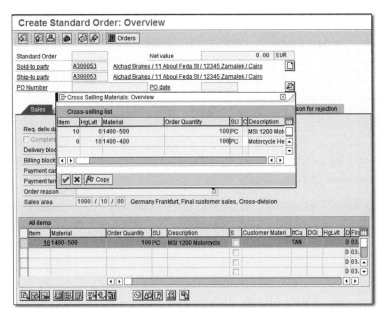

Figure 3.20 Create Standard Order with Cross Selling

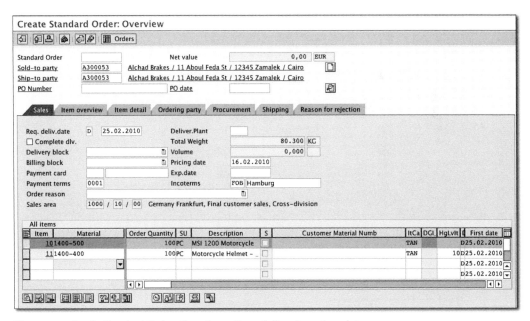

Figure 3.21 Create Standard Order: Overview – Cross Selling Item Complete

3.3.5 Listings and Exclusions in Sales

The last piece of master data that we'll demonstrate by creating a sales order is the record for listings and exclusions. As you remember from Chapter 2, this piece of data will prevent or restrict you from accidentally selling an item to a customer due to geographic, political, or physical restrictions (such as different electrical power standards in voltage).

To see how this works, let's create a sales order starting again with Transaction VA01 (Create Order), or by following the menu path LOGISTICS • SALES AND DISTRIBUTION • SALES • ORDERS • CREATE. Follow these steps:

1. On the CREATE SALES ORDER: INITIAL SCREEN, enter the sales order document type, such as OR – Standard Order, fill in your sales organization data, and press Enter.

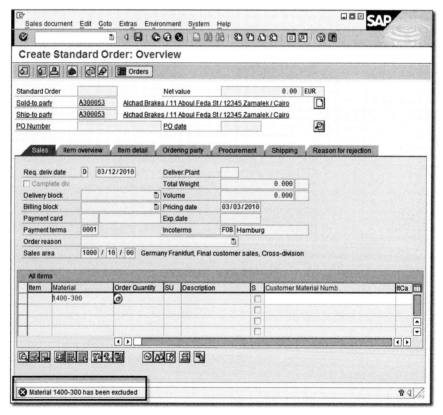

Figure 3.22 Create Standard Order – Exclusion Error

2. On the CREATE SALES ORDER: OVERVIEW SCREEN, enter the number for the customer sold-to that you've maintained in your listing and exclusion record, and press [Enter] to determine the other partners.

3. On the line item, enter the material included in your listing and exclusion record, and press [Enter].

4. You'll run into a "hard stop" error message, which tells you that the material can't be sold to this customer, as shown in Figure 3.22.

3.3.6   Special Orders

So far, we've covered different variations of influencing factors while creating a standard sales order, where the delivery is created upon goods availability date, and the invoice is created after the goods are shipped to your customer.

In addition to the standard sales order, there are also special order types, such as rush order and cash sales, which we'll discuss in the following subsections.

Cash Sale

In cash sales, the goods are paid for immediately when your customer receives them, and the delivery document is created at save. You can define your delivery to be picking relevant or not depending on your business requirements, so you may need to confirm your picks and then post goods issue. Also, when the order is saved, the output condition is triggered to generate the paper invoice as a receipt for your customer.

> **Note**
>
> The invoice output based on the sales order is defined as condition RD03 and triggered automatically by the output determination procedure for sales order type BV.

The subsequent billing document is created at the time of your next billing job in the background with reference to the sales order. You have no account receivables transactions to process because the invoice amount is posted directly to a cash account.

Let's walk through the scenario of creating the cash order, starting again with Transaction VA01 (Create Order), or by following the menu path LOGISTICS • SALES AND DISTRIBUTION • SALES • ORDERS • CREATE. Follow these steps:

1. On the CREATE SALES ORDER: INITIAL SCREEN, enter the sales order document type "BV – Cash Sale", fill in your sales organization data, and press ⸤Enter⸥.

2. On the CREATE SALES ORDER: OVERVIEW Screen, enter the number for the customer sold-to account, and press ⸤Enter⸥ to determine the other partners.

3. On the line item, enter the material and quantity.

4. Enter the price if the pricing conditions aren't maintained, and save your order.

   Upon saving, the delivery document type BV is immediately created using the current system date for the delivery, and the billing dates and system issues output prints an invoice document as a receipt for your customer, as shown in Figure 3.23. You can see the sample of document flow showing order and delivery that was automatically created upon saving.

5. The cash sale is completed with the creation of the billing document BV, created when the billing due list is processed, but an invoice output isn't processed.

Figure 3.23 Cash Sale – Document Flow with Delivery and Transfer Order

---

Note

Consider changes to the standard configuration, for example:

▶ DELIVERY NOT RELEVANT FOR PICKING: If your customer received the goods.

▶ DELIVERY RELEVANT FOR PICKING: If your process requires the customer to pick up the goods from the warehouse or if you have to send the goods.

Rush Order

In a rush order, your customer picks up the goods, or you deliver them the same day the order is placed, but you invoice the customer later.

In the standard SAP system, you define the sales document type SO for rush orders. The subsequent delivery document type LF is created immediately at order save. You then execute picking, removing goods from storage, and posting goods issue. The goods are delivered to or picked up by your customer. Then, the billing documents are created most likely during your standard billing run batch processing, and invoices are printed and sent to your customer.

We'll start the rush order, again with Transaction VA01 (Create Order), or by following the menu path LOGISTICS • SALES AND DISTRIBUTION • SALES • ORDERS • CREATE. Follow these steps:

1. On the CREATE SALES ORDER: INITIAL SCREEN, enter the sales order document type SO – Rush Order, fill in your sales organization data, and press Enter.

2. On the CREATE SALES ORDER: OVERVIEW SCREEN, enter the number for the customer sold-to account, and press Enter to determine the other partners.

3. Add the material, quantity data for the line item, and price if no pricing conditions are maintained, and save your order.

4. Upon save, delivery document type LF is immediately created using the default system date for the delivery and billing dates.

Now that we've walked you through the use of a variety of master data objects described in earlier chapters, let's get to another group of sales documents: scheduling agreements.

3.4   Scheduling Agreements

If you're providing your customers with goods at pre-negotiated time intervals, you're probably using scheduling agreements in the form of an outline agreement that contains delivery dates and preset quantities. Once ready for delivery, you'll transfer these delivery schedule lines into the delivery document on the due date.

> **Note**
>
> You can create scheduling agreements without schedule lines. You can always maintain them later.

Table 3.9 provides a list of a standard scheduling agreement document types you can use out-of-the-box.

Document Type	Item Category
LK – Sched.Agreement ExAg	LKN – SchedAgr w.ExtAgent
	KEN – Consignment Issue
LP – Scheduling Agreement	LPN – Sched.Agreement Item
LZ – SchedAg. w/ del.schd	LZN – Sched.Agreement Item
LZM – SchedAgrt w/Dlv Ord.	LZMA – Dlv. SchedAgree item
LZS – SA:Self-Bill w/Inv.	LZSN – SAlt-SelfBill w/Inv.

Table 3.9 Scheduling Agreements — Document Types and Item Categories

Scheduling agreements are very frequently used in the component supplier industry (e.g., automotive) with heavy use of EDI to communicate with customers. Some of the requirements include the following:

▸ EDI communication

▸ Forecasted or just-in-time (JIT) delivery schedule

▸ Packing instructions

Transaction	Menu Path
VA31 – Create	LOGISTICS • SALES AND DISTRIBUTION • SALES • SCHEDULING AGREEMENT • CREATE
VA32 – Change	LOGISTICS • SALES AND DISTRIBUTION • SALES • SCHEDULING AGREEMENT • CHANGE
VA33 – Display	LOGISTICS • SALES AND DISTRIBUTION • SALES • SCHEDULING AGREEMENT •DISPLAY

Table 3.10 Scheduling Agreements Transactions and Menu Path

You can create a scheduling agreement by executing Transaction VA31 or by following the menu paths listed in Table 3.10. Follow these steps:

1. On the CREATE SCHEDULING AGREEMENT: INITIAL SCREEN, enter the document type LP – Scheduling Agreement, fill in your sales organization data, and press Enter.

2. On the CREATE SCHEDULING AGREEMENT: OVERVIEW SCREEN, enter the number for the customer sold-to account, and press Enter to determine other partners.

3. Add the customer purchase order number if required.

4. Specify the agreement validity dates.

5. Add the material, quantity data for the line item, and price if no pricing conditions exist.

6. To enter the delivery dates, you have to access the schedule line details screen by using the SCHEDULE LINE icon, as highlighted in Figure 3.24, or by going to GOTO • ITEM • SCHEDULE LINES.

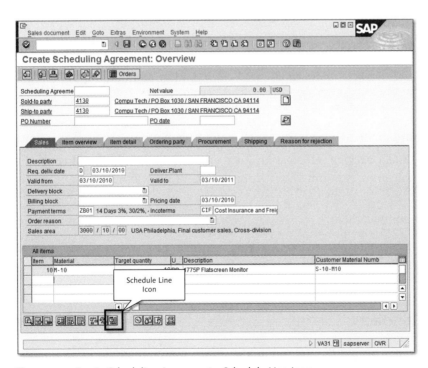

Figure 3.24 Create Scheduling Agreement – Schedule Line Icon

7. Enter the necessary schedule lines, and specify the delivery periods (in days, months, weeks, etc.) and the dates and expected quantities, as shown in Figure 3.25.

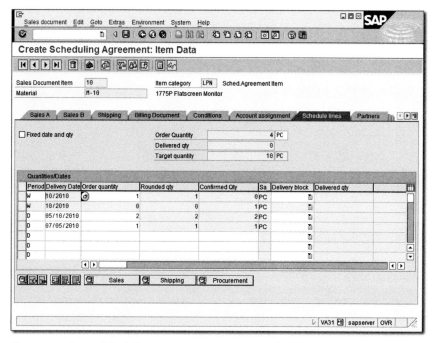

Figure 3.25 Create Scheduling Agreement — Maintain Schedule Lines

8. To return to the overview screen, click the BACK button or press F3.

9. To maintain packing information for your agreement, which will copy into your deliveries, you can select from the menu path EXTRAS • PACKING PROPOSAL.

10. Save your document.

Now that you've completed the scheduling agreements, you're ready to move on to the contracts.

3.5 Contracts

We've already covered the definition and use of contracts as part of the master data objects. You can go back to Chapter 2 and review the functional use for contracts and how they fit into the sales processes. In this section, we'll walk you through an example of contract document creation.

Table 3.11 lists the contract document types you can use as delivered and available in the standard SAP system.

Document Type	Item Category
GK – Global Contract	n/a
CQ – Quantity Contract	KMN – Qty Contract Item
MV – Rental Contract	MVN – Lease Item
WK1 – Value Contract Gen	WKN – Value Contract Item
WK2 – Matl-Rel Value Contract	WKC – ValContrItem-Config.
WV – Service and Maintenance	WVC – Service Contr – conf.
	WVN – Maint.Contract Item
	TAN – Standard Item

Table 3.11 Contract Document Types and Item Categories

You can create a contract by using Transaction VA41 or by following the menu paths listed in Table 3.12.

Transaction	Menu Path
VA41 – Create	LOGISTICS • SALES AND DISTRIBUTION • SALES • CONTRACTS • CREATE
VA42 – Change	LOGISTICS • SALES AND DISTRIBUTION • SALES • CONTRACTS • CHANGE
VA43 – Display	LOGISTICS • SALES AND DISTRIBUTION • SALES • CONTRACTS • DISPLAY

Table 3.12 Contracts – Maintenance Transactions

1. On the CREATE QUANTITY CONTRACT INITIAL screen, enter the document type CQ – Quantity Contract, fill in your sales organization data, and press Enter.

2. On the CREATE QUANTITY CONTRACT OVERVIEW screen, enter your customer sold-to account, and press Enter. The system will determine the other partners.

3. Add the customer purchase order number if required.

4. Specify the contract validity date range.

5. Add the material and quantity data for the line item, enter the price if no pricing conditions exist, and save your document.

Now that you've created a contract document, let's move on to backorders.

3.6   Backorders

Backorder processing allows you to change the committed quantities and overwrite already promised assignment of stock quantities on sales documents and deliveries. This functionality gives you the flexibility in the situation when you receive an order from an important customer for a material, but the entire quantity has already been committed to another customer. Backorder processing will help you change the commitment and assign part or an entire quantity of stock to the sales order placed by a priority customer.

> **Note**
>
> You can process backorders only for materials for which the availability check is set to INDIVIDUAL REQUIREMENTS (usually 02 is standard systems). You can maintain this field in the material master transaction on the SALES GENERAL PLANT view or MRP 3 view.

Your backorder processing transactions use configuration objects such as checking rule and scope of check, which control which documents and requirements are taken into account during the availability check. We'll talk about availability check in detail in later chapters.

You can perform backorder processing in a couple of ways: via manual backorder processing and in automated mass mode using rescheduling functions.

3.6.1   Backorder Processing

You can initiate manual backorder process by using a couple of transaction; each transaction is designed to look at the same commitment issue using different selection criteria. Table 3.13 provides a reference list of the transactions and menu paths.

Transaction	Menu Path
V_RA – SD Documents	LOGISTICS • SALES AND DISTRIBUTION • SALES • BACKORDERS • BACKORDER PROCESSING • SD DOCUMENTS
CO06 – Material	LOGISTICS • SALES AND DISTRIBUTION • SALES • BACKORDERS • BACKORDER PROCESSING • MATERIAL

Table 3.13 Backorder Transactions List

To process backorders with a selection of SD documents, start by using Transaction V_RA or by following the menu path LOGISTICS • SALES AND DISTRIBUTION • SALES • BACKORDERS • BACKORDER PROCESSING • SD DOCUMENTS. Follow these steps:

1. On the initial screen, specify material or the material number range you want to review. You can also specify the plant or range of plants, as shown in Figure 3.26.

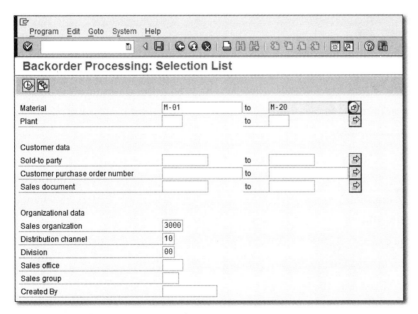

Figure 3.26 Backorder Processing Selection Screen

2. To narrow down your selection, fill in the CUSTOMER DATA section of the screen (it's not mandatory).

3. Your ORGANIZATIONAL DATA section may also limit the number of records returned for processing, so fill in the SALES AREA data whenever possible.

4. Once ready, click the EXECUTE button or press F8.

5. On the BACKORDER PROCESSING SELECTION LIST screen, you'll see a list of the materials that meet your selection criteria. Each line includes the material number and all of the relevant information, including sales document, first delivery date, order quantity, confirmed quantity, and open quantity, as shown in Figure 3.27.

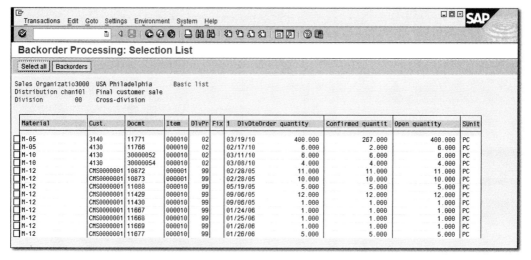

Figure 3.27 Backorder Processing Selection List

6. Here, you can drill into the individual sales documents displaying the order details by double-clicking on the line. You'll access these orders in change mode, for example, running Transaction VA02 (Order Change).

7. You can also access different features by using pull-down menus:

   ▶ Sales document change: ENVIRONMENT • DOCUMENT

   ▶ Display document status: ENVIRONMENT • DOCUMENT STATUS

   ▶ Display document flow: ENVIRONMENT • DOCUMENT FLOW

   ▶ Display changes: ENVIRONMENT • DOCUMENT CHANGES

8. After you select the line for processing, click the BACKORDER button or press F8, and the BACKORDER PROCESSING OVERVIEW appears (Figure 3.28).

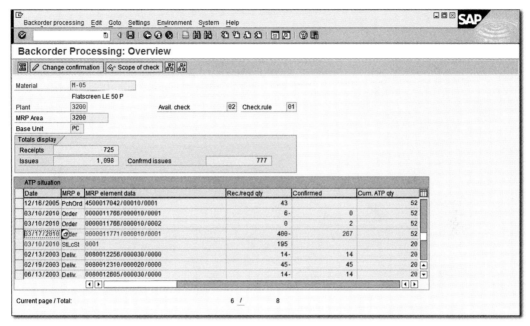

Figure 3.28 Backorder Processing Overview

This overview displays all requirements and relevant dates, purchase orders and production orders, received quantities, the quantities confirmed for the sales order, and deliveries. Your sales order will be highlighted, and this will be the only element that you'll be allowed to change or update.

9. Select the element you want to update (make sure you're selecting the highlighted order line), and click the CHANGE CONFIRMATION button or press F2.

10. Deliveries, purchase orders, and MRP elements other than the sales order relevant for change can't be processed as backorders, so the overview doesn't contain any confirmed quantities for them. However, the system does take the size of the delivery, purchase order, and production order quantities into account when calculating the ATP quantity.

11. When you're satisfied with the updated committed quantities (Figure 3.29), press Enter, and you'll be returned to the BACKORDER OVERVIEW screen.

12. Save your changes.

Figure 3.29 Backorder Processing Committed Quantity Change

3.6.2 Rescheduling

Another form of backorder processing is rescheduling. This automated method is based on the delivery priority settings proposed from the customer master record. The system sorts the orders based on the delivery priority by reshuffling committed quantities to orders of a higher priority. It's recommended that you run this job in background mode because it can dramatically affect the system performance. See Table 3.14 for the list of available rescheduling transactions.

Transaction	Menu Path
V_V2 – Execute	LOGISTICS • SALES AND DISTRIBUTION • SALES • BACKORDERS • RESCHEDULING • EXECUTE
V_R2 – Evaluate	LOGISTICS • SALES AND DISTRIBUTION • SALES • BACKORDER • RESCHEDULING • EVALUATE

Table 3.14 Rescheduling Transactions

When you execute rescheduling Transaction V_V2, you'll get to the initial selection screen when you set your criteria. When running this as a background job, you set a variant that will be executed at the scheduled time. As an example, you can set your criteria on the initial screen of the rescheduling transaction and run it in the foreground, as shown in Figure 3.30. Let's walk through an example of rescheduling in the foreground mode.

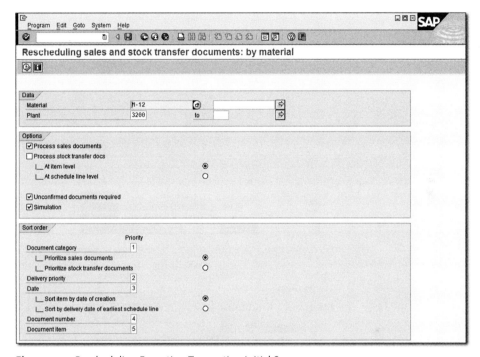

Figure 3.30 Rescheduling Execution Transaction Initial Screen

> **Tip**
>
> Rescheduling should not be done frequently due to the huge consumption of processing power this transaction uses. Narrow down your selection criteria, and run in the time intervals that are outside the normal business hours.

1. In the DATA section of the screen, select your material or range of materials and plant(s) you're processing the rescheduling for.

2. In the OPTIONS section, select what kind of documents you're rescheduling. Select PROCESS SALES ORDERS, as shown in Figure 3.30. If you want to include stock transfer documents, you also need to specify if the line item or a schedule line detail will be taken into consideration.

3. If you select unconfirmed documents required, you'll be carrying out rescheduling for documents with at least one unconfirmed transaction. If you choose to make this selection, you'll increase the number of records for processing.

4. If you choose SIMULATION, you'll be able to review the proposed changes. When ready, simply deselect this option before the true execution takes place and updates your documents.

5. In the SORT ORDER part of the screen, you can define the priority for processing your items. The items and schedule lines found in the selection are sorted according to these criteria: document category, delivery priority, date (i.e., creation date of the item or earliest schedule line date), document number, and document item. Priority 1 is highest priority and priority 5 is the lowest. If you don't want the specific criteria to be used in processing at all, simply enter "0" into the PRIORITY field.

6. When you're ready to execute your simulation, click the EXECUTE button or use [F8]. You'll get the list of the proposed changes for your review, as shown in Figure 3.31.

Figure 3.31 Backorder Processing by Material – Simulation Mode

Behind the scenes, checking rule A is used as a basis for rescheduling sales orders. Exceptions are rush orders (which use checking rule B) and orders with individual customer stock (which use checking rule AE).

▸ A list of proposed changes will be presented for you that shows materials, customer account numbers, documents, order quantities, and old and new confirmed dates.

▸ You can also drill into any of the orders displayed—opening them in change mode allows you to make changes as needed on the fly—by clicking on the listed sales orders or selecting the CHANGE DOCUMENT button.

▸ If you noticed any errors that occurred during processing, you can review the log by using the pull-down menu EDIT • ERROR LOG.

▸ You can also change the scope of the list by clicking on the Improvements or DETERIORATION buttons.

▸ You can use the LIST ORDERS button to link directly to Transaction VA05 (Order List).

If you want to review your rescheduling simulation results again, you can run Transaction V_RA (Evaluation), which specifies the criteria you've used for the simulated rescheduling (shown in Figure 3.32).

Figure 3.32 Rescheduling – Evaluation Selection Screen

If you like the results of the proposed changes, you can go back to the initial re-scheduling Transaction V_V2. Execute it with the original selection criteria, deselect the SIMULATION flag, and run the update.

3.7 Credit Management

SAP Credit Management in conjunction with SAP Risk Management enables you to minimize the risk of delivering your goods to customers that won't be able to pay for them. Maintaining credit limits helps you mitigate those risks. It's defined in the SAP enterprise structures as a credit control area and is assigned to the sales area. You can refresh your memory be going back to Chapter 1, where we covered these structures.

> **Note**
>
> In this section, we won't cover configuration behind SAP Credit Management and SAP Risk Management, which is a part of Financial Accounting Accounts Receivable in SAP ERP Financials. We won't cover the configuration settings that make this functionality applicable and integrated with Sales and Distribution. This functionality is normally maintained and customized by FI team (or system analysts), and is therefore way out of our jurisdiction.

This functionality is very useful if you're dealing with financially difficult customers, or if you do business in the multicurrency markets and countries that have political and financial instabilities. With the available functions of SAP Credit Management, you can define your customer credit limits and apply automatic credit control configuration settings in related business transactions. These controls may result in blocking processing of sales documents in sales and shipping.

In the sales process, you can use the credit status to block the following functions during order processing when creating these documents:

▸ Material reservations

▸ Purchase requisitions

▸ Production orders/planned orders

▸ Output

▸ Deliveries

In shipping, you can use the credit status to block the following subsequent functions:

- Picking
- Packing
- Posting goods issue
- Issuing output

For particularly important or urgent credit problems, you can use output control to specify that email messages are automatically sent to the appropriate credit representative. The credit representative can then process important transactions by reviewing the lists of blocked documents and taking appropriate actions, such as the release of documents, increase of credit limits, and so on.

In the standard SAP system, total credit exposure is calculated based on the system document criteria, combining total commitments, as shown in the following list.

- **Open order value:** This is the value of all order items that haven't yet been delivered. The open order value is based on confirmed quantifies (*Confirmed quantities × Credit price = Open order value of an order*). An order that has been blocked due to a credit check doesn't have any valid confirmed quantities.

- **Open delivery value:** Total value of all delivery items that haven't been billed yet.

- **Open billing value:** Value of all billing items not yet transferred to accounting.

- **Special Liabilities:** This includes receivables from special GL transactions that are transferred from special commitments to total commitments.

- **Receivables:** These are included in total commitments and include incoming payments, for example.

3.7.1 Credit Management Master Data

To use the SAP Credit Management functionality, you have to maintain relevant master data such as risk category and credit limit. Table 3.15 lists the commonly used transactions for SAP Credit Management.

Transaction	Menu Path
FD32 – Change	LOGISTICS • SALES AND DISTRIBUTION • CREDIT MANAGEMENT • MASTER DATA • CHANGE
F.34 – Mass Change	LOGISTICS • SALES AND DISTRIBUTION • CREDIT MANAGEMENT • MASTER DATA • MASS CHANGE
FD33 – Display	LOGISTICS • SALES AND DISTRIBUTION • CREDIT MANAGEMENT • MASTER DATA • DISPLAY

Table 3.15 Credit Management Master Data Transactions

Now let's walk through an example of customer credit management master record change. Start off using Transaction FD32.

1. On the initial screen, enter your customer account number and credit control area. Also, select data sections that you're going to maintain, as shown in Figure 3.33, and press Enter.

Figure 3.33 Customer Credit Management Change – Initial Screen

2. On the OVERVIEW screen, as shown in Figure 3.34, you can see the summary of your credit management data displayed. You can switch between the sections you're trying to maintain by using pull-down menus, or simply by using pressing Shift + F1 to switch between pages.

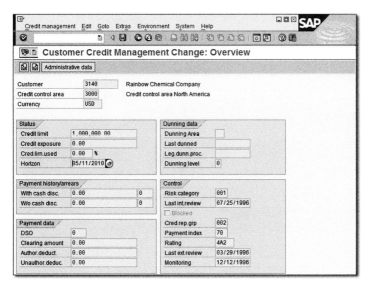

Figure 3.34 Customer Credit Management Change – Overview Screen

3. The STATUS section of you master record allows you to maintain credit limit, risk category, credit representative group, credit control group, texts, and so on (see Figure 3.35).

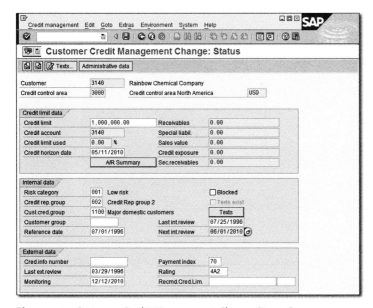

Figure 3.35 Customer Credit Management Change Status Screen

3.7.2 Processing Blocked Sales and Distribution Documents

In the previous section, we covered the master data required for credit management functions to work. Now let's get to the actual process of interacting with the orders on hold that were blocked due to credit restrictions you set in configuration and the credit master data. There are a few transactions that allow you to process sales documents on credit hold, as shown in Table 3.16.

Transaction	Menu Path
VKM1 – Blocked SD documents	LOGISTICS • SALES AND DISTRIBUTION • CREDIT MANAGEMENT • EXCEPTIONS • BLOCKED SD DOCUMENTS
VKM2 – Released	LOGISTICS • SALES AND DISTRIBUTION • CREDIT MANAGEMENT • SALES AND DISTRIBUTION DOCUMENTS • RELEASED
VKM3 – Sales Documents	LOGISTICS • SALES AND DISTRIBUTION • CREDIT MANAGEMENT • SALES AND DISTRIBUTION DOCUMENTS • SALES DOCUMENTS
VKM4 – All	LOGISTICS • SALES AND DISTRIBUTION • CREDIT MANAGEMENT • SALES AND DISTRIBUTION DOCUMENTS • ALL
VKM5 – Delivery	LOGISTICS • SALES AND DISTRIBUTION • CREDIT MANAGEMENT • SALES AND DISTRIBUTION DOCUMENTS • DELIVERY

Table 3.16 Processing Blocked SD Document Transactions

We'll walk through an example of processing blocked orders using Transaction VKM1 (Blocked SD Documents), as discussed in Table 3.16.

1. On the initial screen, at the minimum, enter your credit control area number and if possible any other criteria, such as the customer account number to help narrow down your selection (see Figure 3.36). Press F8 to continue.

2. On the next screen, you'll get a list of all blocked orders waiting for credit management action, as shown in Figure 3.37. You can perform different actions from this one screen, which you can see if you use the EDIT option pull-down menus or function buttons (see Figure 3.38). The following functions can be performed:

   ▹ Release the sales document to approve the transaction.

   ▹ Reject credit and cancel the document.

   ▹ Forward a blocked document to another processor.

▶ Recheck a blocked sales document.

▶ Reassign the blocked document and specify a new sequence.

Figure 3.36 Blocked SD Documents – Initial Screen

Figure 3.37 Blocked SD Documents List

After you perform an action of choice, your report will be updated with the status icon representing the action you're intending to perform. The system displays a processing status icon in the first column of your report, as shown in Figure 3.39.

You have to save the report to apply all of your actions. This results in a log update that you'll see at the end of the process, as shown in Figure 3.40.

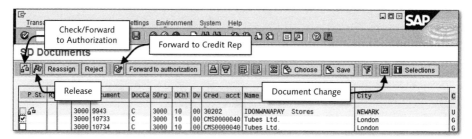

Figure 3.38 Credit Review Action Buttons

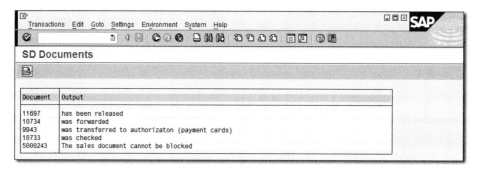

Figure 3.39 Credit Release – Status Update

Document	Output
11697	has been released
10734	was forwarded
9943	was transferred to authorizaton (payment cards)
10733	was checked
5000243	The sales document cannot be blocked

Figure 3.40 Release SD Documents – Processing Log

Note

As of SAP ERP 6.0 EHP 6, Transactions VKM1 through VKM5 have been enhanced with a much more versatile search screen. You can search all listed sales documents more precisely for a specific partner function, which classifies the responsible people or partners. In the selection results, the output list is displayed using the SAP List Viewer in the current version. This allows you to process the list with more versatility and change the layout in different ways. There are multiple layout variants for the individual transactions.

With EHP 6, you now have a much bigger list of fields for selection and all right there on the main screen; which means that you don't need to jump through pop-up screens making it, as SAP calls it, a flat navigation.

3.8 Foreign Trade

Foreign trade (which we also refer to as FT) is a standard SAP ERP functionality that's included in the Sales and Distribution component. In this section, we'll shed some light on what's available in the core foreign trade and customs functionality. In general, the out-of-the-box solution can provide enough functionality for your import and export transactions to make sure they are handled in accordance with the current laws and regulations.

Like most SAP functionalities, foreign trade processes are also based on configuration and master data settings. As we did before, the following section explains some of the most important configuration settings to allow you to understand how these settings impact your day-to-day work.

3.8.1 Configuration Objects

The static data set in configuration is used in the foreign trade functionality, as you'll see when you maintain foreign trade master data for the material master or customer master.

▶ GEOGRAPHICAL INFO: Foreign trade data comes from the route, then from Customizing (default header data), and finally from enhancements if none of the standard procedures work for you.

▶ COMMODITY CODE: You can use internationally standardized codes developed based on the Harmonized Schedule (HS) for classification of goods since 1988. You can assign the commodity codes to your material master records.

▶ MODE OF TRANSPORT: The mode of transport defines the way your goods will enter the destination country. This can be stored on the route record or in Customizing for default data for a business transaction.

- ► CUSTOMS OFFICE: The customs office is the location where your export delivery must be registered before it leaves the jurisdiction of a country. The office is assigned to the office of departure and registered at the destination where the goods have to report to the office of destination. The customs office can be saved on the route or can be configured as part of the default data for a business transaction.

- ► PROCEDURE: The procedure defines the customs procedure for the transfer of goods and the customs procedure for incoming goods. Maintenance of these procedures controls what can be used in import and export documents.

- ► BUSINESS TRANSACTION TYPE: This is a two-digit code identification required for the EU Intrastat reporting of import and export data. When an export license is assigned to an item in a sales document, the business transaction type of the item must match that of the export license.

3.8.2 Foreign Trade Master Data

You'll be applying the configuration data that we described in the previous section to master data, including vendor master, purchasing info records, the material master, routes, and the customer master. In the next few sections, we'll briefly describe where to find the master data connections to foreign trade settings related to SD objects.

- ► **Customer master:** Contains geographical data in the address section and, for example, the VAT registration number.

- ► **Route:** In route data, you store the geographical information needed for foreign trade processing but also, as we discussed in Chapter 2, you have the option to maintain connection points. There you can maintain data for customs offices, as you can see in Figure 3.41.

- ► **Material master:** You can maintain data for both imports and export. Here you can maintain data such as the commodity code, country of origin, customs tariffs data, and export certificates. Again, all of this will be accessed during the sales document processing, which triggers actions that will follow up with export documents, EDI transmissions reporting to the customs authorities, and so on. See Figure 3.42 for the export view of a material master.

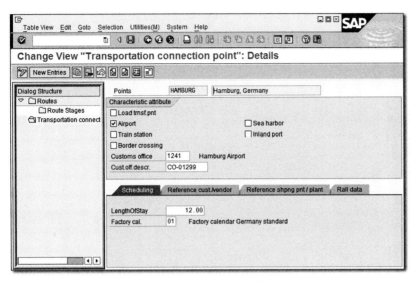

Figure 3.41 Route Transportation Connection Point Data

Figure 3.42 Material Master Foreign Trade Export Data Tab

3.8.3 Foreign Trade in Sales Order, Delivery, and Billing

Foreign trade data is relevant to the sales order, delivery, and billing documents in Sales and Distribution. In this section, we'll talk about how each component of the customer master and the material master, described in previous sections, will be a key component in the success of the sales cycle (sales order, delivery, post goods issue, and invoice), or will also fail based on the incompletion procedure defined in configuration.

Sales Orders

You can find foreign trade data-relevant fields in the header as well as the item levels of a specific sales order, some of them calculated by the system and others are copied from the customer master, material master, and the route. These fields are always available, even if foreign trade is not active.

You can find fields that are specific to foreign trade in the sales order header data under the BILLING tab. Locate yourself inside the sales order by changing or displaying your order via the menu path LOGISTICS • SALES AND DISTRIBUTION • SALES • ORDER (Change [VA02] or Display [VA03]). Once you're inside the sales order, you can select GOTO • HEADER • BILLING (see Figure 3.43). You can see that most of the fields are filled automatically from the partner data and material master.

> **Note**
>
> PAYMENT TERMS as well as risk management data such as PAYMENT GUARANTEE PROC are determined via the partner-payer in the sales header. Although both fields are maintained at the sales order, they are important for foreign trade billing.

Other important foreign trade data is determined at the item level, especially from the route determination and geographic conditions. You can locate foreign trade item fields inside the sales order by choosing GOTO • ITEM • SALES. One of the most important fields at the item level is the BUS.TRANSACTION type. The business transaction is mainly used within the European Union as required for Intrastat import and export data.

Let's discuss how the foreign trade data impact the rest of the process steps, including the delivery header and item as well as the invoice.

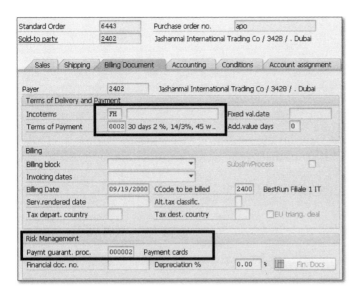

Figure 3.43 Sales Order Header Billing Tab, Foreign Trade Fields

Deliveries

Although you can find foreign trade relevant fields in the sales order, it's only at the delivery levels where the incompletion procedure kicks in. This procedure will alert you if any fields haven't been filled in correctly. You'll be notified so that you can react accordingly.

You're able to see the incompletion procedure at both header and item of a specific delivery. If you'd like to display the details of the procedure, go to LOGISTICS • SALES AND DISTRIBUTION • SHIPPING AND TRANSPORTATION • OUTBOUND DELIVERY • CHANGE (VL02N) or DISPLAY (VL03N). Once you're in the DELIVERY screen, select GOTO • HEADER • FOREIGN TRADE. See Figure 3.44. You can easily review what data and fields are relevant for foreign trade by simply accessing the INCOMPLETENESS ANALYSIS button.

Based on what fields are configured, you can find a detailed list and track down the problem. Proceed to adjust the information in the fields by typing in missing or corrected data, until the incompletion procedure is flagged as completed or the traffic light for foreign trade status turns green.

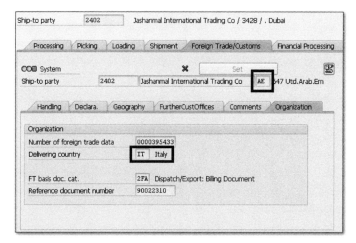

Figure 3.44 Delivery Header Foreign Trade Tab, Origin, and Destination Country

> **Note**
>
> You can process several deliveries simultaneously and expedite the incompletion procedure adjustments using the FT Cockpit under INDIVIDUAL MAINTENANCE to display the incompletion logs at the header via the incompleteness analysis. To access the FT Cockpit follow this menu path: LOGISTICS • SALES AND DISTRIBUTION • FOREIGN TRADE/CUSTOMS • GENERAL FOREIGN TRADE PROCESSING • COCKPIT – GENERAL FOREIGN TRADE PROCESSING or use Transaction EN99. You can experiment with this transaction based on your specific needs.

FT-relevant information is determined by the system in the background. You may find it interesting that SAP considers the *country* to be the departing country where the associated plant is located. The country where the goods will be delivered is based on the ship-to country.

> **Note**
>
> FT HEADER/ITEM fields are activated in both the delivery and billing document automatically when the system notices a difference between the departing country and destination.

Let's now discuss how the foreign trade data impacts the delivery item and how the FT data comes from the sales order.

Delivery Item

At the delivery item, you can find similar incompletion checks as in the sales order header. An incompleteness analysis is provided when you access the details of the delivery item. See the menu path in the previous section (Transaction VL02N and VL03N). You can get the details by highlighting the item and following GOTO • ITEM • FOREIGN TRADE. You then navigate on to the tabs. You can easily review what data and fields are relevant for foreign trade by simply accessing the INCOMPLETENESS ANALYSIS button. According to what item fields are configured, you can find a detailed list and related problems. Proceed to adjust item fields as necessary until the incompletion procedure if flagged as completed or the traffic light for foreign trade status turns green.

The last step of the SD process, the invoice, is also impacted by the FT data from the sales order. Let's find out how the invoice header and item will copy FT data from sales orders, deliveries, and master data.

Invoice Header

At the invoice level, you are able to see the FT procedure and logs. Invoice generation and releasing to accounting is where the final FT check is done. It's very common to find customer invoices not being released to accounting due to FT incompletion logs and procedures. You may also find that these kinds of problems are sometimes a bit hidden inside the details of the invoice. Following the below steps, you'll find an easier way to catch and correct those errors.

1. Access the invoice from the SAP menu LOGISTICS • SALES AND DISTRIBUTION • BILLING • BILLING DOCUMENT • CHANGE (VF02) or DISPLAY (VF03).

2. Type in the invoice number and then follow the menu GOTO • HEADER • FOREIGN TRADE/CUSTOMS. Upon configuration and individual needs, you'll see a set of different fields applicable to specific FT checks. As default, MODE OF TRANSPORTATION or EXPORT OFFICE will be some of the fields FT checks in the standard system. However, you may also find some other fields are applicable. See Figure 3.45 for header FT data.

> **Note**
>
> If you want to see a list of invoices with FT incomplete logs, follow the menu path above to change or display (VF02/VF03). Select the matchcode <F4> in the upper right corner, and select TRANSFERRED TO ACCOUNTING/ACCRUAL NOT YET COMPLETED. You'll get a list of

invoices that haven't been transferred. Proceed individually to complete FT logs. Additionally, the FT Cockpit can provide a similar report for mass processing.

Figure 3.45 Billing Header Foreign Trade Tab, Mode of Transport

Invoice Item

It's very common that you find errors are the invoice item level, some applicable to FT checks. As with the delivery items, at the invoice item, you can find incompletion checks. An incompleteness analysis is provided when you access the details of the invoice item. See the menu path in the previous section to access the invoice (Transaction VF02 or VF03).

1. You can get the details by highlighting the item and following GOTO • ITEM • FOREIGN TRADE ITEM. You then navigate on to the tabs. A commonly missing FT field is COMMODITY CODE OF THE HARMONIZED SYSTEM, typically stored in the material master.

2. Navigate and review what other FT data could be missing by simply accessing the INCOMPLETENESS ANALYSIS button. According to what item fields are configured in your system, you can find a detailed list and related problems.

3. Proceed to adjust the content of the item fields as necessary until the item incompletion procedure is flagged as completed, or the traffic light for foreign trade status turns green.

> **Note**
>
> Any changes to the delivery FT fields should be done before the invoice is created. Once created, you won't be able to change any fields, including FT.

3.8.4 Foreign Trade Cockpits

As in many other areas in SAP, cockpit transactions have been developed to make the functionality as simple as possible and cover functions such as master data maintenance, inbound and outbound shipment processing, periodic processing, and more. We won't go into too much detail about the foreign trade functionality because it's so vast and so specific to the geography and economic region you're operating in and out of. It would be impossible to cover it all, so you're free to explore the transactions if you're planning or already using the standard core component.

3.9 Returns

Your customers' complaints can be executed by one of several available processes. The provided documents as listed in Figure 3.46 include returns, free-of-charge deliveries, free-of-charge subsequent deliveries, credit and debit memos, and invoice correction requests. In this section, we'll cover returns order processing only. The other forms of complaints documents will be covered in the corresponding chapters covering deliveries and billing documents.

You create returns orders when your customer is sending goods back to you because they were damaged during shipment, were the wrong items, or were outside of the allowed shelf life. The process starts with the customer returning the goods. You create a return order to process it, and then, if the customer wants a refund for the amount you've invoiced, you create a credit memo with reference to the returns order. If the customer still wants to replace the originally shipped goods, you create a free-of-charge subsequent delivery referencing your returns sales order.

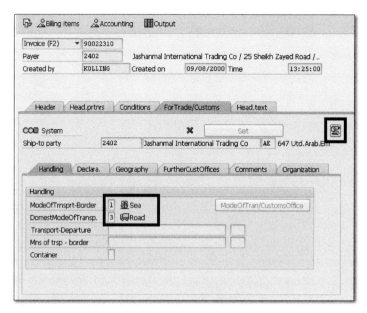

Figure 3.46 Returns Order Document Flow

3.9.1 Returns Order

Start with Transaction VA01 (Create Order), or follow the menu path LOGISTICS •
SALES AND DISTRIBUTION • SALES • ORDERS • CREATE. Follow these steps:

1. On the CREATE SALES ORDER: INITIAL SCREEN, enter the sales order document
   type RE – Returns, fill in your sales organization data, and then press Enter.
   You can also create the return with reference to the original sales order and
   select the items you're getting back from the customer. You may be required to
   enter the reason for this document, and it may also be blocked for billing pending quality or credit approval before the billing document gets created,
   depending on your business process.

2. On the CREATE SALES ORDER: OVERVIEW SCREEN, enter the number for the customer sold-to account, and press Enter to determine the other partners.

3. On the line item, enter the material and quantity if the item didn't copy from
   the reference sales order, as shown in Figure 3.47.

4. If you're referencing the original order, all pricing information will be copied
   into the returns order. If the item you're getting back needs a price, add it, and
   save your order.

Figure 3.47 Create Returns Order Overview

3.9.2 Returns Delivery

Next, if you're expecting the delivery of goods from your customer, you create a returns delivery. You can do this directly at the end of the sales order creation by going to SALES DOCUMENTS • DELIVER. You can also do this by running Transaction VL01N (Create Outbound Delivery), or by running the transaction for collective processing of documents due for delivery, such as VL10A (Sales Orders). For more details on delivery processing, see Chapter 4.

Next, we'll walk you through the steps of creating of delivery using Transaction VL01N (Create Delivery with Reference to Sales Order).

1. On the CREATE OUTBOUND DELIVERY WITH ORDER REFERENCE initial screen, specify the shipping point number, shipping date, and sales order number you want to process delivery for, and then press ⌊Enter⌋ (see Figure 3.48).

2. On the next screen, RETURNS DELIVERY CREATE: OVERVIEW, notice that all of the order header and item data relevant for the delivery document is copied straight from the returns order. Verify the entries, and click the SAVE button to complete, as shown in Figure 3.49.

Figure 3.48 Create Returns Delivery Initial Screen

Figure 3.49 Returns Delivery Overview Screen

3. The follow-up function of creating the transfer order is required if your item category definition requires pick confirmation, and you're receiving your returns into a warehouse managed location. If you are in the non-WM location, you may have to confirm the pick quantities on the DELIVERY PICKING tab instead of transfer orders, confirming the quantities received back from the customer.

4. After you're done with the pick confirmation, you can post goods receipt by clicking the POST GOODS RECEIPT button on the delivery screen. This posts material and financial documents to complete the delivery-processing portion of your return order.

3.9.3 Billing Document

The last step required in the process is creation of the credit memo with reference to the returns sales order. We'll discuss billing documents in detail in Chapter 5, but you can find details for credit memo creation for returns in this section. Start by running Transaction VF01 (Create Billing Document), as shown in Figure 3.50.

Figure 3.50 Create Billing Document Initial Screen

1. On the CREATE BILLING DOCUMENT: INITIAL SCREEN, enter the sales order document number in the DOCUMENT column, and press Enter .

2. On the CREDIT FOR RETURNS CREATE OVERVIEW OF BILLING ITEMS screen, verify that all data copied from the returns order is correct. Once verified, click SAVE to complete your credit memo document. The refund will be issued to your customer.

3.9.4 Subsequent Delivery Free of Charge Order

A free-of-charge subsequent delivery is a sales document, like a standard order, which is created to supply your customer with replacement goods, if the customer wants a replacement product. To do this, you must enter a free-of-charge subsequent delivery with reference to the return document created earlier as a complaint. Let's start with running Transaction VA01 (Create Sales Order).

1. On the CREATE SALES ORDER: INITIAL SCREEN, enter the sales order document type SDF – Subsequent Delivery Free of Charge, fill in your sales organization data, and press ⌈Enter⌋. Create this order with reference to the original returns sales order by using the original order number and then click the CREATE WITH REFERENCE button.

2. On the pop-up window, specify the source returns document number. If you need to choose only specific line items, click the ITEM SELECTION button to check which item(s) you'll be using in your free-of-charge sales order. If you don't plan on making any item selections, click the COPY button to continue.

3. On the main screen of CREATE SUBSEQUENT DELIVERY FREE OF CHARGE, verify the data that was copied from your source returns order, such as the following:

   ▸ Material numbers or text in the DESCRIPTION field if no material number exists

   ▸ Quantities

   ▸ Note item categories determined

4. When ready to complete the process, click SAVE, and you can process the delivery for your order. For more details on delivery processing, see Chapter 4.

3.10 Special Processes in Sales

SAP supports several unique sales processes such as make-to-order, third-party, configurable products, and others. These all differ, with steps you need to perform to complete the process from order taking to billing, but in essence the sales process remains the same: The sales document type uses a special item category that triggers a special subsequent function that is unique to your needs.

> **Note**
>
> Although there are many different flavors of these processes as listed here, we'll describe some of the most common ones in more detail in the upcoming sections.

▶ **Cross-company sales**

This process is widely used when you have to move goods or provide services to a sister company. Your order will have a delivery—just like any other sales order—and you'll execute picking when dealing with goods, and then post goods issue. You sales process will end with a cross-company billing document, and FI documents behind will post to the corresponding company codes books. We'll cover this process in detail in Section 3.10.1.

▶ **Third-party order**

Your company doesn't deliver the goods ordered by your customers; instead, you pass the customer requirements to a third-party supplier who then ships the goods directly to the customer and bills you. In SAP ERP, your order will have a third-party item category defined to immediately create a purchase requisition. The standard Materials Management process would take that requisition via your standard procurement processes, creating a purchase order for your vendor. Upon delivery, your vendor will notify you that the goods left its facilities. This triggers your receiving process, which then ends up with an invoice and payables to your supplier. You finish by creating the billing document for your customer. We'll cover this process in detail in Section 3.10.2.

▶ **Make-to-order**

You manufacture a relatively small number of products with a huge number of characteristics, crafting them uniquely to a customer's request. Basically, your products are made to the customer's order. Each time you take an order, your requirements will be translated into a production order tied to your order as a unique sales order stock identified by your sales order number. Integration with Production Planning will ensure that your production department gets the requirements the minute the order is saved. Upon completion, you'll be notified to start delivery processing and complete this process with the standard billing run. We'll cover this process in Section 3.10.3.

▶ **Consignment process**

You're using SAP consignment when you store your goods at the customer location but the goods are owned by your company. The customer won't pay for these goods until they remove them from consignment stock to consume them. Then you'll bill your customer, and possibly replenish the quantities stored at customer's site. We'll discuss this process in detail in Section 3.10.4.

▶ **Configurable materials**

Configurable materials are complex products that you can manufacture with many variations. Configurable materials using variant configurations allow you to build an order for a car, for example, where you get to choose from predefined body styles, paint colors, interior styles and colors, equipment options, engine, and transmission. All that information together with the BOM can then be used to transfer the requirements to a production order that then will be used to manufacture the requested product. Variant configuration gives you a lot of flexibility and can be extremely complex.

▶ **Sales bill of material**
A sales BOM lists components that together create a saleable product—or a kit—without transferring any requirements and translation to production order(s). You could use it, for example, when selling computers as a kit together with an LCD monitor, wireless keyboard, and a mouse. You're not really putting any assembly work into building your kit; you're just picking the components and shipping them together to the customer. Use sales BOMs where components are relatively high-level materials that can be sold separately.

Now, as promised, let's move to a more detailed overview of the processes that are widely used across different business scenarios and by different industries. We'll cover cross-company sales, third party, make-to-order, custom consignment, and sales order with BOM scenarios.

3.10.1 Cross-Company Sales

Before we get to the details, we'll start by describing the requirements that need to be filled, such as Customizing and master data. This scenario requires certain configuration settings that permit shipping from a sister company code plant on behalf of the company code that created a sales order for a customer, which is done in Customizing.

In our scenario, we'll have two company codes (1000 and 2200) and two sales organizations (1000 and 2200) assigned to corresponding company codes, and there will be plants assigned to the company codes and sales organizations as well. Plant 1200 will be shared by both sales organizations as a permitted delivery plant. See Figure 3.51 for an overview of the organizational components involved in this scenario. The assignment will give your sales organizations the ability to process your sales orders across multiple business units. All parties involved in this process also must have corresponding customer master data maintained and assigned in Customizing.

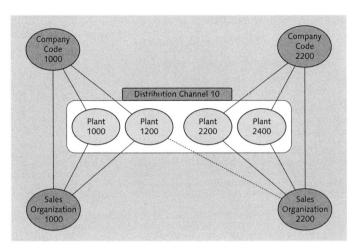

Figure 3.51 Delivery Plant Assignment for Cross-Company Code Sales

Your customer master record for the ordering company code must have all relevant information for the billing process to take place. In the example, our sister company payer is defined as Customer 22000.

Another important piece of information used during this scenario will be contained in pricing conditions. We'll be using intercompany pricing conditions PI01 in the sales order and IV01 during internal invoice billing. The values are transferred from the sales order to the billing document using the copy procedures defined in Customizing.

Let's walk through a business scenario where a customer orders goods from sales organization 2200. The goods, however, are produced in your production plant 1200, which belongs to company code 1000. Sales organization 2200 has an agreement that a particular type of goods will be furnished directly to the customer from sister company code 1000 and specifically plant 1200. The sales requirements are transferred directly to plant 1200. You then create the delivery, pick the goods, and ship directly to the customer of sales organization 2200. Sales organization 2200 issues the invoice, which is sent to the customer, and your sales organization 1000 (supplying company code) issues an invoice to sales organization 2200 (the ordering company code). See Figure 3.52 for a flow chart depicting the transactions and steps in this scenario.

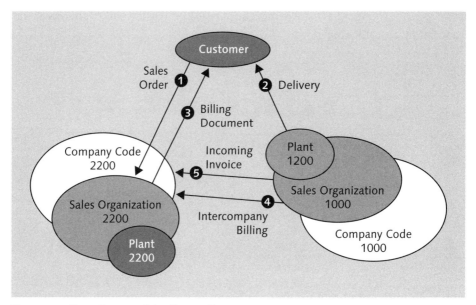

Figure 3.52 Cross-Company Sales Process Flow

Step 1

Create a sales order starting with Transaction VA01 (Create Order) or by using the menu path LOGISTICS • SALES AND DISTRIBUTION • SALES • ORDERS • CREATE. To complete the transaction, follow these steps:

1. On the CREATE SALES ORDER initial screen, enter the sales order document type, such as OR – Standard Order, and fill in your sales organization data, where your selling organization from the scenario described before is 2200, distribution channel is 10, and division is 00. Press Enter.

2. Enter the number for the customer sold-to (for example, 2500), and press Enter to determine the other partners.

3. On the line item, enter the material and quantity.

4. Enter the price if pricing conditions aren't maintained.

5. Replace the delivery plant with the supplying company code plant; in our example, enter plant 1200, as shown in Figure 3.53.

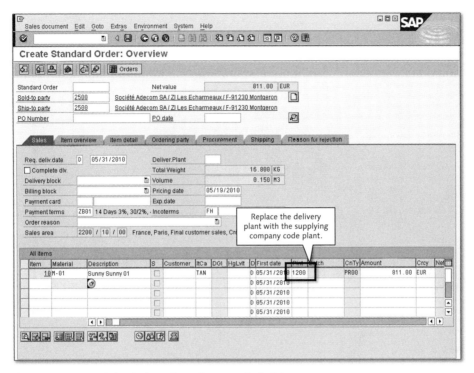

Figure 3.53 Create Sales Order – Cross-Company Code Sales

6. Check your pricing condition details. Unlike a standard order, you'll have additional conditions showing. The condition type PR00 represents the price that is to be billed to the customer. But you'll find other conditions such as PI01, as shown in Figure 3.54.

7. This condition is used to capture the price that the ordering company code 2200 has to pay to the supplying company code 1000. This value will then appear in the internal intercompany billing document. The standard SAP system provides you with two condition types for the intercompany prices: PI01 (based on quantity) and PI02 (based on percentage of price). These condition values are determined using standard condition technique (detailed in Chapter 2), and, in this example, they are accessed based on the sales organization, delivering plant, and material. They also have no impact on the final price determination for the customer.

8. You can now save your order.

Figure 3.54 Cross-Company Sales Order – Intercompany Pricing Record

Step 2

Create an outbound delivery starting with Transaction VL01N (Create Outbound Delivery) or by following the menu path LOGISTICS • SALES AND DISTRIBUTION • SHIPPING AND TRANSPORTATION • OUTBOUND DELIVERY • CREATE • SINGLE DOCUMENT • WITH REFERENCE TO SALES ORDER. Follow these steps:

1. On the CREATE OUTBOUND DELIVERY WITH ORDER REFERENCE initial screen, specify the shipping point number, shipping date, and sales order number you want to process delivery for, and then press Enter.

2. On the next screen, you'll see all of the order header and item data relevant for the delivery document copied straight from the sales order. Verify the entries, and click the SAVE button to complete.

3. The follow-up function of creating the transfer order is required if your item category definition requires pick confirmation and you're receiving your returns into a warehouse-managed location. If you're working within a non-WM managed location, you also may have to confirm the pick quantities for the customer order on the delivery PICKING tab. Figure 3.55 shows the delivery PICKING tab of a WM managed location after pick confirmation of transfer orders.

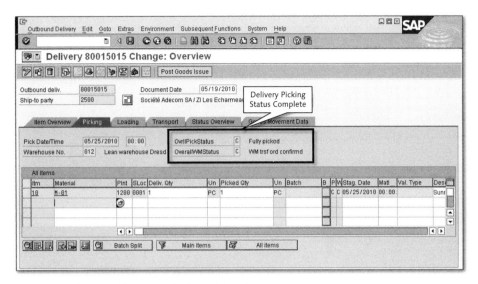

Figure 3.55 Outbound Delivery – Picking Status Complete

4. After you're done with the pick confirmation, you're ready to post goods issue by clicking the POST GOODS ISSUE button on the delivery screen. This will post material and financial documents.

Step 3

Create a billing document for the customer in the ordering company code with these steps:

1. On the CREATE BILLING DOCUMENT initial screen, enter the outbound delivery number from the previous step in the DOCUMENT column, and press Enter.

2. On the INVOICE CREATE OVERVIEW OF BILLING ITEMS screen, you can verify that all data copied from the returns order is correct. Note the billing document type—F2 – Invoice—used for standard customer orders (see Figure 3.56).

3. This invoice will be submitted to the customer by company code 2200 (see the header data showing the sales organization presenting the invoice) as shown in Figure 3.57. Notice that the original intercompany conditions are copied into your billing document. They aren't used for any calculation though; they are purely statistical and will be used by accounting to calculate profitability.

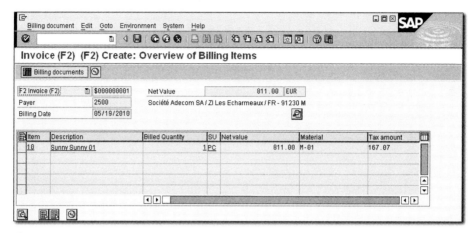

Figure 3.56 Invoice Create – Overview Screen

Figure 3.57 Billing Documents – Header Data General Information

4. Once verified, click SAVE to complete your billing document.

Step 4

Create an intercompany invoice. After the invoice for the end customer is created, the same outbound delivery document used before is entered in the billing

due list of the sales organization of the supplying company code 1000. An intercompany invoice is created for the ordering company code. This invoice uses the
intercompany price from your sales order captured in condition PI01 or PI02
depending on your scenario. Use Transaction VF01 (Billing Document Create),
and follow these steps:

1. On the CREATE BILLING DOCUMENT initial screen, enter the same outbound
   delivery number from the previous billing step in the DOCUMENT column, and
   press Enter . On the INVOICE CREATE OVERVIEW OF BILLING ITEMS screen, you
   can see all master data and data copied from the sales order. Note the billing
   document type is now IV-Intercompany Billing (see Figure 3.58).

Figure 3.58 Intercompany Billing – Overview Screen

2. Use the ITEM PRICING CONDITIONS button or the pull-down menu path GOTO •
   ITEM • ITEM CONDITIONS. You'll see that the price used for billing came from the
   sales order condition PI01 and the values are copied into IV01 – Intercompany
   Price pricing conditions (see Figure 3.59).

3. In the intercompany pricing procedure—condition type PR00—PRICE is inactive because of the subsequent intercompany price, and you can view it for
   informational purposes. Condition type IV01 with the values copied from the
   original sales order condition PI01 carries the price that will be used for the
   billing document you're preparing for the ordering company code customer
   (in our example, customer 22000). Also, for accounting purposes, the value
   from condition IV01 will be used in accounting to capture the sales revenue for
   the supplying company code (in our example, company code 1000).

Figure 3.59 Intercompany Billing Document Create – Pricing Conditions

4. The revenue is also calculated from subtracting VPRS cost value from your IV01 intercompany price entry. This represents your profit margin posted to the CO/PA component.

5. Upon review of all this data, you can save. The financial document is released to accounting as well, if you allow the automatic release.

Step 5

Create the incoming AP invoice. Upon receipt of the billing document, the ordering company code (in our example, company code 2200) has to create the accounts payable invoice to pay the supplying company code 1000 for the goods shipped to the external customer. You can enter this invoice manually by creating the FI invoice. You can also automate this process by providing the output routine, which creates an incoming EDI message that the ordering company code recognizes as an incoming invoice.

Manual Invoice

If you're using a manual process, the ordering company code (2200 in our example) will have to enter the invoice manually based on the printed or faxed intercompany billing document. An invoice document can be printed in the supplying company code (1000) using output message type RD00–Invoice. You can issue output and print immediately or use Transaction VF02 (Billing Document Change), for example, to issue it at your leisure. For more on standard output functions, see Chapter 2 and Appendix B.

Automatic Invoice Receipt

If you're planning on automating the invoice receipts creation, your output conditions will require RD04 – Invoice Receipt MM to be defined and determined during intercompany billing document creation (see Figure 3.60). Automatic posting to vendor account is triggered when message type RD04 is processed into an EDI (Electronic Data Interchange) document. This document will use a message category (INVOIC – invoice) and will use an internal processing variant (FI), which allows you to post the translated incoming invoice receipt directly in Financial Accounting. Also, remember that the payee vendor master record must exist for your supplying company code.

Figure 3.60 Intercompany Billing Output – RD04 Condition for MM Invoice

Now that we've thoroughly covered the cross-company code sales process, let's talk in detail about the third-party order scenario.

3.10.2 Third-Party Sales Order

The third-party sales orders are common in the business world. You're basically arranging to ship goods direct from your supplier on your behalf. Just as in the previous scenario, we also have to have certain configuration settings and master data in place before you can execute this model. One of the most important will be the component of the sales order type that you may want to be defined specifically for this process if you need to isolate this activity at the document header level. You may also decide to standard sales document type like OR – Standard Order, and use the pre-delivered item category TAS – Third-Party Item instead. Also, the other important component is the schedule line category CS – Leg (see Figure 3.61 for configuration details of the schedule line). These settings are maintained using Customizing Transaction VOV6 (Maintain Schedule Line Categories) by your SAP system analyst or configuration team (see Figure 3.61).

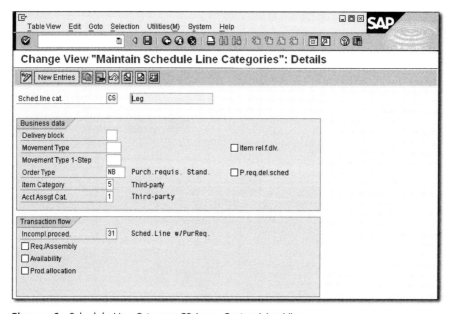

Figure 3.61 Schedule Line Category CS-Leg – Customizing View

The schedule line makes a connection to the purchasing side of this scenario and defines the behavior of to-be-generated purchase requisitions. You can also look for more details on sales document types, item categories and schedule lines, the determination of the relevant categories, and more by going back to the beginning of this chapter.

The configuration settings allow you to transition from your sales order to purchase requisition and finally, upon approval—using release strategies in purchasing—to a purchase order. Table 3.17 shows how data is passed between these documents and what item categories and account assignment are applied on the purchasing side of this scenario.

Sales Order	Purchase Requisition	Purchase Order
Material	Material	Material
Quantity	Quantity	Quantity
Item Category – TAS Schedule Line – CS	Item Category – S Account Assignment – X	Item Category – S Account Assignment – X
Delivery Date	Delivery Date	Delivery Date

Table 3.17 Data Transfers from Sales Order to Purchase Order

This leads us to another component needed to complete this process: material master data. If required by your business requirements, you can permanently default the item category to TAS – Third-Party Item by using standard configuration values in your material master SALES ORG 2 view and setting the item category group field to BANS – Third-Party Item. Figure 3.62 shows the material master view and the SALES: SALES ORG 2 tab. You can access this screen using Transaction MM02 (Material Master Change).

Figure 3.62 Material Master – Sales View Maintenance

This setting causes your item category determination to always select item category TAS for orders with materials to be exclusively procured from an external supplier and shipped directly to your customers. If you need the flexibility of processing your orders in a variety of different ways, however, and only sometimes have your supplier send the goods to your customers, you can leave the settings alone. Make sure, however, that you allow for a manual selection of item category TAS in your item category determination, which is normally done by a system analyst in Customizing. You can also refer to the beginning of this chapter, which details the item categories and schedule lines.

Another very important setting buried in configuration is *billing relevancy*. If your billing relevance setting in configuration for your item category TAS is set to F, your billing document will reflect what your vendor invoice entries had for quantities. So, for example, if your sales order was for a quantity of 10 pieces of material, and your supplier delivered and billed you for a partial of 5, the system will allow you to create a billing document to a customer only for the quantity of 5. If you don't need this level of detail, or if your vendor always fulfills the complete order shipments, you can set your billing relevancy configuration to B, which is order based, and regardless of whether the invoice receipt is for a partial or not, your customer will be invoiced for the total order quantity (e.g., if order placed was for a quantity of 10 pieces, your next billing run will scoop this order up and will invoice your customer for 10 pieces). All of these rules can be fine-tuned by maintenance of the copy control mechanism between sales order and billing documents. Again, this is the area that is normally in the jurisdiction of system analysts and configurators, so we'll stop here.

> **Note**
>
> The default SAP system settings for third-party items are set to match your customer invoice to the invoice receipt from your supplier.

Let's get back to our scenario. Figure 3.63 details the process overview and the steps to execute it. You're a marketing company that doesn't have any manufacturing or inventory capability. You're leveraging your relationship with a supplier to fulfill your requirements and ship directly to the customer on your behalf. Your customer (in our example, customer 4130) places a sales order with your sales organization 3000. The sales order item category is determined to be TAS, and, upon saving, a subsequent purchase requisition and finally a purchase order is issued to your supplier (in our example, vendor 1015). Your vendor ships the goods from its warehouse directly to your customer and notifies you about the completed delivery. This could be a manual step requiring a phone call, fax, email, and so on. The vendor then presents you (company code 3000) with the subsequent invoice, which is received by your accounts payable department. You can then complete you scenario by issuing the standard billing document to your customer and collecting receivables.

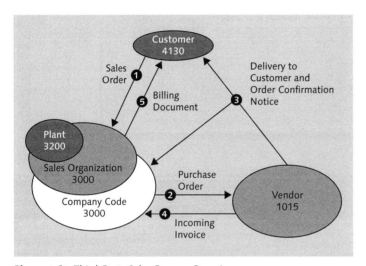

Figure 3.63 Third-Party Sales Process Overview

Now let's walk you through the execution of all of the required steps in detail.

Step 1

Create a sales order with Transaction VA01 (Create Order) or by using the menu path LOGISTICS • SALES AND DISTRIBUTION • SALES • ORDERS • CREATE. To complete the transaction, follow these steps:

1. On the CREATE SALES ORDER initial screen, enter the sales order document type, such as OR – Standard Order, and fill in your sales organization data (your selling organization from the scenario described before is 3000, distribution channel is 10, and division is 00). Press Enter.

2. Enter the number for the customer sold-to (in our example, we used 4130), and press Enter to determine the other partners.

3. On the line item, enter the material and quantity.

4. Enter the price if pricing conditions aren't maintained.

5. In our example, we did use a standard item, so the TAS item category has to be manually selected. Replace the standard item category TAN with TAS as shown in Figure 3.64.

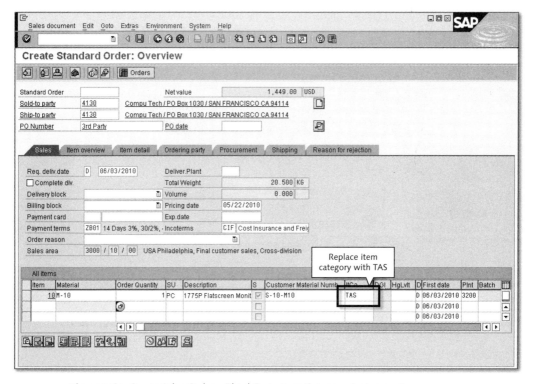

Figure 3.64 Create Sales Order – Third-Party Item Category Assignment

6. Now you can review the details of the schedule lines created. Note that the CS-Leg schedule line category has been determined (see Figure 3.65). To get to this screen, select your item on the OVERVIEW screen, and click on the SCHEDULE LINES FOR ITEM icon 🔳 on the bottom of the screen or use pull-down menus to select GOTO • ITEM • SCHEDULE LINES, and click on the PURCH REQUISITION icon on the bottom portion of the screen.

7. In the detailed overview of the purchase requisition, you'll see all of the data proposed for the purchase order to be created upon conversion of the purchase requisition (see Figure 3.66).

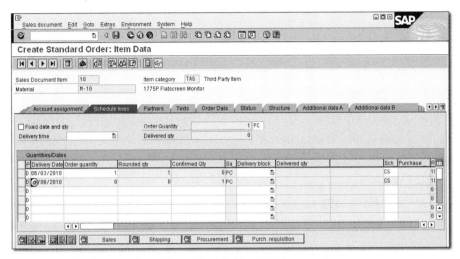

Figure 3.65 Third-Party Sales Order – Schedule Line Details

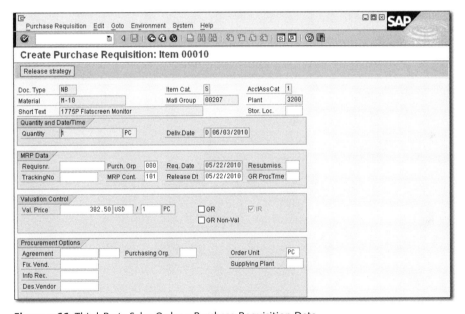

Figure 3.66 Third-Party Sales Order – Purchase Requisition Data

8. After you're done reviewing all your entries, save your order. Not only is your sales order created and saved, but so is the corresponding purchase requisition. You can verify this by going back to the schedule line details to see the actual document number in the PURCHASE REQUISITION column.

Step 2

Create a purchase order. We already created the purchase requisition, so now all we need to do is show you how we convert the purchase requisitions to purchase orders. This is a typical purchasing function so we won't spend much time detailing the entire procedure.

This can be done manually using Transaction ME21N (Create Purchase Order) or by using a conversion Transaction ME59N (Automatically via Purchase Requisitions).

In the end, you'll have a purchase order issued to your vendor (in our test scenario, it's vendor 1015) specifying the delivery address to be of your customer. Figure 3.67 shows the DELIVERY ADDRESS tab of the purchase order we just created.

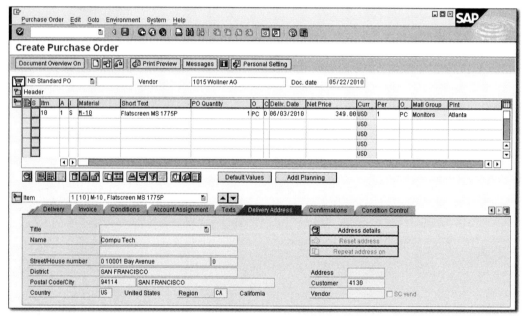

Figure 3.67 Purchase Order Create – Delivery Address Tab

Please note the purchase order item columns A – ACCOUNT ASSIGNMENT with value 1 – THIRD-PARTY and column I – ITEM CATEGORY showing value S – THIRD-PARTY. These are the results of the configuration settings described earlier.

Step 3

Deliver the goods to the customer. The vendor sends the goods to your customer and notifies you that the delivery has been completed. This will be a good trigger to execute the goods receipt transaction for your purchase order. Again, we're not going to spend much time on the details and how-to for this transaction. This is another of the Materials Management functions heavily used for your receiving purposes.

1. If your Materials Management process requires you to do so, you can perform goods receipt using Transaction MIGO (Goods Receipt for PO) by selecting goods receipt for the purchase order. You'll have to specify the purchase order number created in the previous steps.
2. Verify that all of the data is correct and mark the ITEM OK checkbox on the bottom of the MIGO screen. Figure 3.68 shows the PARTNER DATA tab during the goods receipt entry transaction.

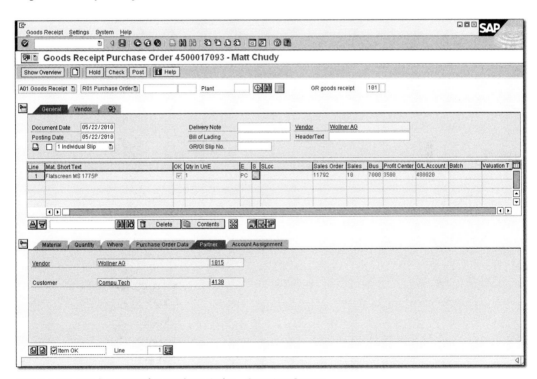

Figure 3.68 Goods Receipt for Purchase Order – Overview Screen

Step 4

Enter the incoming invoice. The next step is to enter the incoming invoice into the system. This is also a function processed by Materials Management or even the accounting group depending on your organizational setup, so we'll only give you a brief overview of this transaction. Normally it's done using Transaction MIRO (Enter Incoming Invoice). See Figure 3.69 for an example of the invoice creation.

Figure 3.69 Enter Incoming Invoice – Transaction Overview Screen

1. Specify the invoice date, and then on the bottom portion of the transaction screen, select the PO REFERENCE tab. Enter your purchase order number from the previous steps.

2. Specify the invoice amount in the BASIC DATA tab of the transaction, and you can either simulate posting to check for errors or click the SAVE button to create the invoice document for your PO.

Step 5

Create the customer invoice. Back on familiar turf, you can create the billing document for the customer using Transaction VF01 (Create Billing Document).

1. On the CREATE BILLING DOCUMENT initial screen, enter the sales order number from the previous steps in the DOCUMENT column, and press Enter.

2. You can verify the pricing condition details by locating condition type VPRS – Cost, which should equal the purchase price you've been invoiced for from your supplier. This value will be used for calculations of your profits that will ultimately post to CO/PA (see Figure 3.70).

3. Save your billing document to complete the process.

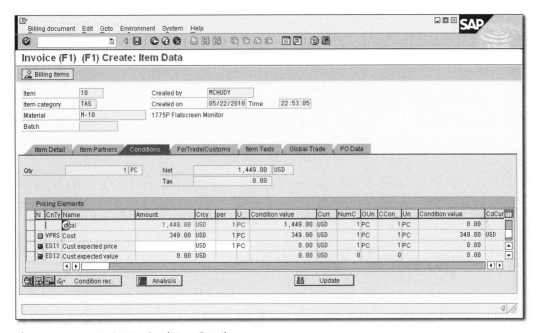

Figure 3.70 Invoice Pricing Conditions Details

Upon completion of all steps, as always, document flow will be updated to capture all your steps along the way. This one was the last step in our third-party process scenario, and now we're ready to move on to an overview of the make-to-order scenario.

3.10.3 Make-to-Order Sales Process

In the previous section, we covered the scenario where your sales requirements are fulfilled by an external procurement; in contrast, this scenario uses internal procurement (that is, production), to make the product and deliver it to your customer. There are two distinct types of processes and supporting strategies for the make-to-order scenario that are defined in the Production Planning component:

► **Make-to-order production**
Defined as strategy 20, which translates to lot-for-lot sizing procedure. A planned order will be created for each sales order item, and the planned order quantity will reflect the sales order item quantity.

► **Assembly processing with production order**
Defined as strategy 82, which uses components that are either manufactured or purchased and stocked. During order processing, the availability check verifies that all components are ready and determines the delivery date. The assembly order quantity also reflects the sales order item quantities.

We aren't going to cover the Production Planning side of this process in elaborate detail, but we'll describe the steps required to complete this scenario in SD. So just as with the previous third-party scenario, we're depending on some configuration settings as well as master data settings.

One of the most important steps will again be the definition of the sales order, in which the order type could be specific to the make-to-order if you need to isolate this activity at the document level, or you can use the standard document type OR – Standard Order to verify the usage of item category TAK – Make-To-Order Prod. The default schedule line category in the standard system is CP – Deterministic MRP (see Figure 3.71 for configuration details of the schedule line). These settings are again maintained using Customizing Transaction VOV6 (Maintain Schedule Line Categories).

The second influential component to this process is just like the previous scenarios: material master data. Again, more than likely you'll permanently default the item category on your sales orders for this process to TAK – Make-To-Order Prod by using the standard configuration values in your material master SALES ORG 2 view and setting the item category group field to 0001 – Make-to-order. Figure 3.72 shows the material master view for the SALES: SALES ORG 2 tab using Transaction MM02 (Material Master Change).

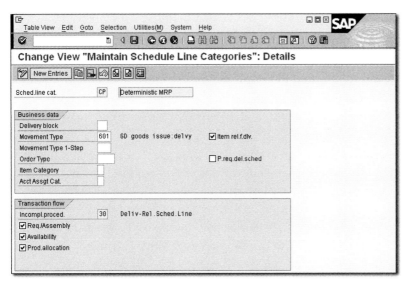

Figure 3.71 Schedule Line Category Definition

Figure 3.72 Material Master Item Category Group Make-to-Order Setting

In this scenario, the billing relevancy is standard and set to delivery related so whatever you produce, stage and ship will be reflected on your billing document type F2 – Invoice.

Figure 3.73 details the process overview and steps to execute the make-to-order scenario. Let's imagine you're a manufacturing company (company code 1000) that produces standard components and assemblies them in a variety of different ways using assembly orders in plant 1200. Your customer (in our example, customer 1900) places a sales order with your sales organization 1000 and distribution channel 12. The sales order item category is determined to be TAK, and, upon saving, a subsequent production order is created that will be sent to the assembly floor. Upon order completion and receipt of goods into the warehouse, your goods are assigned to the sales order stock, category E, reserving them for your specific customer order. The shipping process is then executed, where you pick, pack, load, and send your goods to the customer and post goods issue as a final step. The subsequent billing run creates billing documents to your customer, and finally you collect receivables. Now let's go through the execution of all of the required steps in detail.

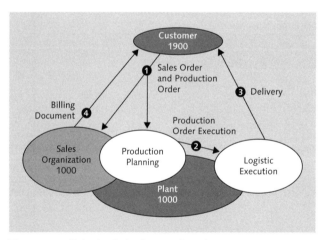

Figure 3.73 Make-to-Order Process Overview

Step 1

Create the sales order with Transaction VA01 (Create Order) or by using the menu path LOGISTICS • SALES AND DISTRIBUTION • SALES • ORDERS • CREATE. To complete the transaction, follow these steps:

1. On the CREATE SALES ORDEr initial screen, enter the sales order document type, such as OR – Standard Order, fill in your sales organization data (selling organization is 1000, distribution channel is 12, and division is 00) and press ⎡Enter⎤.

2. Enter the number for the customer sold-to (in our example, 1900), and press ⎡Enter⎤ to determine the other partners.

3. On the line item, enter the material, quantity, and price if pricing conditions aren't maintained

4. Note the item category was automatically set to TAK (see Figure 3.74).

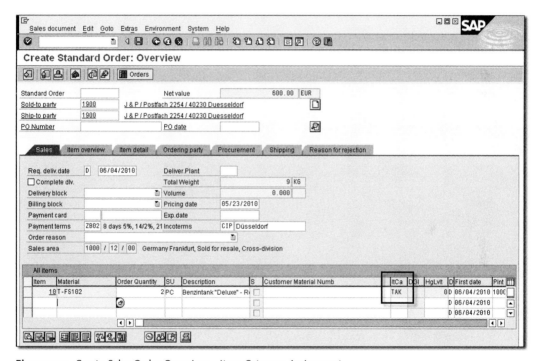

Figure 3.74 Create Sales Order Overview – Item Category Assignment

5. Now you can review the details of the schedule lines created (see Figure 3.75). Note that the CP-DETERMINISTIC MRP schedule line category has been determined. To get to this screen, select your item on the Overview screen, and click on SCHEDULE LINES FOR ITEM icon on the bottom of the screen, or use the pull-down menus and select GOTO • ITEM • SCHEDULE LINES, and click on the

production order on the bottom portion of the screen. Remember the production order number will be assigned after you save your sales order. Note the production order type is PP04 – Production Order as Assembly Order.

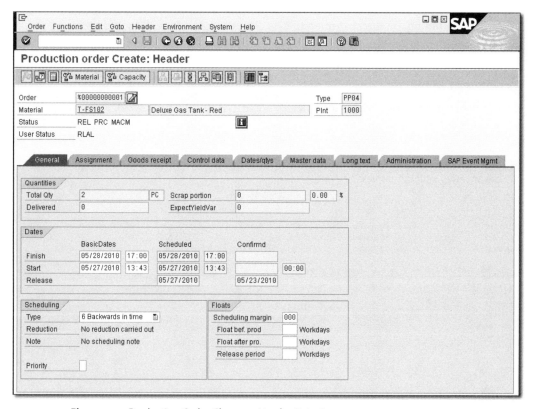

Figure 3.75 Production Order Change – Header Data Screen

Step 2

Execute production by running MRP and scheduling the production order execution. Either the Materials Management person or the production planner will execute the MRP to ensure that all components are ready and available for the assembly process to take place.

Resources are scheduled, and the production order process is initiated. We won't talk in detail about these steps, but we'll mention that production orders also have their own lifecycle, statuses, and so on.

1. Figure 3.76 shows the production change transaction screen. You can get there by executing Transaction CO02 (Production Order Change). You can also use the following menu path: LOGISTICS • PRODUCTION • SHOP FLOOR CONTROL • ORDER • CHANGE. Notice the link to our demo sales order number in the SALES ORDER section of the screen.

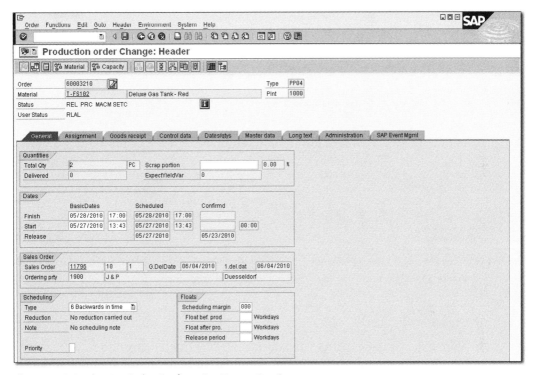

Figure 3.76 Production Order Confirmation Transaction Screen

2. Components goods issue for this order can be posted using Transaction MIGO (Goods Issue To Order).

3. Final goods receipt of the completed product is posted either by a confirmation Transaction CO15 (For Order) (you can access it using the menu path LOGISTICS • PRODUCTION • SHOP FLOOR CONTROL • CONFIRMATION • ENTER • FOR ORDER) or by using Transaction MIGO (Goods Receipt for Order).

4. On the confirmation Transaction CO15 screen, confirm your yield and click the SAVE button. This will post goods receipt of your material to the sale order reserved stock inventory.

5. Figure 3.77 shows Transaction MMBE (Stock Overview), which displays the sales order quantity that you just received from the production order. You can also get to this transaction by using the following menu path: LOGISTICS • MATERIALS MANAGEMENT • INVENTORY MANAGEMENT • ENVIRONMENT • STOCK • STOCK OVERVIEW.

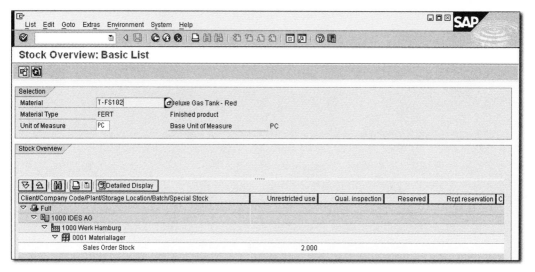

Figure 3.77 Stock Overview After Goods Receipt from Production

Step 3

Ship to the customer. After your stock has been posted to inventory, you can execute the actual shipment to the customer. The standard delivery due list is usually executed, and outbound delivery is created. We'll cover the delivery process in a lot more details in the coming chapters, so let's assume we're using Transaction VA02 (Sales Order Change) by going to SALES DOCUMENTS • DELIVER.

1. Execute your picking transaction. If warehouse management is active, you'll have to create and confirm the transfer order (see Chapter 4, where we detail outbound delivery processes).

2. After your picking activities are completed, you can post goods issue to complete the shipping transaction. Material document and Financial Accounting postings are automatically executed behind the scenes.

Step 4

Create the billing document for your customer using Transaction VF01 (Create Billing Document) just as in the previous examples.

1. On the CREATE BILLING DOCUMENT initial screen, enter the sales order number from the previous steps in the DOCUMENT column, and press ⌈Enter⌉.

2. You can verify the pricing condition details by locating the condition type EK02 – Calculated Cost, which comes from the costing related to the processing of your production order. This value instead of the VPRS condition will be subtracted from the customer price condition PR00 and will be used for calculations of your profit margin that will ultimately post to CO/PA (see Figure 3.78).

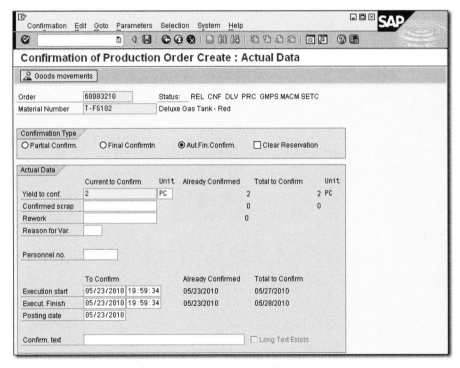

Figure 3.78 Invoice Create Item Data – Conditions Detail

3. Save your billing document to complete the process.

Now that we've covered the three special sales processes, you should be able to easily apply them in your day-to-day operations or review the feasibility for a future use.

3.10.4 Customer Consignment

Consignment is a sales scenario in which the selling party (consignor) agrees to provide goods to a distributor or reseller (consignee) who will pay the seller only after the goods are sold. In this arrangement, the seller remains the owner of the goods until they are paid for in full.

In some arrangements, whatever goods are not sold can be returned to the consignor and the consignee incurs in no charges. In other cases, there is a maximum time for the goods to remain in consignment and after that time, whatever stock is left should be paid by the consignee.

In the SAP ERP system, there's a stock category under special stocks for this type of relations. In this scenario, orders are entered manually by a sales clerk using the Transaction VA01 (Sales Order Create). The goods are initially posted to the customer consignment stock, and thus remain the property of the company (consignment fill-up). At regular intervals, the customer reports how many articles he or she has sold, or how many articles are in his or her current stock (inventory). When the inventory is carried out, if the goods are batch managed, the batch number may also have to be entered to carry out a correct material posting (see Figure 3.79). The process is divided in the fill-up of the consignment stores and the actual sale, which issues and bills the goods.

Every time the consignee reports a sale of the consigned goods, a corresponding order is entered in the ERP system to document the issue from the customer consignment stock, meaning that the goods are no longer the property of the company (consignment issue).

Goods that are not required can be returned from the consignment stock to the central warehouse. The goods must not be defective. They are posted directly into unrestricted stock (consignment pick-up).

It may happen that goods are returned to the customer consignment stock (by its own customer) after the consignment issue has already happened. In this case a return order is created (consignment return).

In the following subsections, we'll walk you through the steps to fill a consignment order.

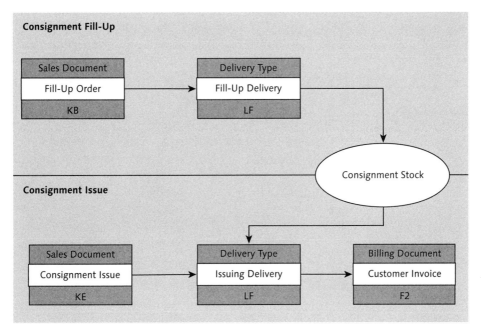

Figure 3.79 The Consignment Process

Step 1

Create a sales order with Transaction VA01 (Create Order) or by using the menu path LOGISTICS • SALES AND DISTRIBUTION • SALES • ORDERS • CREATE. To complete the transaction, follow these steps:

1. On the CREATE SALES ORDER initial screen, enter the sales order document type, such as KB – Consignment Fill-up, and fill in your sales organization data (your selling organization from the scenario described before is 3000, distribution channel is 10, and division is 00). Press Enter. See Figure 3.80.

2. Enter the number for the customer sold-to (in our example, we used 4130), and press Enter to determine the other partners.

3. On the line item, enter the material and quantity.

4. Item category KBN is determined automatically when you press Enter.

5. This type of order does not require a price; you will need to enter the price later in the consignment issue order.

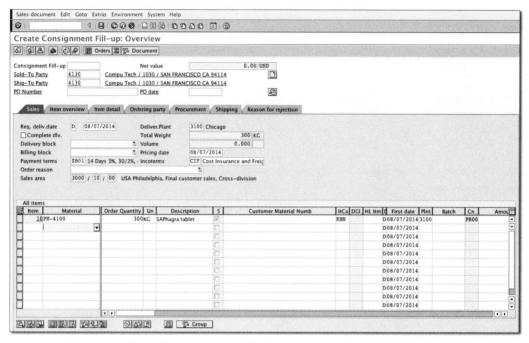

Figure 3.80 Create the Consignment Fill-Up

Step 2

Create an outbound delivery for the consignment fill-up order via Transaction VL10A. The steps are described in Section 3.8.2, so we won't go over them again here.

Step 3

Confirm picking for the delivery and post goods issue. This is done in Transaction VL02N, and the process depends on the setup of your warehouse. If you have either full Warehouse Management or Lean Warehouse Management installed, you'll have to create a transfer order and confirm it in order to have the picking complete. Otherwise, you can enter the picked quantity manually in the PICKING tab of the delivery (see Figure 3.81).

Once you post the goods issue for the delivery, the stock of the material is moved to customer consignment stock. To look at this stock, you can use Transaction MMBE, as shown in Figure 3.82. You can double-click on the line for the consignment stock to check which customer's account it was moved to.

Figure 3.81 Picking Tab

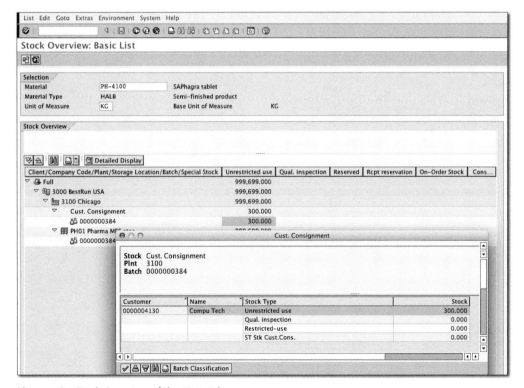

Figure 3.82 Stock Overview of the Material

Step 4

Once the consignee notifies you that a part of the stock has been sold, you have to create a consignment issue order. This is another sales order; to create it you have to once again go to Transaction VA01 (Create Order) or use the menu path LOGISTICS • SALES AND DISTRIBUTION • SALES • ORDERS • CREATE. To complete the transaction, follow these steps:

1. On the CREATE SALES ORDER initial screen, enter the sales order document type, such as KE – Consignment Issue, and fill in your sales organization data (your selling organization from the scenario described before is 3000, distribution channel is 10, and division is 00). Press Enter. See Figure 3.83.

2. Enter the number for the customer sold-to (in our example, we used 4130), and press Enter to determine the other partners.

3. On the line item, enter the material and quantity.

4. Enter the price if pricing conditions aren't maintained.

5. Item category KEN is determined automatically when you press Enter.

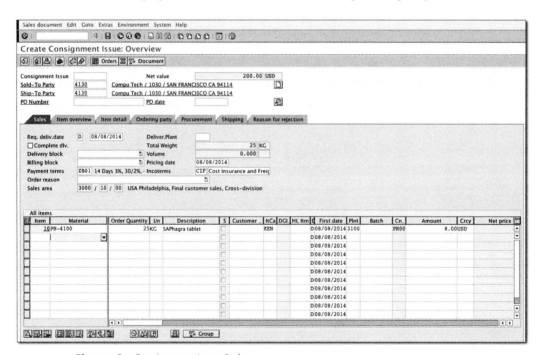

Figure 3.83 Consignment Issue Order

Step 5

Create an outbound delivery for the consignment issue order according to the steps described in Section 3.8.2, which will guide you through Transaction VL10A and post goods issue.

Deliveries for consignment issue orders are not relevant for picking so you don't need to enter the picked quantity; you only need to push the POST GOODS ISSUE button at the top of the screen. See Figure 3.84. Once the goods issue is posted, the customer consignment stock is reduced by the delivery quantity, reflecting the fact that the goods have changed ownership. See Figure 3.85.

Figure 3.84 Post the Goods Issue Directly from the Create Overview Screen

Step 6

Now that the goods have changed ownership, it's time to execute the billing. The billing document is created in Transaction VF01 as described in Section 3.8.3. Once you have created the billing document, the consignment process is complete.

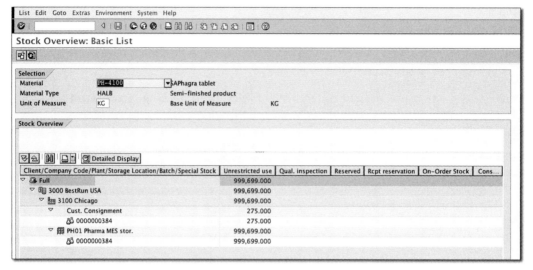

Figure 3.85 Reduced Customer Consignment Stock

3.10.5 Sales Orders with Bills of Materials

As mentioned earlier in this chapter, you can put together bills of materials for items that are to be sold together as a kit. The process is simple and consists of a pair of steps that you have to complete as prerequisites before creating the sales order.

Step 1

Create a new material in the material master, which represents the kit. This material is a regular finished good (FERT); the only differences are the ITEM CATEGORY GROUP and the GENERAL ITEM CATEGORY GROUP that are used.

The material master record needs specific values for ITEM CATEGORY GROUP and GENERAL ITEM CATEGORY group in the SALES 2 view. In Figure 3.86, you can see how the values are ERLA and LUMF.

These values from the material master will trigger the inclusion of the BOM components during the sales order creation.

Figure 3.86 Change Material

Step 2

Now it's time to create a bill of materials. Bills of materials, or BOMs, are normally master data for production, but they can be used for other activities like sales. When you create a bill of materials in Transaction CS01, you have to tell the system that you are creating a BOM to be used for sales purposes.

BOMs are created for specific plants, so you need to enter a plant number, as shown in Figure 3.87, along with the kit material number (which is also called the header material), the plant and the BOM usage. In this case, it is always 5.

The second screen of this transaction, shown in Figure 3.88, is where you'll enter the list of components that have to be packaged together to make up a kit. For each of them, you need to indicate in the item category column whether the component is a stock item or not. Normally, BOM components are stock items since you need to pick them from the warehouse.

Figure 3.87 Create a Bill of Materials with Usage 5 for Sales

Figure 3.88 Enter the Components in the Item Overview Screen

Next, enter the material number and the quantity that has to be packaged into the kit.

Once you're done with all the components, save and you are done. You can proceed to create your sales order.

Step 3

When you create your sales order, as shown in Figure 3.89, there are two things that you need to keep in mind. The first thing is that the header material of a sales BOM will have a new item category, TAP, which is not relevant for pricing. This means that you can neither create a pricing condition record, nor enter a manual price for it. The price of the kit comes from the sum of the prices of the items, so be sure to maintain those pricing conditions correctly.

Figure 3.89 BOM Components are Copied Automatically

The other thing that you need to keep in mind is that also because of that new item category, the BOM items will be copied automatically to the sales order the moment you press Enter after entering the kit material.

After this, the sales and distribution process continues normally. You will create a delivery order, it can be picked with or without a transfer order, depending on your warehouse settings, the delivery will be post goods issued, and then it will be billed.

3.11   Summary

You just completed the core of this book—a chapter that walked you through sales activities. In those pages, you found information on creating sales orders using standard SAP functions, applying different pieces of master data using your knowledge from Chapter 2, using cross-selling and customer material info records, naming materials using customers numbers, and so on. Now you should be able to review and finish any of your presales activities by firming the customers' request into a valid sales order. We'll give you an overview of the follow-up functions—shipping and billing—in the next two chapters. You'll then have the complete picture that will give you all of the information you need to complete your sales order from order to cash.

You've sold the goods. Now all you have to do is deliver them to the customer. How exactly do you do that?

4   Shipping and Transportation

So far, we've covered quite a lot of terrain on the sales side of Sales and Distribution, so now it's time to start discussing the distribution side.

After the availability of the product has been confirmed in the sales order, and the customer has passed the credit checks, it's time to start preparing for the shipping of the goods. In SAP ERP, two main components help you execute the shipping of the goods to our customers: shipping and transportation, as illustrated in Figure 4.1.

Figure 4.1 SAP ERP Logistics Processes

The shipping component consists of several tasks that, when put together, can pass the product needs to the warehouse and determine the shipping methods and routes that the product will follow after dispatch from your warehouse.

> **Note**
>
> Shipping can't be executed if the product isn't made available by the warehouse. In SAP ERP, shipping is also supported by the Warehouse Management functionality, which we'll refer to as WM throughout this chapter.

Shipping monitors the shipping deadlines of preceding or reference documents, such as sales orders or return purchase orders. It uses these deadlines in conjunction with the material availability dates to schedule the delivery creation and execution of outbound deliveries. Shipping also ensures that the materials are picked and packed according to the scheduled dates. It allows you to print and transmit the shipping documentation to customers and freight partners, post the issue of the product from stock, and serve as the basis for creating the billing documents.

The transportation functionality in SAP ERP takes care of determining which is the best carrier to move the product from your company's warehouse to the customer's expected delivery point, handles all of the truck scheduling by setting appointments for trucks to arrive at the loading dock, schedules when the loading of those trucks has to start and finish, and finally records when the truck has to be dispatched.

Transportation also outlines all of the connection points in the transportation route and highlights the different modes of transportation that might take place. It keeps track of any customs clearing points and any loading and unloading points. And it does all this while tracking each and every cost involved in the process.

> **Note**
>
> Shipping and Transportation don't have any new updates with SAP ERP 6.0, EHP 7. The reason for this is all of the new developments for these two modules are now part of SAP SCM Transportation Management. SAP ERP's shipping and transportation functionalities haven't received any updates since EHP 5. The EHP 5 enhancement allows you to connect with and take advantage of SAP SCM Transportation Management's functionalities, connecting seamlessly and allowing the exchange of information. Transportation Management is explained in more detail in Section 4.4.

Now that you have an overview of the shipping and transportation functionalities in SD, we'll go through all of the processes that you'll need to be aware of in your job.

4.1 Outbound Delivery

The outbound delivery is the initial step in the logistics process and is created as the material becomes available and matches the various deadlines in the sales order approach. The system back-schedules based on this deadline and sets new deadlines in the delivery order to ensure that the items will be picked, packed, and shipped on time, so that the customer will receive the ordered items on the requested delivery date.

Delivery orders are linked to a shipping point, which is the responsible unit within the SAP system to monitor and process deliveries. This link can be automatic, based on the plant and storage location entered in the sales order, or it can be assigned manually. Figure 4.2 shows an outbound delivery screen, which you can get to by choosing LOGISTICS • SALES AND DISTRIBUTION • SHIPPING AND TRANSPORTATION • OUTBOUND DELIVERY • DISPLAY. The outbound delivery outlines the materials to be picked, quantities, picking dates, warehouse status, transportation status, and much more.

Figure 4.2 Outbound Delivery

4.1.1 Checks on Delivery Creation

To create a delivery, the system performs the following checks to make sure the information is complete and the delivery can be created:

- Possible delivery blocks (sales order blocks due to credit or other manual blocks set by the Sales and Finance areas)
- Sales orders incompleteness
- Material availability
- Picking date

If these checks are passed, the delivery order is created. At that time, the system will recalculate the deadlines, execute the batch determination (if applicable), calculate the shipping route, assign a picking location, calculate volumes and weights, and update the sales order by reducing the confirmed quantity, updating the document flow, and changing the delivery status.

The information in the delivery order includes the following:

- Ship-to address
- Picking location (the warehouse from which the goods are to be picked)
- Shipping point (the place the truck departs)
- Route (the path the truck will follow along with the total volume and weight of the shipment)

The delivery order also contains foreign trade information so that all necessary documentation that must travel with the goods can be put together. This information can be printed on the bills of lading and invoices screen, as shown in Figure 4.3.

All of these data comes from a collection of sources, mainly the material master, customer master, sales agreements, sales order data, and route information. They determine the customer defaults for processing deliveries.

If the customer requires complete delivery, the order should be delivered in a single delivery—all items should be delivered at the same time. When you create an outbound delivery, if all of the order items can't be shipped with the full order quantity, you'll receive a warning that the customer requires complete delivery.

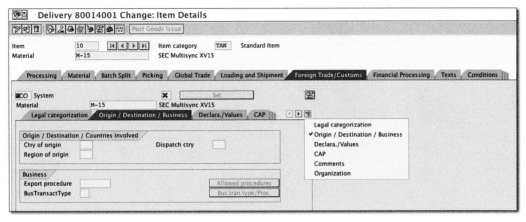

Figure 4.3 Delivery Orders Include Foreign Trade Information

If the customer doesn't require complete delivery, you can define a partial delivery agreement with the customer.

If the customer allows orders to be combined, orders are combined in the outbound deliveries when using the delivery list. Combining items from different sales orders is possible only if the items have several common characteristics, such as the following:

▶ SHIPPING POINT: Goods issue from the same place in your enterprise.

▶ DATE THAT DELIVERY IS DUE: Date on which shipping processing should begin, either material availability date or transportation planning date, must be within the selection dates on the delivery list initial screen.

▶ SHIP-TO PARTY: Outbound deliveries have the same destination.

▶ ROUTE: Same method of transport and route.

▶ INCOTERMS: International Chamber of Commerce terms of liability for freight in-transit.

▶ SHIPPING CONDITIONS: Communicates the customer's shipping requirements.

▶ CUSTOMIZING: The list of common characteristics is maintained in Customizing.

Figure 4.4 illustrates the various options for outbound delivery creation: delivery complete, partial delivery, and order combination.

Figure 4.4 Customer Requirements Dictate How Deliveries Need to Be Created

These data also include information that helps confirm the delivery date to the customer, which is known as the *confirmed delivery date*.

To calculate this confirmed delivery date, the system takes into account different lead times such as the material availability date, pick/pack time, loading time, transportation planning time, and transit time.

The following dates play a role in delivery and transportation scheduling:

▶ ORDER DATE: Date on which the order was placed.

▶ MATERIAL AVAILABILITY DATE: Date on which sufficient goods should be available to begin picking and packing.

▶ TRANSPORTATION PLANNING DATE: Date on which the means of transportation planning must begin (e.g., call the trucking company so a truck is available on the loading date).

▶ LOADING DATE: Date on which picking and packing should be completed (and the mode of transport should be there), for loading to begin.

▶ GOODS ISSUE DATE: The date on which the goods must leave the delivering plant to arrive at the customer's location on time.

▶ DELIVERY DATE: Date at which the goods arrive at the customer location. A difference is made between:

  ▶ REQUIRED DELIVERY DATE: Date on which the customer wishes to receive his goods.

  ▶ CONFIRMED DELIVERY DATE: Date on which the arrival of the goods at the customers can be confirmed by the system.

To calculate the confirmed delivery date, the system has the option of performing either backward scheduling or forward scheduling.

In backward scheduling, the material availability date and transportation planning date are calculated from the required customer delivery date by subtracting the various lead times. The outbound delivery must be created on the earlier of the two dates (selection date of the outbound delivery).

If both dates are after the order date, and the material is available on the materials availability date, the required delivery date is confirmed to the customer. One schedule line is created for a sales line item. The schedule line date matches the confirmed delivery date, which corresponds to the required customer delivery.

If one of the two dates is before the order date, the required delivery date can't be confirmed. Therefore, the system tries to determine the next possible date (forward scheduling).

If the result of backward scheduling is that the delivery date required by the customer can't be confirmed, the system executes forward scheduling. Forward scheduling takes into consideration the time parallels of the workflows for transportation planning and picking/packing of materials. The longer of the two periods is relevant for scheduling. The selection date for the outbound delivery is the earlier of the material availability date or the transportation planning date.

The earliest time at which the material is available in the warehouse is the new material availability date. This is the outgoing point for new delivery scheduling.

Two schedule lines are generated for the sales line item:

▶ The date of the first schedule line corresponds to the customer's required delivery date and has no confirmed quantity.

▶ The date of the second schedule line shows the confirmed delivery date and the confirmed amount.

4.1.2 Create an Outbound Delivery

To create an outbound delivery, go to the menu path LOGISTICS • SALES AND DISTRIBUTION • SHIPPING AND TRANSPORTATION • OUTBOUND DELIVERY • CREATE • SINGLE DOCUMENT • WITH REFERENCE TO SALES ORDERS.

In the initial screen, enter the shipping point, delivery date as confirmed by the sales order, and the sales order number, as shown in Figure 4.5. This will bring you to the delivery screen, as shown in Figure 4.6.

Figure 4.5 Outbound Delivery with Order Reference

The delivery items have data organized into various tabs. Figure 4.6 shows the ITEM OVERVIEW tab, which lists the materials and quantities to be delivered. The second tab, PICKING, is illustrated in Figure 4.7.

This tab shows the delivery quantity, picked quantity, and the picking date (Stag. Date). In this instance, the picked quantity is grayed out so that it can't be manually updated. This is dictated by the Overall WM Status. In this case, the value of this status is A, which makes it relevant for WM transfer orders. The picked quantity is updated by these transfer orders.

Figure 4.6 Delivery Create: Overview

Figure 4.7 Picking Tab for Deliveries

The TRANSPORT tab contains the estimated shipping date, shows the route of the truck, and shows the transportation planning status, as shown in Figure 4.8.

Figure 4.8 Transport Tab for Deliveries

When the transportation planning status isn't blank, the delivery is also linked to the transportation functionality in SAP ERP. This status will be updated as the shipment is executed, as we'll discuss further in Section 4.4.

The GOODS MOVEMENT DATA tab shows you the planned and actual goods issue date, and the total goods movement status, as shown in Figure 4.9. These statuses allow you to monitor the progress of your delivery. The most important status might be the goods movement status because you can't create an invoice until all of the items in a delivery have been issued.

When you save the delivery, the document flow in the sales document gets updated, as shown in Figure 4.10.

Table 4.1 lists the outbound delivery maintenance transactions and menu paths.

Figure 4.9 Goods Movement Data for Deliveries

✅ Delivery 80014999 has been saved

Figure 4.10 After Saving, the Delivery Number Is Shown in the Status Bar

Transaction	Menu Path
VA01 – Create Delivery with Reference to Sales Orders	LOGISTICS • SALES AND DISTRIBUTION • SHIPPING AND TRANSPORTATION • OUTBOUND DELIVERY • CREATE • SINGLE DOCUMENT • WITH REFERENCE TO SALES ORDERS
VL10C – Collective Processing of Documents due for Delivery	LOGISTICS • SALES AND DISTRIBUTION • SHIPPING AND TRANSPORTATION • OUTBOUND DELIVERY • CREATE • COLLECTIVE PROCESSING OF DOCUMENTS DUE FOR DELIVERY • SALES ORDERS ITEMS
VL02N – Change	LOGISTICS • SALES AND DISTRIBUTION • SHIPPING AND TRANSPORTATION • OUTBOUND DELIVERY • CHANGE • SINGLE DOCUMENT

Table 4.1 Outbound Delivery Maintenance

Transaction	Menu Path
VL03N – Display	LOGISTICS • SALES AND DISTRIBUTION • SHIPPING AND TRANSPORTATION • OUTBOUND DELIVERY • DISPLAY
VL06O – Outbound Delivery Monitor	LOGISTICS • SALES AND DISTRIBUTION • SHIPPING AND TRANSPORTATION • OUTBOUND DELIVERY • LISTS AND LOGS • OUTBOUND DELIVERY MONITOR

Table 4.1 Outbound Delivery Maintenance (Cont.)

Now that you understand outbound deliveries, let's move on to the next process: picking.

4.2 Picking

Picking refers to the activities that are executed by the warehouse to collect and stage all of the items requested by the delivery order in the correct quantities and prepare them for shipping.

Depending on your system configuration, the delivery can interface with your warehouse in several ways:

▶ **No Warehouse Management**
When your system is configured to handle only inventory management, the outbound delivery requires only that the picking quantity is confirmed. In this case, the warehouse clerks would pick the items and update the delivery directly.

▶ **Lean Warehouse Management (Lean WM)**
This allows the warehouse to create simple picking lists with quantities per material SKU. After all of the items have been picked, the warehouse clerks need to confirm the picking quantities in a separate document called a transfer order. This transfer order can update the delivery quantities in case the picked quantity is different from the original delivery quantity. The delivery can't have the picking quantity confirmed manually.

▶ **Full Warehouse Management (WM)**
This is a fully functional functionality in SAP ERP that links into the shipping process. It includes a full representation in the system of all of the storage areas in the warehouse, including all racks and storage bins.

Like lean WM, full WM also produces transfer orders for picking, but in this case they contain the specific coordinates where each quantity of each product is stored in the warehouse. To confirm the delivery picking, the warehouse clerks have to confirm the transfer orders. The delivery picking can't be confirmed directly in the outbound delivery.

When a transfer order is created, its WM status changes from *Not Yet Processed* to *Partially Processed*.

We'll go over the different kinds of picking you can use in the following sections.

4.2.1 Wave Picks

Wave picks allow the warehouse to consolidate picking requirements. To do this, you first have to group deliveries together based on the time when they have to be processed.

> **Note**
>
> Wave picks are not for everyone. Some companies' products allow for direct picking for each customer's orders; in other cases, consolidated picking is a very good option. If, for example, your company's products are packed in pallets or boxes that contain multiple items, and each of your customers orders large multiples of them, then you may want to execute consolidated picking. This is true when selling to distributors and not directly to end customers.

To use wave picks, you need to have other functionalities of SAP ERP installed as prerequisites. The simplest configuration can be based on a lean WM implementation, but if you have a very complex warehouse, then your company can benefit from a full WM implementation.

Another prerequisite for wave picking is times slots. *Time slots* help you plan wave picks according to the working calendar at your warehouse facility. These time slots can be, for example, linked to routes so that all of the deliveries for a certain shipping route are picked at the same time, and the trucks can be loaded and dispatched on schedule.

Because time slots have a predefined duration and your picking capacity is just so much at a given time of the day, you can set limits to the number of articles that can be processed. You can set up these capacity restrictions in two ways:

▶ Maximum number of delivery items to be picked in a wave

▶ Maximum number of picking transactions per wave

These restrictions are set in configuration and only the system analysts can change them. The simplest way to create a wave pick is to use the Outbound Delivery Monitor, which we'll describe next. To create a wave pick, follow these steps:

1. Choose LOGISTICS • SALES AND DISTRIBUTION • SHIPPING AND TRANSPORTATION • PICKING • WAVE PICKS • CREATE • VIA OUTBOUND DELIVERY MONITOR. The Outbound Delivery Monitor is your single-point-of-contact with all of the delivery order related statuses (see Figure 4.11).

Figure 4.11 Outbound Delivery Monitor

2. Click on the FOR PICKING button. Once inside the picking section (Figure 4.12), you'll be able to enter selection parameters so that the resulting worklist shows the deliveries that you're looking for.

3. The search screen allows you to enter several different parameters to narrow down your search results. The basic two parameters you have to enter in this search screen are the SHIPPING POINT and PICKING DATE RANGE. Figure 4.13 shows the deliveries that matched our search. Here you see the global information that totals the item's data.

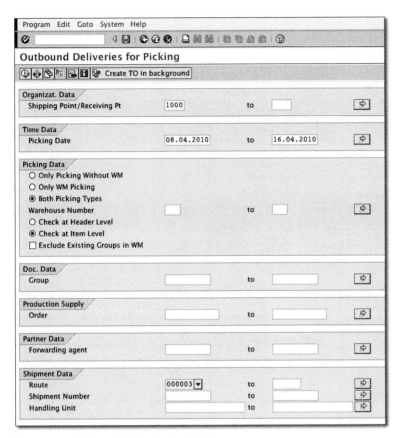

Figure 4.12 Outbound Deliveries for Picking

Figure 4.13 Day's Workload for Picking

4. Select the ITEM VIEW button (Figure 4.14), which displays detailed information for each item.

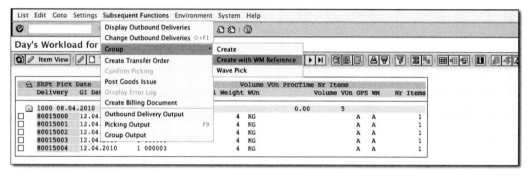

Figure 4.14 Item View

5. Select all of the items, and choose SUBSEQUENT FUNCTIONS • GROUP • CREATE WITH WM REFERENCE, as shown in Figure 4.15. In this example, we're selecting a WM group because it's simple.

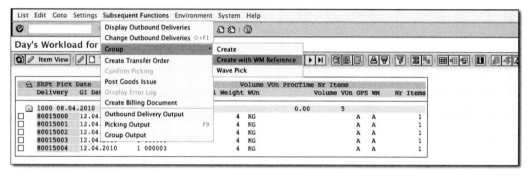

Figure 4.15 Create Delivery Group with WM Reference

6. Enter a description for the group and the warehouse number, as shown in Figure 4.16. After you've done this, the status bar will show you the group number after it's created, which in this case is Group 5940, shown in Figure 4.17.

Figure 4.16 Group Type and Description

| Group 5940 with reference to WM saved |

Figure 4.17 Status Bar Showing the Group

Table 4.2 illustrates the various transactions and menu paths for wave picks maintenance, for your easy reference.

Transaction	Menu Path
VL35 – Create According to Delivery Time	LOGISTICS • SALES AND DISTRIBUTION • SHIPPING AND TRANSPORTATION • PICKING • WAVE PICKS • CREATE • ACCORDING TO DELIVERY TIME
VL35_S – Create According to Shipment	LOGISTICS • SALES AND DISTRIBUTION • SHIPPING AND TRANSPORTATION • PICKING • WAVE PICKS • CREATE • ACCORDING TO SHIPMENT
VL35_ST – Create According to Shipment	LOGISTICS • SALES AND DISTRIBUTION • SHIPPING AND TRANSPORTATION • PICKING • WAVE PICKS • CREATE • ACCORDING TO SHIPMENT AND COMPARE TIME
VL06P – Via Outbound Delivery Monitor	LOGISTICS • SALES AND DISTRIBUTION • SHIPPING AND TRANSPORTATION • PICKING • WAVE PICKS • CREATE • VIA OUTBOUND DELIVERY MONITOR

Table 4.2 Wave Picks Maintenance

4.2.2 Two-Step Picking

After the wave picks are created, you can start two-step picking. Two-step picking is a way of separating the picking activities in the warehouse into two phases: collective picking of material and separation into individual customer orders.

For example, you could have 30 different customers that ordered the same product for a total of 1,500 pieces. In this scenario, a wave pick would consolidate the customers' requirements, and the forklifts would go out and bring all 1,500 pieces. Then, in the picking area, individual orders would be sorted and trucks loaded and dispatched. This allows for a more efficient use of the warehouse resources. As you can see in Figure 4.18, two-step picking moves large quantities of products that need to be sorted.

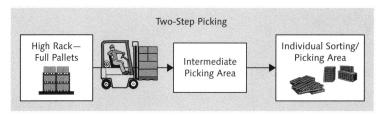

Figure 4.18 Two-Step Picking

The first step creates the consolidated transfer orders so that the pickers can start moving multi-unit packages (i.e., boxes, cases, pallets, sacks, etc.) for each material number that is included in the delivery items that form the wave pick. These transfer orders don't update the WM status in the delivery (see Figure 4.18). The second step starts after the consolidated quantities have been moved from the warehouse into the picking area. At this point, we have to break out and pick the individual delivery item quantities by creating picking lists by delivery. In the SAP system, two-step picking lists are defined as *transfer orders*. The creation of transfer orders updates the WM status from *Not Yet Processed* to *Partially Processed*. Two-step picking (see Figure 4.19) also requires that the functionality is enabled in WM configuration. Ask your IT analyst whether this functionality is active in your system.

Figure 4.19 Two-Step Picking Flow with Transaction Codes

Let's walk through an example so you can visualize this process in the SAP system.

1. Choose LOGISTICS • SALES AND DISTRIBUTION • SHIPPING AND TRANSPORTATION • PICKING • CREATE TRANSFER ORDER • VIA 2-STEP PICKING, to get to the CREATE REMOVAL TO FOR 2-STEP PICKING screen as shown in Figure 4.20.

Figure 4.20 Create Removal TO for 2-Step Picking Screen

2. For this transaction, enter the warehouse number and the group number, and press ⌈Enter⌉; in our example, we created group 5940 earlier in Figure 4.17. This will take you to the screen shown in Figure 4.21. The quantities displayed are the consolidated quantities for all of the deliveries that require each material.

3. Click on the SAVE button. The system will let you know how many TOs were created, as shown in Figure 4.22. It's important to know that this consolidated TO doesn't update the delivery statuses.

Figure 4.21 All Materials and Total Quantities for Each

35 transfer orders were created

Figure 4.22 The Number of TOs Created Is Shown in the Status Bar

4. Go to the two-step picking monitor by choosing LOGISTICS • SALES AND DISTRI-BUTION • SHIPPING AND TRANSPORTATION • PICKING • WAVE PICK • TWO-STEP PICK-ING • ANALYSIS, which brings you to the screen shown in Figure 4.23.

5. The two-step monitor shows you the status for the pick or consolidated picking, and also for the allocation or individual picking, as shown in Figure 4.24.

6. Click on the DISPLAY 2-STEP RELEVANCE button, which brings you to the screen in Figure 4.25. By doing so, you can see how each delivery and each material qualifies for consolidation in two-step picking, along with the consolidated quantities.

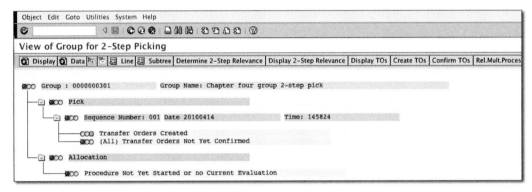

Program Edit Goto System Help

Evaluation of Groups for 2-Step Picking and Update Status

Warehouse Number	T01
Group	301 ▼ to
Reference Document Category	
Creation date	04/14/2010 to 04/14/2010
Display Log	
Display Result of Evaluation	X

Figure 4.23 Evaluation Groups for 2-Step Picking and Update Status Screen

Object Edit Goto Utilities System Help

View of Group for 2-Step Picking

Display | Data | Line | Subtree | Determine 2-Step Relevance | Display 2-Step Relevance | Display TOs | Create TOs | Confirm TOs | Rel.Mult.Proces

Group : 0000000301   Group Name: Chapter four group 2-step pick

└─ Pick

    └─ Sequence Number: 001 Date 20100414   Time: 145824

        ├─ Transfer Orders Created
        └─ (All) Transfer Orders Not Yet Confirmed

└─ Allocation

    └─ Procedure Not Yet Started or no Current Evaluation

Figure 4.24 View of Group for 2-Step Picking Screen

Display 2-Step Picking Relevance for Group

Choose | Save

Display 2-Step Picking Relevance for Group
Warehouse Number T01
Group :   0000000301

2st	Material	Plnt	Batch	GrV	Stock Category	S	S	Requested qty AUn	Reqmt qty AltUn	Qty picked in AUn	AUn	N
2	10030	0010	0000000259	EMERD10				0	9	9	EA	
2	10030	0010	0000000261	EMERD14				0	9	9	EA	
2	10030	0010	0000000263	RED 12				0	9	9	EA	
2	10030	0010	0000000264	RED 14				0	9	9	EA	
2	10030	0010	0000000269	EMERD04				0	9	9	EA	
2	10030	0010	0000000270	EMERD05				0	9	9	EA	
2	10030	0010	0000000272	RED 04				0	9	9	EA	
2	10030	0010	0000000273	RED 05				0	9	9	EA	
2	10030	0010	0000000274	RED 16				0	9	9	EA	
2	10030	0010	0000000275	RED 18				0	9	9	EA	
2	10171	0010	0000000723	AEG 4				0	9	9	EA	
2	10171	0010	0000000724	AEG 5				0	8	8	EA	
2	10171	0010	0000000725	AEG 6				0	8	8	EA	
2	10171	0010	0000000726	AEG 7				0	8	8	EA	
2	10171	0010	0000000727	AEG 8				0	8	8	EA	
2	10171	0010	0000000728	AEG 9				0	8	8	EA	
2	10171	0010	0000000729	BER 4				0	9	9	EA	

Figure 4.25 Display 2-Step Picking Relevance for Group Screen

Create Individual Transfer Orders for Individual Deliveries

Let's now create the individual transfer orders for the individual deliveries. In two-step picking, this is referred to as an *allocation*. To create the individual transfer order, go to Logistics • Sales and Distribution • Shipping and Transportation • Picking • Create Transfer Order • Collective Processing, as shown in Figure 4.26, or go to Transaction LT42 and enter the group number. It's a prerequisite that all transfer orders for consolidated picking are confirmed at this time.

Figure 4.26 Create TOs by Multiple Processing: Initial Screen

If you choose to run this transaction in the foreground, you'll be prompted to create a TO for each delivery, as shown in Figure 4.27. Because we normally process hundreds or thousands of deliveries, it's a good idea to run it in the background.

At the end of the background processing, you'll see the summary information, as shown in Figure 4.28. You can also display the list of transfer orders by clicking on the Disp. Details button.

The detailed information, shown in Figure 4.29, shows you which transfer orders were create for each delivery.

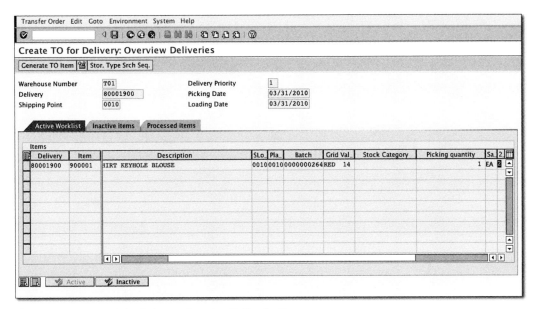

Figure 4.27 Create TO for Delivery: Overview Deliveries Screen

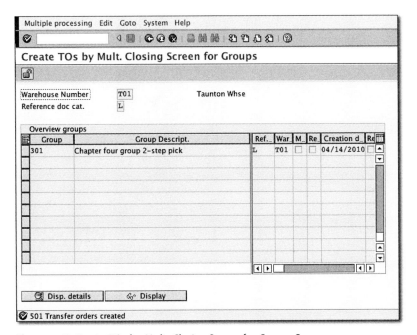

Figure 4.28 Create TOs by Mult. Closing Screen for Groups Screen

Figure 4.29 Create TO by Mult. Processing: Doc. Closing Info Screen

Table 4.3 lists the two-step picking maintenance transactions and menu paths for your easy reference.

Transaction	Menu Path
LT72 – Redefine Two-Step Picking	LOGISTICS • SALES AND DISTRIBUTION • SHIPPING AND TRANS-PORTATION • PICKING • TWO-STEP PICKING • REDEFINE 2-STEP PICKING
LX39 – Two-Step Picking Analysis	LOGISTICS • SALES AND DISTRIBUTION • SHIPPING AND TRANS-PORTATION • PICKING • TWO-STEP PICKING • ANALYSIS
LT0E – Create Consolidated Transfer Orders (two-step first step)	LOGISTICS • SALES AND DISTRIBUTION • SHIPPING AND TRANS-PORTATION • PICKING • CREATE TRANSFER ORDER • VIA 2-STEP PICKING
LT42 – Create Individual Transfer Orders for Group (two-step second step)	LOGISTICS • SALES AND DISTRIBUTION • SHIPPING AND TRANS-PORTATION • PICKING • CREATE TRANSFER ORDER • COLLECTIVE PROCESSING

Table 4.3 Two-Step Picking

4.2.3 Planning Replenishments

Some companies need to supply odd quantities to their customers. This means that they don't supply full pallet or full box quantities. In this situation, the SAP system provides what is known as a *large/small quantities* picking.

The *large* part refers to the full pallet or box quantity, and the *small* part refers to a partial quantity of that larger container. The system indicates two different sections of the warehouse as dependent on each other. The small quantity area has to be replenished from the large quantity area when the stock level reaches a certain threshold. The system will guide the picking into these sections or storage types by creating separate transfer orders for the large quantity containers and for the partial container quantities, respectively.

Let's walk through an example to help explain this better. You sell a product in cases of 12, there are 32 cases in a pallet, and your client ordered 300 cases. To fulfill this quantity, the system will create 1 TO in the large quantities storage type for 9 pallets for a subtotal of 288 cases. Then it will create a second TO for the small quantities area for the remaining 12 boxes.

This way, you don't have to break a new pallet and return the remaining partial pallet to the pallet storage area, as illustrated in Figure 4.30.

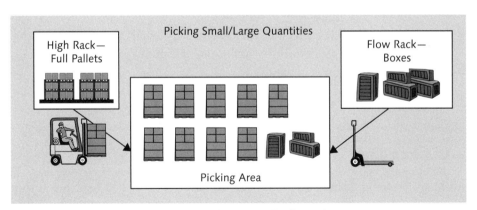

Figure 4.30 Picking Small/Large Quantities from the Full Pallet and Box Storage Areas

This all sounds nice and neat, but how does the small quantity area get those 12 cases? Well, we have to replenish this area. Normally, we'd wait until the stock here goes below a minimum threshold, and then we would request that at least one full pallet be moved from the pallet storage area.

In the SAP system, we need to indicate these parameters in the WAREHOUSE 2 view of the material master (LOGISTICS • MATERIALS MANAGEMENT • MATERIAL MASTER • MATERIAL • CHANGE • IMMEDIATELY), as shown in Figure 4.31, for each of the products you want to pick in this manner.

Figure 4.31 Storage Bin Stock from the Warehouse Management 2 View

First, we need to create a new view for the specific small quantities storage type and then enter the values that will guide both the replenishment and the split picking.

The fields we need to update are as follows:

▶ MAXIMUM BIN QUANTITY: The maximum quantity that this storage type can hold for this material.

▶ MINIMUM BIN QUANTITY: Threshold quantity to trigger the replenishment.

▶ REPLENISHMENT QTY: The quantity of this material that will be moved from the pallet storage type to the box storage type.

▶ CONTROL QUANTITY: The quantity that will dictate when to split the picking. Normally, it's a full pallet quantity minus one. From our example, if a pallet is 32 cases, then our control quantity would be 31 cases.

Now that you understand picking, let's move on to packing.

4.3 Packing

Although you might think all your products have to be packed before you ship them out to your customer, in SAP this isn't necessarily the case. Packing in SAP ERP helps you keep track of individual shipping units. A shipping unit is also known as a *handling unit* (see Figure 4.32), and it can refer to a box, a pallet, a container, or any other packaging that you serialize and keep track of for your client.

Each of these containers maintains the following characteristics about the products that are packed inside of it:

▶ **Material number**
  Refers to the SKU number that uniquely identifies a product within the SAP system.

▶ **Quantity**
  Refers to the partial quantity of the material that is contained in that specific package.

▶ **Batch**
  If your company sells materials that require batch management, then the batch number will be included in the handling unit data.

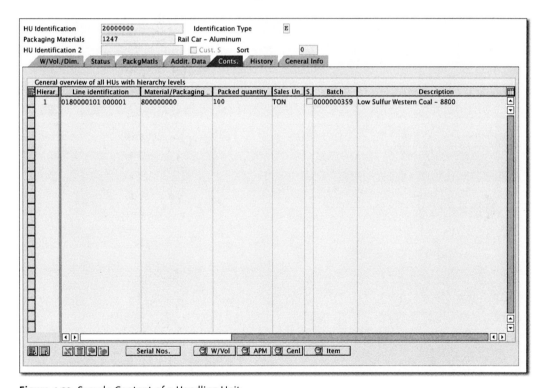

Figure 4.32 Sample Content of a Handling Unit

Packing takes place either in SAP-defined packing stations, which are defined in configuration, or directly in the delivery order. There is also the option to have the system automatically pack each delivery upon creation. You should ask your functional analyst whether this is activated in your system.

Packaging materials are also defined in the material master; they have a pre-defined capacity in weight and volume as shown in Figure 4.33.

Figure 4.33 Packaging Material Data from the Sales/Plant Data View in the Material Master

To pack your product before shipping to your customer, you first have to go to the packing screen in the delivery order. From the item overview, click on the PACKING button (see Figure 4.34). When you are on the packing screen, choose a packaging material, which is typically a pallet or case, depending on your company's needs.

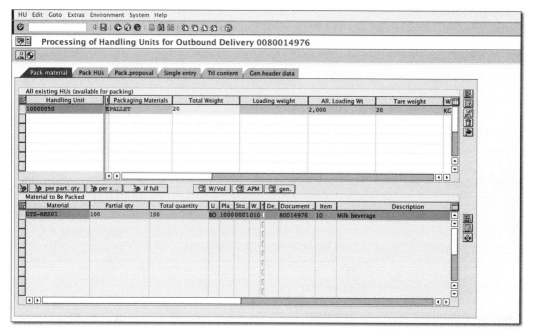

Figure 4.34 Packing Screen in a Change Delivery Transaction

After you've selected a packaging material, you need to select the materials and quantities that are to be packed in each handling unit. After packing your materials, the weight of the handling unit is updated with the weight of the packed materials (see Figure 4.35). Save the delivery.

Figure 4.35 Weight of the Packed Handling Unit Updated After Packing

In Section 4.4, we'll discuss the transportation functionality in SAP ERP. At that point, you'll learn about shipments and how they represent trucks carrying your company's products to your customers. For now, we'll only mention that those trucks are also handling units, and you'll need a packaging material for each truck type you use. In them, you'll pack multiple deliveries.

Note

If you're using batch management in your company, you can't pack a delivery until the batch determination has taken place.

Table 4.4 lists the packing transactions and menu paths for your easy reference.

Transaction	Menu Path
VL02N – Outbound Delivery	LOGISTICS • SALES AND DISTRIBUTION • SHIPPING AND TRANSPORTATION • PACKING • OUTBOUND DELIVERY
VT02N – Shipment	LOGISTICS • SALES AND DISTRIBUTION • SHIPPING AND TRANSPORTATION • PACKING • SHIPMENT
HUPAST – Packing Station	LOGISTICS • SALES AND DISTRIBUTION • SHIPPING AND TRANSPORTATION • PACKING • PACKING STATION

Table 4.4 Packing Transactions and Menu Paths

Now that you understand packing, let's move on to shipments.

4.4   Shipment

Another very important component of the logistic chain in the SAP system is the transportation functionality. This functionality allows you to create shipments that represent trucks for sending multiple delivery orders for your customers. Shipments can inherit the route in the delivery orders if all of the deliveries have the same shipping route. The shipment will then have a set of stops based on the customers' addresses.

The transportation functionality in SAP ERP allows your company to plan and execute transportation activities to ensure that shipments will be dispatched and will arrive timely to your customer.

To use the transportation functionality, you need to make specific configurations for your company in your system. Ask your systems analysts whether this functionality is activated and configured in your company.

EHP 7 Updates: SAP Transportation Management (TM)

As mentioned earlier, SAP won't enhance the transportation functions in SAP ERP any longer. Instead, they recommend clients with complicated transportation needs to move to SAP SCM Transportation Management. SAP Transportation Management (SAP TM) is an advanced logistics system that supports you in all activities connected with the physical transportation of goods from one location to another. Efficient deliveries depend on informed route planning, freight consolidation, and enhanced visibility. By providing managers with appropriate tools like route optimization, load building, and track and trace, the right TM can improve fleet performance and reduce supply chain expenditures. Along with warehouse management solutions and truck routing solutions, TM solutions constitute the logistics side of an overall supply chain management system.

You can use SAP TM to perform the following activities, for example:

► Create forwarding orders for your ordering parties
► Transfer orders and deliveries from an ERP system
► Create freight bookings
► Plan the transportation and select carriers
► Tender transportation services
► Dispatch and monitor the transportation
► Calculate the transportation charges for both the ordering party and the supplier side
► Consider foreign trade and dangerous goods regulations

You can use SAP TM to create and monitor an efficient transportation plan that fulfills the relevant constraints (for example, service level, costs, and resource availability). You can determine options to save costs and to optimize the use of available resources. You can react to transportation events and find solutions to possible deviations from the original transportation plan.

The first important point in transportation planning in SAP ERP is the *transportation planning point*, which represents the place where trucks are loaded and dispatched from the warehouse. It's essentially the place where you'll create shipments.

Shipments are documents that hold the information about the movement of goods to the customer; this information includes carrier information, truck type, truck license plates, and the name of the truck driver. It also contains all of the information about the shipping route, including mode of transportation, connection points, loading and unloading points, and total weight, along with the list of all of the deliveries loaded in the truck, which themselves contain the lists of materials and handling units shipped to each customer.

There are three different types of shipments:

▶ **Individual shipments:** Can contain one or more deliveries that go from one point of departure to one point of destination with one mode of transportation.

▶ **Collective shipments:** Can perform several drop stops to several points of destination with one mode of transportation.

▶ **Transportation chain:** Can be very useful when shipping of deliveries has to deal with several modes of transportation, which is very common in exports.

The transportation chain normally has different legs, one for each loading and unloading point. For example, if you have to ship goods to Europe, then you'll have to use a truck to move the goods to the port, and then use a ship carrier to move the goods to Europe, and most likely then you'll need to load the shipment onto a train so it gets to the final destination.

In this example, there are three modes of transportation involved: truck, ship, and train. There are also three legs of the trip, one for each mode of transportation, and at least two loading and unloading points, which represent the ports. The route stages are illustrated in Figure 4.36.

Figure 4.36 Overview of the Route Stages

As part of the logistics chain, the shipments are linked to the deliveries, so each time that a delivery is made part of a shipment, its transportation planning status changes from *Not Started* to *Partially Processed*. The main screen in Transaction VT01N prompts you for the transportation planning point and the shipment type, as shown in Figure 4.37.

Figure 4.37 Create Shipment: Initial Screen

When you create a shipment, you have to select the shipment type and the transportation planning point. From there, SAP provides you with a selection screen for selecting the deliveries you want to include in it. You can filter deliveries using several parameters. You can select deliveries, for example, by route, delivery date, customer (ship-to), planned goods issue date, and several others, as shown in Figure 4.38.

Figure 4.38 Delivery Selection Screen for Shipments

After the selection, you'll find a list of the deliveries provided based on your search parameters, and from there you can manually add or remove deliveries. This screen (Figure 4.39) is very important because it will show you the total weight and volume occupied by each delivery so you know whether they will all fit in a single truck or other shipping container.

After you're satisfied with the list of deliveries in the shipment, then you can use the planning screen to set the shipment deadlines shown in Figure 4.40. These deadlines can later be used to communicate with the shipping carriers to schedule the right trucks at the right time.

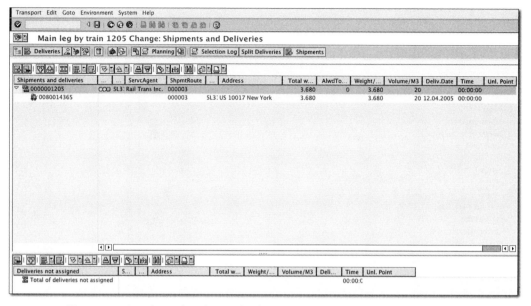

Figure 4.39 Search Result with List of Deliveries in Shipment

Figure 4.40 Shipment Deadlines from the Shipment Overview Screen

With deadline planning, you can schedule the following:

▶ CHECK-IN: THE truck appointment.

▶ LOADING START: The time the loading activities must start.

▶ LOADING END: The time the loading activities must finish.

▶ SHIPMENT COMPLETION: The truck closing time.

▶ SHIPMENT START: The truck dispatch time.

▶ SHIPMENT END: Related to the shipment cost functionality, which isn't a mandatory setting for using transportation.

Later, when the shipment is executed, the shipment has to be updated by the transportation clerks at the warehouse. Each button in the shipment overview (Figure 4.41) updates the actual dates and times for each of the deadlines. Additionally, you can ask your system analyst to link tasks to these buttons.

Figure 4.41 Complete Overview of the Shipment Status

The types of tasks that can be linked range from printing different formats such as the individual packing lists, the consolidated packing lists, the list of dangerous materials included in the shipment, to posting the actual goods issue for all of the deliveries in the shipment, and to executing the billing and printing the invoices and other documents that must travel with the goods.

Shipments, like other SAP documents, can be treated either individually or collectively.

Table 4.5 lists some transactions for creating, updating, and listing shipments.

Transaction	Menu Path
VT01N – Create Shipment Single Document	LOGISTICS • SALES AND DISTRIBUTION • SHIPPING AND TRANSPORTATION • SHIPMENT • CREATE • SINGLE DOCUMENT
VT02N – Change Shipment Single Document	LOGISTICS • SALES AND DISTRIBUTION • SHIPPING AND TRANSPORTATION • SHIPMENT • CHANGE • SINGLE DOCUMENTS
VT06 – Mass Change	LOGISTICS • SALES AND DISTRIBUTION • SHIPPING AND TRANSPORTATION • SHIPMENT • CHANGE • MASS CHANGES
VT03N – Display Shipment Single Document	LOGISTICS • SALES AND DISTRIBUTION • SHIPPING AND TRANSPORTATION • SHIPMENT • DISPLAY
VT70 – Print	LOGISTICS • SALES AND DISTRIBUTION • SHIPPING AND TRANSPORTATION • SHIPMENT • PRINT
VT11 – Transportation Planning List	LOGISTICS • SALES AND DISTRIBUTION • SHIPPING AND TRANSPORTATION • SHIPMENT • LISTS AND LOGS • TRANSPORTATION PLANNING LIST
VT14 – Utilization List	LOGISTICS • SALES AND DISTRIBUTION • SHIPPING AND TRANSPORTATION • SHIPMENT • LISTS AND LOGS • UTILIZATION LIST
VT15 – List of Free Capacity	LOGISTICS • SALES AND DISTRIBUTION • SHIPPING AND TRANSPORTATION • SHIPMENT • LISTS AND LOGS • LIST OF FREE CAPACITY
VT16 – Check-In List	LOGISTICS • SALES AND DISTRIBUTION • SHIPPING AND TRANSPORTATION • SHIPMENT • LISTS AND LOGS • CHECK-IN LIST
VT11 – Shipment Completion List	LOGISTICS • SALES AND DISTRIBUTION • SHIPPING AND TRANSPORTATION • SHIPMENT • LISTS AND LOGS • SHIPMENT COMPLETION LIST

Table 4.5 Shipment Transactions

4.5 Shipment Cost Document

Costing transportation shipments is an optional function in the SAP system. If your company chooses to use it, then you'll be able to track each invoice from each of your transportation partners and relate it to individual shipments. This, like many of the steps described before, also requires the system to be configured to handle shipping costs.

Shipping costs are tracked in a separate SAP document called a *shipping cost document*. This cost document collects all of the costs involved in a specific shipment, including freight, insurance, and customs. These costs are calculated based on previously negotiated prices with your transportation partners for each route and transportation mode.

When the shipment cost document is created, it will look up all of the conditions included in the shipment document and use the data available, such as shipping partner, route, stages, distance, weight, volume, and so on, to determine the value for each of those conditions, which include prices, surcharges, and discounts; and are stored in condition records.

Shipment pricing takes those condition records and determines prices and surcharges/discounts and allows the user to influence these conditions manually. You can define conditions at any level. A level corresponds to the fields in the condition table in which a condition record is stored. Therefore, the level represents the key fields for the access to a condition. Common levels at which price agreements are made are predefined in the standard system.

Through Customizing, you can add any levels that you may need. You can make conditions dependent on any fields of the shipment document. You'll need the assistance of your IT systems analyst to make any of these changes to the field catalogs. By specifying a validity period, you can restrict a condition to a specific period.

You can maintain the values within a condition record (e.g., price, surcharge, and discount) depending on a scale (weight-based, volume-based, or value-based). You can also use multi-dimensional scales. There is no limit to the number of scale levels.

For each condition record, you can define an upper and lower limit that will allow you to manually change a pricing element within the limits specified.

All condition types supported for pricing are determined in the pricing procedure (determined in Customizing), which is decided automatically based on different criteria:

▸ Transportation planning point of the shipment

▸ Shipping type (grouped in a shipping type procedure group)

▸ Forwarding agent (grouped in a service agent procedure group)

▸ Shipment cost item category (grouped in an item procedure group)

Shipment cost documents can be created one at a time or collectively. In either case, there will be one cost document created for each shipment document in a one-to-one relationship.

To create a shipment cost document for a shipment, the shipment must be relevant for shipment costs (at header and/or stage level). The shipment must also have the required *overall status* set in the definition of the shipment cost type. As a minimum, it must have *planned* status.

The shipment cost document consists of the following sections:

▸ **Shipment cost header**
This contains general information on the entire document. Status, reference, and administrative information are provided. As far as the status information is concerned, the statuses are cumulated statuses that are derived from the individual items.

▸ **Shipment cost item**
This contains general data for shipment cost calculation and settlement, such as service agent, pricing and settlement date, tax amount and tax base amount, and organizational data such as company code, plant, and purchasing organization. Each item has its own status for the shipment cost calculation, account assignment, and transfer functions.

▸ **Shipment cost subitem**
Shipment costs are calculated at shipment cost subitem level. The calculation result is also recorded at this level.

After the document is complete, it can be settled against the transportation partners (also known as service agents) and accounts, and the cost is passed either to an internal transportation costs account or billed to the customer.

If you choose to bill your customer for the shipping and handling charges, then you need to also have the system configured to carry those costs included in the *shipping cost document* to the customer's invoice. These can either be totaled up or itemized, depending on your company's policies.

Another very interesting functionality in transportation costs is the creation of a purchase order issued to the transportation partner for the services described in the shipment document. When the invoice for these services is presented, it has to reference either the shipment number or the purchase order number so that it can be approved by the transportation department. To execute this approval, the transportation department creates a service entry sheet, which is the equivalent of a goods receipt for services, and allows the accounts payable area to process the payment.

Each of your service agents that will receive payment through this functionality must be created as a vendor in the SAP system. These vendors are maintained either by the Purchasing or the Accounts Payable departments. To create the shipment cost document, the shipment must have a status of *Shipment Complete*. Then follow the path LOGISTICS • LOGISTICS EXECUTION • TRANSPORTATION • SHIPMENT COSTS • CREATE • SINGLE DOCUMENTS. When prompted, enter the shipment for which you want to create the cost document and the shipment cost type, as shown in Figure 4.42.

Figure 4.42 Create Shipping Costs

The shipment cost document receives the value of the conditions that were previously established for the route/partner, and you'll get the screen shown in Figure 4.43.

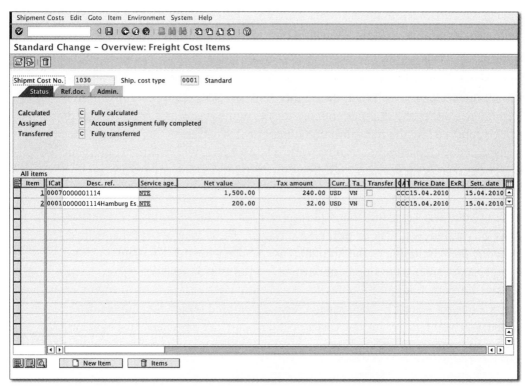

Figure 4.43 Shipment Cost Document After Calculation of the Price Conditions

To settle the costs, you first need to transfer them, as shown in Figure 4.44.

Item	ICat	Desc. ref.	Service age	Net value	Tax amount	Curr	T	Transfer		Price Date	ExR	Sett. date	
1	0007	0000001114	NTE	1,500.00	240.00	USD	VN	☑		CCA15.04.2010		15.04.2010	▲
2	0001	0000001114Hamburg Es	NTE	200.00	32.00	USD	VN	☑		CCA15.04.2010		15.04.2010	▼

Figure 4.44 Transferring Costs

After the document is saved, the costs are transferred, and the status is updated, as shown in Figure 4.45.

In the shipment costs settlement list (Transaction VI12), shown in Figure 4.46, you can see how the document was updated with the purchase order that was created automatically when the cost was transferred.

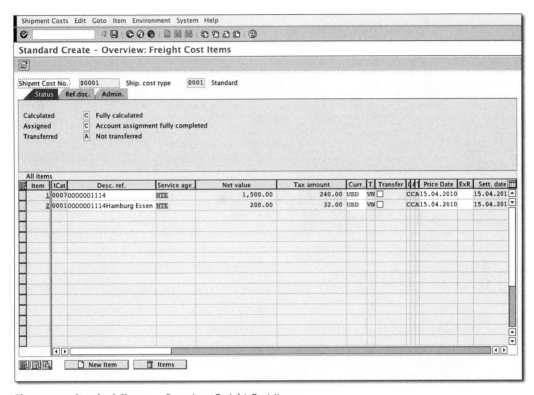

Figure 4.45 Standard Change – Overview: Freight Cost Items

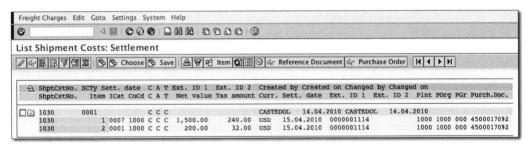

Figure 4.46 Shipment Costs Settlement List

By displaying the purchase order history in Transaction ME23N (see Figure 4.47), you can see how a goods receipt for the services was posted. Now the vendor can submit an invoice for payment, and it can be posted in the SAP system.

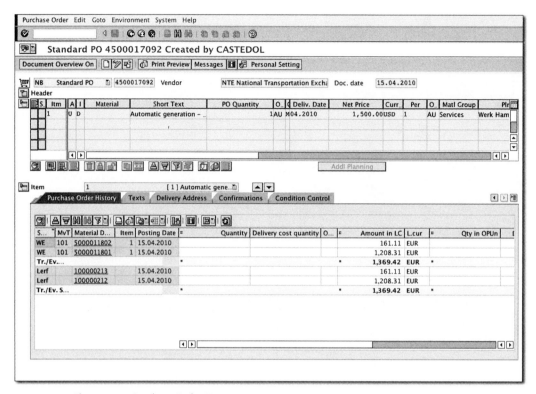

Figure 4.47 Purchase Order History

Table 4.6 lists some transactions for creating, updating, and listing shipment cost documents.

Transaction	Menu Path
VI01 – Create Single Document	LOGISTICS • LOGISTICS EXECUTION • TRANSPORTATION • SHIPMENT COSTS • CREATE • SINGLE DOCUMENTS
VI04 – Create Multiple Processing	LOGISTICS • LOGISTICS EXECUTION • TRANSPORTATION • SHIPMENT COSTS • CREATE • COLLECTIVE PROCESSING
VI02 – Change Single Document	LOGISTICS • LOGISTICS EXECUTION • TRANSPORTATION • SHIPMENT COSTS • CHANGE • SINGLE DOCUMENTS

Table 4.6 Shipment Cost Document Transactions

Transaction	Menu Path
VI05 – Change Multiple Processing	LOGISTICS • LOGISTICS EXECUTION • TRANSPORTATION • SHIPMENT COSTS • CHANGE • COLLECTIVE PROCESSING
VI03 – Display Single Document	LOGISTICS • LOGISTICS EXECUTION • TRANSPORTATION • SHIPMENT COSTS • DISPLAY
VI11 – Calculation List	LOGISTICS • LOGISTICS EXECUTION • TRANSPORTATION • SHIPMENT COSTS • LISTS AND LOGS • CALCULATION LIST
VI12 – Settlement List	LOGISTICS • LOGISTICS EXECUTION • TRANSPORTATION • SHIPMENT COSTS • LISTS AND LOGS • SETTLEMENT LIST

Table 4.6 Shipment Cost Document Transactions (Cont.)

4.6   Goods Issue

Goods issue occurs when inventory is taken off from the General Ledger (GL). The inventory is no longer part of the company's assets at this time. Therefore, it's very important that this activity matches the actual physical exit of the goods from the warehouse. From the shipping and transportation point of view, it's normally right before the truck is dispatched that the goods issue is posted. This activity also precedes one other very important activity: billing. Billing can't be executed until the goods issue is posted.

When you're sending out one single delivery, it's very easy to pick, pack, goods issue, bill, and dispatch. But in large distribution environments, it can become complicated to follow up each of these activities for hundreds or thousands of deliveries.

SAP ERP provides several ways to execute them, one of which is the Outbound Delivery Monitor. This allows you to search and select several deliveries at once and change the status for them all. From here, you can create transfer orders for picking, confirm those transfer orders, and post the goods issue (see Figure 4.48 and Figure 4.49).

Another way of handling deliveries collectively is, as discussed earlier in this chapter, the use of shipments in the transportation functionality.

Figure 4.48 One of the Multiple Functions of the Outbound Delivery Monitor is to Post the Goods Issue

Figure 4.49 Deliveries Ready for Goods Issue Listed in the Outbound Delivery Monitor

As part of the Inventory Management component, SAP ERP creates a material document for each goods issue that is posted. This material document outlines the change in stock that just happened. It details the material that was affected, the movement type that affected it, the quantity for which the movement took place, the plant and storage location where the material was issued from, and the reference document (in this case, the delivery).

Along with this material document, the system also creates an accounting document, which shows the effects to the GL. Normally, the value of the goods is taken out from the stock account and at the same time affects the cost of goods sold account. For each entry in the journal, the document shows whether it was a credit or a debit, as well as the amount in local currency for the total quantity issued.

If you want to review how this information flows, you can review the document flow in a delivery document in Transaction VL02N and select EXTRAS • DOCUMENT FLOW, as shown in Figure 4.50. The document flow is consistent across all logistics documents and shows the relationship among them.

Figure 4.50 Document Flow

The document flow outlines the relationship among all of the logistics documents, from the sales order to the invoice, with the delivery and goods issue in the middle. As you can see in Figure 4.51, the material document shows the details of the goods issue. You can see the material that was issued, plant, storage location, quantity, movement type, and delivery number that created it.

The accounting document (Figure 4.52), on the other hand, is linked to the material document and shows the GL accounts that were debited and credited along with other financial details.

Figure 4.51 Material Document

Figure 4.52 Accounting Document

Table 4.7 lists the important transactions to process goods issue.

Transaction	Menu Path
VL02N – Change Delivery Single Document	LOGISTICS • SALES AND DISTRIBUTION • SHIPPING AND TRANSPORTATION • POST GOODS ISSUE • OUTBOUND DELIVERY SINGLE DOCUMENT
VL06G – Collective Processing via Outbound Delivery Monitor	LOGISTICS • SALES AND DISTRIBUTION • SHIPPING AND TRANSPORTATION • POST GOODS ISSUE • COLLECTIVE PROCESSING VIA OUTBOUND DELIVERY MONITOR
VL09 – Cancellation/ Reversal	LOGISTICS • SALES AND DISTRIBUTION • SHIPPING AND TRANSPORTATION • POST GOODS ISSUE • CANCELLATION/ REVERSAL

Table 4.7 Goods Issue Transactions

In those cases in which you reverse a goods issue, if you want to also reverse the picking for that delivery, you need to do so in Transaction LT0G.

4.7 Proof of Delivery

Some companies apply the guidelines suggested by the Generally Approved Accounting Principles (GAAP), which require that a company can't issue an invoice to its customers until the customer has confirmed the receipt of goods or services.

If this is the case in your company, then your system is very likely configured to support proof of delivery (POD). In configuration, delivery item categories are marked as relevant for POD. So when you create a delivery order that is relevant for POD because of the delivery item, the system won't let you create a billing document for that delivery until the POD from the customer has been received. As you can see in Figure 4.53, the customer master requires the POD-relevant indicator in the SALES and SHIPPING tabs of the customer master.

You also need to make sure that each customer is marked as POD-relevant. After the configuration is set and the customer master record updated, then the SAP system will take care of the rest automatically.

Figure 4.53 Relevant POD Field in the Shipping Tab of Customer Master Data

Proof of deliveries can be posted either manually or automatically. In the case of small customers without automated ways of sending your company a POD, you can get a signed and dated delivery slip from the truck driver. In SAP ERP, you'll create a POD document and that will confirm the outbound delivery and release it for billing.

Proof of delivery is also useful in business scenarios where the materials you ship to your customer may suffer quantity variances. This may be due to different causes, but in any case where the shipped-out quantity may vary from the quantity received by your customer, you may be able to enter the actual quantity by entering a POD and then bill for the quantity they received to avoid constant reconciliation.

Table 4.8 lists the proof of delivery transactions and the corresponding menu paths for easy reference.

Transaction	Menu Path
VLPOD – Change Single Document	LOGISTICS • SALES AND DISTRIBUTION • SHIPPING AND TRANSPORTATION • PROOF OF DELIVERY • CHANGE SINGLE DOCUMENT
VLPODA – Display Single Document	LOGISTICS • SALES AND DISTRIBUTION • SHIPPING AND TRANSPORTATION • PROOF OF DELIVERY • DISPLAY SINGLE DOCUMENT
VLPODL – Worklist Outbound Deliveries	LOGISTICS • SALES AND DISTRIBUTION • SHIPPING AND TRANSPORTATION • PROOF OF DELIVERY • WORKLIST OUTBOUND DELIVERIES
VLPOF – Worklist for Subsequent Document	LOGISTICS • SALES AND DISTRIBUTION • SHIPPING AND TRANSPORTATION • PROOF OF DELIVERY • WORKLIST
VLPOQ – Automatic POD Confirmation	LOGISTICS • SALES AND DISTRIBUTION • SHIPPING AND TRANSPORTATION • PROOF OF DELIVERY • AUTOMATIC POD CONFIRMATION

Table 4.8 Proof of Delivery Transactions

4.8 Customer Returns

All businesses run into complaints from customers, and these complaints typically have to do with receiving the wrong merchandise, damaged merchandise, or simply an incorrect invoice. To resolve these situations, adjustments have to be made in the system. If the complaint involves valuable goods, then the goods must be sent back. Once returned, they will be put in stock under a different stock category, which will block them from being available for sale again until they are inspected, and the customer will receive a credit.

Blocked stock is the category where the stock is received and it's represented in the system with an S. This is one of the stock categories available within Inventory Management. Customers will receive a credit when they have a justifiable reason for their complaint. They might have been overcharged, or they might have received damaged goods. You must, of course, make sure that the correct amount is credited to the customer account.

Returns, credit memo requests, debit memo requests, or invoice correction requests are created with reference to the original document. The credit and debit memo processes are the same. You can create credit and debit memo requests by referencing either the invoice or sales order. The system can then transfer the correct amount from the preceding document.

In the standard system, a *return order* will be created with a *billing block*. This will ensure that someone reviews the order and releases it. After approval of the returns, the credit memo and required accounting documents are created by billing the transaction, which can happen independently of the inbound delivery.

During the posting of the billing documents (credit memo or debit memo), the corresponding accounting documents are created. By doing this, the correct amounts are credited or debited against the customer's AR account. This will also add to the originating document's document flow (Figure 4.54) so that you have a complete view of the history of the order.

Document Flow

| Status overview | Display document | Service documents |

Business partner 0000004130 Compu Tech
Material M-05 Flatscreen LE 50 P

Document	Quantity	Unit	Ref. value	Currency	On	Status
▽ Inquiry 0010000003 / 10	10	PC	825.00	USD	17.02.2010	Completed
▽ Quotation 0020000015 / 10	10	PC	830.00	USD	17.02.2010	Being processed
▽ Standard Order 0000011766 / 10	6	PC	498.00	USD	17.02.2010	Open
▽ ⇒Returns 0060000081 / 10	1	PC	83.00	USD	19.03.2010	Completed
Credit for Returns 0090036104 / 10	1	PC	83.00	USD	19.03.2010	
▽ Returns delivery 00£ ...., ..	1	PC			20.03.2010	Completed
GD ret.del. returns 4900034956 / 1	1	PC	0.00	USD	20.03.2010	complete
Cancel Credit Memo 0090036105 / 10	1	PC	83.00	USD	20.03.2010	
Credit for Returns 0090036106 / 10	1	PC	83.00	USD	20.03.2010	Open

Figure 4.54 Document Flow of a Return Order

Returns orders are sales orders but of a different kind because they are created with reference to a billing document or an order. This will provide the correct quantities and price agreements from the original document. In this way, the correct amount can be processed further. Return orders, as shown in Figure 4.55, are always created with reference to one of the original documents, normally the billing document.

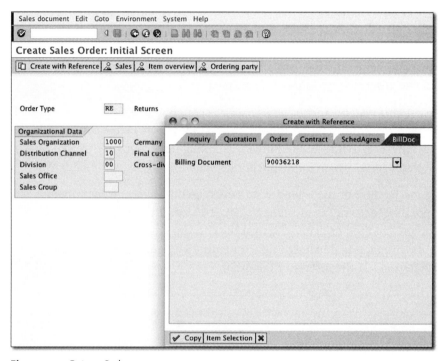

Figure 4.55 Return Orders

After copying the document you'll need to enter an order reason (see Figure 4.56), which will automatically copy all of the items from the original billing document.

The billed prices are also copied into the return order, as illustrated in Figure 4.57.

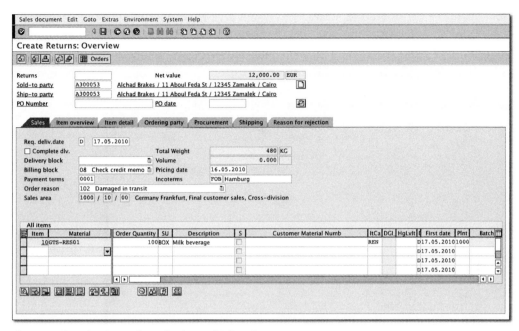

Figure 4.56 Order Copies from the Original Billing Document

Figure 4.57 Return Order

Once created, you can proceed to create a return delivery in the path: SALES AND DISTRIBUTION • SHIPPING AND TRANSPORTATION • OUTBOUND DELIVERY • CREATE • SINGLE DOCUMENT (Figure 4.58). This will allow your company to receive the goods and put them back in inventory. As we already mentioned, these goods won't be available for sale until they are inspected and a decision is made about them.

Figure 4.58 Return Deliveries

The posting of the goods receipt can be carried out either before or after the credit memo has been created. As opposed to standard outbound deliveries, return deliveries have a POST GOODS RECEIPT button instead of a POST GOODS ISSUE button (Figure 4.59).

Invoice correction is used to carry out corrections to quantities or values that have already been invoiced to the customer. An invoice correction request is always created with reference to the incorrect billing document.

The customer receives a document, which lists the original quantity and price, the correct quantity and price, as well as the amount credited to or debited from the customer account. The return sales order is created with a billing block, as shown in Figure 4.60. The credit memo can't be created until the block is removed.

A credit memo item and a debit memo item are created in the invoice correction request for every item in the incorrect billing document. At the start of processing, the net value of the document is zero because all credit memo items and all debit memo items are listed.

Figure 4.59 Return Deliveries Have the Post Goods Receipt Button

Figure 4.60 Return Sales Order with a Billing Block

The credit memo item reflects the original (incorrect) price and quantity. The debit memo item will reflect the quantity and price that should have been charged. The net value of the document is the difference between the credit memo items and the debit memo items.

Credit memo and debit memo items are always deleted in pairs. You can delete all item pairs that have not experienced any changes.

4.9 Summary

In this chapter, you learned about the logistic functions related to delivering your product to your customer. These functions, although not directly linked or executed by sales areas, are a very important component of the logistics chain, and without them your customers would never be able to receive the products they bought from your company.

You've learned about outbound deliveries and their relationship with both sales orders and the warehouse. You also learned how the warehouse executes picking and about the different types of picking available in SAP ERP.

Later, we introduced you to shipments and the value they add to the chain by planning and executing transportation activities and how to handle transportation costs. You also were exposed to how the system creates a purchase order for services after the costs are transferred from the shipment cost document for settlement.

We also discussed materials movements out of the warehouse through goods issue, how they affect the stock and the accounting at the same time, and how the appropriate GL records are registered in the system.

Last, this chapter included a brief description of how customer returns are handled and how items are handled in blocked stock after they are put back in inventory.

In the next chapter, we'll discuss the last step in the sales process: billing.

Billing is the last step in the sales process, where you request customer payment for products or services that you provided. After this step, the accounts receivables process hands it over to Financial Accounting.

5   Billing

Billing is the final function in the sales process, and it's based on predecessor documents such as orders or deliveries. Billing integrates with the Financial Accounting component of SAP ERP Financials. All of your financial transactions are posted at the company code level using a predefined chart of accounts.

Due to the configuration settings, your unique assignment made between sales organization and company code allows you to automatically determine the company code when you populate your sales organization data in sales orders. This also guarantees that financial postings are created for the right company code at the time of billing document creation. In this chapter, we'll introduce you to different billing document types, billing methods, and settlement types that are available for your business scenarios. Again, we'll focus on some of the pre-delivered SAP functions and explain the influencing factors that play key roles during invoice processing as we walk through examples of day-to-day billing transactions.

5.1   Billing Types

Just as with sales documents and delivery documents, in billing, you'll deal with a lot of different document types, as illustrated in Figure 5.1.

Billing document types also control the behavior of the business transaction during billing document creation, as well as help you determine the subsequent document types. Table 5.1 lists some of the standard billing document types delivered by SAP.

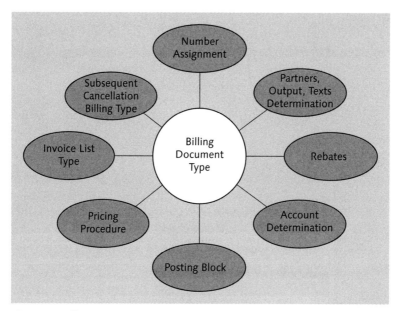

Figure 5.1 Billing Document Type Control Functions

Document Type	Description
B1	Rebate Credit Memo
CS	Cash Sale
F1	Invoice (F1)
F2	Invoice (F2)
F5	Pro Forma for Order
G2	Credit Memo
IV	Intercompany Billing
L2	Debit Memo
LG	Credit Memo List
LR	Invoice List
LRS	Cancel Invoice List
RE	Credit for Returns

Table 5.1 Billing Document Types

Document Type	Description
S1	Invoice Cancellation
S2	Credit Memo Cancellation

Table 5.1 Billing Document Types (Cont.)

We won't cover Customizing transactions and details on setting up billing types, but we do want you to understand some of the most important factors Customizing will influence during billing. The most generic thing you assign here is, for example, a document number range. Maintenance of the billing document types is done in logical sections, as described in the following lists.

General data section settings influencing factors include the following:

▶ SD DOCUMENT CATEGORY: This assigns a document type to a business transaction and specifies whether you're dealing with the invoice or a cancellation document, for example.

▶ TRANSACTION GROUP: This is related to the document category and is also responsible for the document behavior during processing.

▶ POSTING BLOCK: This controls whether a billing document will be blocked for you automatically at the time of creation preventing it from posting to Financial Accounting. Manual release is required.

▶ INVOICE LIST TYPE: This setting enables you to control whether this document can be processed using invoice lists; if you decide to do so, you assign a type of Invoice List Allowed.

▶ RELEVANT FOR REBATE: This controls whether your billing document is relevant during rebate processing.

The cancellation section factors include the following:

▶ CANCELLATION BILLING TYPE: This setting assigns the cancellation document type proposed automatically when you want to cancel a billing document.

▶ COPYING REQUIREMENTS: This setting enables you to specify any special copying routines, which checks whether certain requirements are filled from either SAP predefined ones or those you create.

Account assigning and pricing section factors include the following:

▶ ACCOUNT DETERMINATION PROCEDURE: This setting allows you to assign an account determination procedure that will be applied during document processing when posting, which enables you to create the financial document.

▶ DOCUMENT PRICING PROCEDURE: This setting enables you to assign a key that specifies the pricing procedure for your billing document. This helps determine the pricing procedure. If this factor is different from the sales order or the preceding document pricing procedure, then a new pricing procedure will be determined. Most of the scenarios for the billing document pricing procedure are the same as the sales order document pricing procedure.

> **Note**
>
> Remember that during pricing, the system determines the pricing procedure by taking the following into account:
> ▶ Sales area data
> ▶ Pricing procedure key from the sales document header
> ▶ Pricing procedure key from the customer master

Output, partners, and texts section options include the following:

▶ OUTPUT DETERMINATION PROCEDURE: This is the procedure assigned to your document type that drives which output types are to be generated for your billing document and in what sequence they will be issued.

▶ OUTPUT TYPE: This setting enables you to maintain a default output type for your billing document.

▶ HEADER PARTNERS: This setting controls the partner determination procedure that will be used for the header data of your billing document.

▶ ITEM PARTNERS: This setting, if needed, enables you to also specify the partner determination procedure for your document items.

▶ TEXT DETERMINATION PROCEDURE: This text determination procedure also determines what text types appear in your document header.

▶ TEXT DETERMINATION PROCEDURE ITEM: This text determination procedure is used to determine what text types appear in your document items.

5.2   Billing Relevance

You can create billing documents with reference to a sales order, delivery, or external EDI transactions. You can also refer to an entire document, individual items, or even partial quantities of items. This means that you can distinguish between order-related invoices and delivery-related invoices.

Your sales document type definition and copy controls defined in SAP Customizing drive the process of invoice creation.

5.2.1   Order-Related Invoice

Use the order-related invoice if you invoice a customer for services you performed, or where delivery items aren't required for your billing process, as illustrated in Figure 5.2.

Figure 5.2 Sales Order-Related Invoices

The billing type defaults from the sales document type definition, and item relevancy for order type billing comes from your sales document item categories configuration, which we discussed in detail in Chapter 3. In this scenario, your item category BILLING RELEVANCY field would have one of the following values, for example:

▶ **B**
Relevant for order-related billing documents; used for order billing as a default in item categories such as REN, Returns and BVN, and Cash Sales. Order-required quantity defines the status of billing.

▶ **C**
Relevant for order-related billing documents. This is used for credit and debit memo processing. For example, item categories Credit Memo (G2N) and Debit

Memo (L2N) are set up as this type of relevance. Target quantity defines the status of billing.

▶ **F**
Relevant for order-related billing documents that use incoming purchasing quantities from a vendor invoice. They are then transferred as billing quantities during invoice creation. The standard item category TAS (third-party business transaction) is defined in this way.

▶ **G**
Relevant for order-related billing of the delivery quantity. Here your order is relevant for billing, but only for the quantity already delivered to your customer. This allows you to combine multiple deliveries of sales orders into one billing document.

5.2.2   Delivery-Related Invoice

If you want to make sure your goods have already been shipped to your customer before an invoice is created, you create an invoice with reference to a delivery, as illustrated in Figure 5.3.

Figure 5.3 Delivery-Related Invoices

Just as with order-related billing, your item category BILLING RELEVANCY field would have one of these values:

▶ **A**
Relevant for delivery-related billing documents. Your outbound delivery is the basis for billing.

▶ **H**
Relevant for delivery-related billing documents with no zero quantities. You can use this to prevent items with zero quantities (no-ship items) from being included in your invoice.

- ▶ **K**

    Relevant for delivery-related partial billing documents. You can use this if you need to bill your customer for partial quantities despite deliveries being complete, and change the billing document quantity as needed.

5.2.3 Order- and Delivery-Related Invoice

You can create an invoice that refers to a sales order and a delivery at the same time, such as one invoice for delivered goods and services, as shown in Figure 5.4. For several items to be used in a billing document, the header fields must match to make sure that your partner data and billing dates are the same.

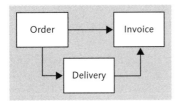

Figure 5.4 Simultaneous Order- and Delivery-Related Billing

5.3 Billing Processing

When we talk about billing processing, we're referring to the processes where you create, change, and delete billing documents. That may include customer invoices, credit memos, or debit memos. Also during billing processing, you can define whether your system will generate individual billing documents for single sales orders or will combine multiple orders into one invoice.

SAP ERP provides you with multiple ways to create your billing documents:

- ▶ INDIVIDUAL: This isn't a common practice in real business scenarios. It allows you to create a billing document for an individual sales document or delivery and is typically used in training and testing.

- ▶ MANUAL MASS PROCESSING: This function allows you to process the entire billing due list manually.

- ▶ AUTOMATIC BILLING DUE LIST: Your billing due list is processed in the background mode scheduled as a background job selecting relevant documents based on your selection variant data.

> **Note**
>
> Automatic billing batch job can be set up in Transaction SM36 (Define Background Jobs) by using program RV60SBAT. You can also set it up using Transaction VF06 (Creating Background Jobs for Billing).

Depending on your settlement type settings, your results will end up with different numbers of billing documents. You can influence processing by defining whether you want the following:

- INDIVIDUAL BILLING DOCUMENT: One invoice for each sales document or delivery to your customer.
- MULTIPLE BILLING DOCUMENTS: Split invoices, created for one or more sales orders or delivery documents driven by a distinct data object, such as a material, material group, or others definable in Customization. Also if the reference documents (sales orders or deliveries) differ from the header fields of billing document, then the system splits the invoice.
- COLLECTIVE BILLING DOCUMENT: Created for several sales or delivery documents, when header data such as payer and terms of payment of billing document are the same for all of the predecessor documents.

All of these rules also have applicable rules around billing dates. Some of these functions are customer master data driven. Figure 5.5 shows a customer master billing data overview showing the INVOICING DATES field using the Agreement Monthly billing calendar, which will cause your billing due process to be executed at the end of each month.

You can invoice your customers immediately upon delivery, on order completion, or at a specific time interval:

- Periodically (e.g., weekly or monthly)
- Time specific (e.g., at a particular day and hour of the week)

Taking this information into consideration, you can choose a billing transaction that will be applicable for your invoicing process. Table 5.2 lists the commonly used billing document transactions.

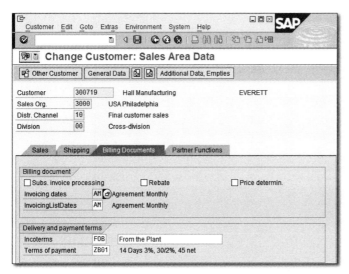

Figure 5.5 Customer Master – Billing Documents Invoicing Dates Setup

Transaction	Menu Path
VF01 – Create	LOGISTICS • SALES AND DISTRIBUTION • BILLING • BILLING DOCUMENT • CREATE
VF02 – Change	LOGISTICS • SALES AND DISTRIBUTION • BILLING • BILLING DOCUMENT • CHANGE
VF03 – Display	LOGISTICS • SALES AND DISTRIBUTION • BILLING • BILLING DOCUMENT • DISPLAY
VF04 – Process Billing Due List	LOGISTICS • SALES AND DISTRIBUTION • BILLING • BILLING DOCUMENT • PROCESS BILLING DUE LIST
VF06 – Background Processing	LOGISTICS • SALES AND DISTRIBUTION • BILLING • BILLING DOCUMENT • BACKGROUND PROCESSING

Table 5.2 Billing Transactions

Let's walk through an example of creating billing documents via Transaction VF04 (Process Billing Due List).

1. On the initial screen of the billing due list transaction, enter the selection criteria, starting with the billing data, where you specify the billing dates (see Figure 5.6). You can also restrict the billing document types that are in scope of the run, and, if need be, the range of sale documents you're trying to process.

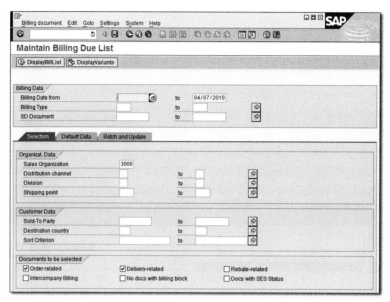

Figure 5.6 Maintain Billing Due List – Initial Screen

2. On the SELECTION tab, specify the sales area data, range of customers, and destination countries. This is where you can also restrict the transaction to either order-related or delivery-related, and allow both types to be processed by selecting the relevant options.

3. To execute your selection, click the DISPLAYBILLLIST button or press F8. The following screen will display all of the sales orders and delivery documents that meet your criteria and are ready for processing, as shown in Figure 5.7.

4. Here you can make a choice of your next steps by selecting or deselecting the documents you want to process, reformat the list using standard grid processing function buttons, re-sort and reorganize your work list, and display document details. After you make your document selection, you can choose to perform a few different functions.

5. Simulate billing document creation by clicking on the SIMULATION button or by pressing Shift + F5. By using this function, you can make sure that the document is ready for further processing and that there is no missing data or other errors that otherwise would prevent you from processing the invoice. If successful, your simulated posting will take you inside the Billing Document Create transaction, where you can review the accuracy of the data before the real invoice is created, as shown in Figure 5.8.

Figure 5.7 Maintain Billing Due List – Document List

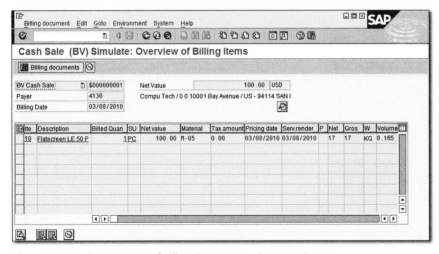

Figure 5.8 Simulate Creation of Billing Document – Overview Screen

▷ **Create individual billing document**

By clicking the INDIVIDUAL BILLING DOCUMENT button or pressing [Shift] + [F6], you can create an individual invoice for selected sales orders or delivery documents. The subsequent screen will look just like the simulation screen, except that the SAVE button is now available.

▷ **Create collective billing document in the background**

You can do this by selecting a range of documents and clicking COLLECTIVE BILLING DOCUMENT or pressing [F9]. Your invoices will be created according to your master data and configuration settings that drive your settlement types, producing either individual invoices or collective billing documents.

▷ **Create collective billing document in the online mode**

This is the same type of process as before, but you can preview the results before saving the documents and review the error log by selecting a range of documents and clicking on the COLLECTIVE BILLING DOC/ONLINE button (or pressing [Shift] + [F2]). The system will run the functions to create invoices, collect the messages, and display them on the follow-up screen. Figure 5.9 shows a screen with exception messages in the PROCESSING STATUS column.

Figure 5.9 Create Collective Billing Documents Online – Exception Messages

6. If you didn't get any exception messages during online processing, your screen will display document types and totals for invoices to be created (shown in Figure 5.10). After you review these messages, save the list, and your invoices will be created according to your master data and configuration settings with the correct settlement types applied. This will produce either individual invoices or collective billing documents.

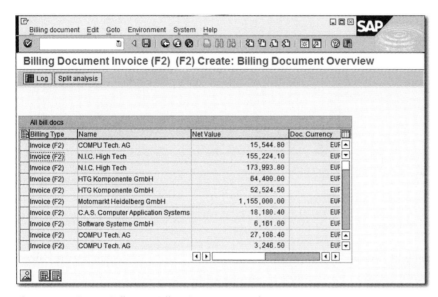

Figure 5.10 Create Collective Billing Documents Online – Overview

For all of the transactions that allow you to create invoices, you have a log function available to review messages posted when exception messages are returned and displayed in the PROCESSING STATUS column.

1. To review system messages in detail, you have to select the document displayed after you attempt to create invoices (refer to Figure 5.9). Note the line with the NOT PROCESSED status; you can review the log for details of the system message stored for this failed transaction.

2. After you select the document line, choose EDIT • LOG, or press ⌈Shift⌋ + ⌈F1⌋.

3. On the detailed message screen, you can review the messages, and to see the technical data details, you can simply click on the little folder icon, which will expand showing more information for you. Figure 5.11 shows a sample of error log messages.

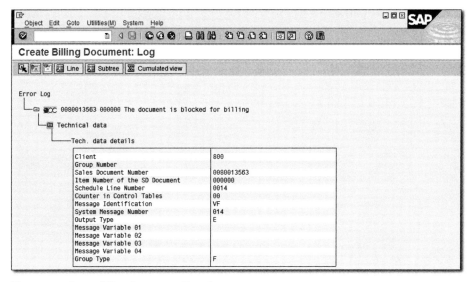

Figure 5.11 Create Billing Document Error Log

5.4 Invoice List

The invoice list allows you to create a list of billing documents such as invoices, credit memos, and debit memos at specified time intervals or on specific dates and then send them to a particular payer (e.g., a statement that summarizes all of your invoice activity).

The documents in the invoice list can be single or collective billing documents. As you remember from a previous section, collective invoices combine items from more than one delivery or more than one order.

> **Note**
>
> The predelivered standard SAP system allows the following documents to be grouped together using the following billing document types:
>
> ▶ **LR:** For invoices and debit memos
> ▶ **LG:** For credit memos
>
> During processing of the invoices, debit memos, and credit memos at the same time, the system will automatically create two separate invoice lists—one for credit memos and another for invoices and debit memos combined.

The billing document type definition contains the information about which billing document type allows it to be used in the invoice list (see Section 5.1). This is the number-one driving factor that will recognize whether your billing documents are subjects for the invoice list.

For the invoice list to be generated, you also need master data to be maintained, such as the assignment of the factory calendar to the INVOICING DATES field of the payer master record (refer back to Figure 5.5).

Another important set of master data will depend on the maintenance of pricing conditions and pricing records for condition types:

▶ **RL00** – Factoring Discount

▶ **MW15** – Fact. Discount Tax

We covered pricing in detail in Chapter 2. You should review the information again if you need to refresh your knowledge on pricing maintenance. If you want to create a printed version of your invoice list, you have to maintain output condition records for these condition types:

▶ **LR00** – Invoice List

▶ **RD01** – Single Invoice List

In Table 5.3, you'll find a list of invoice list transactions for your reference.

Transaction	Menu Path
VF21 – Create	LOGISTICS • SALES AND DISTRIBUTION • BILLING • INVOICE LIST • CREATE
VF22 – Change	LOGISTICS • SALES AND DISTRIBUTION • BILLING • INVOICE LIST • CHANGE
VF23 – Display	LOGISTICS • SALES AND DISTRIBUTION • BILLING • INVOICE LIST • DISPLAY
VF26 – Cancel/Reverse	LOGISTICS • SALES AND DISTRIBUTION • BILLING • INVOICE LIST • CANCEL/REVERSE
VF24 – Work List for Invoice Lists	LOGISTICS • SALES AND DISTRIBUTION • BILLING • INVOICE LIST • WORK LIST FOR INVOICE LISTS

Table 5.3 Invoice List Transactions

Let's walk through an example of creating an invoice list by grouping billing documents via Transaction VF24 (Work List for Invoice Lists).

1. On the initial screen of the work list transaction (see Figure 5.12), enter the selection criteria, starting with the BILLING DATA section, where you specify the billing dates and can restrict the billing document types that are in scope. If you need to, you can also restrict the range of the billing documents for which you're trying to create the invoice list.

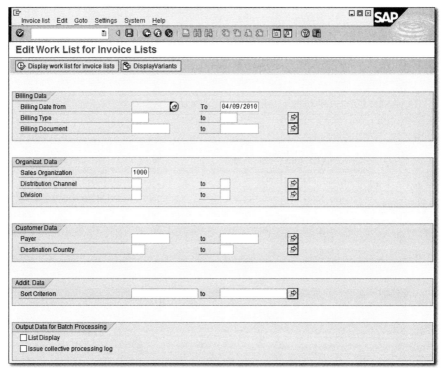

Figure 5.12 Work List for Invoice Lists – Initial Screen

2. In the ORGANIZATIONAL DATA section, specify the sales area data, and in the CUSTOMER DATA section, pre-set a range of customers and destination countries. To execute your selection, click the DISPLAY WORK LIST FOR INVOICE LISTS button or press F8.

3. The following screen displays all relevant billing documents that meet your criteria (see Figure 5.13). By default, all documents that met your criteria will be selected for further processing. You can, however, select only documents you

want to process. To do so, use the standard grid functions and icons available at the top of the screen:

S	BICat	SOrg.	Billing Date	Sold-to pt	BillT	DstC	Document	DChl	Dv	DocCa	Address	Sold-to pt	Sold-toLoc	Sort term	Counter	ShPt	POD status	Net Value	Curr.	Billing Date	BillT	Stat	Group
X	R	1000	03/31/2004	1050	LR	DE	90034526	10	00	M		Becker AG	Berlin			1000		520,817.80	EUR	03/31/2004	LR		
X	R	1000	03/31/2004	1050	LR	DE	90034527	10	00	M		Becker AG	Berlin			1000		92,215.80	EUR	03/31/2004	LR		
X	R	1000	04/30/2004	1050	LR	DE	90034609	10	00	M		Becker AG	Berlin			1000		115,205.60	EUR	04/30/2004	LR		
X	R	1000	05/31/2004	1050	LR	DE	90034670	10	00	M		Becker AG	Berlin			1000		115,205.60	EUR	05/31/2004	LR		
X	R	1000	06/30/2004	1050	LR	DE	90034755	10	00	M		Becker AG	Berlin			1000		72,890.40	EUR	06/30/2004	LR		
X	R	1000	09/30/2004	1050	LR	DE	90034964	10	00	M		Becker AG	Berlin			1000		229,348.80	EUR	09/30/2004	LR		
X	R	1000	10/31/2004	1050	LR	DE	90035039	10	00	M		Becker AG	Berlin			1000		411,284.50	EUR	10/31/2004	LR		
X	R	1000	11/30/2004	1050	LR	DE	90035117	10	00	M		Becker AG	Berlin			1000		503,692.60	EUR	11/30/2004	LR		
X	R	1000	12/31/2004	1050	LR	DE	90035206	10	00	M		Becker AG	Berlin			1000		429,411.60	EUR	12/31/2004	LR		
X	R	1000	12/31/2004	1050	LR	DE	90035207	10	00	M		Becker AG	Berlin			1000		99,130.40	EUR	12/31/2004	LR		
X	R	1000	01/31/2005	1050	LR	DE	90035289	10	00	M		Becker AG	Berlin			1000		512,549.40	EUR	01/31/2005	LR		
X	R	1000	03/31/2005	1050	LR	DE	90035432	10	00	M		Becker AG	Berlin			1000		92,215.80	EUR	03/31/2005	LR		
X	R	1000	04/30/2005	1050	LR	DE	90035497	10	00	M		Becker AG	Berlin			1000		115,205.60	EUR	04/30/2005	LR		
X	R	1000	06/30/2005	1050	LR	DE	90035674	10	00	M		Becker AG	Berlin			1000		469,815.20	EUR	06/30/2005	LR		
X	R	1000	07/31/2005	1050	LR	DE	90035737	10	00	M		Becker AG	Berlin			1000		197,494.80	EUR	07/31/2005	LR		
X	R	1000	08/31/2005	1050	LR	DE	90035794	10	00	M		Becker AG	Berlin			1000		520,817.80	EUR	08/31/2005	LR		
X	R	1000	08/31/2005	1050	LR	DE	90035795	10	00	M		Becker AG	Berlin			1000		92,215.80	EUR	08/31/2005	LR		
X	R	1000	09/30/2005	1050	LR	DE	90035863	10	00	M		Becker AG	Berlin			1000		538,907.50	EUR	09/30/2005	LR		

Figure 5.13 Work List for Invoice Lists – Edit Processing List

▶ **Simulate invoice list creation:** By using the Simulation button or the ⌷Shift⌷ + ⌷F5⌷ function, you can make sure that the billing documents selected are ready for the invoicing list. If successful, your simulated posting will take you inside the Invoice List Create transaction, where you can review the total amount to be posted on the invoice list (see Figure 5.14). If you get any status messages, as you did during invoice creation, review the error log.

Figure 5.14 Create Invoice List – Simulation Overview

▶ **Create individual billing document:** By using the Individual Billing Document button or ⌷Shift⌷ + ⌷F6⌷, you can create an individual invoice list for a selected billing document. The subsequent screen will look just like the simulation screen with the exception of the SAVE button being now available.

▷ **Create collective billing document in the background:** You can do this by selecting a range of documents and then selecting the COLLECTIVE BILLING DOCUMENT button or using ⌈Shift⌉ + ⌈F9⌉. Your invoice list will be created in background mode, and the processing status will be updated.

▷ **Create collective billing document in online mode:** This is the same type of process as the background process, but you can preview the results before saving the invoice list, review the error log, and perform split analysis. You can select a range of documents or select all and click the COLLECTIVE BILLING DOC/ONLINE button or use ⌈Shift⌉ + ⌈F2⌉. Figure 5.15 shows a review screen. You can perform split analysis, which will review consistency between documents selected and verify whether the invoice list will potentially drop some of the selected documents that didn't make the criteria (e.g., outside of the invoice list schedule calendar, etc.). After you review your data, click the SAVE button to create the invoice list.

Figure 5.15 Create Invoice List in Online Mode – Overview Screen

5.5   Rebates Processing

We discussed rebate agreements in Chapter 2, but let's quickly walk through the rebate process in the following sections.

5.5.1 Standard Rebate Processing

You can create a material rebate agreement with a customer and store condition records with the rebate rate and the accrual rate within a validity period by using Transaction VBO1 (Create), as we discussed in Chapter 2. Figure 5.16 shows the change view of the material type rebate agreement.

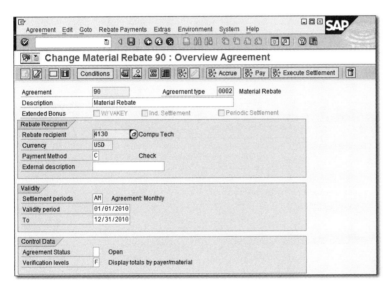

Figure 5.16 Change Rebate Agreement – Overview Screen

These valid rebate records will be determined by the billing document pricing procedure during the billing run when processing either sales orders or delivery documents for materials sent to your customer.

During billing, your system will copy all of these rebate condition records (e.g., BO02) into the billing document, the rebate accrual amount will be calculated (percentage or scale values used in the creation of the condition records will be applied), and the system will post an accrual to Financial Accounting when your billing document is released to accounting. Figure 5.17 provides an example of rebate conditions, and Figure 5.18 shows the material rebate condition applied.

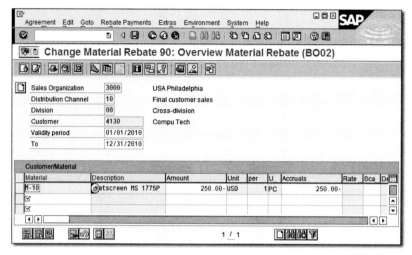

Figure 5.17 Material Rebate Condition Maintenance Screen

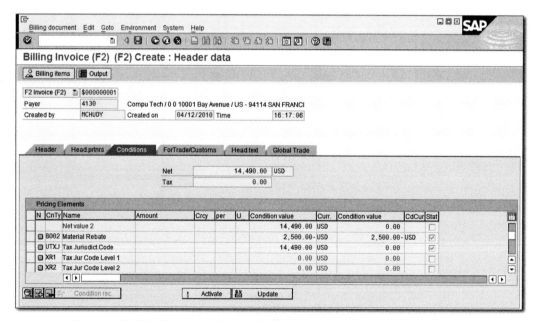

Figure 5.18 Billing Document Create – BO02 Rebate Condition Applied

At the same time, the system updates the rebate agreement, showing the rebate basis and the accrual amount on the sales volume screen of the Rebate Agreement transaction, as shown in Figure 5.19. If your rebate agreement isn't updated, run Transaction VBOF (Update Billing Documents) to perform a data update.

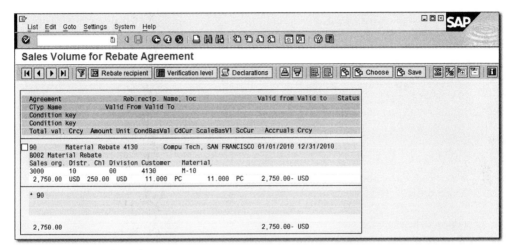

Figure 5.19 Sales Volume for Rebate Agreement

The last step in the rebate agreement processing is settlement using accumulated amounts. Figure 5.20 shows the entire rebate process overview. It's a common business practice to send a payment to your customer on the payment schedule date. Before this can be done, you have to change the status of your agreement to B, Released for Payment.

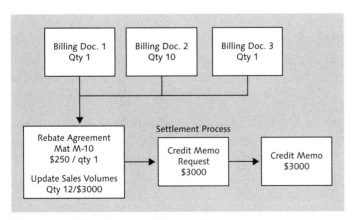

Figure 5.20 Rebate Agreement Process Flow

You can run a final settlement for the rebate agreement (see the list of transactions in Table 5.4):

▶ **Manually:** Use Transaction VBO2 (Rebate Agreement Change).

▶ **Automatically:** Use Transaction VB(7 (Rebate Settlement).

▶ **In the background:** Create a batch job for your choice of programs RV15C001 and RV15C002.

Transaction	Menu Path
VBO2 – Change	LOGISTICS • SALES AND DISTRIBUTION • MASTER DATA • AGREEMENTS • REBATE AGREEMENT • CHANGE
VB(7 – Rebate Settlement	LOGISTICS • SALES AND DISTRIBUTION • BILLING • REBATE • CHANGE
VBOF – Update Billing Documents	LOGISTICS • SALES AND DISTRIBUTION • BILLING • REBATE • UPDATE BILLING DOCUMENTS

Table 5.4 Rebate Processing Transactions

You can execute a manual partial settlement by running Transaction VBO2 (Change), using the PAY icon, or `Shift` + `F12`. All of your settlement runs will create the credit memo request (sales document type B4), which will be automatically generated in the background. You can review the posted credit memo requests by choosing REBATE PAYMENTS • REBATE DOCUMENTS, and selecting the rebate document type you're querying for. Figure 5.21 shows a sample credit memo document posted for a rebate agreement.

If your process requires the credit memo requests to be blocked for billing, you need to release the billing block using Transaction VKM3 (Release Blocked SD Documents) before you can continue to create billing documents. See Chapter 3, Section 3.6 for more details on credit management and release transactions.

You can also change the blocked status using Transaction VA02 (Sales Order Change), by updating the billing block. You then remove the billing block on the ITEM OVERVIEW tab when given the authorization to do so (see Figure 5.22). You can also use Transaction VKM3 (Release Sales Documents) to release SD documents blocked for credit restrictions.

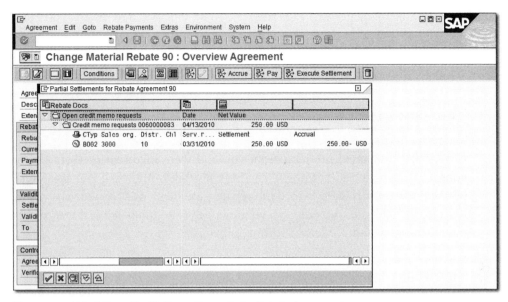

Figure 5.21 List of Open Credit Memo Requests for Rebate Agreement

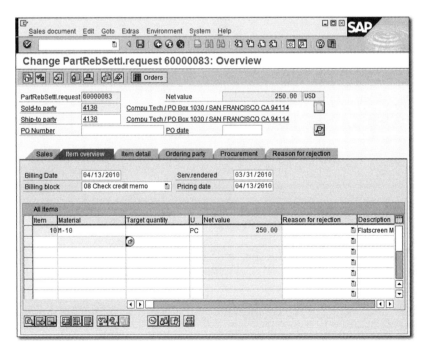

Figure 5.22 Sales Order Change – Remove Billing Block

Your last step in the process is to create the credit memo and release it to accounting. This will also cancel your accruals in your rebate agreement. This is done either in mass by the background job, as mentioned in the earlier part of this chapter, or manually by running Transaction VF01 (Create Billing Document).

5.5.2 Retroactive Rebate Agreements

The retroactive rebate agreement process allows you to extend the rebates to customers that purchased products from you and were invoiced for them before your rebate program went into effect. This will allow you to take into account all billing documents created before the rebate agreement was created. The rebate basis for the billing documents created previously is accumulated and recorded in the rebate agreement. Let's walk through this scenario.

You have created orders and delivered the goods to your customer already. You also created billing documents for these deliveries. You've decided to initiate a rebate agreement that includes billing documents created in the past. To do so, execute Transaction VBOF (Update Billing Documents) to update the previously posted billing documents with rebate pricing condition values, as shown in Figure 5.23.

Figure 5.23 Update Billing Documents

The accrual amount isn't automatically updated for billing documents created prior to agreement creation because it has to be entered manually. The rest of the process is pretty much the same as for standard agreements, and you end up with the settlement and posting of the credit memo. All subsequent billing documents created after the retroactive agreement will also post in the standard way.

5.6 Other Billing Processes

In this section, we'll focus on special billing processes and transactions that are frequently used by most of the SAP installations. We'll cover canceling billing documents, canceling credit and debit memos, correcting invoices, creating billing plans, and handling down payments.

5.6.1 Canceling Billing Documents

To cancel any billing document, you have to create a cancellation document that records the reverse postings into Financial Accounting as well. The most commonly used billing document cancel transaction is Transaction VF11 (Cancel), which you can get to by choosing LOGISTICS • SALES AND DISTRIBUTION • BILLING • BILLING DOCUMENT • CANCEL.

If you pick a sample sales order with completed billing status, you can use the cancellation transaction to walk through this process. Let's start with the review of the document flow for the sales order to verify the status of the order (see Figure 5.24).

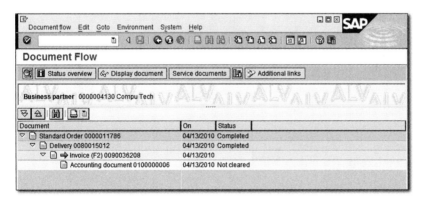

Figure 5.24 Document Flow Screen

1. Start the transaction and enter the billing document number for cancellation (Figure 5.25).

2. After you've accepted your entry and pressed ⌜Enter⌝, you'll get to an overview screen containing the original billing document as well as the new cancellation document to be created. This screen will allow you to review differences between the two documents before you post the cancellation (see Figure 5.26).

Figure 5.25 Cancel Billing Document – Initial Screen

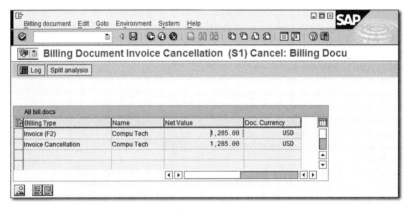

Figure 5.26 Billing Document Cancellation Review Screen

3. Here you can also make the decision to cancel individual items by removing the unwanted items from the proposed cancellation document (Figure 5.27).

4. Finally, click the SAVE icon or press ⎵Shift⎵ + ⎵S⎵. This will save your cancellation document and will attempt to release the document to accounting.

> **Note**
>
> Standard invoices can be cancelled with document type S1 (Invoice Cancellation), and credit memos can be cancelled with document type S2 (Cancel Credit Memo).

The completion of cancellation allows you to make necessary corrections and re-bill your delivery or sales order.

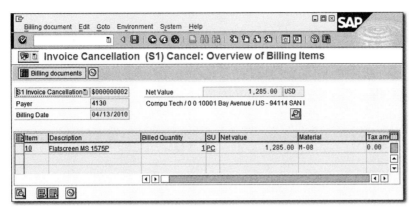

Figure 5.27 Cancellation Document Overview

5.6.2 Credit and Debit Memos

The credit and debit memo billing documents are created with reference to credit or debit memo requests sales document types. If your business process allows it, you can also create both document types directly with reference to a billing document. You can create credit and debit memo requests referencing previous business transaction such as an order or a billing document, as shown in Figure 5.28.

Figure 5.28 Credit and Debit Memo Processing Overview

You can create the credit or debit memo request with or without reference to previous transactions, using Transaction VA01 (Sales Order Create).

You have to specify the document type desired:

- ▸ CR – Credit Memo Request
- ▸ DR – Debit Memo Request

When you create the credit memo requests, you can define whether the system will set the billing block automatically, which forces an approver to open the document, either release the request or reject it, and specify the reason code for each item. Figure 5.29 shows the billing block applied to a credit memo request. It's a standard practice to block credit memo requests for billing because it requires you to send the money back to the customer. You can define the release procedure to be value driven, for example:

- ▸ If the value of the credit memo request is below a predefined minimum limit, it can be released automatically.
- ▸ If the value of the credit memo request is above a certain value, the workflow process routes the credit memo requests to the approver.

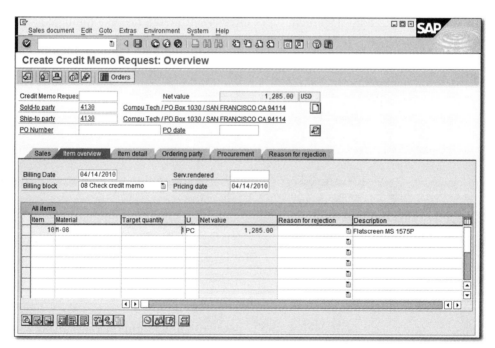

Figure 5.29 Create Credit Memo Overview – Automatic Billing Block

The final step in this process is to create the actual credit memo. You can do it just as we described in the billing overview using several methods. Refer to Table 5.2 for billing document transactions. For example, you can run Transaction VF01 (Create Billing Document), and then specify the credit memo request you want to process on the initial screen and continue. The billing document type will be determined for you automatically based on the Customizing settings converting your credit or debit memo requests to the following:

▸ G2 – Credit Memo

▸ L2 – Debit Memo

Debit memo request sales documents and debit memo billing documents are processed exactly the same way as credit memos and credit memo requests.

5.6.3 Invoice Corrections

The invoice correction request represents a combination of credit and debit memo requests applied with reference to a billing document, as illustrated in Figure 5.30.

Figure 5.30 Invoice Correction Request Process Flow

When you create the invoice correction request, the billing document items copied into the request are automatically duplicated, so for every item in the billing document, you'll see a credit item reversing fully the incorrect line and second debit item, allowing you to make quantity and value corrections. The difference between the two lines created will show you the final correction amount to be credited back to your customer. You can create this document with reference to a billing document using Transaction VA01 (Sales Order Create), where you set the document type to RK (Invoice Correction Request). As you can see in the example provided in Figure 5.31, first the credit memo items will appear and then all the debit memo items.

If you're expecting your customer to send the goods back to you in your business scenario, you should be using a returns order (which we discussed in Chapter 3).

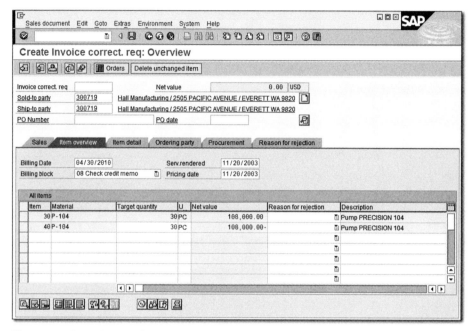

Figure 5.31 Create Invoice Correction Overview

Note

A credit memo item can't be changed, whereas a debit memo item quantity and price can be adjusted as needed.

If you need to delete any of the items, you have to delete them in pairs, including credit and corresponding debit memo items.

You can perform quantity difference adjustments when a customer complaint is due to damaged or inaccurate delivery by changing the debit line quantity. You can use price difference adjustments if your customer complaint is due to incorrect pricing by changing the pricing value on the pricing details part of the screen (access this screen by clicking the ITEM CONDITIONS button).

The last step in the process is creating the credit memo. As with any other billing document creation, you have multiple methods available, as we discussed in Section 5.3.

5.6.4 Billing Plans

The purpose of the billing plan is to establish and firm a billing schedule with your customer either in the contract or another type of a sales document. This is controlled in Customizing for billing plans. Two of the most frequently used billing plans are predelivered in standard SAP systems:

▶ **Periodic billing**
This is often used for rental and service agreements that charge full amounts periodically at certain dates, such as the end of the month.

▶ **Milestone billing**
This is frequently used in construction projects to bill your customer based on the milestone completion dates.

The different billing plans can be created as needed together with your custom rules as well, which you can maintain in SAP Customizing—see Table 5.5 for available standard plans. We only mention this because billing plans can be relevant for processing the entire sales order (e.g., maintenance contract, service contract) by assigning the billing plan to the document type; or you can make it specific to the line item by assigning your billing plan to an item category.

Billing Plan	Description
01	Milestone Billing
02	Periodic Billing

Table 5.5 Billing Plan Types

Let's walk through an example of a periodic billing plan in the service contract. You can start by executing Transaction VA41 (Contract Create) or menu path: LOGISTICS • SALES AND DISTRIBUTION • MASTER DATA • AGREEMENTS • CONTRACTS • CREATE.

1. On the initial screen, choose document type WV (Service and Maintenance Contract) and specify your sales area data. (See Chapter 2 to review sales agreements if needed.)

> **Note**
>
> When processing an order, instead of storing a single billing date, you can store a detailed billing plan with several billing dates in the sales document at the item level.

2. Depending on the business transaction you're processing, the system will automatically propose one of the two billing plan types. In this instance, your contract will be for PC maintenance services with periodic billing.

3. To access the billing plan details, click on the BILL PLAN icon located on the bottom of the CONTRACT ITEM screen (see Figure 5.32). You can also access this section by choosing GOTO • ITEM • BILLING PLAN.

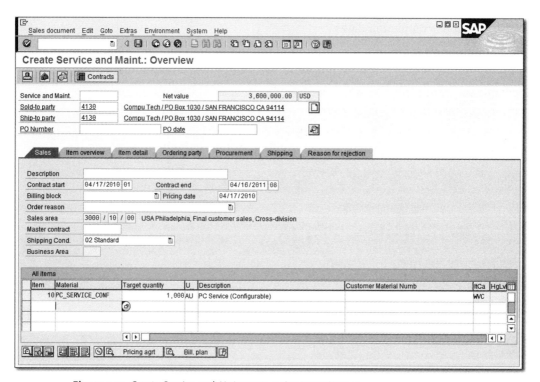

Figure 5.32 Create Service and Maintenance Contract Overview

4. On the details of the BILLING PLAN tab, you'll find information about the type of plan defaulted into your transaction, the start and end date, and the horizon code (see Figure 5.33). Based on these configuration settings, the system will determine the settlement dates for you and the billing amounts that will be proposed during the execution of the billing due lists.

Figure 5.33 Billing Plan Details Screen

5. To display details of individual settlement lines, you can select the line and click on the SELECT DATE button (magnifying glass) on the bottom of the screen.

6. You can also review pricing, which also stores data relevant for you subsequent processes, such as pricing condition PPSV that uses calculation type M for a monthly price that is quantity dependent. See Figure 5.34 for pricing condition details.

7. Finally, create the invoice on the due date. The successfully processed billing document will also update the billing plan's billing status, which sets the settlement line item to C, Complete Status.

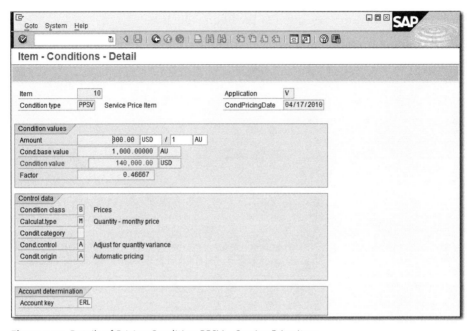

Figure 5.34 Details of Pricing Condition PPSV – Service Price Item

5.6.5 Down Payment Processing

In this section, you'll see how down payments in SAP ERP are created, processed, and settled. You can use the down payment process if your business provides customer with big, time-consuming, and expensive jobs such as plant engineering, construction, startup or, in general, capital goods. Down payment processing is carried out using the billing plan functions we've talked about in the earlier sections. This time, however, they're based on milestone billing. Also, for this process to work, the item you're selling must have a material master sales view setting defined for milestone billing or be specified as one of the SAP-defined item categories relevant for this process, such as TAO (Milestone Billing). You maintain all of these settings in SAP Customizing, and these settings will default into your document when processing sales order items. Your sales order item can have one or more down payment agreements stored as a date in a billing plan.

This type of payment processing is applicable only for order-related billing and *not* delivery-related billing. Also, you can enter the value of the agreed down payment as either a fixed amount or as a percentage of the value, which is controlled by your billing rule set in Customizing:

▶ **Billing Rule 4:** Down payment in milestone billing on percentage basis.

▶ **Billing Rule 5:** Down payment in milestone billing on a value basis.

The down payment agreement can be assigned directly to an item, or it can be defined as valid for all items in the order.

Let's start with creating a sales order and walk through the subsequent steps explaining the whole process (see Figure 5.35):

1. Start by creating a sales order using Transaction VA01 (Create Sales Order). (See Chapter 3 for more details on order creation.) The material specified will inherit the item category TAO required for milestone billing to be used.

2. Your billing plan will be generated with suggested dates, percentage values, calculated down payment amounts, and the required billing document type for the down payment request based on your Customizing settings. See Figure 5.36 for a generated billing plan.

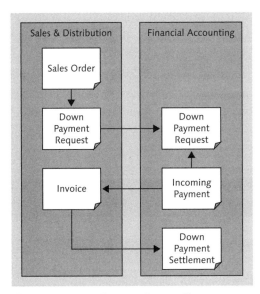

Figure 5.35 Down Payment Process Flow

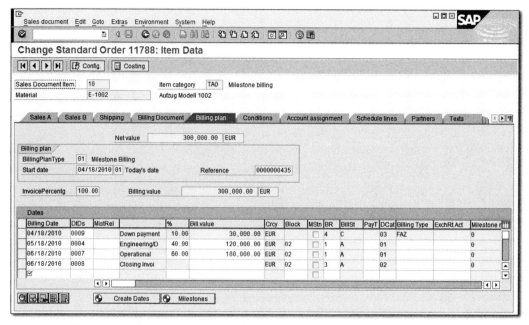

Figure 5.36 Billing Plan Overview with Down Payment

3. On your order billing due date, the system will create a down payment invoice and send it to the customer. Billing type FAZ is used to create the down payment request. If you were forced to reverse this document, billing document type FAS would be used to cancel the down payment request.

4. During the billing process, the special condition type AZWR (Down Payment/ Settlement) is used for down payment items. When this condition type is determined, all of the other conditions are set to inactive.

5. The down payment request billing document is automatically released to accounting and posted in Financial Accounting as a down payment request. The item has a special General Ledger (GL) indicator F, which ensures that the posting is statistical and made to a different reconciliation account (see Figure 5.37). This allows you to differentiate down payment requests from other account receivables.

6. To receive incoming payments, use Transaction F-29 (Down Payment) or menu path: ACCOUNTING • FINANCIAL ACCOUNTING • ACCOUNTS RECEIVABLE • DOWN PAYMENT • DOWN PAYMENT.

Figure 5.37 Accounting Document Posting to Special GL

7. On the initial screen of the transaction, specify the document date and customer account number, set the special GL indicator to A – Down Payment, and enter the bank account number and down payment amount, as seen in Figure 5.38. Click the REQUESTS button, or use F6 to select the down payment request created earlier from the list. Next, click on the CREATE DOWN PAYMENTS button, or use Shift + F1.

Figure 5.38 Post Customer Down Payment Initial Screen

8. The incoming payment is deducted from the special reconciliation account and entered in the standard reconciliation account. The down payments for clearing then appear as open items for the customer and reduce the receivables total (see Figure 5.39). In addition, the billing plan status is updated.

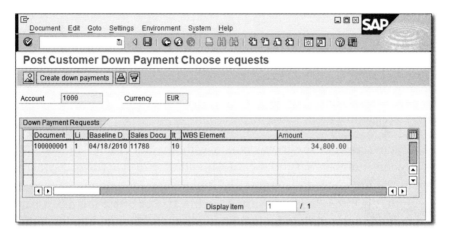

Figure 5.39 Down Payment Requests Selection List

9. After that is done, execute the milestone billing process for the first settlement period. If it's subject to release, remove the billing block for the settlement deadline in your billing plan.

10. When creating the billing document, choose a date that falls after the first but before the second partial billing period. The down payment amount that you already deposited will be deducted from the invoice.

5.7 Integration with Financial Accounting

The integrated nature of the SAP system is also evident in Sales and Distribution transactions. You interact with Materials Management when executing deliveries, picking materials, and updating stock levels and financial postings at the time of goods issue transaction. You also integrate with Logistics Execution by executing WM transactions during picking and by using shipments to process your deliveries to internal and external customers using SAP Transportation Management (SAP TM). You also use integration with Financial Accounting by performing account determination postings that you've set up for your pricing conditions in

Customizing. Your field transfer settings for the SD/FI interface are also defined in configuration and allow you to control whether the accounting document is created immediately or the process gets stopped if the requirements aren't met.

In order for the FI and SD integration to work during automatic account determination, several components have to be defined that includes configuration and master data objects (see Figure 5.43 showing influencing objects), like:

▶ CUSTOMER MASTER

One of the fields used in G/L account determination is the ACCT ASSIGNMENT GROUP. Figure 5.40 shows the maintenance screen of the customer master using Transaction XD02. The field is located in the SALES AREA DATA section on the BILLING DOCUMENTS tab.

▶ MATERIAL MASTER

Another field used in G/L account determination is the ACCT ASSIGNMENT GROUP on material master located on the SALES ORG DATA 2 in the GROUPING TERMS part of the screen section (see Figure 5.41).

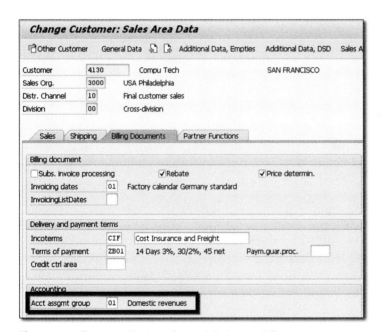

Figure 5.40 Customer Master – Account Assignment Group

Figure 5.41 Material Master–Account Assignment Group

- ▸ **G/L Accounts**

  Another necessary master data object needed for automatic account determination are the actual G/L accounts themselves. They're maintained using Transaction FS00. You can also access it using the following menu path: ACCOUNTING • FINANCIAL ACCOUNTING • GENERAL LEDGER • MASTER RECORDS • G/L ACCOUNTS • INDIVIDUAL PROCESSING.

- ▸ **Pricing Procedure**

  We already talked about the pricing procedures in Section 2.4.5 of Chapter 2, so you can revisit the details, but in essence the procedure is applied during document creation and use pricing conditions in calculations in the sequence they will be processed. Figure 5.42 shows the pricing procedure definition and account key assignments which we will talk about in the next section. So when talking about account determination, we're talking about mapping the account keys to GL accounts using condition technique.

- ▸ **Condition Records**

  Condition records provide values maintained for specific condition type combinations of data fields required to call for them when pricing procedure is executed. You can check for more on condition record maintenance Chapter 2, Section 2.4.6.

Figure 5.42 Pricing Procedure Control Data – Account Key Assignment

5.7.1 Account Determination

Account determination is usually defined in SAP Customizing by the Financial Accounting team and covers multiple functionalities.

To configure all your SD-related FI postings, your configuration team needs to understand and collect information for the following:

▶ Chart of accounts

▶ Sales organization enterprise structure

▶ Account assignment group for customer payer partner, BILLING SCREEN, ACCOUNT GROUP field

▶ Account assignment group for your materials, SALES 2 screen, ACCOUNT ASSIGNMENT GROUP field

▶ Account keys

▶ GL and profit center reporting requirements

Figure 5.43 provides an overview of the standard criteria in account determination. One of the driving forces behind the integration is account keys. *Account keys* are assigned to the condition types in the pricing procedures to help you direct the conditions to the correct revenue accounts. You can revisit Chapter 2 to review pricing and condition technique basics. Each of the condition types can be assigned to an account key, or, if you're using rebates, two account keys.

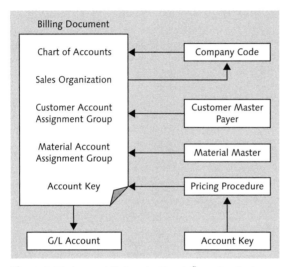

Figure 5.43 Account Determination Influencing Factors

Also, you can have multiple condition types assigned to the same account key. Some of the predefined account keys are listed here:

▶ ERF – Freight Revenues

▶ ERL – Revenues

▶ ERS – Sales Deductions

▶ EVV – Cash Settlement

▶ MWS – Sales Tax

5.7.2   SD/FI Interface

SD to FI interface configuration settings control how certain fields are transferred and how you can prevent the system from automatically creating accounting documents.

For example, in the standard SAP scenarios, you're posting billing data in invoices, credit memos, and debit memos to Financial Accounting and posting them to predetermined accounts, as we described in the previous section. Your data gets automatically transferred to Financial Accounting, but, if needed, you can set a posting block for the billing documents you don't want to process automatically. The determination of automatic posting blocks is set in the billing type configuration.

The following fields can be updated before you create the accounting document:

▶ PRICING

▶ BILLING DATE

▶ ACCOUNT DETERMINATION

▶ OUTPUT DETERMINATION

Your process will require you to release the block so the system can generate the accounting document. You can do this by executing Transaction VF02 (Billing Document Change). After you released the document to accounting, you can only change output data. This is why some of your billing documents have to be processed using explicit selection to release the document to accounting immediately after billing document creation. In certain industries individual document release process would not be efficient to large amount of billing documents that may need corrections.

SAP provides you with a way to execute this function en masse by using Transaction VFX3 (Blocked Billing Docs) or menu path: LOGISTICS • SALES AND DISTRIBUTION • BILLING • BILLING DOCUMENT • BLOCKED BILLING DOCS.

> **Warning**
>
> Make sure that the actual errors reported during initial posting to accounting have been resolved. This transaction re-post the documents and it doesn't provide you with the interface to fix the errors.

1. On the initial screen of the transaction, provide your selection criteria and press ⌑F8⌑ to execute. See the selection screen example in Figure 5.44.

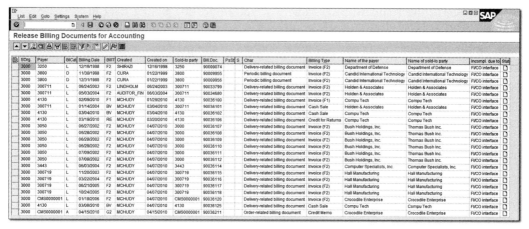

Figure 5.44 Release Billing Documents–Selection Screen

2. On the folloing screen you'll get the list of all documents fitting your search criteria. You can either select all or pick individual documents for processing, and when ready click on the RELEASE TO ACCOUNTING button shown in Figure 5.45. You can also execute the same function using ⟨Shift⟩ + ⟨F6⟩.

Figure 5.45 Release Billing Document to Accounting Document List

3. A successful attempt of release to accounting will be marked in the STAT column with a number "1" and you will get a red "X" if the document fails to post to accounting.

4. You can review processing logs showing the detailed description of what happened during processing by clicking on the NOTES button or by using ⟨Shift⟩ + ⟨F5⟩.

5.8 Summary

This chapter described the standard use of billing functions in Sales and Distribution. We covered some of the most frequently used billing processes, so you should now have a good understanding of billing document creation, billing document cancellation, rebate agreements, invoicing plans, billing plans, and down payment processes. Although your company-specific requirements may be different, the core process remains the same. Also, you should now be able to describe the integration of billing and Financial Accounting.

Now, let's move on and discuss reporting with SD.

Information is made out of data, but data by itself doesn't tell us anything. It's not until we filter it and put it together with other bits and pieces that it provides an added value.

6   Reporting

Standard SAP functionality allows you to attain several reports based on the transactional data produced in Sales and Distribution (SD). Because the SAP system is real time, report results often vary and become obsolete almost immediately.

It's important for SAP customers to display SAP reports on screen or download the reports onto their computer for further analysis in a spreadsheet program or some other kind of tool. In short, the reports shouldn't be printed. SAP customers also commonly feel the need for more reports. Sometimes companies invest a lot of money because of a lack of familiarity with the system or because they're used to look at information in a certain way and it's very difficult for them to adapt to a new format.

In this chapter, we'll try to give you a quick view of the most common reports, which will provide a good view of your operation. We'll also discuss a couple of tools that can help you get more information out of the system.

6.1   Master Data

In this section, we'll review some useful reports to review sales master data. These reports will help you identify records that need maintenance and are also valuable for analysis.

6.1.1 Display Customer Hierarchy (VDH2)

Customer hierarchies are used during sales order processing and billing for determining pricing, including rebates. Customer hierarchies may be useful for your organization if you trade with customers who have complex, external structures that need to be taken into account for pricing. This report allows you to visualize the structure as it's mapped in the SAP ERP system.

To run this report, go to LOGISTICS • SALES AND DISTRIBUTION • MASTER DATA • INFORMATION SYSTEMS • SINGLE DOCUMENT • DISPLAY CUSTOMER HIERARCHY. From there, follow these steps:

1. Select Customer Hierarchy Type A for the standard hierarchy, as shown in Figure 6.1.

Figure 6.1 Display Customer Hierarchy

2. Enter the customer you want to display, and click EXECUTE. The results, as shown in Figure 6.2, show a tree view of the customer hierarchy.

The report will also notify you of any errors on the hierarchy assignments, as shown in Figure 6.3.

Note

You can edit the customer hierarchy in Transaction VDH1.

Figure 6.2 Display Customer Hierarchy Result

```
300010    3020 30 00 REMA US Inc.
Hierarchy node incorrect
 -300011   3020 30 00 REMA DC West
 Hierarchy assgmnt for 0000300010 3020 30 00 not allowed
  -300013   3020 30 00 REMA Superstore

  -300014   3020 30 00 REMA Store

  -300015   3020 30 00 REMA Retail

  -300016   3020 30 00 REMA Market

 -300012   3020 30 00 REMA DC East
 Hierarchy assgmnt for 0000300010 3020 30 00 not allowed
  -300017   3020 30 00 REMA Denver

  -300018   3020 30 00 REMA C&C

  -300019   3020 30 00 REMA Shopping

  -300020   3020 30 00 REMA Food

  -300021   3020 30 00 REMA Drink
```

Figure 6.3 Report with Error Notifications

6.1.2 Display Condition Record Report (V/I6)

We discussed condition records in depth in Chapter 2. The Display Condition Record (V/16) report is an effective tool for displaying several of these condition records at one time. For example, you can display all of the materials with sales promotions that apply for one customer in a specific sales organization.

To run this report, go to LOGISTICS • SALES AND DISTRIBUTION • MASTER DATA • INFORMATION SYSTEMS • CONDITIONS & PRICING • DISPLAY CONDITION USING INDEX, and follow these steps:

1. Select the condition type that you want to display, and click the KEY COMBINATION button to select a key combination, as shown in Figure 6.4.

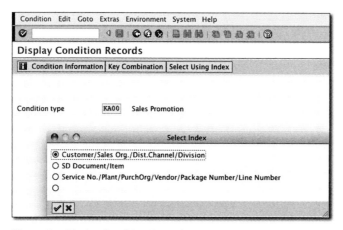

Figure 6.4 Display Condition Records

2. Press ⌈Enter⌋ again to go to the next screen, as shown in Figure 6.5. Enter the relevant data according to the key combination you selected. In this example, we've entered the customer number, sales organization, and distribution channel.

3. Execute.

The result is a list of all of the materials for this customer who have a sales promotion (see Figure 6.6). The report shows the condition record value, validity dates, and the calculation type.

Figure 6.5 Select Condition Records Using a Condition Index

Material	Description	Amount	Unit	per	U	C	S	Valid From	Valid to	Tax	W/t	Lic. no.	Lic. date	D	S	S	T	E	Pay
CP-0001	ineva Creme 100 ml	15.000-%				A		07.05.200	31.12.9999										
CP-0002	Skineva Shower Gel 250_	15.000-%				A		07.05.200	31.12.9999										
CP-0003	Skineva Shower Gel 250_	15.000-%				A		07.05.200	31.12.9999										
CP-0004	Skineva Shower Gel Disp_	15.000-%				A		07.05.200	31.12.9999										
CP-0010	Froglo French Fries 2,5 K_	15.000-%				A		07.05.200	31.12.9999										
CP-0011	Froglo Beans 2,5Kg froze_	15.000-%				A		07.05.200	31.12.9999										
CP-0012	Cookies	15.000-%				A		07.05.200	31.12.9999										
CP-0020	Soladrink Orange Juice 1_	15.000-%				A		07.05.200	31.12.9999										
CP-0021	Soladrink Orange Juice 1_	15.000-%				A		07.05.200	31.12.9999										
CP-0030	Floor Wiper	15.000-%				A		07.05.200	31.12.9999										
CP-0031	Sprange	15.000-%				A		07.05.200	31.12.9999										
CP-0032	Bucket	15.000-%				A		07.05.200	31.12.9999										
CP-1000	Dummy	15.000-%				A		07.05.200	31.12.9999										
CP-1001	Dummy	15.000-%				A		07.05.200	31.12.9999										
CP-1002	Dummy	15.000-%				A		07.05.200	31.12.9999										
CP-1003	Dummy	15.000-%				A		07.05.200	31.12.9999										

Figure 6.6 Display Sales Promotion KA00: Overview

6.1.3   Pricing Report (V/LD)

The pricing report (V/LD) also displays condition records information, focusing on pricing. In this report, you can display the price information for all of the materials for a specific organizational structure.

1. Let's follow this path and take a look at the report: Logistics • Sales and Distribution • Master Data • Information Systems • Conditions & pricing • Pricing Reports (see Figure 6.7).

Figure 6.7 Description of List Reports for Conditions

2. In the selection screen, select the report you want to display. In this example, we selected pricing report 15: Materials Price.

3. Now you have a selection screen for the report itself. Enter the sales organization and distribution channel, as well as the price validity range, as shown in Figure 6.8.

4. The report lists the pricing conditions for each material, including scales, as illustrated in Figure 6.9.

Figure 6.8 Material Price

Figure 6.9 Material Price Report with Conditions and Sales

6.1.4 Customer Analysis Basic List (MCTA)

The Customer Analysis Basic List (MCTA) report is part of the Sales Information System (SIS) that will be described in more detail later in this chapter. In this specific report, you can display the basic information about the volume of transactions by customer. This is especially useful when a customer is trying to negotiate greater discounts or better conditions.

To run this report, go to Logistics • Sales and Distribution • Sales Information System • Standard Analysis • Customer, as shown in Figure 6.10. In the selection screen, you can enter the organizational level that you want to display the information for, along with the time period. Typically, you'll display this one month at the time.

Figure 6.10 Customer Analysis: Selection

The resulting report shows the key figures totaled by client and period, as you can see in Figure 6.11.

If you double-click on any line or column, the report will open a pop-up window, shown in Figure 6.12, with all of the key figures for that client.

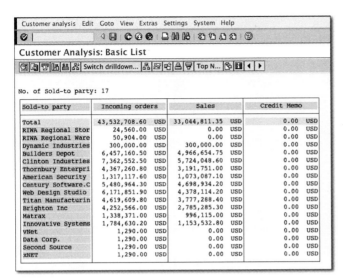

Figure 6.11 Customer Analysis Report Results

Figure 6.12 Report Pop-Up Screen Displaying Key Figures

You can also display the pop-up window by selecting the ALL KEY FIGURES option in the EXTRAS menu, shown in Figure 6.13.

Figure 6.13 All Key Figures

One useful feature of the SIS reports is the TOP N option. When you select a key figure and click the TOP N button (Figure 6.14), you indicate for the report to show the top 3, top 10, or Top N customers for that key figure. The result is shown in Figure 6.15.

Figure 6.14 Top N Option

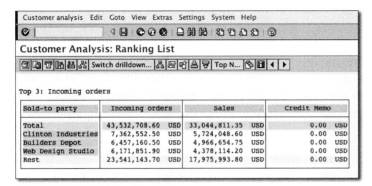

Figure 6.15 Top Three Report Example

From here, you can add or remove key figures by clicking on the icon, which is shown in Figure 6.16.

Figure 6.16 Add/Remove Key Figures

6.1.5 Sales Organization Analysis (MCTE)

The Sales Organization Analysis (MCTE) report is also part of the SIS and provides information about how the sales organization is performing. This information can tell you which sales organization is performing better and which customers are contributing to this. You can also identify other areas of your company's business that need improvement. This way, you may focus either on presales or support resources to strengthen or create more customer relationships.

Like other SIS reports, the sales organization report has various levels of information, the highest being the sales org. From there, you can drill down to monthly periods, distribution channels, divisions, sales districts, customers, and finally into amounts per material.

To run this report, go to Logistics • Sales and Distribution • Sales Information System • Standard Analysis • Sales Organization. In the selection screen (Figure 6.17), enter the organizational level for which you want to display the information. At the minimum, you must enter the sales organization and a date range.

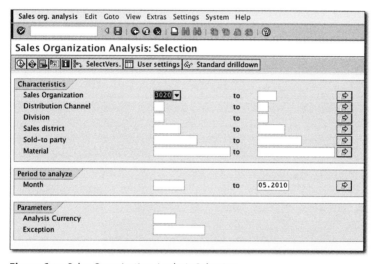

Figure 6.17 Sales Organization Analysis Selection

At the highest level, the information is totaled by the sales organization. From here, you can drill down by double-clicking on the sales organization, as shown in Figure 6.18.

As you drill down, the information becomes more granular and allows you to perform different analysis (see Figure 6.19).

Figure 6.18 Sales Organization Analysis – Basic List

Month	Incoming orders		Tot.order qty		Sales	
Total	43,532,708.60	USD	209,367.000	***	33,044,811.35	USD
09.2002	1,413,981.25	USD	7,519	PC	35,057.20	USD
10.2002	1,289,975.95	USD	6,082	PC	1,091,251.95	USD
11.2002	945,125.85	USD	4,056	PC	998,837.85	USD
12.2002	1,086,535.15	USD	5,413	PC	1,069,268.55	USD
01.2003	1,122,940.45	USD	5,413	PC	1,096,068.15	USD
02.2003	1,294,716.80	USD	6,737	PC	2,362,823.40	USD
03.2003	1,122,940.45	USD	5,413	PC	1,116,229.35	USD
04.2003	1,122,940.45	USD	5,413	PC	1,111,886.55	USD
05.2003	729,173.70	USD	2,796	PC	191,099.20	USD
06.2003	1,181,270.85	USD	7,260.000	***	598,898.85	USD
07.2003	1,122,940.45	USD	5,413	PC	1,122,940.45	USD
08.2003	1,122,940.45	USD	5,413	PC	1,122,940.45	USD
09.2003	1,122,940.45	USD	5,413	PC	962,524.80	USD
10.2003	1,122,940.45	USD	5,413	PC	1,013,380.55	USD
11.2003	1,223,575.45	USD	5,332	PC	785,794.45	USD
12.2003	1,422,940.45	USD	5,413.000	***	1,348,232.85	USD
01.2004	796,172.90	USD	3,111	PC	710,729.20	USD
02.2004	1,122,940.45	USD	5,413	PC	1,030,832.75	USD
03.2004	1,105,806.85	USD	5,380	PC	980,466.05	USD
04.2004	1,122,940.45	USD	5,413	PC	885,989.35	USD
05.2004	1,122,940.45	USD	5,413	PC	258,339.80	USD
06.2004	1,122,940.45	USD	5,413	PC	1,056,781.65	USD
07.2004	1,083,747.45	USD	5,381	PC	0.00	USD
08.2004	1,122,940.45	USD	5,413	PC	1,049,978.55	USD
09.2004	1,122,940.45	USD	5,413	PC	1,049,978.55	USD
10.2004	1,128,100.45	USD	5,453	PC	1,122,940.45	USD
11.2004	1,122,940.45	USD	5,413	PC	1,122,940.45	USD
12.2004	1,122,940.45	USD	5,413	PC	1,122,940.45	USD
01.2005	1,087,410.35	USD	5,349	PC	1,087,410.35	USD
02.2005	1,122,940.45	USD	5,413	PC	1,122,940.45	USD

Figure 6.19 Sales Organization Analysis – Drilldown

The further you drill down, the more interesting the data becomes. In Figure 6.20, you can see the distribution channel and division. By slicing and dicing data, you can better decide where to focus resources to improve sales.

Here we see the sales district and customer, or sold-to party. We're also able to see which districts perform better and which companies are the largest customers (see Figure 6.21).

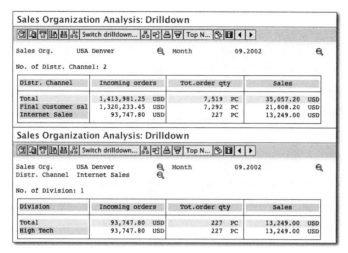

Figure 6.20 Sales Organization Analysis – Further Drilldown

Figure 6.21 Sales Organization – Sales District

The lowest level that you can drill down to is material, as shown in Figure 6.22. At this level, you can see the customer's preferences, and you can then plan promotions or special pricing for materials, or perhaps bundle additional materials to sell to the customer.

Figure 6.22 Sales Organization – Material

6.2 Sales

This entire chapter is dedicated to Sales and Distribution (SD) reports, but this section is the most relevant for the sales function. You'll learn about the reports that give you a view of the operation, as well as statistical reports from the SIS that allow you to have better tools for your decision making.

6.2.1 Sales Summary (VC/2)

The Sales Summary (VS/2) report gives you a complete view of the master data and latest sales activity for a customer or a range of customers (see Figure 6.23). This gives you a quick one-screen view of data that you would normally need to display in several different transactions and then probably match and put together in an external tool such as a spreadsheet.

To run this report, go to LOGISTICS • SALES AND DISTRIBUTION • SALES SUPPORT • INFORMATION SYSTEM • SALES SUMMARY.

In the selection screen, you can enter the customer or customers along with the sales organization. The distribution channel and division are optional. The report starts with a view of the master data and sales information (Figure 6.24). Also included is the assignment to sales organizational structures.

Figure 6.23 Sales Summary Report

Figure 6.24 Master Data and Sales Information

In addition, you can view additional product information, such as pricing and transportation, as shown in Figure 6.25.

This report also contains billing document, payment, and delivery information, as well as partner functions and the last sales document in the system, as shown in Figure 6.26.

Figure 6.25 Pricing, Shipping, Delivery, and Transportation

Figure 6.26 Sales Summary – Billing Document and Payment Information

You also can see the quick view of the latest sales activity and any backorders that might be opened, as shown in Figure 6.27.

Figure 6.27 Sales Summary – Quick View

6.2.2 List Customer Material Info (VD59)

The List Customer Material Info (VD59) report is a simple list of customer-material info records. You can display info records by customer, sales organization/distribution channel, or material. To run this report, go to LOGISTICS • LOGISTICS EXECUTION • MASTER DATA • CUSTOMER MATERIAL INFORMATION • LIST. You can also search the info records by using the customer's material number and description, as shown in Figure 6.28.

The result is the list of materials with info records that match your search criteria, as shown in Figure 6.29.

Figure 6.28 Customer Material Info Report

Figure 6.29 Customer Material Info Record Search Results

6.2.3 List of Sales Order (VA05)

The List of Sales Orders (VA05) report is possibly one of the most useful reports for your day-to-day operations. With this report, you can look at all of the sales orders posted for a given customer or, even better, sales orders for a given material. To run this report, go to LOGISTICS • SALES AND DISTRIBUTION • SALES SUPPORT • INFORMATION SYSTEM • LIST SALES ORDERS. In the screen, you can either enter the customer or the material you want to search for in the sales orders (Figure 6.30).

This report makes it difficult to miss a sales order. The report, as shown in Figure 6.31, lists all of the items for each sales order. From here you can reach the sales order maintenance Transaction VA02. If you have the proper access permissions, you can make changes to the order.

Figure 6.30 List of Sales Orders – Search Screen

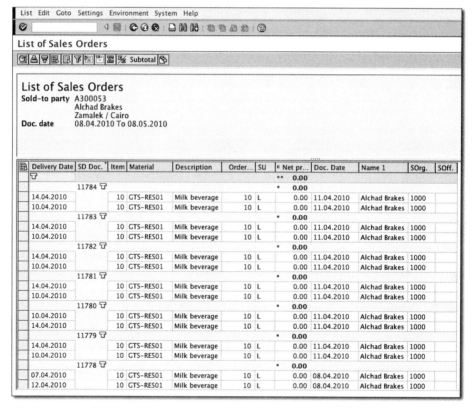

Figure 6.31 List of Sales Orders

Some of the most frequently used reports have been optimized in enhancement package 6 for SAP HANA SP01. The changes affect the selection of data. To get access to these changes, your technical support group will have to activate the business function LOG_SD_REPORT_OPT and add the entries for VA05, VA15, VA25, and VA45.

> **Note**
>
> As of SAP ERP 6.0 EHP 6, this report has been enhanced with a much more versatile search screen. If your system is running prior to EHP 6, when you push the button Fur-
> ther Sel. Criteria, you'll see a list of seven fields, from which you can pick three to make your selection more specific.

With EHP 6, you now have a much bigger list of fields for selection and all right there on the main screen; which means that you don't need to jump through pop-up screens making it, as SAP calls it, a flat navigation. See Figure 6.32.

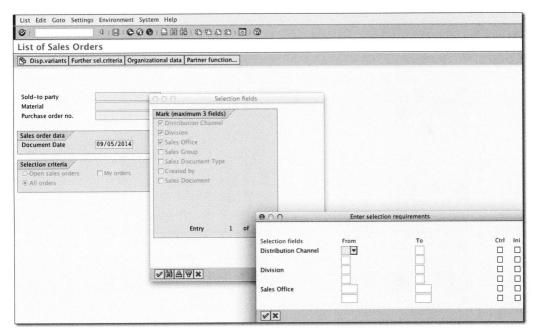

Figure 6.32 Pop-Up Screens Prior to EHP 7

The new VA05, as shown in Figure 6.33, allows the use of wild cards, value ranges, and also selection by partners. This provides the flexibility to look up data when you know it contains certain characters, list information for a set of values, including customers, which in the old selection screen was limited to one customer. This will make your search for sales orders much easier in your daily experience.

Figure 6.33 Additional Selection Options

> **Warning**
>
> With the implementation of this change, the old transactions are not available anymore and any customer-specific changes made to these transactions will be lost.

Other reports with the same changes include:

- Inquiries List (VA15)
- Quotation List (VA25)
- Contracts List (VA45)
- Orders With Time Period (SD01)

In the same manner, the activation of this function activates changes on other transactions, like:

- List of documents with credit management (VKM1 to VKM5)
- List of sales documents blocked for deliveries (VL14L)
- List of sales documents blocked for billing (V23)
- List of sales documents by object status (V.26)
- And also the output from orders report (SD70AV1A)

6.2.4 Inquiries List (VA15)

The Inquiry List (VA15) report is very useful and allows you to list all of the inquiries that are opened by customer or by material. It displays the inquiry number and all of the items for each sales document. To run this report, go to LOGISTICS • SALES AND DISTRIBUTION • SALES • INFORMATION SYSTEM • INQUIRIES • INQUIRIES LIST.

In the selection screen, enter the customer number or the material number, as shown in Figure 6.34. Enter the validity period for the document and the document date or document range, if applicable. If you select the MY INQUIRIES checkbox, the results will only show the documents that you've created.

The result, as shown in Figure 6.35, is a list of inquiry documents that includes all of the items for each of the inquiries. You can use this information to follow up with your customer as part of the sales cycle.

> **Note**
>
> As of SAP ERP 6.0 EHP 6, this report has been enhanced with a much more versatile search screen. If your system is running prior to EHP 6, when you push the button FURTHER SEL. CRITERIA, you'll only be able to choose up to three fields to make your selection more specific.

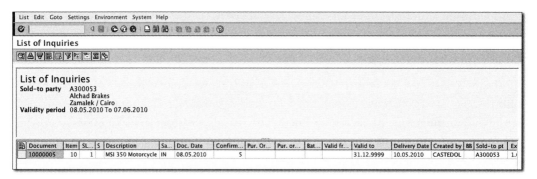

Figure 6.34 List of Inquiries

Figure 6.35 List or Inquiries Result

6.2.5 Quotation List (VA25)

Just like the Inquiries List report, the Quotation List (VA25) report displays all of the open quotations for a given customer or material. You can also use this report to follow up with your customer as you progress in the sales cycle. To run the report, go to Logistics • Sales and Distribution • Sales • Information System • Quotations • Quotations List. In the selection screen, enter the sold-to party (customer) number or the material number. Enter the validity period for the document. You can also enter the document date or date range if applicable (see Figure 6.36). If you select the My Quotations checkbox, the results will only show the documents that you've created.

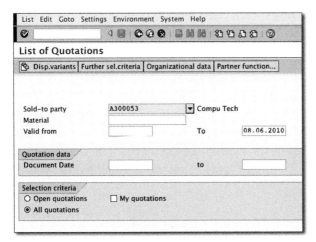

Figure 6.36 List of Quotations Report

The result is a list of quotation documents, which includes all of the items for each quotation, as shown in Figure 6.37. Again, this report helps you assess the progress you get with a customer in the sales cycle.

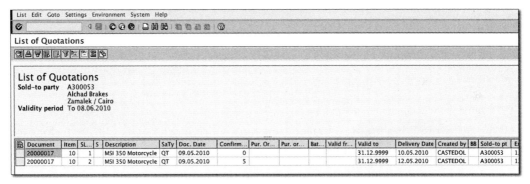

Figure 6.37 List of Quotations Results

> **Note**
>
> As of SAP ERP 6.0 EHP 6, this report has been enhanced with a much more versatile search screen. If your system is running prior to EHP 6, when you push the button FURTHER SEL. CRITERIA, you'll only be able to choose up to three fields to make your selection more specific.

6.2.6 List of Contracts (VA45)

This report displays all of the open contracts, the ones created by you, or just all of the contracts for a given customer or material. You can also use this report to follow up with your customer as contracts age. To run the report, go to LOGISTICS • SALES AND DISTRIBUTION • SALES • INFORMATION SYSTEM • CONTRACTS • LIST OF CONTRACTS. In the selection screen, enter the sold-to party (customer) number or the material number. Enter the validity period for the document. You can also enter the document date or date range if applicable (see Figure 6.38). If you select the MY CONTRACTS checkbox, the results will only show the documents that you've created.

Figure 6.38 Selection Screen for Contracts

The result is a list of contract documents, which includes all of the items for each contract, as shown in Figure 6.39. This transaction helps you monitor your contracts for each client.

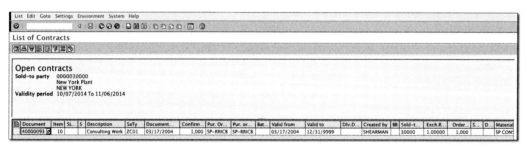

Figure 6.39 Resulting List of Contracts

6.2.7 Orders with Time Period (SD01)

This report displays a list of all the orders that were created within a certain time period. You can also use this report to find all the orders that have been entered into the system within a given date range. To run the report, go to LOGISTICS • SALES AND DISTRIBUTION • SALES • ORDERS • ORDERS WITHIN TIME PERIOD.

In the selection screen (Figure 6.40), enter the document type, the date range, a user ID, the sales area or areas that will be part of your selection criteria, and the result will be a list of sales documents created by the user in the selection criteria, or by all users if you decided to leave it blank.

Figure 6.40 Selection Criteria

The result is a list of sales documents with their items that show the material ordered, the quantity and the price, as shown in Figure 6.41.

Figure 6.41 Resulting List of Contract Items by Item

If you select the check box at the left of any given item, you can display the order, look at the originals, document status, the document flow, or the master data. See Figure 6.42; use the ENVIRONMENT menu.

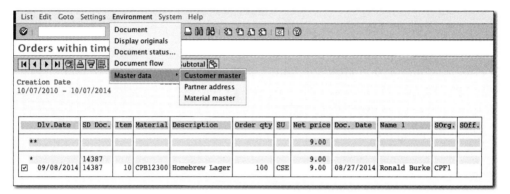

Figure 6.42 Detailed Information about Each Item

6.2.8 Incomplete Sales Orders (V.02)

The Incomplete Sales Orders (V.02) report allows you to find documents that have missing information or that haven't completed the sales cycle.

A very useful feature in this report is that it's an interactive list, which allows you to modify any of the resulting documents directly from the list. This means you don't have to open a second session to work on the document of your choice.

To run the report, go to LOGISTICS • SALES AND DISTRIBUTION • SALES • ORDERS • INCOMPLETE ORDERS. Enter the sales organization, distribution channel, division, or any combination of the sales structure to narrow your search down in the selection screen, as shown in Figure 6.43. In the INCOMPLETENESS section of the screen, select the incompleteness information that you would like displayed in the report. You can choose between general information or information specific to sales orders, deliveries, billing, and pricing.

The status groups are predefined selections of these parameters (Figure 6.44). If you leave it blank, the report will contain the default fields.

Incomplete SD Documents

Incompleteness
- ☑ General
- ☑ Delivery
- ☑ Billing document
- ☑ Price determination
- ☑ No assignment
- Status group [ ] to [ ] →

Organizational data
Sales organization	1000	to	→
Distribution channel	10	to	→
Division	00 ▼	to	→
Sales office		to	→
Sales group		to	→

Document Information
Created by	CASTEDOL		
SD transaction	2	to	→

Execute
- Display variant [ ]

List variation
- ☑ Safety query

Figure 6.43 Incomplete Sales Orders Report

Figure 6.44 Incomplete Sales Orders Report – Status Group

The result is a list of incomplete sales documents, as shown in Figure 6.45. The X in the various fields indicates the type of incompleteness for each of them.

By clicking on the document number, you can see the maintenance screen and the incompleteness log (Figure 6.46). From here, you can start editing the document to complete it.

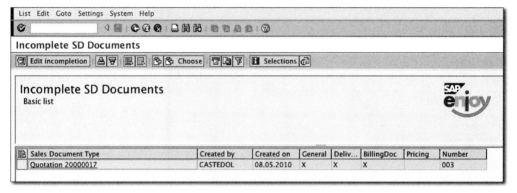

Figure 6.45 Incomplete Sales Orders Report Results

Figure 6.46 Incompletion Log

6.2.9 Backorders (V.15)

The Backorders (V.15) report allows you to display all those sales documents that are past their shipping due date and are still opened. This report allows you to intervene and work toward expediting these orders so that you can minimize the impact on your customer's satisfaction.

To run the report, go to Logistics • Sales and Distribution • Sales • Information System • Orders • Display Backorders. Enter the sales organization, and select the display values that you want for the currency amounts (Figure 6.47). You can also select the currency in which you want to display the report. If you select the Fast Display/Document Overview checkbox, then the result will be a list of all of the backorders by sales document number.

Figure 6.47 Backorders Report

If you don't select the Fast Display checkbox, the initial report screen gives you a list with the total backorder values per month and a total value of the backorders (see Figure 6.48). You can select any of these lines and click the Customer or Material buttons.

If you click the Customers button, you get a list of the customers with backorders for the selected period (Figure 6.49). The list includes the order number, the value, and the planned goods issue date. By double-clicking on the order number or selecting a line and clicking on the Display Document button, you'll go directly to the sales document.

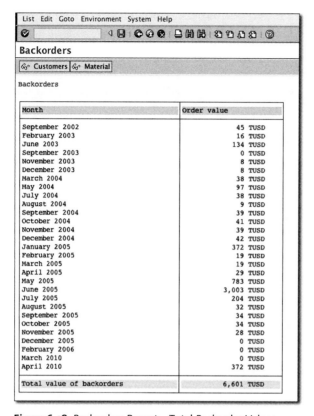

Figure 6.48 Backorders Report – Total Backorder Values

List Edit Goto Environment System Help

Backorders

Display document

Backorders   04.2010

Order	Ship-to party	Order value	Goods issue date
11788	Becker Berlin	372 TUSD	22.04.2010
11778	Alchad Brakes	0 TUSD	12.04.2010
11777	Alchad Brakes	0 TUSD	12.04.2010
11776	Alchad Brakes	0 TUSD	12.04.2010
11775	Alchad Brakes	0 TUSD	12.04.2010
11774	Alchad Brakes	0 TUSD	12.04.2010
Total value of backorders		372 TUSD	

Figure 6.49 Backorder Report – Customers

You can obtain a very similar result by clicking on the MATERIALS button. In this case, instead of a list of customers, you'll see a list of materials with backorders for the period (Figure 6.50).

Figure 6.50 Backorder Report – Materials

6.2.10   Blocked Orders (V.14)

The Blocked Orders (V.14) report provides a list of those orders that are blocked for shipping with order values.

Important
The order value is determined not by the conditions in the order, but by the confirmed quantities. Some delivery block reasons don't allow for quantities to get confirmed, such as credit limits, even if the material is available.

To run the report, go to LOGISTICS • CUSTOMER SERVICE • SERVICE PROCESSING • ORDER • CUSTOMER REPAIR • DOCUMENT EVALUATIONS • DELIVERY-BLOCKED ORDERS. Enter the delivery block reason and the organizational structure level that you want to search blocked orders for (Figure 6.51). Also, clear the FAST DISPLAY checkbox. For this example, we've selected delivery block 04, which allows confirmed quantities.

The result is a list of the value of all blocked orders by monthly period (Figure 6.52). From here, you can select a period and select the DISPLAY CUST. or DISPLAY MATL buttons to display the detail of the blocked orders.

Figure 6.51 Blocked Orders Report

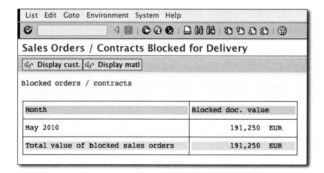

Figure 6.52 Blocked Orders by Monthly Period

When you click on the DISPLAY CUST. button, you get a list of orders with the description of the delivery block reason, order number, customer, and order value (Figure 6.53). Blockings can be set either manually or automatically, but in either case, they prevent any further treatment of an order. This report allows you to identify orders that can't continue their normal processing. By identifying and acting toward the resolution and elimination of the blocking reason, you ensure that your customer will receive the goods on time.

| List | Edit | Goto | Environment | System | Help |

Sales Orders / Contracts Blocked for Delivery

Disp. doc.

Blocked orders / contracts   05.2010

Blocking reason	Doc.	Ship-to party	Blocked doc. value
Export papers missng	11790	Alchad Brakes	191,250 EUR
Total value of blocked sales orders			191,250 EUR

Figure 6.53 List of Blocked Orders – Customers

When you click on the DISPLAY MATL button, you get a list of the blocked orders with the description of the delivery block reason, order number, material, and order value (Figure 6.54).

| List | Edit | Goto | Environment | System | Help |

Sales Orders / Contracts Blocked for Delivery

Disp. doc.

Blocked orders / contracts   05.2010

Blocking reason	Doc.	Material	Blocked doc. value
Export papers missng	11790	MSI 1200 Motorcycle	191,250 EUR
Total value of blocked sales orders			191,250 EUR

Figure 6.54 List of Blocked Orders – Materials

When in the selection of the blocking reason, you enter the reason that doesn't allow quantity confirmation in the order, such as the 01 Credit Limit, as shown in Figure 6.55. When you do this, the report shows no order value.

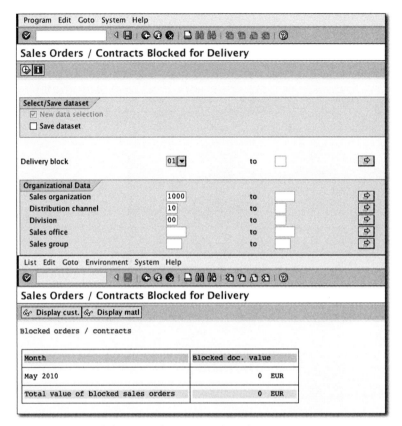

Figure 6.55 List of Blocked Orders – No Order Value

6.2.11 Duplicate Sales Orders (SDD1)

The Duplicate Sales Orders (SDD1) report allows you to identify possible errors in the creation of customer orders. This report can identify similar orders and alert you of a possible duplication. After these duplicate orders have been identified, you can verify with your customer if these orders were created in error or if they are valid requirements. To run the report, go to INFORMATION SYSTEMS • GENERAL REPORT SELECTION • SALES AND DISTRIBUTION • SALES • ORDERS • DUPLICATE ORDERS.

In the selection screen shown in Figure 6.56, enter the customer, date range, and organizational structure for which you want to look for duplicates, and execute.

Figure 6.56 Duplicate Sales Document in Period Report

The resulting list (Figure 6.57) will have one line per customer. If you expand each line, you'll see a list of orders with traffic lights. The green ones are correct, and the yellow are possible duplicates for you to investigate further.

Figure 6.57 Duplicate Orders Report – Stop Lights

If you select two suspicious orders and click on the COMPARE ORDERS icon, then the system will take a closer look and alert you with red status lights if the orders are identical (Figure 6.58).

Figure 6.58 Compare Orders

In this example, when we open both orders (Figure 6.59), we can see that they belong to two different periods, so they are probably correct.

Figure 6.59 Orders in Two Different Periods

6.2.12 Customer Returns-Analysis (MC+A)

The Customer Returns-Analysis (MC+A) report is also part of the SIS, and it gives you statistical information about customer returns for a period of time. The information you can get from this analysis may help you identify problems with clients that are making too many returns. You may even identify quality problems when many customers return purchases in a short period of time. To run the report, go to INFORMATION SYSTEMS • LOGISTICS • SALES AND DISTRIBUTION • CUSTOMER • RETURNS. In the selection screen shown in Figure 6.60, enter the organizational levels and periods for which you want to display information. You may also use the EXCEPTION field, which uses preconfigured scenarios defined by combining characteristics or characteristic values to identify only the data that falls below or above a threshold value, or that represents a trend, such as a decrease in orders or order values.

> **Note**
>
> You can display information in a specific currency so that international sales are translated to your company's main currency.

Figure 6.60 Customer Returns Analysis Report

The result is a list of customers with returns movements during that period (Figure 6.61). In this example, we sorted the returns quantity key figures in descending order. In this type of analysis, we see key figures with similar names but that refer to very different information. For example, we can differentiate between the returns quantity, which tells you how many pieces have been returned, and the return items, which identify the number of different material numbers that have been returned.

Figure 6.61 List of Returns Movements by Customer

Similar to other SIS reports, you can double-click on any customer to drill down into the different organizational levels. As shown in Figure 6.62, you can see the sales organization and distribution channel levels.

If you continue with the drilldown, Figure 6.63 shows the division and material levels. This level of the drilldown can be useful to identify which materials have a higher incidence of returns in each of your divisions.

Figure 6.62 Returns by Sales Organization and Distribution Channel

Figure 6.63 Returns by Division and Material Levels

6.2.13 Customer Analysis—Sales (MC+E)

The Customer Analysis–Sales (MC+E) report gives you statistical data about sales amounts for a given period. It includes totals for sales, billed quantities, gross sales, and other key figures that will let you make better decisions when you plan your promotions or discounts, for example. To run the report, go to INFORMATION SYSTEMS • LOGISTICS • SALES AND DISTRIBUTION • CUSTOMER • SALES. Enter the organizational structure and the period of the analysis, as shown in Figure 6.64.

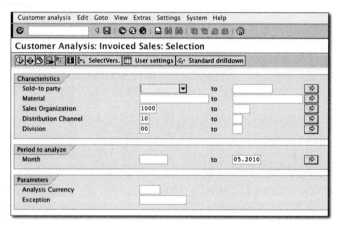

Figure 6.64 Customer Analysis – Sales

The resulting report is a list of customer's sales activities that occurred during the analysis period (Figure 6.65).

No. of Sold-to party: 12

Sold-to party	Sales		Billing qty		Gross Sales		Inv.sales: cost	
Total	27,312,651.95	EUR	77,179	PC	27,312,651.95	EUR	11,744,818.35	EUR
Becker Berlin	0.00	EUR	0	PC	0.00	EUR	0.00	EUR
Institut fuer Umwe	2,858,401.30	EUR	915	PC	2,858,401.30	EUR	485,401.58	EUR
CBD Computer Based	2,860,003.75	EUR	15,800	PC	2,860,003.75	EUR	2,081,514.64	EUR
Becker Koeln	1,488,876.60	EUR	465	PC	1,488,876.60	EUR	224,148.43	EUR
Becker Stuttgart	5,502,628.70	EUR	1,795	PC	5,502,628.70	EUR	934,476.05	EUR
Amadeus	2,613,509.90	EUR	13,695	PC	2,613,509.90	EUR	1,874,690.44	EUR
C.A.S. Computer Ap	2,935,652.45	EUR	16,504	PC	2,935,652.45	EUR	1,855,099.80	EUR
Carbor GmbH	3,474,639.10	EUR	1,100	PC	3,474,639.10	EUR	542,697.71	EUR
Software Systeme G	2,820,654.90	EUR	14,420	PC	2,820,654.90	EUR	1,903,609.72	EUR
COMPU Tech. AG	2,758,285.25	EUR	12,485	PC	2,758,285.25	EUR	1,843,179.98	EUR
CompuMax GmbH	0.00	EUR	0	PC	0.00	EUR	0.00	EUR
Etelko Texti	0.00	EUR	0	PC	0.00	EUR	0.00	EUR

Figure 6.65 Customer Analysis – Sales Results

If you double-click on any line, you'll get a list of the values for all key figures in the report, as shown in Figure 6.66.

Sold-to party	Sales		Billing qty
Total	27,312,651.95	EUR	77,179
Becker Berlin	0.00	EUR	0
Institut fuer Umwe	2,858,401.30	EUR	915
CBD Computer Based	2,860,003.75	EUR	15,800
Becker Koeln	1,488,876.60	EUR	465
Becker Stuttgart	5,502,628.70	EUR	1,795
Amadeus	2,613,509.90	EUR	13,695
C.A.S. Computer Ap	2,935,652.45	EUR	16,504
Carbor GmbH	3,474,639.10	EUR	1,100
Software Systeme G	2,820,654.90	EUR	14,420
COMPU Tech. AG	2,758,285.25	EUR	12,485
CompuMax GmbH	0.00	EUR	0
Etelko Texti	0.00	EUR	0

No. of Sold-to party: 12

All Key Figures

Bill. docmt: PS5	0.00	EUR
Billing docmt: PS6	0.00	EUR
Billing quantity	77,179	PC
CrdMems: subtotal 5	0.00	EUR
CrdMems: subtotal 6	0.00	EUR
Cred.memos: freight	0.00	EUR
Credit Memo	0.00	EUR
Credit memos qty	0	PC
Credit memos: cost	0.00	EUR
Credit memos: gross	0.00	EUR
Gross orders	31,685,147.75	EUR
Gross returns	0.00	EUR
IRPricSubTot5 SC	0.00	EUR
Incoming orders	31,685,147.75	EUR
Incoming orders qty	86,588	PC
Incoming returns	0.00	EUR
Inv. freight chrgs.	0.00	EUR
Invoiced sls: cost	11,744,818.35	EUR
Invoiced sls: gross	27,312,651.95	EUR
Net credit memos 1	0.00	EUR
Net credit memos 2	0.00	EUR
Net invoiced sls 1	27,312,651.95	EUR
Net invoiced sls 2	27,312,651.95	EUR
Net orders 1	31,685,147.75	EUR
Net orders 2	31,685,147.75	EUR
Net returns 1	0.00	EUR
Net returns 2	0.00	EUR
Open orders	30,793,963.75	EUR
Open orders qty	86,302	PC
Order items	1,073	
Orders: cost	13,519,804.90	EUR
Orders: freight	0.00	EUR
Orders: subtotal 5	0.00	EUR
Orders: subtotal 6	0.00	EUR
Returns Quantity	0	PC

Figure 6.66 All Key Figures

By clicking on the SWITCH DRILLDOWN button, you can see the different levels (Figure 6.67), and you can switch directly to the one that most interests you without double-clicking on any line.

357

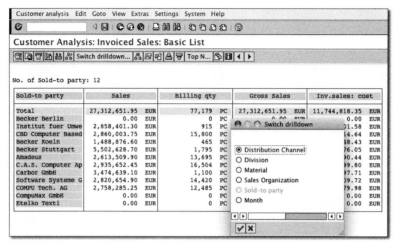

Figure 6.67 Switch Drilldown

6.2.14 Credit Memo Analysis for Customers (MC+I)

The Credit Memo Analysis for Customers (MC+I) report allows you to evaluate the credit memos issued for a customer in response to customer returns or other processing errors. We described the returns process in detail in Chapter 4. To run the report, go to INFORMATION SYSTEMS • LOGISTICS • SALES AND DISTRIBUTION • CUSTOMER • CREDIT MEMOS. As shown in Figure 6.68, enter the organizational structure, customer, materials, and any other characteristics you may want to use to narrow your search.

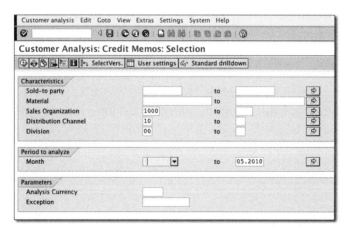

Figure 6.68 Credit Memo Search Selection

The result is a list of customers with their credit memo activity, as you can see in Figure 6.69.

Customer Analysis: Credit Memos: Basic List

No. of Sold-to party: 12

Sold-to party	Credit Memo	Credit memo qty	CredMemos: cost	Gross crd memos
Total	0.00 EUR	0 PC	0.00 EUR	0.00 EUR
Becker Berlin	0.00 EUR	0 PC	0.00 EUR	0.00 EUR
Institut fuer Umwe	0.00 EUR	0 PC	0.00 EUR	0.00 EUR
CBD Computer Based	0.00 EUR	0 PC	0.00 EUR	0.00 EUR
Becker Koeln	0.00 EUR	0 PC	0.00 EUR	0.00 EUR
Becker Stuttgart	0.00 EUR	0 PC	0.00 EUR	0.00 EUR
Amadeus	0.00 EUR	0 PC	0.00 EUR	0.00 EUR
C.A.S. Computer Ap	0.00 EUR	0 PC	0.00 EUR	0.00 EUR
Carbor GmbH	0.00 EUR	0 PC	0.00 EUR	0.00 EUR
Software Systeme G	0.00 EUR	0 PC	0.00 EUR	0.00 EUR
COMPU Tech. AG	0.00 EUR	0 PC	0.00 EUR	0.00 EUR
CompuMax GmbH	0.00 EUR	0 PC	0.00 EUR	0.00 EUR
Etelko Texti	0.00 EUR	0 PC	0.00 EUR	0.00 EUR

Figure 6.69 Customers with Credit Memo Activity

By double-clicking on any line in the list, the system provides you with a list of all of the key figures included in the report, as shown in Figure 6.70.

Customer Analysis: Credit Memos: Basic List

No. of Sold-to party: 12

All Key Figures		
Bill. docmt: PS5	0.00	EUR
Billing docmt: PS6	0.00	EUR
Billing quantity	77,179	PC
CrdMems: subtotal 5	0.00	EUR
CrdMems: subtotal 6	0.00	EUR
Cred.memos: freight	0.00	EUR
Credit Memo	0.00	EUR
Credit memos qty	0	PC
Credit memos: cost	0.00	EUR
Credit memos: gross	0.00	EUR
Gross orders	31,685,147.75	EUR
Gross returns	0.00	EUR
IRPricSubTot5 SC	0.00	EUR
Incoming orders	31,685,147.75	EUR
Incoming orders qty	86,588	PC
Incoming returns	0.00	EUR
Inv. freight chrgs.	0.00	EUR
Invoiced sls: cost	11,744,818.35	EUR
Invoiced sls: gross	27,312,651.95	EUR
Net credit memos 1	0.00	EUR
Net credit memos 2	0.00	EUR
Net invoiced sls 1	27,312,651.95	EUR
Net invoiced sls 2	27,312,651.95	EUR
Net orders 1	31,685,147.75	EUR
Net orders 2	31,685,147.75	EUR
Net returns 1	0.00	EUR
Net returns 2	0.00	EUR
Open orders	30,793,963.75	EUR
Open orders qty	86,302	PC
Order items	1,073	
Orders: cost	13,519,804.90	EUR
Orders: freight	0.00	EUR
Orders: subtotal 5	0.00	EUR
Orders: subtotal 6	0.00	EUR
Returns Quantity	0	PC

Figure 6.70 Key Figures Included in the Report

By clicking on the SWITCH DRILLDOWN button in Figure 6.71, you can display the drill-down levels available. You can also use this window to switch between levels without having to double-click your way to the desired level.

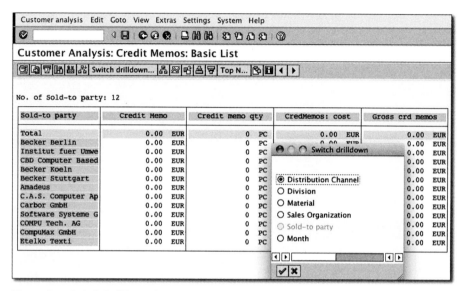

Figure 6.71 Switch Drilldown Option

6.2.15 Sales Org Analysis for Invoiced Sales (MC+2)

In the Sales Org Analysis for Invoiced Sales (MC+2) report, you can find the statistical information about the sales orders that have gone through the complete sales cycle and made it all of the way to invoicing. To run the report, go to INFORMATION SYSTEMS • LOGISTICS • SALES AND DISTRIBUTION • SALES ORGANIZATION • SALES ORGANIZATION • SALES. As shown in Figure 6.72, enter the organizational structure, customer, materials, and any other characteristics you may want to use for narrowing your search.

The result, shown in Figure 6.73, is a list of customers with their sales activity, including sales and billing activity for the selected period.

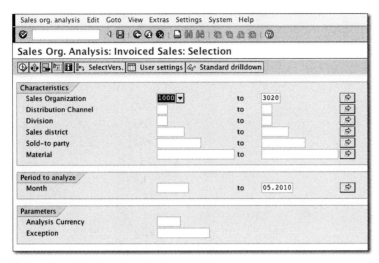

Figure 6.72 Sales Org Analysis Characteristics

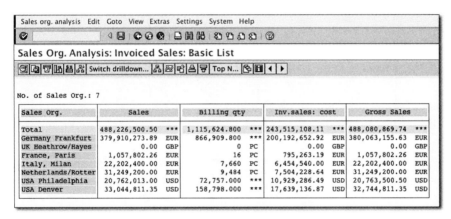

Figure 6.73 Customers Listed with Sales Activity

By double-clicking on any line, you get a list of all key figures included in this report, as shown in Figure 6.74.

By clicking on the SWITCH DRILLDOWN button, you can display the drill-down levels available (Figure 6.75). You can also use this window to switch between levels without having to double-click your way to the desired level.

Figure 6.74 Sales Org. Analysis – All Key Figures

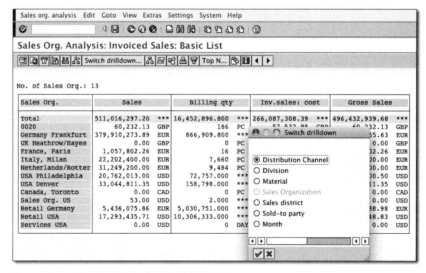

Figure 6.75 Sales Org Analysis – Switch Drilldown

6.2.16 Material Analysis—Incoming Orders (MC(E)

The Material Analysis – Incoming Orders report is based on orders received for materials in a sales organization. It can help you identify those materials that are having a better or a worse performance than others. This performance can be evaluated at different levels of the organizational structures. To run the report, go to INFORMATION SYSTEMS • LOGISTICS • SALES AND DISTRIBUTION • MATERIAL • INCOMING ORDERS. As shown in Figure 6.76, you can enter the materials, organizational structure, and period for which you want the analysis. Remember, you can also enter a currency for displaying the analysis.

Figure 6.76 Material Analysis – Incoming Orders

The result, as shown in Figure 6.77, is a list of materials with their sales activities listed for the selected period.

Figure 6.77 Materials with Sales Activities Listed

As you've seen with other reports, if you double-click on any line, you get a list of all key figures included in this report, as shown in Figure 6.78.

Figure 6.78 All Key Figures

By clicking on the SWITCH DRILLDOWN button in Figure 6.79, you can display the drill-down levels available. You can also use this window to switch directly to that level without having to double-click your way to the desired level.

Figure 6.79 Switch Drilldown

6.3   Logistics

The logistics reports will help you identify the status of an order in the different steps of the logistics chain. You'll be able to display deliveries in different statuses, such as ready for picking, confirmation, packing, loading, goods issue, or even transportation planning. In this section, we'll discuss the reports that can be used to evaluate delivery orders in their different processing statuses.

From the warehouse point of view, the most important report is the Delivery Due List, which we'll discuss first.

6.3.1   Delivery Due List (VL10A)

The Delivery Due List (VL10A) report is one of the most important reports for the warehouse. It's the one tool that communicates the shipping requirements generated by sales orders and also allows them to plan the picking capacity. To run this utility, go to Logistics Execution • Outbound Process • Goods Issue for Outbound Delivery • Outbound Delivery • Create • Collective Processing of Documents Due for Delivery • Sales Orders. In this selection screen, as shown in Figure 6.80, the most important element is the shipping point. In addition, delivery dates are very sensitive, so the report will find all those sales orders with delivery dates within the selection date range.

Figure 6.80 Collective Processing of Documents Due for Delivery

The resulting report (Figure 6.81) lists all of the orders that comply with the selection parameters. Each order has a traffic light status next to it. The different color statuses indicate whether the sales order is past its delivery date (red), if the order is past its picking date but not its delivery date (yellow), or if the order is being processed in time according to the picking date (green).

Figure 6.81 Orders That Comply with the Selection Parameters

To create the deliveries, select the orders you want to process (shown in Figure 6.82), and click on the BACKGROUND button.

Figure 6.82 Create the Deliveries

When the system finishes the processing, it will highlight those orders that were successfully processed in green, as shown in Figure 6.83. Click on the SHOW/HIDE DELIVERY icon to make the delivery numbers appear on the screen. You also have the option of using the totaling functionality on the WEIGHT and VOLUME columns. This can serve as a good estimate for warehouse and shipping activities.

Li...	Goods Issue	DP...	Ship-to	Route	Origin...	Gr...	WUn	Volu...	V...	Document
OΛO	12.05.2010	1	A300053		11747	48	KG			
OΛO			A300053		11772	100	KG			
OΛO			A300053		11774	100	KG			
OΛO			A300053		11775	100	KG			
OΛO			A300053		11776	100	KG			
OΛO			A300053		11777	100	KG			
OΛO			A300053		11778	100	KG			
⌀CO	30.03.2010		A300053	R00030	11772	0	KG			80014999
⌀CO	12.04.2010		A300053	000003	11778	0	KG			80015004
⌀CO			A300053	000003	11777	0	KG			80015003
⌀CO			A300053	000003	11776	0	KG			80015002
⌀CO			A300053	000003	11775	0	KG			80015001
⌀CO			A300053	000003	11774	0	KG			80015000
COD	12.05.2010		A300053		11747	0	KG			80015013
COD			A300053		11772	0	KG			80015014
COD			A300053		11774	0	KG			80015014
COD			A300053		11775	0	KG			80015014
COD			A300053		11776	0	KG			80015014
COD			A300053		11777	0	KG			80015014
COD			A300053		11778	0	KG			80015014

Figure 6.83 Successfully Processed Orders

As you can see in Figure 6.84, the Delivery Due List report simplifies the shipping process. In this example, because all of the orders belonged to the same customer's ship-to address, all of them had the same shipping date. So, the system grouped all of the orders under two deliveries instead of seven. Another important factor in this grouping of sales orders in few deliveries is the creation date of the sales orders.

COD	12.05.2010	A300053		11747	0	KG		80015013
COD		A300053		11772	0	KG		80015014
COD		A300053		11774	0	KG		80015014
COD		A300053		11775	0	KG		80015014
COD		A300053		11776	0	KG		80015014
COD		A300053		11777	0	KG		80015014
COD		A300053		11778	0	KG		80015014

Figure 6.84 Two Deliveries Instead of Seven

6.3.2 Outbound Delivery Monitor (VL06O)

After the deliveries are created, they will go through different steps. The Outbound Delivery Monitor (VL06O) report is valuable because it displays and processes deliveries in each of those statuses. To run this utility, go to LOGISTICS

EXECUTION • OUTBOUND PROCESS • GOODS ISSUE FOR OUTBOUND DELIVERY • OUT-
BOUND DELIVERY • LISTS AND LOGS • OUTBOUND DELIVERY MONITOR. The Outbound
Delivery Monitor is divided in eight sections, as shown in Figure 6.85. Each
section has a different tool for a different purpose in delivery processing.

Figure 6.85 Outbound Delivery Monitor

The first two sections of the Outbound Delivery Monitor are the deliveries FOR
CHECKING and FOR DISTRIBUTION. These two sections won't be covered in this text
because they are only used when working with a decentralized warehouse. So,
when the WM functionality is running in a separate server, these two sections
would create interface communication documents called IDOCs.

The first button that will be relevant for your needs is the FOR PICKING button.
FOR PICKING, shown in Figure 6.86, lists all of the deliveries that are due for picking in the warehouse. The main parameter in this selection screen is the shipping
point; remember that the delivery orders are very sensitive to dates, so the date
range you enter here will only find deliveries with picking dates that fall within
that range.

Figure 6.86 For Picking

The selection screens in all of these tools in the Outbound Delivery Monitor allow you to narrow your search by providing a wide variety of fields to choose from. In previous chapters, we've discussed routes, groups, and shipments. You can use these values to get a list of deliveries that match those prerequisites. To process the search, click on the EXECUTE button.

When you're in the resulting delivery list (Figure 6.87), you have a chance to choose the deliveries you want to process. You might find that your list was too extensive, and your warehouse personnel only have the capacity for a limited number of picks.

By clicking on the ITEM VIEW button, you get a list of all of the items in the deliveries that resulted from the search, as shown in Figure 6.88.

Figure 6.87 List by Default Ordered by the Delivery Number

List Edit Goto Settings Subsequent Functions Environment System Help

Day's Workload for Picking

ShPt Pick Date		Total Weight WUn		Volume VUn ProcTime		
Delivery	Item Mat.Av.Dt. Delivery quantity SU	Material		Plnt SLoc Description		
1000 10.05.2010		600 KG		0.00		
80015014	10 10.05.2010	1 KG GTS-RES02		1000 0001 milk powder		
80015014	20 10.05.2010	1 KG GTS-RES02		1000 0001 milk powder		
80015014	30 10.05.2010	1 KG GTS-RES02		1000 0001 milk powder		
80015014	40 10.05.2010	1 KG GTS-RES02		1000 0001 milk powder		
80015014	50 10.05.2010	1 KG GTS-RES02		1000 0001 milk powder		
80015014	60 10.05.2010	1 KG GTS-RES02		1000 0001 milk powder		

Figure 6.88 Workload for Picking

If you don't have the capacity to constrain or just want to generate a large worklist, you can select all of the deliveries and click the TO in Background button. This will create the transfer orders you need to execute the picking in the warehouse.

After the system finishes processing, it will come back and highlight the successfully processed deliveries in green, as shown in Figure 6.89.

List Edit Goto Settings Subsequent Functions Environment System Help

Day's Workload for Picking

Figure 6.89 Successful Deliveries

In our example in Figure 6.90, we're picking from a fixed bin, so the TO was created and confirmed immediately.

Figure 6.90 Picking from a Fixed Bin

The next relevant button from Figure 6.85 is FOR CONFIRMATION. This is where you typically find the same deliveries from the previous step so that you can confirm the picking through confirming the transfer orders, as shown in Figure 6.91. As in all other selection screens, in the Outbound Delivery Monitor, make sure you at least enter the shipping point and the date range.

Figure 6.91 Outbound Deliveries for Confirmation

Again, you can review the list of deliveries, select only those deliveries you want to process (Figure 6.92), and click on the CONFIRM IN BACKGROUND button (which resembles a forklift with a checkmark on top).

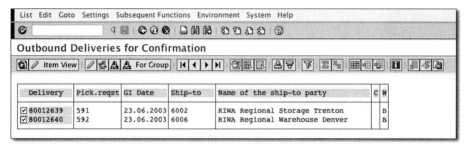

Figure 6.92 Confirm Background

After processing, the list will highlight the items that were successfully processed in green, as shown in Figure 6.93.

Figure 6.93 Successfully Processed Items Listed

The next tool we'll review is FOR LOADING. Here you'll again search for deliveries to form a worklist, as shown in Figure 6.94. You need to select the deliveries you want to load into the truck.

From the resulting list shown in Figure 6.95, select the deliveries you want to load into the truck, and click on the CREATE FREIGHT LIST button. Enter a description when the pop-up window appears, and press [Enter].

Figure 6.94 Outbound Deliveries for Loading

Figure 6.95 Create Group Description

The system will highlight in green those deliveries that were successfully processed, as shown in Figure 6.96.

Figure 6.96 Successfully Processed Deliveries

At this point, the system created an output for the freight list. The standard output is shown in Figure 6.97. This image of the freight list output was taken from the spool. To reach your spool, go to Transaction SP02.

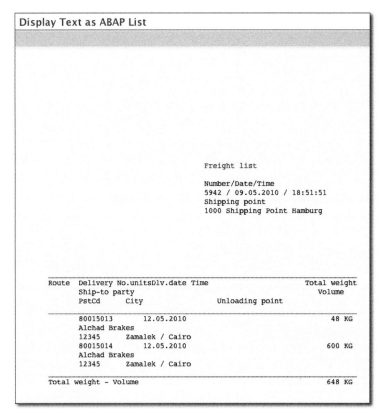

Figure 6.97 Standard Output for the Freight List

After the deliveries have been picked and loaded into the trucks, it's time to post the goods issue. To do this, you can use the next tool in the Outbound Delivery

Monitor: FOR GOODS ISSUE, shown in Figure 6.98. Once again, use the selection screen to select those deliveries that you want to post the goods issue for.

Figure 6.98 Outbound Deliveries for Goods Issues

From here, you can select the deliveries you want to process and click on the POST GOODS ISSUE button (see Figure 6.99).

Figure 6.99 Goods Issue for Outbound Deliveries to Be Posted

As you've seen with other tools, the system will process in the background and highlight in green those items that were successfully processed. During this step, the materials are issued from stock creating material documents and accounting documents. In addition, the document flow, as shown in Figure 6.100, is updated for each of the delivery orders.

Figure 6.100 Document Flow

The last tool that's available for use in the Outbound Delivery Monitor is FOR TRANSPORTATION PLANNING, which offers no added value and simply displays the list of deliveries that can at this point be added to a shipment. Refer to Chapter 4 for a detailed explanation on shipments.

6.3.3 Display Delivery Changes (VL22)

The Display Delivery Changes (VL22) report can be useful when you run into inconsistencies. It shows any changes that have occurred in the delivery, both at the header and item level. These changes are most likely in the dates, quantities, or status. To run this report, go to LOGISTICS EXECUTION • OUTBOUND PROCESS • GOODS ISSUE FOR OUTBOUND DELIVERY • OUTBOUND DELIVERY • LISTS AND LOGS • CHANGES. In the selection screen shown in Figure 6.101, enter the delivery you want to display the changes for, and select a display option.

The result (Figure 6.102) is a list of changes that has occurred in the delivery since it was first created.

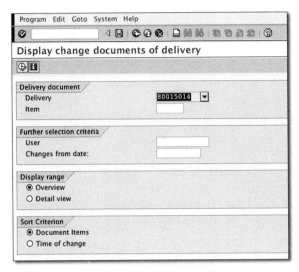

Figure 6.101 Display Change Document of Delivery

Figure 6.102 Changes to the Delivery

6.4 Billing

In this section, we'll cover an important report that will help you monitor and execute billing activities.

The Billing Due List (VF04) report is very useful for the invoicing team. Whether your company creates and prints invoices directly at the warehouse or somewhere in Finance, they can look at this report and process the deliveries that have made it to this point.

To run this report, go to LOGISTICS EXECUTION • OUTBOUND PROCESS • GOODS ISSUE FOR OUTBOUND DELIVERY • BILLING • BILLING DOCUMENT • PROCESS BILLING DUE LIST. In the selection screen shown in Figure 6.103, enter at least the sales organization, the customer (sold-to party), and the date range.

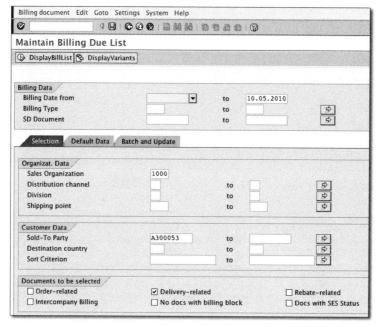

Figure 6.103 Billing Due List – Selection Screen

From the resulting list of deliveries, select the ones you want to process, and click on INDIVIDUAL BILLING DOCUMENT or COLLECTIVE BILLING DOCUMENT (Figure 6.104). The selection depends on how your company and your customers prefer to execute this function. It may also depend on other factors; for example, deliveries for international orders are typically billed individually because of customs requirements.

Figure 6.104 Selected Deliveries for Processing

6.5   SIS and LIS Overview

We've already covered several reports that we mentioned were part of the Sales Information System, but what *is* about the Sales Information System?

The Sales Information System is so vast that complete coverage would take a book in itself, but in an attempt to be succinct; the SIS is a collection of databases called info-structures formed by key figures, which are essentially fields in a database. The info-structures collect statistical information every time a transaction is posted in SD, based on specific rules.

The different infostructures provide different ways for you to view the same data. Each report, or analysis as they are defined in the SIS, aggregates the data up to different organizational structure levels and gives you different key figures, which are the analytical tools for decision making.

The SIS is part of a bigger collection of data analysis tools called the Logistics Information System (LIS); both have to be activated by your company's IT analysts as part of the system's configuration and base their data collection on statistical groups that are assigned in the different master data components, such as the material master and vendor master.

The LIS and SIS might very well represent the foundation of the more modern SAP Business Suite or SAP Business Warehouse product, and as such, has been neglected of any updates in the latest versions of SAP ERP.

LIS is a wider collection of analyses that cover the following:

- Purchasing Info System
- Quality Info System
- Warehouse Management Info System
- Transportation Info System

It's important to keep in mind that the info systems collect statistical information and is normally not updated online, so you can't find the most up-to-date data in them.

From the info system, you can view the aggregate data for each key figure, but you can't go down to the individual document detail. So from the SIS, you can't display an individual sales order, delivery, accounting documents for a goods issue, or billing documents.

What you can do is create your own analyses through the flexible analyses and even your own info-structures. The latter you could probably do with the help of your IT analyst. This gives you incredible flexibility.

6.6 Summary

Throughout this chapter, we discussed the reports and tools that will help you in your day-to-day SAP experience. The list of reports available in SAP is much more extensive than we covered here, so we encourage you to try other reports and see how they fit into your daily activities.

Be careful with those reports in which you see buttons that "create" or "post." Those are processing tools, and you might end up processing documents at the wrong time. Talk to your IT systems analysts if you need any further guidance.

We also introduced you to the Logistics Information System and the Sales Information System. When these components are active in the SAP system, they are very valuable tools for statistical analysis and decision making. Remember, however, not all companies implement these two components as part of their SAP solution. The reasons are varied, from trying to avoid extra load in the system and trying to save in the size of the hardware, to companies that go the extra mile and implement the full data warehouse solution from the SAP Business Suite.

Again, ask your IT systems analysts and try to get access to those systems. They will provide you with invaluable information.

This chapter discusses the importance of the SAP CRM component and how it applies to Sales and Distribution. You'll learn about Marketing, Sales and Services, and essential CRM functionalities, in addition to the latest CRM technologies, such as analytics and the Customer Interaction Center.

7 Customer Relationship Management in Sales and Distribution

In Chapter 1, we provided a brief overview of the CRM component of SAP. You learned that CRM stands for Customer Relationship Management (SAP CRM) and that it's an application that typically sits in a separate box from SAP ERP.

In this chapter, we'll bring you to a better understanding of this important SAP application. We'll start by defining CRM concepts and definitions, and provide an overview and highlights of the component. In addition, we'll address how SAP CRM integrates with Sales and Distribution (SD) and SAP ERP processes in your daily job. In the second section of this chapter, you can find more details on each of the CRM modules, along with the primary functionalities they offer.

Let's begin by defining what we can understand about SAP Customer Relationship Management.

7.1 Understanding SAP CRM

The SAP CRM application is integrated customer relationship management (CRM) software created by SAP that focuses on your most valuable asset, your customers. CRM is part of the SAP Business Suite; unlike other CRM software, the SAP CRM application not only helps you reduce cost and improve your decision-making process, but also helps to improve your capacity to compete effectively.

SAP CRM manages the principal aspects of the customer relationship across the marketing, sales, and services departments of your company (which we discuss later, starting in Section 7.3). It's common to find the following as major CRM advantages: increased market value, share, and profitability by improving customers' experience and providing a 360-degree view of customers via analytics. Figure 7.1 illustrates how CRM covers sales, services, and marketing and determines valuable analytics and reports to classify customers and better detect their needs.

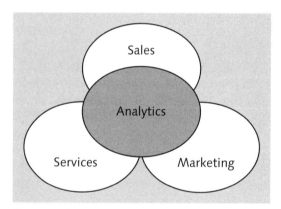

Figure 7.1 SAP CRM 360-Degree Customer View

CRM and SD systems have some similar functions, as you'll find out. There are several advantages to having a CRM system, especially SAP CRM, compared to the regular SD Order-to-Cash solution. You can see that while SD is oriented to processes from sales order-delivery to billing and AR, CRM is concentrated on your customers' needs: for example, it centralized sales orders, order entry and services, and presents customers with a simplified and customer-oriented platform and interface. Table 7.1 compares the traditional SD functionality and the SAP CRM solution in terms of a user's typical day-to-day operation.

Regular SD Order-to-Cash	SAP CRM
Sales/orders and services traditionally are in different departments or different system platforms.	Orders, order entry, and services are centralized.
Focused on the process. Order-Delivery-Billing-AR.	Focused on customers and customers' needs; processes are handled in ECC.
Information and workflow are limited to a given department and the people involved in such activity. Limitations based on system architecture.	Centralized information, unifying database and platform with one customer-facing application.
Globalization based on ECC deployed system.	Globalization, similar platform across countries.
Forecast based on previous sales.	Customers' behavior and forecast including customers' predictions.
Oriented to processes.	Higher customer satisfaction.

Table 7.1 Comparison of Traditional SD and CRM Functionality: Highlights

Even though SAP CRM is a more sophisticated tool, Sales and Distribution plays a key role in the CRM system, especially since SD covers the processes, such as logistics and billing. The invoice is commonly produced in SAP ERP rather than CRM. We will discuss the SD and CRM integration in more detail next.

7.1.1 SAP CRM Integration with SD and SAP ERP

Previously we addressed Sales and Distribution as a core SAP ERP component. If you want to make a sale, source inventory, and invoice, you need to use SD. However, SAP CRM directly interacts with SD and other SAP ERP components, such as FSCM and AR. Figure 7.2 shows how a sales order replicates automatically and flows from the CRM system into the SD to get inventory sourced, delivered and post-of goods issued. You may notice as well that while the replicated sales order is processed in SD, the order and delivery completion status could be fed back into CRM for display purposes.

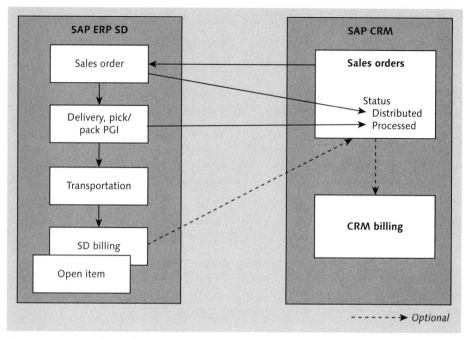

Figure 7.2 CRM and SD Sales Cycle Integration

The last step of the order cycle is billing. Here, you have two choices that you and your company need to make, regarding where the invoice is created. The SD order cycle includes the customer invoice generation in SD, which is the method most typically used.

Alternatively, you can create the customer invoice in CRM and replicate it into SAP ERP Billing. However, this method is used less often, mainly due to the SD Billing capabilities and the AR integration that happens in the ECC box. Therefore, it's very common to find billing in SAP ERP SD and replicated into CRM, either at the invoice status only or the full billing document.

7.1.2 Master Data

SAP CRM synchronizes master data with SAP ERP. When CRM is implemented, your company needs to decide which system will be the master and replicate the system for master data objects and others.

Figure 7.3 illustrates key master data object master data replication based on typical CRM implementations. The customer master in SAP ERP is typically the master of records, replicated into the CRM BPs. The same is true for the product master, which is replicated into the product catalog and pricing IPC. However, it's very common to identify the customer contacts to be the master in CRM, since the customer contacts are received at the Interaction Center and then replicated into SAP ERP. Other combinations are also possible between the master data objects and your specific needs for CRM data objects.

Figure 7.3 Relationship between SAP ERP SD and CRM for Master Data Replication of Key Master Data Objects

7.1.3　CRM Software Components

The number of SAP CRM solutions have significantly increased in the latest releases of CRM. The software package is expected to continue growing and offering new solutions for CRM users. Table 7.2 lists the main components available in CRM, and indicates whether or not a given component will be described in this chapter. Although it's a comprehensive list of CRM components, the key ones are Sales, Marketing, Services, Analytics, and Customer Interaction Center.

CRM Component	Described in This Chapter?
Marketing	Yes
Sales	Yes
Service	Yes
Analytics	Yes
CRM Customer Interaction Center	Yes
CRM Web Channel (E-Marketing, E-Commerce, and E-Service)	No
Partner Channel Management	No
Web Client UI	Yes
Social Service	No
ICM – Investigative Case Management	No
LM – Loyalty Management	No
RTOM – Real Time Offer Management	No
Mobile Solutions	No
TPM – Trade Promotion Management	No
CRM solutions for small/midsize business	No
CRM On Demand	No

Table 7.2 List of CRM Components Discussed in This Chapter

We'll cover details of the key CRM components in the following sections. Coming next, we'll highlight the main functionality in each CRM key component, and emphasize what you can do with it in your daily work activities. First, however, we'll discuss SAP CRM's user interface and help you become familiar with it so you can perform your daily routine more quickly.

7.2 CRM Web User Interface and Concepts

Today, the Web Client solution is the one you'll most likely use in your day-to-day activities when performing tasks in SAP CRM. Therefore, it's important that you learn some basic concepts in this area.

7.2.1 Web Client Homepage

Figure 7.4 shows the Web Client interface homepage. You can see that it looks and feels just like a commercial web page. It's a secure page, so you need to be granted related access via the security team.

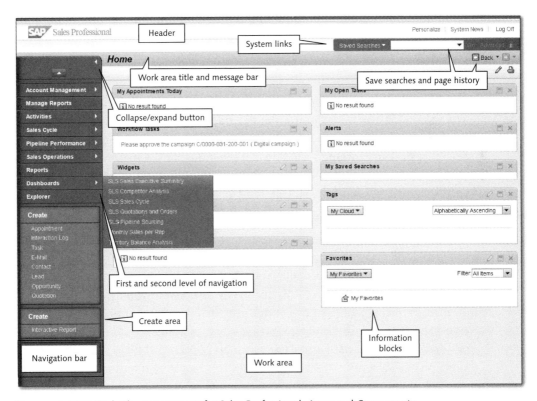

Figure 7.4 CRM Web Client Homepage for Sales Professional, Areas and Components

The homepage is the place where you'll create orders, billing, and sales agreements, see open tasks, and search for customers and contacts, among other activities. The user interface and homepage are divided into three areas (header area, work area, and navigation bar). We discuss each in the following subsections.

> **Note**
>
> Any additions or changes to this screen are controlled via the confirmation and enhancements done for your specific company and associated roles that have been assigned.

Header Area

This is the area at the top of the page, which contains the general information needed and historical data, including logo area, saved searches, system links, page history, work area title, work area toolbar, and message bar. Figure 7.4 shows you where each of the header components is located. The Logo area is where your company logo and information is situated. You can navigate back and forward based on your navigation history during each session.

Navigation Bar

The navigation bar is located on the left side of the Web Client. The navigation bar cannot be changed, but it can be expanded, contracted, or even hidden so you see more of your working area. You can see in Figure 7.4 that the navigation bar is divided into three well-defined areas on the left side: first level navigation (main menus), second level navigation (submenus), and the direct links or creation area.

One important thing you may notice is that the navigation bar in CRM Web Client is flexible, based on the tasks and roles that have been assigned to you. The navigation bar menu options will vary based on the CRM business role you chose when you first logged on to CRM, or the one assigned to you by default based on your individual activities and security profile. Table 7.3 shows how the navigation bar varies according to the business role selected. Marketing Professional will have additional marketing analysis menu options; similarly, Service Professional will have service orders and service contracts menu options.

Standard Business Roles	Navigation Bar Menu Options
Marketing Professional MARKETINGPRO	Default navigation bar and MARKETING ANALYSIS: ▶ Home ▶ Worklist ▶ Calendar ▶ Marketing ▶ Fund Management ▶ Accounts & Products ▶ Reports ▶ Dashboards ▶ Manage Reports ▶ Central Sharing Tool
Sales Professional SALESPRO	Default business role navigation bar: ▶ Home Calendar ▶ E-Mail Inbox ▶ Account Management ▶ Manage Reports ▶ Activities ▶ Sales Cycle ▶ Pipeline Performance ▶ Sales Operations ▶ Reports ▶ Dashboards ▶ Explorer
Service Professional SERVICEPRO	Default navigation bar and SERVICE ORDERS and SERVICE CONTRACTS: ▶ Home ▶ Worklist ▶ Calendar ▶ E-Mail Inbox ▶ Accounts & Products ▶ Service Orders ▶ Manage Reports ▶ Service Contracts

Table 7.3 CRM Standard Business Roles and Navigation Bar Menu Options

Standard Business Roles	Navigation Bar Menu Options
	▸ Complaints & Returns
	▸ Service Operations
IC Agent IC_AGENT	▸ Account Identification
	▸ Account Fact Sheet
	▸ Account Overview
	▸ Interaction Record
	▸ Interaction History
	▸ Lead
	▸ Fax
	▸ Sales Order
	▸ Letter
	▸ Unfinished E-Mails
	▸ Sales Order ERP
	▸ Complaint
	▸ Service Order
	▸ Case
	▸ Knowledge Search
	▸ Product Catalog
	▸ Script
	▸ Index
	▸ Inbox

Table 7.3 CRM Standard Business Roles and Navigation Bar Menu Options (Cont.)

Note

In this chapter, we'll use the standard CRM business role SALESPRO – SALES PROFESSIONAL.

Work Area

The work area is located at the center of the Web Client, which contains information blocks (see Figure 7.4). The work area allows you to move the page around to give you some flexibility and personalization. Drag-and-drop technology is used in the Web Client. You can customize the elements to better fit your individual needs and information blocks. This feature provides you with the unique opportunity to customize what you see on the screen without any further configuration or enhancements. Your changes will be saved and available the next time you log on. Let's discuss how you can navigate using Web Client.

7.2.2   Navigation in Web Client

Typically, the homepage is displayed immediately after you log on and it's the place where you can find your tasks, appointments, and other personalized objects.

> **Note**
>
> The homepage is the initial screen and entry point for all users. The homepage cannot be removed via customizing. It's the starting point of the CRM Web Client navigation.

Starting on the homepage, on the left side (navigation bar) you can select any of the roles available, such as ACCOUNT MANAGEMENT, SALES CYCLE, PIPELINE PERFORMANCE, or REPORTS, to mention some examples; then you will see the second level of navigation. Each will have SEARCH, CREATE, and REPORT information blocks. If you select SEARCH, then you'll enter the third level of navigation, while listing the OBJECT LIST SEARCH. Inside each listed element, you can also double-click to discover further details, get an overview, or even edit some of them. Figure 7.5 presents the Web Client navigation levels.

On the one hand, from the homepage you can either work on pages in the work area at the center of the screen, or search for your information. The search will give you a result list. If you click on any resulting object list, you access the lowest-level pages. Once you reach the lowest level, you have the choice to display or edit any listed elements accessed.

Regardless of which level you're on, you can use the BACK TO THE PREVIOUS PAGE ◼ Back ▾ and FORWARD ◼ ▾ buttons. Alternatively, you can select from the BACK TO THE PREVIOUS PAGE dropdown list the selected screen you want to jump to; the same applies to the FORWARD item in the dropdown list.

On the other hand, you can also use the CREATE page. The CREATE page is located from the information block of the Work Center page. You can also directly access the CREATE page when creating a new business object, e.g., Sales, Contacts, or Opportunities.

Figure 7.5 shows a linear navigation in the Web Client from the first level to the third level and to the overview (edit/create) of the listed objects, in addition to the creation path. One example of linear navigation is when you navigate from your homepage to an overview page, custom information blocks or others. Another example is when you go from SEARCH operation to the overview pages of the selected business objects.

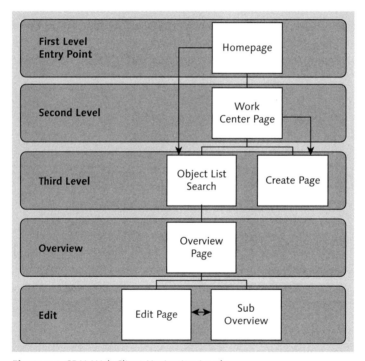

Figure 7.5 CRM Web Client Navigation Levels

You'll find the best navigation paths based on your system settings, customization levels, or simply your personal choices and information blocks. Let's discuss personalization.

7.2.3 Personalization of Web Client

In contrast to SD screens, where most of the elements are fixed, the SAP CRM Web Client allows you flexibility and personalization to meet your specific needs and preferences. Although personalization doesn't mean you can completely redesign the web interface, it does allow you to change how information is displayed to each individual user, rather than a customized view intended for all users.

The personalization in CRM Web Client is called up by selecting the PERSONALIZE link in the header of the user interface. Figure 7.6 shows the options you have for personalization and flexibility.

Figure 7.6 CRM Web Client Personalization Information Blocks

Table 7.4 summarizes the personalization activities you can perform in the SAP Web Client. We suggest that you explore each of them to find the perfect combination that matches your needs, including the skin colors and Web Client appearance that fits your own preferences.

Information Block	Description	Subareas	Object List Details
MY DATA	The information block is used to personalize your general data, user information, communication as well as to change passwords.	▸ Personalize My Data ▸ Change Password	▸ General Information ▸ Communication Information ▸ Organizational Information ▸ Change Password
SETTINGS	This information block sets your profile settings, including time zone, data format, decimal, screen reading mode, etc.	▸ Personalize Settings	▸ General Settings ▸ Screen Reader Mode ▸ Tab Order Definition Mode ▸ Dropdown Lists Configuration Mode ▸ Tag Clouds and Favorites ▸ Messages
GROUPWARE INTEGRATION	You can define synchronization between SAP CRM and a GROUPWARE application, in this case, MS Outlook and Lotus Notes, including emails, calendar, tasks, and contacts.	▸ Set Up E-Mail Transfer ▸ Edit Synchronization Settings ▸ Install Synchronization Software	

Table 7.4 Personalization, Information Block, and Subarea Description

Information Block	Description	Subareas	Object List Details
LAYOUT	This information block give you the ability to change the skin color and enable performance mode as well as personalization on links at the navigation bar.	▶ Personalize Layout ▶ Personalize Navigation Bar	▶ Skin ▶ Performance Settings ▶ Skin color ▶ Navigation Bar Links ▶ Link Type ▶ Available Links ▶ Displayed Links
SHORTCUTS	Keyboard settings and fast-keys settings. You can personalize your own shortcuts.	▶ Personalize Shortcuts	▶ Focus Shortcuts ▶ Navigation Shortcuts
PREFERENCES	This information block allows you to personalize application links, web links, and widgets you can display.	▶ Personalize Application Links ▶ Personalize Web Links ▶ Personalize Widgets	▶ Application Links ▶ Link Type ▶ Available Links ▶ Displayed Links ▶ Web Links ▶ Link Type ▶ Available Links ▶ Displayed Links ▶ Widgets ▶ Available Links ▶ Displayed Links
FEED	Set up your own feeds.	▶ Personalize feed settings	▶ Feed ▶ Customize Your Feed

Table 7.4 Personalization, Information Block, and Subarea Description (Cont.)

Note

Your company may also decide to prevent the use of certain features of personalization. You can use Transaction SM30 with maintenance view PERSCV_PROFILE to deactivate personalization options.

Now that you have a good understanding of some fundamental CRM concepts, homepages, components, and Web Client navigation, let's individually discuss each CRM component described in Table 7.2, starting with Marketing.

7.3 Marketing

CRM Marketing is the component that allows your company to plan, budget, and execute the vast majority of your marketing needs. In addition, CRM Marketing allows you to analyze and optimize your marking strategy and campaign execution.

In the native Sales and Distribution functionality, you can also find some basic functionality associated with Marketing. Among others, you can find the Sales Support functionality in SD Marketing as part of sales promotions and sales activities, both activities oriented to determine pricing conditions and promotional discounts on customer invoice. Table 7.5 describes frequently used sales support transaction codes.

SD Sales Support	Transaction and Description
Sales promotions	▶ VC01N_M – Edit Sales Promotions ▶ VC06 – Address List Change ▶ VC10 – Address Assign Sales Reports ▶ SO10 – Standard Texts ▶ VC15 – Crossmatching
Sales activities	▶ VC01N – Edit

Table 7.5 SD Sales Support Transactions

In general, the connectivity between CRM Marketing and SD Marketing is limited to a few pricing conditions defined in CRM. Those discounts come as part of Customer Billing. If your marketing needs are rather simple, then SD Marketing is recommended. Otherwise, CRM Marketing is recommended for larger operations and needs. However, it's important for you to get familiar with the CRM key functions and to understand CRM capabilities, including further exploring the CRM Marketing system and its ability to meet the needs of your company.

We'll describe the CRM Marketing details. SAP has embedded up to eight main components of the Marketing cycle, as shown in Table 7.6. You'll find a tool to support each of the processes of your marketing campaign, segmentation, planning, and budgeting.

CRM Marketing Solution	CRM Path Web Client	Key Functions
Marketing Resource Management	CALENDAR	Allows you to control and forecast your marketing campaigns. Your forecast can include publishing calendars of marketing events. The Marketing calendar tool is used to view, edit, and interconnect promotions and campaigns.
Marketing Planning and Budgeting	MARKETING • MARKETING PLANS	The marketing plan is the top of the Marketing component. It defines strategic products, timelines, and budget. The marketing plan also holds the hierarchy to allocate one or more campaigns, target groups, and even other subcomponents of the marketing plans.
Segmentation	MARKETING • SEGMENTS	CRM provides the segment builder. Customer segments are specially designed to aggregate customers with similar needs and attributes in a customer campaign. This allows you to group customers using marking attributes, including income, age, location or even hobbies, for marketing campaigns. Data sources are Marketing attributes and BI queries, including SAP ERP or other external sources.
List Management	MARKETING • EXTERNAL LISTS	External lists provide data mapping from source data into SAP CRM data fields, in addition to providing checks for duplicates, data cleansing, and address validation. In addition, external lists help you maintain customer master records and data cleansing. The data can be exported to SAP BusinessObjects BI.

Table 7.6 CRM Marketing Solution, Path, and Description

CRM Marketing Solution	CRM Path Web Client	Key Functions
Campaign Management	MARKETING • CAMPAIGNS	Campaign Management helps you set up a campaign from beginning to end, which includes the market analysis, campaign execution and analytics. Campaign Management also allows you to use the graphical interface to provide a clearer overview of the process flow. Monitoring of ongoing campaigns and adjustments is also allowed by the Campaign Management component.
Trade Promotion Management (TPM)	CRM TPM tool	TPM will help you manage in-store retail promotions. One of the major advantages of TPM is that it will allow you to trace your promotions in detail, so you can demonstrate how many product quantities are sold in each related retail location, covering pay-for-promotion scenarios. TPM is mostly associated with Consumer Package Goods (CPG), but also used in other retail industries. Some examples are apparel and footwear, or consumer electronics.
Lead Management	MARKETING • LEADS	This tool allows you to fully manage leads across your marketing channels. CRM leads are especially useful after your campaigns are successfully launched. They are a repository that allocates follow-up contact from your customers. Lead management will also help you qualify leads automatically, and even send them via workflow for qualification.
Marketing Analytics	Reports and Dashboard	CRM Marketing Analytics help you support marketing plan optimization, corrective actions and improvements. Marketing Analytics will allow you to discover market channels, customer behavior, segments, products, market trends, and profitability, among others.

Table 7.6 CRM Marketing Solution, Path, and Description (Cont.)

Importance of the Marketing Role

You can access the CRM Marketing menu by selecting the role MARKETINGPRO, or be assigned to it. For further explanation, see Table 7.3.

You now understand what kind of functionality CRM Marketing offers, and how CRM is a customer-oriented tool, so now let's discuss another important CRM functionality: Sales.

7.4 Sales

Sales is another crucial component of the SAP CRM solution. It's dedicated to supporting the sales department and the sales people, especially to help them attain, grow, and retain customer relationships. You may find that using the CRM Sales application will facilitate your sales cycle and provide you with a broader vision of new areas for potential revenue, and even discover new methods for improving sales productivity.

Needless to say, CRM Sales is the component that most closely parallels the Sales and Distribution functionality; therefore, it's where you'll find the highest degree of CRM-SD integration. Sales orders, opportunities, pricing, and quotations are some examples where you will find CRM-SD integration. Table 7.7 shows you a comprehensive list of CRM Sales key solutions, along with their location and description. We invite you to explore each solution to identify the ones that fit your needs most closely.

CRM Sales Solution	CRM Path Web Client	Key Functions
Accounts and Contacts Management	ACCOUNT MANAGEMENT	Account and Contacts Management allows you capture, track and monitor data on prospects, customers, and partners. You will benefit from having a single, comprehensive view of centralized sales accounts information. Account Management will leverage sales accounts from end to end. It also allows you to record in the system activities and follow-ups, which in turn will be available for your Sales people. An important feature is the Business Partner (BP) RELATIONSHIP, where BP relationships are stabilized, along with their hierarchy.

Table 7.7 CRM Sales Solution, Path, and Description

CRM Sales Solution	CRM Path Web Client	Key Functions
Planning and Forecasting	REPORTS • SALES PLANNING AND FORECASTING	This solution will help you plan and forecast sales along with the budget, opportunities, and resources assignment, in addition to performing strategic planning and monitoring across the planning cycle. The component allows you to achieve enhanced performance with planning and execution of sales activities and projected revenue and sales volume. Sales Planning in CRM has two main components: strategic planning (what, where, and who to sell) and operational planning (demand forecasting based on historic sales data).
Territory Management	SALES OPERATION • TERRITORIES	CRM Sales Territory Management allows you to get a clear vision of your territory definition, all assignments and their scheduling, in addition to full visibility of the distribution of the team. One of the main advantages is that you can react quickly to market demands or changes, by placing the perfect combination of resources and locations. This will help ensure that your top customers are covered by your top sales representatives.
Billing and Sales Contract Management	SALES CYCLE • SALES CONTRACT	CRM Sales Contracts handles the long-term customer contracts and their related daily processes and monitoring ranging from quote to billing completion. This component integrates seamlessly with SAP ERP Financials and accounts receivable for billing, AR payments, credit returns, and process disputes. The contract types available include quantity-based and value-based, collaborative contract negotiation, sales agreements, release-order handling, cancellation and credit management, invoicing, and payment processing.

Table 7.7 CRM Sales Solution, Path, and Description (Cont.)

CRM Sales Solution	CRM Path Web Client	Key Functions
		Billing can be done in CRM or SAP ERP, or even another third-party system. Two main scenarios are supported in billing: transaction-related billing (including usage-based billing) and delivery-related billing (which requires a SAP ERP delivery and post-of good issue to be created). Integrates with SD Sales Orders and Contracts, as well as Delivery and Billing/AR Open items in ECC.
Quotation and Order Management	▶ SALES CYCLE • QUOTATIONS ▶ SALES CYCLE • SALES ORDERS	Quotation and Order Management is another CRM solution that integrates with Sales and Distribution. CRM orders can confirm product availability and track status in real time. Orders also include the product configuration process and related pricing. In CRM, as opposed to SD, a sales order document can be used as an inquiry, quotation or firm order, just by setting the line-item status. You will have one document to handle throughout the sales process, rather than several documents. Availability-check and credit are checked during the order creation, which is yet another integration point with Sales and Distribution.
Incentives and Commissions	ERP • SAP MENU • SALES • INCENTIVE AND COMMISSION MANAGEMENT	Incentives and Commissions allows you and your company to map all types of variable remuneration, including brokerage and bonuses. It's a solution that processes commissions and incentives for employees and partners. Different groups, such as managers, executives, and technicians incentives, are part of this CRM solution. It will give your sales representatives or sales force the advantage of an easy visibility into possible commissions and estimation when the sales deal closes, which includes the "what if" calculation to estimate their own commissions.

Table 7.7 CRM Sales Solution, Path, and Description (Cont.)

CRM Sales Solution	CRM Path Web Client	Key Functions
		In general, you'll see increased accuracy of incentives and commissions, which will improve your sales force and increase your sales levels. Commission splits are part of the CRM solution that includes determination of supervisors and managers throughout the organization. You and your sales force can also see current status on earned and anticipated remuneration via the CRM Incentives and Commissions solution.
Sales Analytics	PIPELINE PERFORMANCE REPORTS	Sales Analytics provides you with a set of analytical data intended for sales managers and the actual sales people. With Sales Analytics, you will be able to forecast revenue and plan accurately, as well as with track pipeline performance and budgets management. We'll cover Analytics in Section 7.6.

Table 7.7 CRM Sales Solution, Path, and Description (Cont.)

The Importance of Sales Role

You can access the CRM Sales menu by selecting the role SALESPRO, or be assigned to it. For further explanation, see Table 7.3.

So far, we've discussed the general CRM Order capabilities and subcomponents. Let's learn about how the CRM Quotation and Orders are created in CRM Sales. We'll concentrate on the steps required to create a sales contract, as the process follows a very similar path for Opportunities and Contracts and Quotations creation in CRM.

1. Log on to SAP CRM. Make sure that you have been granted the role SALESPRO. Immediately after logging in, you may also see a list of roles for which you have been pre-selected. Make sure you select SALESPRO from the list. The selection listing appears only when you have one more role assigned to you; otherwise, the role is proposed based on the one you have been granted.

2. From the CRM homepage, navigate to the sales order via SALES CYCLE • CREATE • SALES ORDER.

3. The sales order in CRM could be created coming from the opportunity, which is a very common scenario. To do so, you can search and locate the opportunity and select CREATE FOLLOW-UP. Otherwise, skip this step.

4. You'll be prompted to enter the transaction type. Transaction types are equivalent to sales order types in SD. That means that you'll see entries in the list such as sales order, credit/debit order, consignment, and others applicable to your customized solution. Select TA – TELESALES as an example.

5. Enter the sold-to party address number, either by typing in the customer number or searching for it using the dropdown list. The system will determine the rest of the partner functions or prompt you for any missing ones.

6. Scroll down to the section ITEMS and enter the PRODUCT ID as well as the QTY.

7. Check for errors: The upper right corner will indicate how many errors exist and their severity. Click on the [icon] icon and resolve the red highlighted items. Common errors you'll find are misssing sales area data or any missing fields in the customer master or pricing. Resolve them until the red errors disappear from the list or save the order for further processing. You can also correct these errors at a later point. In Figure 7.7, you can see a sample order entry screen and the error logs or warnings.

8. You are ready to complete your CRM Order. Click SAVE.

9. The same order is now reflected in sales in SAP ERP. An order is created with the same order number and it's ready for further processing in SAP ERP.

10. Once the sales order arrives in SAP ERP, it will be necessary to process it in the same way as any order via Transaction VA02, followed by a delivery, PGI, and invoice.

Figure 7.7 Sales Order Entry: Warning and Errors

> **Replication to SD**
>
> After a quote or sales order is saved in CRM, it will be replicated into SAP ERP for further processing using SD Quotations, SD Sales Orders, and SD Contracts.

Despite the integration between SD and CRM Orders, both components keep a real-time interface with SAP ERP. Available-to-Promise (ATP) is controlled in SAP ERP. The same is true for credit checks. Sales order credit checks are also performed in SAP ERP.

In the following section, we'll discuss an important aspect of almost any company: services and service revenue. SAP CRM provides the Service component to meet your company's requirements in this area.

7.5 Service

In this section, we'll cover the SAP CRM Service component. In today's critical environment, where services are sold more rapidly than ever, you need a tool to support your operation and to track services all the way through the process. CRM Service supports all the facets of your customer service organization. CRM Service provides you with a better user experience and expedites issues resolution because it has real-time support and integrated complaint management.

There are a number of reasons why CRM Service can be an important tool for your company:

▶ Lets your sales representative retain valuable customers and increase their engagement.

▶ Offers targeted services and products based on customer insights.

▶ Provides integrated complaint management to boost your customers' confidence.

▶ Delivers tiered service levels based on customer value, which will help you increase efficiency.

With SAP CRM Service, you can perform several activities starting from service orders, or appointments for technicians to visit a customer location.

Using SAP CRM Service, you can perform service orders, contracts, and service tickets using a centralized tool, along with complaints and returns. In general, you'll find a functionality in CRM Service to support your daily tasks when handling a service operation. We'll discuss each of them in Table 7.8.

CRM Service Solution	CRM Path Web Client	Key Functions and Tasks
Installed Base Management	ACCOUNT & PRODUCTS • INSTALLED BASES	Installed base (iBase) is a term commonly used in a service environment to allocate all pieces of equipment installed in a company site. The individual pieces of equipment that are not directly part of the installed bases are commonly referred as *individual objects*. One customer could have more than one iBase for the service installation, such as a building and floors. CRM iBase provides a tracking solution to trace customers' installed products via a graphical hierarchical display. In addition, it will help your company to maximize uptime with the use of planned and routine service maintenance.
Warranty and Claims Management	▶ SERVICE CONTRACTS • WARRANTIES ▶ SERVICE CONTRACTS • WARRANTIES CLAIMS	This solution allows you to manage the entire warranty and claims process, including warranties registration, return merchandise authorization (RMA) via the warranty claim, receipt, and inspection. Typically, RMAs involve third-party logistics to issue customer credits. With the use of Warranty and Claims Management, you'll see goodwill allowances lowered to the point where they become a rare occurrence rather than a frequent operation. Your company will also benefit from the control of customer warranties (Manufacturer) and vendor warranties (Supplier); both types of warranties can be customized to meet your customers' requirements. In addition, you'll be able to retrieve warranty entitlement during service-related business and tracking of the entitlement services provided to your customers as warranty cost assignment.

Table 7.8 SAP CRM Service Solution, Path, and Description

CRM Service Solution	CRM Path Web Client	Key Functions and Tasks
Contract & Entitlement Management	SALES CYCLE CONTRACTS •	Service contracts are commonly found as a Service Level Agreement (SLA), where the response time and availability for the customer's entitlements are established. CRM Service Contract will allow your company to manage service agreements and service contracts quotations within the same functionality, including service contracts, parts and labor, and usage-based agreements. CRM Entitlements include system-wide tracking of your customer's enlistments with automatic entitlement verification, and proactive customer engagement on expiring service contracts. Service contracts are replicated into the SD Contracts module for further processing and billing.
Service Order Management	SERVICE ORDER • SERVICE ORDER	Service Orders Management in SAP CRM will provide your company with a tool to handle service repairs, maintenance or installations where a technician is needed. Your company will also benefit from handling multi-level categorization and SLA information in one place: Service Order. SAP CRM Service Order also supports service quotations that outline the pricing and delivery conditions. Once the service order is confirmed, warranty and entitlements are verified, as well as service plan and reference objects such as product and installed base. Replication of the service order happens with SAP ERP under the SD component.
Complaints and Returns	▶ COMPLAINTS & RETURNS • COMPLAINTS ▶ COMPLAINTS & RETURNS • RETURNS	Complaints and Returns provides the tools your company needs to manage customer complaints. It's very common to create complaints with reference to a transaction selected, line items or products. A complaint usually follows the creation of credits and debits, free-of charge replacements, and RMAs, among others. The return process is supported by SAP ERP, especially all the financial impact. Returns and complaints are replicated into SAP ERP SD for further processing.

Table 7.8 SAP CRM Service Solution, Path, and Description (Cont.)

CRM Service Solution	CRM Path Web Client	Key Functions and Tasks
Case Management	SERVICE OPERATIONS • CASES	Cases in CRM Service are considered a central repository to keep track of documentation and information related to a single case or issue. Because it is centralized, your company will benefit from CRM Cases because all agents can share the same up-to-the-minute information. It's also known as a common folder created for tracking purposes.
In-House Repairs	COMPLAINTS & RETURNS • IN-HOUSE REPAIRS	In-House Repairs will provide you with a tool to assist in the repair process from the RMA authorization, receiving the broken product, and even shipping the repaired product to your customers. It also provides your company with an automatic warranty and service contract and entitlement checking. SAP In-House Repair also provides you with a comprehensive assistant for repair steps, diagnosis, and damage, along with the cause codes. Your technicians can leverage previous solutions, avoiding re-creating solutions and thus expediting your repairs. Due to the high degree of integration with Finance, In-House Repairs also replicates into SAP ERP and SD for further processing of the credit/debit memo, or free shipping.
Service Analytics	MANAGE REPORTS	Reports are provided in each of the Service components, including iBases, Service Orders and Contracts, Entitlement Management, Resource Planning, Case Management, Complaints and Returns, and In-House Repairs, among others. We'll discuss CRM Analytics further in Section 7.6.

Table 7.8 SAP CRM Service Solution, Path, and Description (Cont.)

Importance of the Service Role

You can access the CRM service menu by selecting SERVICEPRO – Service Professional role, or it can be assigned to you. For further explanation, see Table 7.3.

Now you understand what the CRM Service main functionality is, and how each part impacts SAP ERP with replication of service orders, contracts, warranties, credit/debit, and repairs, among others. The next section addresses the important topic of analytics. You'll discover the related functionality, and the most important reports available to you.

7.6   Analytics

CRM Analytics is the component that will give you delivery business insights, and empower you with effective analysis. It provides metrics regarding customer behavior, life-time value, customer performance, and products purchased and services requested by the customer. You'll find a data mining capability that can give a 360-degree view of the customer, which is a critical activity when you're trying to determine the quality of your customer relationship. It can help you plan accordingly or adjust to a more personalized view of the customer. One other important feature of CRM Analytics is that the data results can also help you predict a customer's future behavior, which will enable you to engage in a more informed decision-making process.

However, the most powerful tool from CRM Analytics is the closed-loop approach. Closed-loop analytics lends insight into the whole customer lifecycle, because it enables you to measure, predict, plan, and optimize business operations. CRM Analytics provides insights into each of the closed-loop steps, including planning and predicting a customer's response and behavior.

In the following sections, we'll discuss the various analytics that are delivered out-of-the-box for the different components in CRM Marketing, Sales and Services, and IC.

7.6.1   Marketing Analytics

Marketing Analytics will provide you with the marketing insights, standard delivered reports, queries and metrics, including the Customer Lifetime Value (CLTV), and customer satisfaction or churn propensity. Marketing Analytics will help you predict customers' behavior and anticipate their needs. You'll also find out the reason marketing activities succeed, and why others didn't work as expected.

Let's discuss another important component of CRM: Sales Analytics.

7.6.2   Sales Analytics

With Sales Analytics, you'll benefit from full sales circle insights, from territory management all the way to billing. Sales Analytics will provide you with the information you need as a sales manager, but also the data requested by your sales people; not only historical data, but also the tools your team needs to react quickly. Sales Analytics allows you to manage the sales pipeline and respond in real time as needed. Your sales managers also have access to competitive win and loss data for analysis.

We encourage you to explore each of the Sales Analytics reports and dashboards, to determine which set adapts better to your specific needs. Now let's discuss Service Analytics.

7.6.3   Service Analytics

Your company will benefit from Service Analytics by obtaining insights into service-related metrics, customer satisfaction, service revenue, and product quality, among others. Using Service Analytics, you can determine the difference between service revenue and service cost to calculate profitability.

Service managers in your company will also benefit from Service Analytics. They can retrieve historical data on a particular customer or group of customers with regard to the level of service received, and quickly react to it. Service Analytics provides you and your service manager with key information for decision-making, including the effectiveness of existing territories, warranties and service contracts, along with expiration dates. In addition, your company may find it useful to control the early identification of quality issues, or real-time cost control. These reports and more are available to you and your whole sales department.

7.6.4   Interaction Center Analytics

The Interaction Center (IC) Analytics component empowers you with the tools you need to evaluate service issues by analyzing telephone volumes, inbound email, and performance metrics. You can also trigger standard delivered reports to help your company better understand ticket volumes and turnaround time. The component also provides reports to measure email volume, average handling and response time, and service level compliance. One of the major benefits you will receive is that your call center can increase customer loyalty and satisfaction with the use of IC Analytics. This can be achieved by detecting customer problems early, and resolving them in a fast and efficient way, with the help of IC Analytics.

The next section addresses another very important solution, the CRM Customer Interaction Center (CIC) and usage. You'll discover the CIC's key functionality and the most important reports it provides to you.

7.7 SAP CRM Interaction Center

The SAP CRM Customer Interaction Center (CIC) is a tool that provides a very user-friendly environment that helps facilitate communication between your company and your customer. The CRM Interaction Center allows communication via telephone, email, fax, postal letter and, in the current release, web chat, providing your company's customers a multi-channel interaction center.

SAP CRM CIC not only provides a centralized way for CIC agents to work, but also allows each agent to have their own virtual environment. Instead of the traditional call center, centralized in one physical location, now your CIC agents can work virtually anywhere in the world.

CIC is used to facilitate two-way communication. Your customers will benefit from it because it allows them to check placed orders and know their order status, ask questions, request product information, request services, and engage in other communication activities, such as filing complaints and processing returns. In turn, your company will benefit from CIC because it allows you to contact your customers for campaigning, announce new promotions, follow up on sales and opportunities, make services appointments, and even schedule customer deliveries, among other possibilities. Overall, your company makes all channels available, and your customers can select the one that matches their preferences. Figure 7.8 depicts the multiple channels of communication available in CIC.

But what does CIC look like? Figure 7.9 shows the initial screen in CIC. You'll notice that although it's similar to the rest of the CRM screens, there are substantial differences due to the integration of each CIC screen with other CRM components, such as Marketing and Campaigning, CRM Sales Integration, Service Management Integration, and so on.

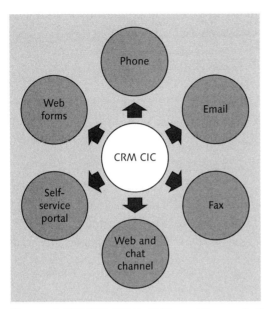

Figure 7.8 SAP CRM CIC Multi-Channel Communication

Figure 7.9 CRM Interaction Screen and Homepage

Now we will describe each of the components in the Figure 7.9 navigation bar. We'll describe them from the CIC agents' point of view, as these are the tasks and capabilities they will use on a daily basis.

▶ ACCOUNT OVERVIEW and ACCOUNT IDENTIFICATION
You can get a complete overview of the customer's account, and search for a specific account that also is used to identify your calling customer. Customer identification can be set to be performed before accepting contacts. The CIC agents will have access to all account details, typically including notes, planned activities, roles, and business partner relationships.

▶ INTERACTION RECORD
You can access a customer-focused overview that includes follow-ups, either from the current interaction or based on the customer's history.

▶ INTERACTION HISTORY
You can use several search criteria to find the business transactions of a specific customer. You also can record data both during and after an interaction.

▶ LEADS
Using a questionnaire, you can determine what type of a lead a customer may be. The agent can view the business context and create associated follow-up actions based on this evaluation.

▶ E-MAIL, LETTER and FAX
You can use this component for processing incoming and outgoing e-mails, letters, and faxes to a customer.

▶ CASE MANAGEMENT
You can search for previous cases, as well as create new ones.

▶ SERVICE ORDERS
Interacting with service orders, you have the ability to enter services and products. The service order that's created also serves as an overview of all data relevant for these processes.

▶ KNOWLEDGE SEARCH and PRODUCT SEARCH
This allows you to search for products and knowledge that match a combination of selection criteria. This will help you quickly respond to customers' needs.

▶ CAMPAIGNS
You can explore details of the current campaign, in preparation for incoming or outgoing customer calls.

▶ CALL LIST MANAGEMENT
Displays the maintenance of calling campaigns created by the managers, who can also maintain the call lists. You usually execute calls based on their assigned call lists.

▶ AGENT INBOX
Incoming and outgoing emails are processed here, along with scheduled activities and work items.

▶ CHAT
Incoming chat sessions can be carried out here.

▶ INTERACTIVE SCRIPTING
Your CIC managers can use the interactive script editor to create scripts to be used in current campaigns. These scripts will guide CIC agents through customer interactions.

▶ SCRATCH PAD
This is an electronic notepad used to record miscellaneous information during an interaction. Any notes created can then be imported into fields in the IC WebClient.

▶ ALERTS
This component provides guides and intelligent alerts to agents during customer interactions.

▶ BROADCAST MESSAGING
CIC managers can send instant messages to agents and can broadcast news.

▶ QUEUE STATUS
This displays the channels and the queues they are assigned to.

▶ IC MANAGER DASHBOARD
The dashboard displays current session-related information specific to the CIC agents.

▶ TRANSACTION LAUNCHER
Your system administrators can configure access to a non-IC WebClient through the IC WebClient, including web pages and other systems.

7.8   Summary

In this chapter, we walked you through SAP Customer Relationship Management (CRM) capabilities that are similar to and integrate with SD. You learned how CRM integrates into SAP ERP, and especially how the orders, contracts, and service orders are replicated into SAP ERP and how master data dependencies happen between SAP ERP and CRM.

We discussed in detail the functionality accessible in each of the key components of CRM, including Marketing, Sales, Service, Analytics, and the Interaction Center. Now you know the facts on the related functionality of each component and, even more importantly, how each component integrates into the Sales and Distribution component.

In the next chapter, we'll introduce you to another important SAP functionality: Financial Supply Chain Management, or FSCM. You'll find out how Biller Direct, Dispute Management, and Credit Management integrate with Sales and Distribution.

SAP Financial Supply Chain Management is another SAP application that has direct integration with Sales and Distribution. In this chapter, you'll find detailed discussion on the modules that are most commonly integrated with Sales and Distribution: Biller Direct, Credit Management, and Dispute Management.

8   SAP Financial Supply Chain Management for Sales and Distribution

In Chapter 1, we introduced you to Financial Supply Chain Management, otherwise known as FSCM. In this chapter, you'll find a broader description of FSCM and its functionality.

> **Note**
>
> FSCM was introduced in 2002 with great success and rapid customer adaptation. In 2012 it was rebranded as SAP Receivables Management (RM) for HANA, as a way to optimize the financial value chain, reduce the cost of AR and collections, and identify late payments while improving customer relationships and handling disputes more accurately. Today, you can find references to both *FSCM* and *SAP RM*, as well as a combination called *SAP Receivables Management, formerly known as FSCM.* In this chapter, we'll continue to refer to FSCM, as it's still the most commonly used term.

We'll concentrate on how the main transaction for each module works, what functionality is associated with each, and the outputs produced.

8.1   SAP Financial Supply Chain Management Overview and Components

FSCM is tightly integrated into Credit Management as a sophisticated tool that provides external integration and faster, more reliable analysis (see Figure 8.1). As we learned in previous chapters, credit check runs at order and delivery and even during posting of goods issue. Billing, on the other hand, integrates with Accounts Receivable to account for open items and collections. FSCM integrates with Biller Direct for invoice presentment and related payment, facilitating expedited cash collection and cash management. Disputes are now integrated with the customer invoice displayed via Biller Direct and the dispute cases that a customer can create via self-service.

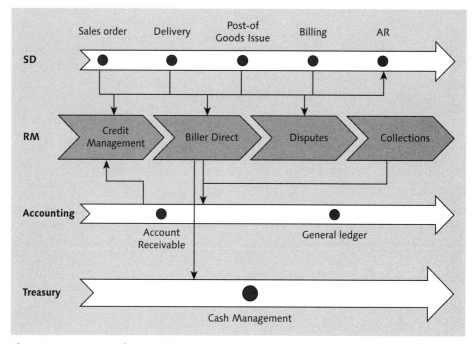

Figure 8.1 Integration of Receivables Management with Sales and Distribution

In previous chapters, you learned how the Sales and Distribution subcomponents flow from the sales order to delivery into billing, and in each, you learned about the interaction with other modules, such as Finance, Treasury, and Accounting. Similarly, FSCM interacts with Sales and Distribution via the following main components:

1. **Credit Management**
   You may be familiar with the traditional credit checks at sales order or at delivery. FSCM Credit Management will eventually fully replace this functionality, since it's greatly enhanced by providing a platform to third-party credit

bureaus, automatic credit rules and risk management, workflows, master data and automatic updates on credit profiles, among others.

2. **Dispute Management**

Provides dispute case management and notes management, along with tight customer correspondence and cross-department workflow.

3. **Collection Management**

Allows a new variety of functionality to help define collection strategies and rules, along with work item assignment and workload monitoring. It also allows a view for the collection specialist to process a daily worklist and prioritization among others.

4. **Biller Direct**

Allows your customers to access a self-service environment, where they can review account status, invoices, payments and credits. They can also self-initiate disputes and even download their own invoices in a 24/7 operation.

> **Note**
>
> Although in Chapter 1 you learned that other SAP FSCM subcomponents are available, we will concentrate on the description of the modules listed above due to their level of integration to the order-to-cash cycle and Sales and Distribution.

In the next part of this chapter, you'll learn about the primary transactions and functionality of FSCM in Biller Direct, Dispute Management, and Credit Management.

8.2   Biller Direct

Electronic bill presentment and payment (EBPP; also known as Biller Direct [BD]) is a component of FSCM that allows your customers to see their invoice, download an invoice PDF, make a payment, or initiate a dispute over a secured website. However, your customers cannot see any open invoices on the website until the invoice is created in the billing area of the SD component or imported from an outside environment. Moreover, the invoice needs to be fully released to accounting in order to be displayed in the web enabled page. Additionally, BD can interface invoices created in CRM and even outside of the main system (we'll use the term *BD* in this book for standardization).

SAP Biller Direct

BD has the ability to manage processes interconnected with FI Account Receivable (AR), Finance Account Receivable and Payable (CA), including related master data connected to both customer and vendor.

You may wonder whether there is a difference between EBPP and Biller Direct, since you can find several references in the literature to one or both concepts. There are indeed differences at the technical level that we will cover only briefly. Both EBPP and SAP Biller Direct feature similar solutions for presenting the billing document, allowing payment, disputes and self-service via a Java webpage. However, the key difference is that EBPP attaches directly to an existing web portal or a pre-existing customized interface in the background system, while BD requires a unique interface to communicate to the main ERP system.

You can see that BD integrates seamlessly with FSCM processes such as Dispute Management, Cash & Liquidity Management, and Collections. Within BD, your customers can execute several different transactions, such as display your open items, download your PDF invoice, and make payments using credit cards or ACH bank transfers. In addition, your customers are empowered to initiate an inquiry about any of the open items or dispute cases. Figure 8.2 illustrates the diverse functionality in the Biller Direct application.

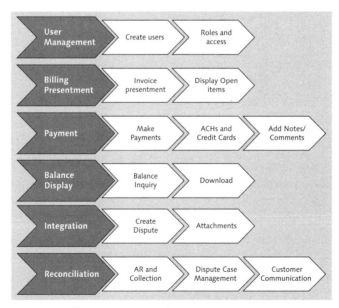

Figure 8.2 Biller Direct Functionality: Overview

The BD web page is a secure Java page, so your customers need to register and provide a user ID and password. Therefore, the BD process starts with the creation and maintenance of the registered users, their role and maintenance. If customers want to pay an invoice or even download the digital version, they'll select BILLING PRESENTMENT AND PAYMENT. Additionally, your customers can check their open balance and recent payments applied to their account. Since Biller Direct is an integrated FSCM module, it has direct real-time connectivity with the backend SAP ERP system, especially to process collections, close open items, and even follow up on dispute cases and customer communication.

As we mentioned before, BD is a webpage that can be displayed at your customer's location without the need to install any additional software. You can expect BD to look like any other commercial webpage or HTTP site because the frontend design is coded in Java and it has the look and feel of any webpage. Figure 8.3 shows the BD main screen. Because BD is a secured website, the initial BD screen requires authentication with a user ID and password. Inside BD, your customers can see several tabs to navigate to, such as OPEN BILLS, CREDITS, PAID BILLS, PAYMENTS, ADDRESS DATA, BANK DATA, CREDIT CARDS and others. In the next section, we'll describe in detail the main functionality of each. You'll be able to understand how BD works, basic concepts, and how your customers will navigate the page.

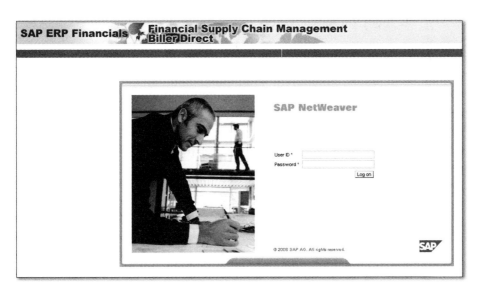

Figure 8.3 SAP Biller Direct: Authenticating Screen

If you compare the BD screen shown with your own BD screen, you'll see some differences in terms of how the screen looks. Some additional functionality may even be available. The configuration of how BD will look is done via the XCM tool that includes any customization done for your company's specific needs or any feature or functionality that has been added to the standard BD. By using the XCM tool, you can also change logos and other trademarking for your own company.

As you've discovered, SAP offers a Java website for SAP transactions. What you'll see in the following pages is a quick overview of the web-enabled SAP Biller Direct. These are instructions that the customer will follow, but we feel that it will be very helpful for you to understand how BD works, and its capacities and operation. Let's begin our discussion with the first BD tab: OPEN BILL.

8.2.1   Open Bill

By using this functionality, SAP provides customers with a way to see their invoices and digital versions at your convenience. BD is a self-service operation and will make it possible for your customers to know what invoices are pending or open, allowing you to plan ahead for payments.

> **Biller Direct is a Real-Time Website**
>
> Your customers can rely on Biller Direct for real, up-to-the-minute data. BD interacts with the SAP ERP system to pull the information in real time and present it to them. Even a newly invoice created in SAP ERP, CRM, or other systems is displayed immediately in BD for your convenience.

Once your customers access the OPEN BILL tab, they're presented with a list of invoices ready for payment. They are coming directly from the Open Items module in AR, Invoices in CRM, or other sources, depending on how your particular system is integrated.

As you can see in Figure 8.4, the list of invoices is presented in a very simplified way to facilitate the payment and make it user friendly. BILLING DESCRIPTION, DUE DATE, BILLED AMOUNT, OPEN, PAYMENT AMOUNT and ACTION are the main columns on this web page. Your customers can sort any of the columns to make it easier to find an invoice by date, for example.

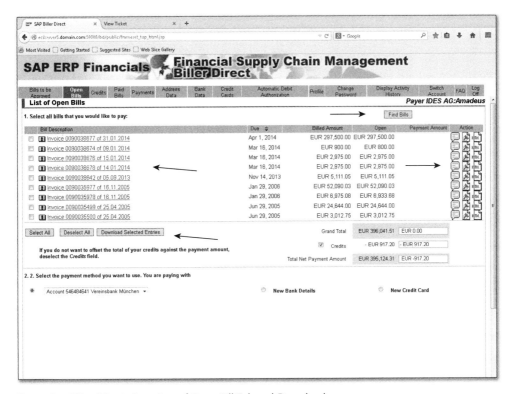

Figure 8.4 Biller Direct: Overview of Open Bill Tab and Downloads

---

Billed Amount versus Open

Billed amount refers to the original amount showed in the invoices; open amount includes any partial payments that have been applied.

In the upper right corner you'll find a FIND BILLS button. This is intended to give your customers a larger range of searching tools and filters that you could apply to recovering invoices. This is especially useful when you have a large number of invoices displayed on the webpage. DISPLAY ALL BILLS, TEXT IN BILL, DUE DATE, BILL AMOUNT and OPEN AMOUNT are some of the search criteria that can be used to search for invoices, as displayed in Figure 8.5.

In addition to the ability to display your customer's invoices, BD also presents the series of credits under their account that are available for immediate application. If you select the CREDIT tab, BD will present you a list with the credit numbers, VALID FROM, CREDIT AMOUNT and AVAILABLE. See Figure 8.6.

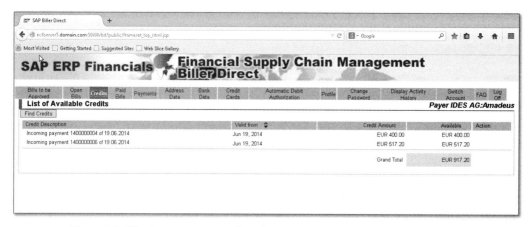

Figure 8.5 Biller Direct: Searching Tool

Figure 8.6 Biller Direct: Overview of Credit Notes

Your customers will also find available credits on the same page as their invoices. BD can display both credits and invoices on the same tab to facilitate payment. This feature entirely depends on how the original BD application was configured and customized.

Downloads

One of the most important features in BD is its downloading capability. In Figure 8.4 you may have noticed the icons to the right of the screen: . These three icons represent the download capability in Biller Direct under the ACTION section.

Another major advantage of BD is that allows the customer a self-service environment, even for downloads. Invoices and credit and other documents can also be attached as a digital copy inside of BD. Your company can benefit from this functionality as a way to save on postal fees and mailing charges, while delivering digital invoices directly to the customer. You can encourage your customers to use this feature even for mass download of digital files. In Figure 8.7 you can see how a digital invoice and PDF look on the BD screen. To retrieve the invoice PDF, follow the next steps:

1. First select the invoice or invoices you would like to display, then click on the PDF icon.

2. The invidual invoice PDF shows in the screen.

3. Alternatively, you can download one or multiple invoices in PDF as a local file by selecting the DOWNLOAD SELECTED ENTRIES button.

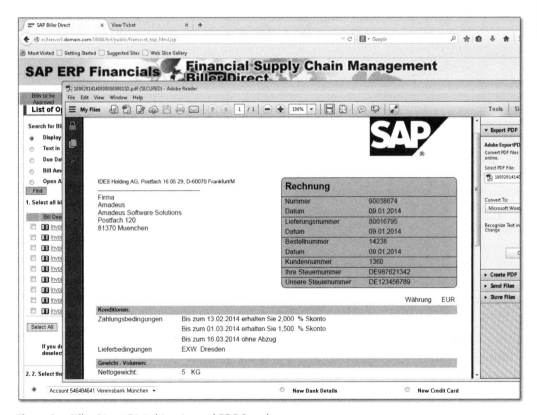

Figure 8.7 Biller Direct Digital Invoice and PDF Sample

Biller Direct Download Formats

You and your customers can use the following electronic download formats:

▶ **PDF**: Invoices and credits for digital invoice PDF file. This file format can include digital sealers for security.

▶ **XML or CSV**: Invoice text file formats that are commonly used in clients' systems, also known as raw invoice data. CSV and XML are both standard format types in the market.

8.2.2 Payment Processing

Can you imagine an operation designed to recover your payments in a fast and convenient way? Biller Direct not only allows your customers to see your invoices, credits, and PDF downloads, but it allows them to accept payments. You and your customers can process ACHs, debits, and even credit card payments via the secure website in Biller Direct in a fast and convenient way.

In the following subsections, we'll discuss the different steps in the payment processing phase with DB.

Step 1: Invoice Selection

Payments can be made under the ORDER BILLS AND CREDITS tab, by simply locating and selecting the invoice(s) to pay. Figure 8.8 illustrates how your customers can do this, by selecting the invoice(s) due for payment on the left side. On the right side, the PAYMENT AMOUNT will reflect the full amount of the individual invoice.

The TOTAL NET PAYMENT AMOUNT on this screen will be updated automatically to reflect the set of invoices you select. Also notice that the CREDITS flag will count all credits under your account with the intent to apply those credits to the current total payment, when selected. If your customers want to see the list of credits and the total credited amount, select the CREDITS tab. We addressed credits details in the previous section.

If you customers decide not to apply the available credits at this time, they could unselect the CREDITS flag, and the TOTAL NET PAYMENT AMOUNT will be updated automatically. Available credits will again be flagged as unapplied, and will be available for the next payment transaction.

Figure 8.8 Invoice Payment Selection Along with Applicable Credit Cards

Step 2: Process the Payment

Are you ready to apply the payment? To do so, scroll down on the OPEN BILLS tab after selecting the desired invoices. The TOTAL NET PAYMENT AMOUNT will reflect the total amount to be charged. Scroll down on the OPEN BILLS tab to discover BD SECTION 2.2, where the payment will be processed (Figure 8.9). If you have previously entered credit card or bank information, you'll see this information on the left side. Select the appropriate payment method from the dropdown list.

However, if this is the first time your customers are paying using BD, they are able to enter their own payment information and type by selecting NEW BANK DETAILS or NEW CREDIT CARDS. Thereafter, your customers can enter the details of the bank or the type and information on the credit card. Typically, bank details are used when a direct debit from a bank account is needed, or a transfer of funds via ACH. Credit cards are accepted in the same way as on any other commercial website for payment. The bank or credit card data will be stored for reuse in the next payment.

Figure 8.9 Section 2.2: Payment Profile and Payment Process

Debit and Credit Card Accepted

In a typical installation on Biller Direct, you'll find common credit card and debit card types, such as American Express, Master Card/Euro and VISA, among others. However, you may see more debit/credit card types available in your system, based on your customized credit/debit card solution. For invoice payments, BD uses debits and credit cards equally.

Step 3: Confirming Payment

Similar to any other website, your customers need to confirm their payment before submitted by selecting SECTION 3.3 CHOSE CONTINUE TO CHECK AND CONFIRM

YOUR PAYMENT. This section will help them confirm and process the invoice amount selected and the payment method selected. When your customers are ready, they will select the CONTINUE button. Your customers will be able to confirm all choices and the system will process the payment. Figure 8.10 shows a payment confirmation. You can always change any of your previous selections by using the GO BACK button on your browser of choice.

Figure 8.10 Payment Confirmation Screen

Step 4: Payment Confirmation

Once you select the PAY button, Biller Direct will process and complete the charge to your invoices and inquire to the bank or credit card your customers selected. Your customers will receive the confirmation screen illustrated in Figure 8.11. Alternatively, they can print the receipt for your own records by selecting PRINT.

Figure 8.11 Payment Receipt Confirmation Screen

Payment History

Biller Direct gives your customers the capacity to check on payments. Whether the payments were recently made or historically applied, your customers will find them here in BD. Your customers can also select the period to review payments (30 days, 12 months, 5 years, etc.).

Select PAID BILLS (see Figure 8.12). If customers recently made the payment via BD, you'll find such payments under Status IN PROCESS. Newly created payments typically could stay for a period of time, whether hours or days, depending on the needs of your company. If you see the column ARRANGED, you can also see some hyperlinks on each of the amounts. Click on them and you'll see a new screen with all your payment details. This feature is available only for payments done via Biller Direct.

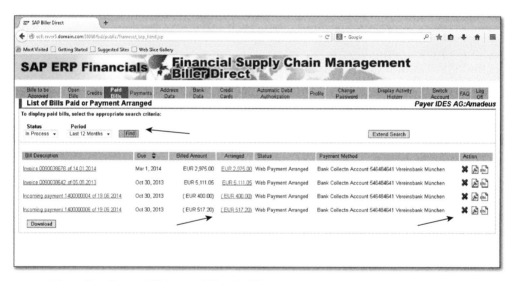

Figure 8.12 Payment History and Historical Data

If you see the ACTION box ✖, it means the payment is still in process and your customers may still cancel it. The invoice will be sent back into OPEN BILLS tab as an open invoice and your bank or credit card may or may not be charged.

The status PROCESSED in BD indicates that the payment has been processed in the backend system or SAP ERP along with your bank or credit card.

8.2.3 Integration with SAP Dispute Management

An important feature of Biller Direct is its integration with other components, in this case SAP Dispute Management (DM). Your customers are empowered to create an inquiry or a dispute regarding any of the open bills. They are capable of starting a full dispute case and researching it via the BD. The dispute case is then created in SAP ERP under Dispute Management. Both your customers and you can see the same dispute case created in BD and processed in SAP ERP. We will discuss Dispute Management and integration with BD in detail later in Section 8.4.4.

To start a new inquiry or dispute, your customers can select the INQUIRY button 🗩 in the ACTION box. A new screen appears (see Figure 8.13) where your customers can enter details of the dispute.

Figure 8.13 Biller Direct Inquiry and Dispute Attachments

First, your customers must provide a reason that the dispute or inquiry is being created. They must select one reason from the list. Additionally, your customers can enter further references, such as invoice number, PO number, or other information in the reference field. You can add your own comments in the COMMENTS box to justify the case or to ask a question.

Attachment Uploads

Your customers have the ability to attach digital documents to support their claim, including receipts, invoice images, or other documents. To do so, follow these steps:

1. Your customers click on BROWSE, select the files to be attached, and then UPLOAD. The system will then upload the files and attach them to the dispute case in SAP ERP. Attachments are optional, and are not required as part of the inquiry.

2. In order to submit the inquiry, your customers have to click on the SEND button. They will obtain a confirmation screen on the dispute case, and will be advised that they will soon receive a response.

3. Once the dispute confirmation is shown, if you or your customers go back to the OPEN BILLS tab, you'll see that in the ACTION box, the dispute icon has now changed to 🗎. This icon is an indication that the inquiry is now accepted and soon will be processed in SAP ERP by the related sales representative or clerk. As the case is assigned and due diligence is completed, or further questions are added to the inquiry, BD will allow responses via the dispute document. You customer will notice that a response is provided when this icon changes in each invoice. Click on it to see the response or to provide further information.

Now that you know how BD attachments work, we'll discuss another important feature, BD master data and the BD customer profile.

8.2.4 Biller Direct Master Data and Customer Profile

By using Biller Direct, your customers now have a faster and more convenient way to let you know about address changes and other contact information updates. We'll briefly discuss how a master data update is done in BD.

Address Update

Follow these steps to change a customer's addess:

1. By selecting ADDRESS DATA button, you're able to access the customer's general information (Figure 8.14).

2. If you select the EDIT button, you'll be able to display and make changes to any of the address fields in the master data. Here's an important reminder: be sure to save your work when you're done, so the changes are actually safe.

3. Customer master data changes via BD such as address will be submitted to the SAP ERP side, where approval needs to be given by a sales representative or clerk and thereafter update other satellite systems.

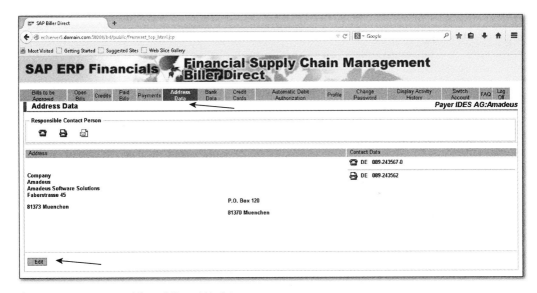

Figure 8.14 Customer Address Edit and Update

Profile

Different features can be activated or deactivated via self-service in Biller Direct. Now your customers can opt in or opt out of the associated features at any time. Profiles are illustrated in Figure 8.15. Your customers can verify the details in each profile option and opt in or opt out, as shown in Table 8.1.

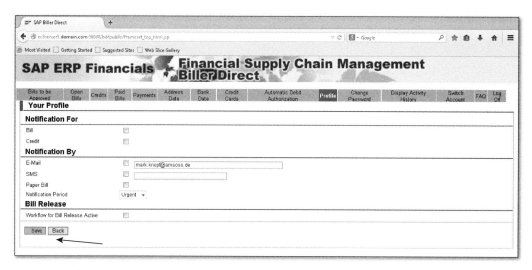

Figure 8.15 Edit Customer Profile: Opt In or Opt Out

Your Profile	Notification for	Description
Notification For	► BILL ► CREDIT	You'll receive an email for a newly created bill or credit. Opt in by selecting each.
Notification By	► E-MAIL ► SMS ► PAPER BILL	Indicate the email address where you would like to receive email about newly created invoices. You can also choose to receive a SMS text message at the number provided here. Opt in by entering email and mobile number. Select PAPER BILL if you prefer to have a printed copy mailed to you.
	► NOTIFICATION PERIOD	Select URGENT, INDIVIDUAL notification, WEEKLY or MONTHLY notifications.

Table 8.1 BD Profile: Opt In or Opt Out Options

In Table 8.2, you can find a list of additional functionality that you can make available for your customers.

BD Additional Functionality	Description
Creation of payment advice	Your customers can assign payments to invoices and submit payment advice notes to a designated reviewer or approver for processing.
Create or change bank details or payment cards	Credit card and bank information maintenance is also allowed at Biller Direct. Your customers is able to add/change or delete any bank data or credit card provided under his or her profile.
Display balances and line items	Your customers can view balance and line item information in a manner similar to how it's displayed in ECC FI-AR (Transaction FD11).
Partial payment	While processing the payment, your customers can also overwrite the quantities for payment and allow partial amounts to be charged to their bank or credit card.
Balance confirmation	With balance confirmation, BD gives you the ability to provide a tool to your customers for year-end preparation of a balance sheet. This will empower your customers to compare the current open items internally with their accounting records. Additionally, your customers can confirm or reject any invoice or explain any variances.
Self-registration	Your customers can subscribe via self-service to the secure website by entering general information and a mailing address via the BD website. Such a registration needs internal approval from the sales representative.
Payer direct	Your BD installation can provide help to your customers and can also be activated to provide self-service to your vendors. If your company decides to activate this feature, your vendors will be able to upload their invoices directly to the website, and monitor their status. Your vendors will be able to see which of their bills have already been entered in your accounting system, for example.
BD interaction and contract accounts receivable	Your customers can see open bills, paid bills, credits, or payments that they have selected, as well as payment history, while integrating with FI Contract Accounts Receivable and Payable (FI-CA).

Table 8.2 BD Additional Functionality

8.2.5 Biller Direct in SAP ERP

Although there is a full Java page for Biller Direct self-service, there are a few transaction codes in SAP ERP (ECC) that are worth running from time to time. Sales representatives are usually the business group that benefits the most from these transactions. Table 8.3 shows the list of common SAP ERP transaction codes in Biller Direct.

Transaction	Menu Path
EBPP_CREATE_USER – Create Users	SAP MENU • ACCOUNTING • FINANCIAL SUPPLY CHAIN MANAGEMENT • BILLER DIRECT • CUSTOMER PORTAL ADMINISTRATION
IQS8 – Worklist Customer Messages	SAP MENU • ACCOUNTING • FINANCIAL SUPPLY CHAIN MANAGEMENT • BILLER DIRECT • CUSTOMER PORTAL ADMINISTRATION
EBPP_LOG_DISP – Display Customer Actions Logs	SAP MENU • ACCOUNTING • FINANCIAL SUPPLY CHAIN MANAGEMENT • BILLER DIRECT • CUSTOMER PORTAL ADMINISTRATION
EBPP_LOG_ORGA – Delete Customer Actions Logs	SAP MENU • ACCOUNTING • FINANCIAL SUPPLY CHAIN MANAGEMENT • BILLER DIRECT • CUSTOMER PORTAL ADMINISTRATION
S_AXB_19000002 – Create Customer Notifications	SAP MENU • ACCOUNTING • FINANCIAL SUPPLY CHAIN MANAGEMENT • BILLER DIRECT • CUSTOMER PORTAL ADMINISTRATION

Table 8.3 Biller Direct ECC Common Transaction Codes

8.3 Credit Management

In Chapter 3, you learned the basics of credit management in the Sales and Distribution component. In this section, you'll learn in more detail how Credit Management (FSCM-CR) can help you to perform better customer checks and credit score management, as well as lower your risk while performing business with your clients.

Table 8.4 compares the key characteristics of Credit Management and SD. You can clearly see how Credit Management offers greater enhanced functionality in comparison with SD credit, which is limited to manual credit score and credit limits only.

Functionality	FSCM Credit Management	SD Credit
Credit checking	Yes	Yes
Credit score	Yes	NA
Credit limit automatic calculations	Yes	NA
Integration platform to third-party credit bureaus	Yes	NA
Credit rules engine for risk scoring	Yes	NA
Workflow on credit events	Yes	NA
Multiple credit limit categories	Yes	NA
Credit limit approval and automatic updates	Yes	NA
BI content and portal integration for analytics	Yes	NA

Table 8.4 Comparison between FSCM-CR and SD Credit Functionality

Note
The following list of business roles illustrates the typical required roles in Credit Management:

- ▶ 000000 – General Business Partner
- ▶ FLCU00 – Customer/Vendor Integration: FI Customer
- ▶ UDM000 – Business Partner for Collections Management
- ▶ UKM000 – Credit Management Business Partner

8.3.1 Master Data

The Business Partners (BP) component in Credit Management master data was created to maintain the customer's credit profile, as well as the internal credit data under the finance accounting, including credit information from external sources and credit bureaus. The BPs will hold the external data of the customer, while the FI master data will hold the internal view of the same customer.

FSCM-CR will be more useful to you if your company has a complex system landscape with frequent difficulties in consolidating credit decisions or information, or if your company has a large number of business partners in addition to having internal and external sources of scoring and rating. This way, Credit Management provides you with a way to operate a centralized credit, and share it evenly across the system landscape, taking into account both internal and external credit information, scores, and risks. Internally, Credit Management uses XML interfaces and SAP NetWeaver to connect internally to SAP ERP components, as well as external credit information providers.

In the following subsections, we'll quickly overview a few different master data subcomponents.

BP Rating and Credit Information

You can consolidate external and internal credit rates in one place for your business partners. The intention is for you to use such sources and feed the credit rules engine. The engine is commonly used to automatically generate BP ratings and scores, or even to calculate credit limits based on previous behavior and external sources.

External Sources of Credit Information

Using Credit Management, you can request external credit information with ease. Once you have established interfaces to the external sources, your company can electronically exchange information via the established interfaces.

Internal Credit Information and Scores

A customer internal score is typically determined for each BP, based on the legacy systems and credit behavior. Alternatively, you can use your company's own rating rules and criteria to help determine your own internal score.

Both internal sources and external information are stored in the Credit Management business partner data. Each BP is also assigned a rating procedure that contains formulas to integrate all sources to calculate the rating.

Score Determination

Scores are typically determined using:

▶ BD master data, i.e., country of origin

▶ Number of dunning notices in a certain period, or other dunning

▶ Average days in arrears and payment behavior

▶ Number of dispute cases in a period

You can check the internal credit score and information easily with the following steps:

1. Via Transaction UKM_BP, enter the business partner number you'd like to see.

2. Select the PERSON, ORGANIZATION, or GROUP icon.

3. From the DISPLAY IN BP ROLE drop down list, select CREDIT MGT BUSINESS PART.

4. Select the CREDIT PROFILE tab. You'll be able to display the credit profile of the customer including the following fields: RULES, SCORE, VALID-TO, RISK CLASS, CHECK RULE, and CUSTOMER GROUP.

Workflow and BP Credit Limit

The credit limits of your BPs are calculated automatically. Via the workflow, you can generate approvals for changes to a credit limit or other master data fields via electronic notifications.

8.3.2 Steps to Create a Business Partner

You should now be comfortable with general master data information. Now that you understand the basic concepts of Credit Management, we'll walk you through the creation of a business partner. We'll include some other concepts needed to understand more about this important feature and other applicable transactions.

Let's begin by saying that a business partner (BP) could be people, organizations, or groups. We'll take you through the main steps of the common Credit Management transactions (see Table 8.5).

Transactions	Menu Path
UKM_BP – Business Partner Master Data	SAP MENU • ACCOUNTING • FINANCIAL SUPPLY CHAIN MANAGEMENT • CREDIT MANAGEMENT • MASTER DATA
UKM_BLACK_WHITE – Negative and Premium Customer Lists	SAP MENU • ACCOUNTING • FINANCIAL SUPPLY CHAIN MANAGEMENT • CREDIT MANAGEMENT • MASTER DATA
SCASE – Credit Limit Request	SAP MENU • ACCOUNTING • FINANCIAL SUPPLY CHAIN MANAGEMENT • CREDIT MANAGEMENT • MASTER DATA

Table 8.5 Credit Master: Processing Transactions

Step 1: Create the General Data for the Business Partner

You can create BPs through the following simple steps. The initial screen of Transaction UKM_BP is shown in Figure 8.16.

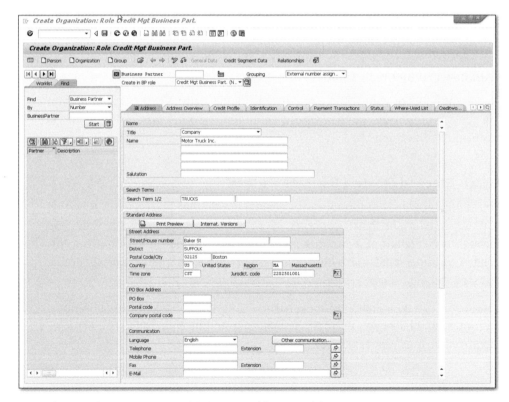

Figure 8.16 Business Partners BP Creation: Address Initial Screen

The first decision you need to make is whether the BP to be created is a person, organization, or group. Organization is mostly commonly used, so we'll concentrate on this one. Click on the ORGANIZATION button. You'll display the ADDRESS tab. Complete the general data of the customer: Title, Name, Search 1 and 2. Those are the basic data to be entered in each BP. Based on your specific configuration, the ADDRESS tab and others shown below could also apply different settings and mandatory fields, per configuration to your company's needs. Please make sure that a full address is entered, including STREET/HOUSE NUMBER, DISTRICT, POSTAL CODE, COUNTRY, and REGION. Continue with the following tab, ADDRESS OVERVIEW.

> **Note:**
>
> In order to see all address fields, click on MORE FIELDS 🔳 .

You can maintain more than one address for each customer. The ADDRESS OVERVIEW tab will help you to enter more addresses, depending on the specific situation of your customers. See Figure 8.17.

Figure 8.17 Business Partners BP Creation: Address Overview Screen

> **BP Field Control**
>
> You can control which fields in the BPs are displayed, and which ones are mandatory or optional, depending on your specific needs as configured. The configuration is based on the field attribute per BP role: e.g., UKM000: IMG • CROSS-APPLICATION COMPONENTS • SAP BUSINESS PARTNER • BUSINESS PARTNER • BASIC SETTINGS • BUSINESS PARTNER ROLES • DEFINE BP ROLES.

Step 2: Create Credit Profile

In this tab (Figure 8.18), you can enter the credit profile of the customer or allow the system to calculate it automatically. Let's go over the specific fields:

▶ RULES: The rules are configurable to your needs and mainly used to calculate the score and the credit limit of a BP. It has a direct impact on how the score will be calculated.

▶ SCORE: Typically it's calculated by the system, including the VALIDITY TO field.

▶ RISK CLASS: This corresponds to the score assigned to the BP internally in FSCM-CR. The risk class is a classification added to the scoring and is associated with the risk category in ECC.

▶ CHECK RULES: A check rule is defined in configuration to your own precise needs. Check rules consist of individual steps to determine parameters used to execute steps and the extent to which they are logged.

▶ CUSTOMER GROUP: A statistical criteria tailored to your needs.

▶ EXTERNAL RATING PROCEDURE: Defines external rating procedures and validity to account for the rating.

Figure 8.18 Business Partners BP Creation: Credit Profile Overview Screen

Step 3: Enter Identification Details

Depending on the customization of the IDENTIFICATION tab, some of the fields could be mandatory, such as LEGAL FORM, INDUSTRY, and EXTERNAL BP IDs. You will have to fill out each field accordingly. See Figure 8.19.

Figure 8.19 Business Partners BP Creation: Identification Overview Screen

▶ CONTROL and PAYMENT TRANSACTIONS: Those two tabs depend on how much information is needed at your BP, especially for reporting.

▶ BP TYPE: Grouping of your BPs accordingly to your own criteria.

▶ PAYMENT TRANSACTIONS: This tab will hold the bank, bank key and other data to store information for payments.

▶ Create segment data by clicking the CREDIT SEGMENT DATA button.

▶ CREDIT LIMIT AND CONTROL: This is one of the most important tabs because it holds the rules and can also be used to either set a fixed credit limit or allow the system to calculate the BP's credit limit. If you wish to automatically calculate the credit limit, leave the credit limit field blank. Other fields may also be required based on your company's specific needs and configuration. Also, under CONTROL DATA, you can see the blocking actions, including Blocked in Credit Management, and the reason for blocking. See Figure 8.20.

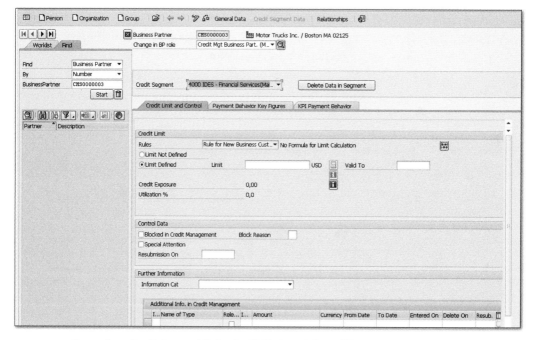

Figure 8.20 Credit Segment Data: Credit Limit and Control Overview

Step 4: Assign Relationships

The last step in the creation of a BP is assigning some relationships at the higher and the lower level. In Credit Management, a relationship can exist between two or more business partners. You can use the RELATIONSHIP CATEGORY tab to describe the relationship among them. You can reach this tab by selecting the RELATIONSHIPS button. See Figure 8.21.

- OVERVIEW: This tab will give you a list of the relationships assigned to a BP. The list will be displayed based on the settings you have assigned for higher-level and for lower-level Credit Management accounts. The list can be also displayed as a hierarchy or as a network format.

- HIGHER-LEVEL CREDIT MANAGEMENT ACCOUNT: As shown in Figure 8.21, you can enter a higher-level relationship to a BP by selecting the credit segment and related relationship BP. Don't forget to select the CREATE button.

- LOWER-LEVEL CREDIT MANAGEMENT ACCOUNT: Just as in the higher-level relationship, you can enter a lower-level relationship to a BP by selecting the credit segment and the related relationship BP. Don't forget to select the CREATE button.

Figure 8.21 Relationships Overview: Higher-Level Credit Management Account

Step 5: BP Save and Replicate

Once you've completed all the previous steps, your business partner should be created and replicated to the databases depending on your system landscape. A good practice is to save your work before you leave the transaction, so that your BP is created.

In the next section, we'll review the mass transactions in Credit Management.

8.3.3 Mass Data Changes

In every company, there's always a need for mass updates of customer master data. Credit Management provides a list of mass updates you can do to a customer master. Although we won't cover every single one of the mass changes that can be done in Credit Management in detail, we will concentrate on the most typically used transactions.

It's important for you to know that SAP provides a centralized mass changes report that you can run to make credit fields adjustments. In the report UKM_MASSDATA_UPDATE, the following mass changes are allowed: score, external credit info updates, assign the role UKM000, and credit limits. Table 8.6 shows the set of transactions to individually execute each action.

Transaction	Menu Path
UKM_MASS_UPD4 – Rule for Scoring and Credit Limit Calculation and Check Rule	SAP Menu • Accounting • Financial Supply Chain Management • Credit Management • Master Data Mass Changes
UKM_MASS_UPD3 – Credit Limit	SAP Menu • Accounting • Financial Supply Chain Management • Credit Management • Master Data Mass Changes
UKM_MASS_UPD2 – Score	SAP Menu • Accounting • Financial Supply Chain Management • Credit Management • Master Data Mass Changes
UKM_MASS_UPD1 – External Credit Information	SAP Menu • Accounting • Financial Supply Chain Management • Credit Management • Master Data Mass Changes
UKM_MONITOR – Update Entries for Ext. Credit Info.	SAP Menu • Accounting • Financial Supply Chain Management • Credit Management • Master Data Mass Changes

Table 8.6 FSCM-Credit Master: Mass Changes Transactions

Some of these transactions will permit you to preview results before you actually execute the mass change. That means you have a way to simulate the run and see the results before you actually execute the changes.

One of the most frequently used mass update lists is the one depicted in Figure 8.22. The test run shows you how the score will be updated to the new value from the old and same the related rule. You can review such report, make any fields adjustments. This list reacts just like any other in SAP: you can change the report layouts, add or remove your own fields by using the ⬛ ⊞ ⊞ ⬛ 🔲 🔲 Selections icons, and finally save the list as a variant.

SAP Credit Management: Mass Update of Credit Data

Test Run

Valid To Maximum 07/01/2014

Without Extract

Cr.Segment	Business Partner	Old Rule	New Rule	Old Score	New Score	Valid To	Old Risk	New Risk	Σ Old Cr. Limit	Σ New Cr. Limit	Σ Cr.Lim.AmtChnge	Cr.LimChge	Valid To	Bloc
	CMS0000001	B2B-EXIST	B2B-EXIST	36	26	02/18/2012	D	D				0.00		
	CMS0000002	B2B-EXIST	B2B-EXIST	45	36		C	C				0.00		
	CMS0000007	B2B-EXIST	B2B-EXIST	40	40		C	C				0.00		
	CMS0000009	B2B-EXIST	B2B-EXIST	40	40		C	C				0.00		
	CMS0000043	B2B-EXIST	B2B-EXIST	10	10		E	E				0.00		
	CMS0000044	B2B-EXIST	B2B-EXIST	10	10		E	E				0.00		
	CMS0000045	B2B-EXIST	B2B-EXIST	10	10		E	E				0.00		
	CMS0000098	B2B-SMALL	B2B-SMALL	30	30		D	D				0.00		
	CMS0000099	B2B-SMALL	B2B-SMALL	36	36		D	D				0.00		
	COL105	B2B-EXIST	B2B-EXIST	10	10		E	E				0.00		

Figure 8.22 Sample of the List: Mass Update of Credit Data: Test Run

Saving Your List

If you chose to save the output list in an extract, use Transaction UKM_MASS_SHOW to display it.

8.3.4 Credit Lists

Similar to the mass changes, SAP provides you with a list of transactions available to display information. SAP uses the centralized report UKM_ MASSDATA_DIS-PLAY to display the BP credit master data and credit segments on one or more BPs. In this section, we'll cover details of some of the most used credit list reports and lists. At your convenience, experiment with them all and see which ones best match your business needs.

Running each of the transactions described in Table 8.7, you'll be able to list or display each centralized credit data. SAP also provides a concentrated transaction by groups and gives you the choice to run them individually or by the concentrated transaction (see Figure 8.23). Use Transaction UKM_MALUS_DSP to discover the customer credit behavior and detect any with a credit limit that has been exceeded.

Transaction	Menu Path
UKM_MASS_DSP1 – Credit Profile	SAP Menu • Accounting • Financial Supply Chain Management • Credit Management • List Displays
UKM_MASS_DSP2 – Credit Segment	SAP Menu • Accounting • Financial Supply Chain Management • Credit Management • List Displays
UKM_MALUS_DSP – Credit Limit Utilization	SAP Menu • Accounting • Financial Supply Chain Management • Credit Management • List Displays
UKM_VECTORS – Payment Behavior Summary	SAP Menu • Accounting • Financial Supply Chain Management • Credit Management • List Displays
UKM_COMMITMENTS – Credit Exposure	SAP Menu • Accounting • Financial Supply Chain Management • Credit Management • List Displays
UKM_BP_DISPLAY – Master Data List	SAP Menu • Accounting • Financial Supply Chain Management • Credit Management • List Displays
UKM_MASS_RECON – Reconciliation of Credit Exposure	SAP Menu • Accounting • Financial Supply Chain Management • Credit Management • List Displays
UKM_LOGS_DISPLAY – Logs in SAP Credit Management	SAP Menu • Accounting • Financial Supply Chain Management • Credit Management • List Displays
UKM_MASS_SHOW – Display Extracts	SAP Menu • Accounting • Financial Supply Chain Management • Credit Management • List Displays

Table 8.7 FSCM-Credit Master: List Displays and Common Transaction Lists

On the other hand, if you want to get a good overview of your customer's credit limits and settings, use Transaction UKM_MALUS_DSP (Credit Limit Utilization). This is where the percentage is displayed, along with the credit warnings and other flags. See Figure 8.23. In Figure 8.24, you'll find an example of the CREDIT LIMIT UTILIZATION screen along with the warning flags.

SAP Credit Management: Selection and Display of Credit Data

Output List

Without Extract

Partner	Cr.Segment	Crcy	Rules	Calculated	Score	Credit Limit	Calculated Limit	Ris.	Risk	Valid To	Valid To	B	Credit Analyst	Submission	S	Changed On
CMS000	0000	EUR	B2B-EXIST	36	36	450.000,00	252.000,00	D	D	18.02.2015	07.06.2012			29.03.2011	X	04.03.2005
CMS00000	1000	EUR	B2B-EXIST	36	36	252.000,00	252.000,00	D	D		18.02.2012					18.02.2011
CMS00000	2000	EUR	B2B-EXIST	36	36	50.000,00	252.000,00	D	D		12.06.2005					14.12.2004
CMS00000	3000	USD	B2B-EXIST	36	36	60.000,00	252.000,00	D	D		01.10.2014				X	23.11.2009
CMS00000	3020	USD	B2B-EXIST	36	36	50.000,00	252.000,00	D	D		14.12.2005					14.12.2004
CMS00000	4000	USD	B2B-EXIST	36	36	0,00	0,00	D	D							14.12.2004
CM111	0000	EUR	B2B-EXIST	40	40	100.000,00	0,00	C	C	25.03.2013						25.03.2011

Figure 8.23 Report: List of Credit Segment

List of Credit Limit Utilization

Without Extract

Partner	Cr.Segment	Crcy	Credit Exposure	Credit Limit	Utilization %	Exposure Amount	Icon	Hedged Cr. Exposure	Calculated Limit	Cr. Gr	Risk Class	Cr.	Block	Sp. Atten.	Reasn	Submissi
B888	0000	EUR	12.495,00	20.000,00	62,5	7.505,00-	COB	0,00	20.000,00	B		2				
B888	1000	EUR	12.495,00	100.000,00	12,5	87.505,00-	COB	0,00	20.000,00	B		2		X		
B889	0000	EUR	12.883,96	40.000,00	32,2	27.116,04-	COB	0,00	40.000,00	B		2				
B889	3000	USD	16.037,54	40.000,00	45,1	21.962,46-	COB	0,00	40.000,00	B		2		X		
B00000	Z001	USD	17.980,00	15.000,00	119,9	2.980,00-	BCO	0,00	0,00	C						
B00100	Z001	USD	12.980,00	5.000,00	259,6	12.980,00-	BCO	0,00	0,00	C				X		

Figure 8.24 Report: List of Credit Limit Utilization

In the event you need to know what your customer's exposure is at a specific time, you could run Transaction UKM_COMMITMENTS (Credit Exposure). Figure 8.25 shows you what the report looks like.

It's very important to bear in mind that when you run this transaction, you have the option to correct credit exposure data, either correcting the totals or the line items. DELETE TOTALS will erase the entire table of totals records, as well as UKM_TOTALS. Please select wisely, as deleting totals of credit exposure implies erasing the table of totals records and (UKM_TOTALS) deletion. In contrast, selecting DELETE LINE ITEMS means the line items (UKM_ITEM) are deleted inside the logical system indicated. Finally, REBUILD TOTALS means the totals table is reconstructed using the line items table.

Credit Exposure									

Credit Exposure Tot.

BP Message	Mess. Sgt	Ty	Cr. Expos. Cat. Σ	Cr. Expos.	Cr. Expos.	Curr	Credit Exposure	Hedged	Mess
255	3000	200	Open Items f..	1.576,43	0,00	EUR	2.207,00	0,00	USD
255	3000	200	Open Items f..	2.207,00	0,00	USD	2.207,00	0,00	USD
Business Partner 255			▪	1.576,43		EUR			
				2.207,00		USD			
257	3000	200	Open Items f..	1.642,14	0,00	EUR	2.299,00	0,00	USD
257	3000	200	Open Items f..	2.299,00	0,00	USD	2.299,00	0,00	USD
Business Partner 257			▪	1.642,14		EUR			
				2.299,00		USD			
471	3000	200	Open Items f..	6.011,07	0,00	EUR	8.415,50	0,00	USD
471	3000	200	Open Items f..	8.415,50	0,00	USD	8.415,50	0,00	USD
Business Partner 471			▪	6.011,07		EUR			
				8.415,50		USD			

Figure 8.25 Report: List Display on Credit Exposure

If you're wondering how you do reconciliation between BPs and the SD master data, who has been created as a BP versus not, then you're right to use the report UKM_MASS_RECON. It provides you with a way to know the exact customers replicated in the FSCM BPs. However, this report requires configuration in the ABAP Query, specifically defining the user groups and sources. If not running, you may have to contact your helpdesk or a consultant on this area. However, it's suggested to begin with reconciliation of the variant's and only displays the differences between SD and BPs.

8.4   Dispute Management

In this section we will discuss Dispute Management (DM) and its integration with SD and other SAP components. DM supports the process that occurs between the customer invoice and the payment. DM drives any discrepancies with the customers. Figure 8.26 refers to the intersection between the Sales and Distribution invoices and Contract Management invoices. In both cases, DM will handle the dispute case to a final conclusion or a credit to the customer.

Common sources of disputes are found in inquiries from customers, payments applied partially or incorrectly, or even intercompany discrepancies. You may find your own source of disputes based on the specific needs of your company and the tools associated with it, including the case authorizations. A common scenario for a dispute case occurs when a customer is either overcharged, or makes an insufficient payment, or none at all. Sometimes these deductions are justified, such as goods arrived damaged, or maybe price differences. Additionally, other cases can be justified if a delivery was not made on time or the price was not right. The DM module will handle each case and related workflow to a final resolution.

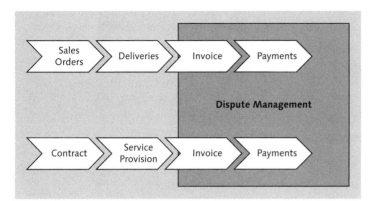

Figure 8.26 Dispute Management: Process Chains Interlaces with DM

Using DM, you can find a centralized component to handle dispute cases. DM cases store all dispute information and documentation or attachments to integrate with other AR, SD, and Biller Direct modules. DM offers you a centralized and up-to date tool for disputed items, providing a centralized view of the case along with the available reports. Dispute Management also provides you with case escalation and case hold actions. You can benefit from a complete dispute case history and internal communication features. We'll discuss these more in the following sections.

First, we'll concentrate on commonly used DM transactions associated with SD. We'll also cover the integration with Credit and Biller Direct. All other DM transactions are listed for your convenience in Table 8.8. We suggest that you explore each DM transaction, list, and report to determine which one best fits your, and your company's, specific needs.

Dispute Management Subareas

DM has two main subareas: Dispute Case Processing and Process Integration with other modules such as Credit Management, Collections, AR, and Biller Direct, among others.

Transaction	Menu Path
UDM_DISPUTE – Dispute Case Processing	SAP Menu • Accounting • Financial Supply Chain Management • Dispute Management
UDM_AUTOWRITEOFF – Automatic Write-Off of Dispute Cases	SAP Menu • Accounting • Financial Supply Chain Management • Dispute Management • Periodic Processing in Dispute Case Processing
SPPFP – Processing of Actions	SAP Menu • Accounting • Financial Supply Chain Management • Dispute Management • Periodic Processing in Dispute Case Processing
UDM_PUBLISH_DISPUTE – Transfer of Dispute Cases	SAP Menu • Accounting • Financial Supply Chain Management • Dispute Management • Periodic Processing in Dispute Case Processing
FDM_AUTO_CREATE – Automatic Creation of Dispute Cases	SAP Menu • Accounting • Financial Supply Chain Management • Dispute Management • Periodic Processing in Accounting
FDM_CREATE_PROPOSAL – Create Assignment Proposal	SAP Menu • Accounting • Financial Supply Chain Management • Dispute Management • Periodic Processing in Accounting • Automatic Assignment of Open Items to Dispute Cases
FDM_PROCESS_PROPOSAL – Edit Assignment Proposal	SAP Menu • Accounting • Financial Supply Chain Management • Dispute Management • Periodic Processing in Accounting • Automatic Assignment of Open Items to Dispute Cases
FDM_LDDB_EXEC–Execute	SAP Menu • Accounting • Financial Supply Chain Management • Dispute Management • Periodic Processing in Accounting • Document Changes through Dispute Cases

Table 8.8 Dispute Management: Commonly used Transactions

Transaction	Menu Path
FDM_LDDB_DISP – Display	SAP Menu • Accounting • Financial Supply Chain Management • Dispute Management • Periodic Processing in Accounting • Document Changes through Dispute Cases
FDM_LDDB_REORG – Reorganize Logging	SAP Menu • Accounting • Financial Supply Chain Management • Dispute Management • Periodic Processing in Accounting • Document Changes through Dispute Cases
UDM_CASE_PROCESSOR – Regular Processor	SAP Menu • Accounting • Financial Supply Chain Management • Dispute Management • Current Settings in Dispute Case Processing

Table 8.8 Dispute Management: Commonly used Transactions (Cont.)

8.4.1 Dispute Cases and Process

Let's begin this section by defining what a dispute case is. A dispute case is a business object related to the DM module which has descriptive attributes. A dispute case is also designed as a centralized folder, to allocate documents and object such as notes, attachments, or other digital components inside the system. The dispute case could be processed by different departments based on roles, such as accounts, dispute manager, and collection manager, among others.

One of the most important transactions in DM in terms of helping us to control dispute cases is UDM_DISPUTE (Dispute Case Processing). Figure 8.27 shows you how the transaction looks. The figure also shows the Records Management System (RMS) as a mandatory set in UDM_DISPUTE. The RMS helps us keep different employee groups that have access to dispute records separate. RMS are configurable and additionally determine how the dispute will behave, including the element displayed and types. You can select or change the RMS by selecting the Change RMS icon ⊞.

The header data in Dispute Management will give you the customer information and general data, including Customer number, Case ID, Title, and Case Type, among others.

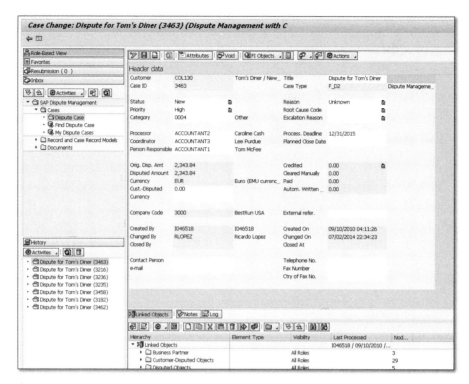

Figure 8.27 Dispute Management: Transaction UDM_DISPUTE

You can see the status of the dispute by looking at the STATUS/PRIORITY section on the screen (see Figure 8.28). The status can be ASSIGNED, BEING PROCESSED, CLOSED, NEW, TO BE COLLECTED, and WAITING FOR INFORMATION. Such status moves according to the information gathered along the way to solving the cases, starting from NEW when the case is newly created.

Status	New		Reason	Unknown	
Priority	High		Root Cause Code		
Category	0004	Other	Escalation Reason		
Processor	ACCOUNTANT2	Caroline Cash	Process. Deadline	12/31/2015	
Coordinator	ACCOUNTANT3	Lee Purdue	Planned Close Date		
Person Responsible	ACCOUNTANT1	Tom McFee			

Figure 8.28 Dispute Management: UDM_DISPUTE: Status, Priority, and Roles

The dispute case PRIORITY can be VERY HIGH, HIGH, LOW, or MEDIUM. The field CATEGORY refers to a further subdivision of the case or your own company search definition (see Figure 8.28).

The dispute case also contains AMOUNT fields in the midsection, as seen in Figure 8.27. This amount can be entered or calculated according to Table 8.9 and the type of amount entered.

Amount Field	Description
Original dispute amount	Amount disputed at the time of the dispute creation
Disputed amount	Amount currently disputed (includes payments, credit memos and write-offs)
Paid	Disputed amount that has being paid
Credited	Disputed amount that has being credited
Cleared manually	Amount entered and cleared manually
Written off	Amount that is written off automatically

Table 8.9 Dispute Management: Amount Types

Figure 8.28 shows the ROLE field. Each role has a specific set of steps and functions to help you process the approvals. See Table 8.10.

Role	Description
The processor	Processor is the people responsible for the next process step. This role may not be used when the process route is present.
Dispute case coordinator	Coordinator is in charge of the dispute case resolution, including some of these tasks: dispute case control and coordination, and finally determining the steps involved in case solution.
People responsible	Primary contract with the customer to resolve the case, many times in coordination with any of the above roles.

Table 8.10 Dispute Management Roles

Following along Figure 8.27, you'll find the section where the logs are stored, which includes dates and time of creation, created by, changed by, etc.

Dispute Attachments and Linked Objects

Each dispute case will have the type of linked object and/or attachments that you can store in the case, based on the configuration and selected RMS. Normally, you'll attach receipts, invoices, and other internal relevant documents provided by you or by your customer that can be used during the dispute approval. You can find an illustration of linked objects in Figure 8.29. Dispute linked objects can be accessed by selecting the LINKED OBJECTS, NOTES, and LOGS buttons. These linked objects include BUSINESS PARTNER as a link, CUSTOMER-DISPUTED OBJECTS, DISPUTE OBJECTS including the invoice, RESOLVED OBJECTS, ITEMS ASSIGNED and OTHER or various objects.

Hierarchy	Element Type	Visibility	Last Processed	Nod...
▼ Linked Objects			I046518 / 09/10/2010 /...	
▸ Business Partner		All Roles		3
▸ Customer-Disputed Objects		All Roles		29
▼ Disputed Objects		All Roles		5
• Residual Item	Accounting Document L...	All Roles		6
• Invoice	Accounting Document L...	All Roles		7
• 3000 1800000213 2010 001 (	Accounting Document L...	All Roles	I046518 / 09/10/2010 /...	7
• Credit	Accounting Document L...	All Roles		8
• Partial Payment	Accounting Document L...	All Roles		9
▸ Resolved Objects		All Roles		10
▸ Items Assigned during Clearing		All Roles		26
▸ Other Objects		All Roles		16
▸ Various		All Roles		23

Figure 8.29 Dispute Management: Linked Objects

You can also add notes to your case by selecting NOTES. You are able to select different types of notes and who can see them if you select the DESCRIPTION button. Notes can be classified as INTERNAL, REPLY, CONCLUDING REMARKS, DESCRIPTION OF CUSTOMER and CUSTOMER REPLY. Based on your specific configuration, some of these notes can be displayed internally for others to see but also to your customers as two-way communication or messaging.

8.4.2 Integration with CRM

FSCM Dispute Management integrates with the SAP CRM system. DM will receive and process cases from CRM Claim Management. Dispute case processing is also integrated with the Interaction Center (CIC).

8.4.3 Integration with Collection Management

Collection Management is a module that can be deployed in SAP ERP or also as part of the CRM landscape you may have available in your own system. It can be integrated with the CRM Interaction Center via the three work centers:

▶ My Worklist

▶ All Worklists

▶ Process Receivables

You can create dispute cases from invoices or even from existing residual amounts to invoices. The dispute cases can also be incorporated into collection rules to show customers in collection worklists.

8.4.4 Integration with SAP Biller Direct

Early in this chapter you learned about Biller Direct (BD) and how you can provide your customers with a self-service environment. You learned that your customers are presented with a list of their invoices, payments, and credits. Your customers can also verify and confirm their balance in BD, and also be able to download digital invoice and PDFs.

Biller Direct also offers you an integrated way to initiate customer disputes directly from the webpage created by your customers. BD disputes are typically created due to:

▶ **Invoices**
Your customers can face several problems with an invoice, including incorrect pricing, late delivery, or incorrect goods delivered.

▶ **Payment deductions**
A customer may short pay any amount or partially pay the invoice amount, without notice or warning.

Section 8.2.3 explains how a customer can create a dispute at their own convenience with a click of a button in Biller Direct. The customer can also indicate a reason, which can be verified in DM, and can attach supporting documents, receipts or other digital media as required. The Biller Direct (BD) then is reflected as part of the DM cases with NEW status.

Processing Biller Direct Disputes

The BD disputes will show in the list of disputes, just like any other dispute. In Section 8.4.1, you learned how to search for a specific case or cases. Also, you learned about case status and how the status gets processed.

BD disputes will be also listed in DM cases and are due to be assigned, approved, and processed like any other case. However, this feature needs to be configured in your system. The DM dispute should be brought to the DM environment via configuration and connectivity, depending on your specific needs and system landscape.

> **Note**
>
> A dispute case created in BD can follow your case process and approvals via the STATUS field, displayed directly in BD. In addition, notes with the description "Reply to Customer" will also be displayed in BD.

Searching for a Dispute Case

There are several ways to search for dispute case, including a series of specific steps tailored to your company. Here, we present the steps required for a simple seach for a dispute case.

1. Using Transaction UDM_DISPUTE, you can select the appropriate RMS (see Section 8.4.1). Select the FIND DISPUTE CASE button to give you a screen as illustrated in Figure 8.30, which shows how a simple case search is proposed.

2. Select CASE ID and enter an asterisk (*) to symbolize all case IDs. Make sure that RESTRICT HITS TO is not left blank or with a question mark, and make sure you enter a number to restrict the search output. Select the SEARCH button.

> **Note**
>
> Other, more detailed searching capabilities are applicable based on your system configuration and sytem landscape.

3. The DM module then presents the dispute cases found. You may wonder which ones are coming from each source, including Biller Direct. It's actually simple. DM has prepared a field you can add to your own report variant by

selecting , changing the current layout to include the field ORIGIN OF DIS-
PUTE CASE, and saving it. Figure 8.31 illustrates how the field is added and
saved. This field will show in the final search results.

Figure 8.30 Dispute Management: Simple Case Searching

Figure 8.31 DM Searching Dispute: Adding Origin of Dispute Case

4. Sort or query by the ORIGIN OF DISPUTE CASE field during DM case processing.

457

Table 8.11 shows you the values in the Origin of the DM. In this case, if you want to know how many disputes from BD you have, you can query based on value 01. That also includes how many came from CRM, value 04, and so forth.

Code	Source Description
Blank	Accounting
01	Biller Direct
02	External Application
04	CRM Service Request
03	ESR Service

Table 8.11 Origin of Dispute Case: Field Content

8.5 Summary

In this chapter, you learned about SAP Financial Supply Chain Management. We selected three of the modules most relevant to Sales and Distribution and picked the transactions that are mostly related to SD: Biller Direct, Credit Management, and Dispute Management.

We introduced Biller Direct (BD) as a module that allows your customers a self-service environment. Biller Direct interacts with SD per customer invoice, with AR on open items, dispute cases with Dispute Management, and even to object storage. FSCM Credit Management (CR) is another module that directly interacts with Sales and Distribution. CR is planned to replace fully the credit functionality from the Sales and Distribution credit. It provides not only the SD basic functionality, but also has been enhanced to store credit scores and ratings.

The last topic in this chapter is the Dispute Management module from the FSCM side. We reviewed how dispute cases are processed and how a dispute case can be initiated from the SD invoices. We gave a detailed description of how a dispute case is created, modified, and processed via the workflow and related status.

Appendices

A   SAP Navigation

In this appendix, we'll describe some additional functions available for Windows users. Be sure to pay attention because not all features may apply to Java and SAP WebGUI versions.

SAP GUI (Figure A.1) is usually installed by the administrator, and all accessible SAP systems are usually already predefined. You don't really need to do anything else but log on to the system, and, if allowed, you can tweak the look and feel of the interface.

Figure A.1 Logon Icon on the Windows Desktop

On your desktop, you'll have at least one icon: SAP Logon (Figure A.2), which starts the actual application. If allowed by administrators, you'll also have Tweak SAP GUI, which enables users to modify the look and feel of the SAP GUI screens.

Figure A.2 SAP GUI Configuration Button on the Windows Desktop

When you click on the SAP GUI CONFIGURATION icon, the visual design feature (Figure A.3) setup will be available for modification. This feature allows you to personalize the look and feel of the application. You can set your GUI theme, fonts, and color schema for your reports. You can also change your interaction design by adjusting keyboard behavior, visualization, and sound settings, as well as your display system information.

When you're ready to access SAP, click on the SAP LOGON icon. You'll see all defined SAP systems for you to access on the SYSTEMS tab. You can click on any of the systems shown. You can also choose the SHORTCUTS tab, where you can click on the transaction shortcuts, starting the SAP session directly in the transaction defined in the shortcut (Figure A.4).

Figure A.3 Visual Design Options and Interaction Details Controls

Figure A.4 SAP Logon Pad Systems and Shortcuts Tabs

Finally, the SAP GUI logon screen starts, and you must specify the SAP client number, enter your account credentials with the user name and password information, and press Enter .

> **Note**
>
> You can pre-set your client, user, and password information by setting up shortcuts and save a few steps. Remember: if you have multiple users accessing SAP from the same computer, all access credentials will default to settings saved in the shortcut.

On the initial screen, enter your user name and password for the appropriate client as provided to you by the security administrator. Always verify the client number when logging on to the system. See the initial screen example in Figure A.5.

Figure A.5 SAP Opening Logon Screen

You can find more details about SAP GUI functions by visiting the extensive library of information in the SAP GUI online help by pressing [F1] in the SAP Logon pad window. You can change your initial password by selecting the NEW PASSWORD button. You'll be prompted during your first login to change your password.

A.1 SAP Easy Access Settings

To make SAP Easy Access settings using your pull-down menus, follow the path EXTRAS • SETTINGS. The SETTINGS dialog box will appear, as shown in Figure A.6.

Figure A.6 Extras Settings Dialog Box

Here you can specify the following:

▶ Whether your favorites should appear before or after the menu.

▶ Whether only your favorites, and not the SAP standard menu, should appear.

▶ Whether technical names (transaction codes) of menu options should appear in the navigation area.

▶ Whether a user or an SAP standard menu should appear. To make this setting, choose either MENU • USER MENU or MENU • SAP MENU.

A.2   The SAP GUI

The SAP graphical user interface (SAP GUI) consists of the technical features that enable you to exchange information with the system by entering data, choosing functions and transactions, and so on.

The SAP GUI consists of two main screen areas: screen header and screen body.

Screen Header

The screen header consists of the following:

▶ Menu bar

▶ System function bar

▶ Title bar

▶ Application toolbar

Let's explore the components of the screen header.

Menu Bar

Menus allow you to access certain functions during SAP processing and appear as dropdowns on the bar. When you choose a menu item, further options become available.

The menu bar has the following clear components for overview and definition (see Figure A.7):

▸ **GUI interaction options:** Located in the top-left portion of your menu bar. After you click there, you'll get options to choose from the following:

　▸ Move the SAP GUI Window

　▸ Size (change the size)

　▸ Minimize

　▸ Maximize

　▸ Close Window

　▸ Create Session (allows you to open another SAP GUI session)

　▸ Stop Transaction (allows you to stop a runaway process transaction)

Figure A.7 Menu Bar Overview

▸ **Pull-down menus:** These menus are dynamic and change as you process transactions, access the standard navigation area, and so on. Sometimes not all of the available menus fit on one menu line. In this case, they wrap to the next line, and you have to click on the dropdown icon to access remaining options.

Table A.1 shows the menu options that are standard on almost every screen.

Menu	Description
SYSTEM	Contains functions for the whole system, such as CREATE SESSION
HELP	Provides access to help files

Table A.1 Standard Menu Components

Table A.2 lists the menus that are standard in most SAP applications.

Menu	Description
<Object>	Named after the object/transaction you are currently working with, such as material. Contains functions for this object such as Display, Change, Print, or Exit.
EDIT	Allows you to edit components of the current object, for example, Select, Edit, Copy, and Cancel
GOTO	Allows you to move directly to additional screens of the current transaction

Table A.2 Additional Pull-Down Menu Options

Finally, Table A.3 lists the menus that may also appear on your pull-down menu options when processing certain transactions.

Menu	Description
EXTRAS	Contains additional functions you can choose to complete the current transaction
ENVIRONMENT	Displays additional information about the current object/transaction
VIEW	Allows you to toggle between display versions, for example, switching between a single-line and double-line display
SETTINGS	Allows you to set user-specific transaction parameters
UTILITIES	Provides access to object-independent processing, such as delete, copy, and print functions

Table A.3 Additional Pull-Down Menu Options

▶ **GUI interaction buttons:** These give you the options to minimize, maximize, and close your GUI screen.

Standard Toolbar

The standard toolbar contains multiple buttons with icons that will be repeatedly used in multiple SAP screens and represent the base of tools accessible in most transactions (see Table A.4). We'll talk about SAP buttons in detail later in this appendix. The most commonly used feature of this portion of the screen is the COMMAND FIELD, as shown in Figure A.8.

Icon	Keyboard Alternative	Function
	Enter	Confirmation
	Ctrl + S	Save your work
	F3	Back to previous screen
	Shift + F3	Exit function
	F12	Cancel; exit current function without saving
	Ctrl + P	Print data from current screen
	Ctrl + F	Find data
	Ctrl + G	Find next; perform extended search
	Ctrl + Pg Up	First page; scroll to first page
	Pg Up	Scroll to the previous page
	Pg Dn	Scroll to the next page
	Ctrl + Pg Dn	Scroll to the last page; same function as the key
	n/a	Create a new SAP session
	n/a	Create shortcut
	F1	Help; provides help on the field where the cursor is positioned
	Alt + F12	Customize local layout

Table A.4 Standard Toolbar Icons

Command field

Figure A.8 Standard Toolbar Area Overview

By default, the COMMAND FIELD is closed or collapsed. To display it and make it available, choose the arrow icon to the left of the SAVE button icon. To hide it, repeat the same. To display a list of the transactions you used last, choose the dropdown arrow located at the right side of the command field.

Screen Body

The screen body is the area below the screen header. It has variable contents and includes the following:

- ▸ Navigation area
- ▸ Transaction screens and data when you execute SAP transactions
- ▸ Status bar on the bottom of the screen.

The screen body is the dynamic part that changes most frequently. Let's talk about the static components of this area.

Navigation Area

In the navigation area, you can expand and collapse menus by choosing the drop-down arrows to the left of the menu items, as shown in Figure A.9.

Figure A.9 SAP Easy Access Navigation Area

To open an application in the navigation area, you can do any of the following:

- ▸ Double-click its node.
- ▸ Select a node, and press the ⎣Enter⎦ button.
- ▸ Choose menu path EDIT • EXECUTE.
- ▸ Choose menu path EDIT • EXECUTE IN NEW WINDOW.

After you've started the transaction, you'll have access to the status bar.

The Status Bar

The status bar is located all the way on the bottom of the SAP GUI screen. It displays information on the transactions you are performing. On the left side of the status bar, system messages are displayed, such as error messages or informational messages. On the right side of the status bar, you have three fields with information about the transaction you are processing, SAP server name, and more, as shown in Figure A.10.

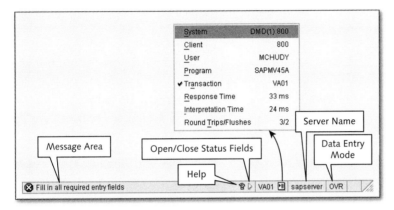

Figure A.10 Status Bar Components

To collapse or open the display portion of the status bar, use the open/close arrow icon, as shown in Figure A.10.

To display the system information, click on the LIST icon next to the transaction code displayed in the status bar. Click on it to get information about the following:

▶ System (information such as instance and client names)

▶ Client (number)

▶ User (session owner name)

▶ Program (open program in your session)

▶ Transaction (transaction code you are running)

▶ Response Time

▶ Interpretation Time

▶ Round Trips/Flushes

The second status field displays the server name you are connected to. Finally, the last status field specifies your data entry mode. You can toggle between the following:

▶ **Insert (INS):** Data to the right of the cursor moves to the right as you type.

▶ **Overwrite (OVR):** Whatever you type will overwrite any data to the right of your cursor.

A.3   Finding Transaction Code Names

Before you can use a transaction code in the command window, you must find the transaction code for the task you want to start. To find a transaction code for a certain task, place the cursor on the requested node with the transaction on the menu path in the SAP Easy Access navigation area, and select one of the following methods:

▶ Use menu path CHOOSE EXTRAS • TECHNICAL DETAILS. A dialog box appears displaying the details for the selected menu item (see Figure A.11).

Figure A.11 Technical Details Display Window

▶ Choose EXTRAS • SETTINGS • DISPLAY TECHNICAL NAMES. Your menu will close and collapse to the initial level. When you reopen it, the system displays the transaction codes not only for the desired original item but also throughout the workplace menu.

▶ From within a transaction, display details that include the transaction code name by choosing SYSTEM • STATUS.

A.4 Creating Favorites

In the SAP Easy Access menu, you can create a favorites containing the following:

- Transactions
- Files/folders
- Web addresses

The first step in the process is to add transactions that you're running to your favorites.

From any transaction in the system, you can go to SYSTEM • USER PROFILE • EXPAND FAVORITES, and that transaction code will be added to the FAVORITES menu.

You can also insert an item from the SAP standard by using drag and drop, to do the following:

1. Select an executable menu item using the mouse, and keep the mouse button pressed.
2. Drag the item to the desired position in your Favorites list, and release the mouse button.
3. The new item appears below the position where you dropped it.
4. Or you can use the menu bar to select a transaction code from the menu, and choose FAVORITES • ADD, and the new item appears at the end of your list.

To insert a transaction, you can choose FAVORITES • INSERT TRANSACTION, as shown in Figure A.12. From here, you can enter the transaction code number, and choose the CONTINUE button. The new item appears at the end of your list and is automatically labeled with the transaction code name.

Figure A.12 Favorites – Insert Transaction

A.5   Managing Favorites

SAP Easy Access allows you to organize your favorites by doing the following:

▶ Creating folders in your Favorites list

▶ Moving, renaming, or deleting favorites and folders

If you want to insert folders, choose FAVORITES • INSERT FOLDER. This produces the new folder, which appears below the currently selected folder.

To move favorites and folders within a single node of the menu hierarchy, follow these steps:

1. Select the favorite or folder you want to move.

2. Choose FAVORITES • MOVE • UP/DOWN or MOVE FAVORITES DOWNWARDS/MOVE FAVORITES UPWARDS.

3. Repeat this step until the favorite or folder is where you want it.

To move favorites or folders between hierarchy levels, use your mouse and apply drag and drop functionality:

1. Select the favorite or folder with the mouse, and keep the mouse button pressed.

2. Drag the favorite or folder to the desired position in the Favorites list, and release the mouse button.

3. The favorite or folder appears below the position where you let it go.

To rename favorites and folders, follow these steps:

1. Select the favorites or folders you want to rename.

2. Choose FAVORITES • CHANGE.

3. A dialog box appears. Enter a new name, and choose CONTINUE.

4. From the context menu, choose CHANGE FAVORITES. To open the context menu, click the right mouse button.

Deleting favorites and folders is just as simple and straightforward. Simply select the favorites or folders that you want to delete, and choose FAVORITES • DELETE. From the context menu, choose DELETE FAVORITES. To open the context menu, click the right mouse button. When you remove a favorite from your favorites list, you aren't actually deleting the respective file, program, or transaction: you are only removing a link to that particular item.

A.6 Transaction Access

When attempting to perform any transactions that aren't included in your security profile, you'll receive an error message at the bottom of your screen. Use Transaction SU53, which displays the authorization object check report, and press the PRT SC button to capture the screen. You can then paste the picture to the email notification that you would then forward to the security administrator for verification of your profile/approved system access.

A.7 Multiple SAP Sessions

A session is basically another SAP instance on your screen. Multiple sessions allow you to work on more than one task at a time. This can save you time and reduces the need to jump from screen to screen. You can open up to six sessions, and do a different task, or even the same task, in each one. You can move around between the open sessions, and you can close any session without having to log off from the system. If you try to work on the same record (e.g., the material master record for a specific material) at the same time in multiple sessions, you may "lock yourself out" of one of the sessions. If this happens, choose EXIT or BACK to move out of the transaction. Then you'll be able to proceed.

Creating a New Session

You can create a session at any time. You don't lose any data in sessions that are already open. As mentioned before, you can create up to six sessions. Each session you create is as if you logged on to the system again, so each session is independent of the others. Closing the first session doesn't cause the other sessions to close.

To create a new session from anywhere in the system, follow these steps:

1. Choose SYSTEM • CREATE SESSION from the menu bar.

2. Click on the CREATE NEW SESSION icon.

3. Use GUI INTERACTION OPTIONS, located in the upper-left portion, and choose the CREATE SESSION option.

Moving Among Sessions

You can move among sessions as often as you like without losing any data. As long as you remain logged on to the SAP system, you can leave a session for as long as you like. Moving to a different session is like putting a telephone call on hold—you can resume the call whenever you're ready. To move from one session to another, click any part of the window that contains the session you want to go to or use ⌊Alt⌋ + ⌊Tab⌋ to switch between windows. The window you choose becomes the active window and moves in front of all the other windows on your screen.

Stopping a Runaway Transaction

Occasionally, a transaction will be executed that runs for an unacceptably long time. Your cursor will be displayed as an hourglass, preventing standard mouse controls. You can stop processing by clicking the GUI Interaction Options icon in the far upper-left corner of the menu bar. Your cursor will become active when hovering over this icon. From the available options, select STOP TRANSACTION, and your transaction will be terminated.

Ending a Session

Before you end a session, save any data you want to keep. When you end a session, the system doesn't prompt you to save your data. If you have only one session open, and you end it, you will log off from the system. You can end your sessions by using one of the following:

1. Choose SYSTEM • END SESSION from the menu bar.

2. Click the CLOSE icon from the GUI Interaction Icons corner of the active sessions menu bar by the SAP logo.

3. Use COMMAND FIELD and enter command "/nEX". This ends the session and logs you off the system in one step.

B   Output Processing in Sales and Distribution

Outputs are a very important part of business. In general, in the SAP ERP system and particularly in SD, you have several options for producing communications with our business partners.

SAP is capable of printing, faxing, e-mailing, EDI, and some other internal options such as SAP Business Workflow, SAP Event Management, and so on. As we discussed in Chapter 2, for every output that you generate a sales document for, you need to create an output condition record.

In this first section, we'll discuss the most important settings for those condition records and other important prerequisites that must be in place for a successful output.

B.1   Output Settings in Condition Records

When you create a condition record independently of the document you want to output, there are some important settings that you need to keep in mind. Let's start with sharing the path for SD output conditions, which is LOGISTICS • SALES AND DISTRIBUTION • MASTER DATA • OUTPUT. Under this menu, shown in Figure B.1, you'll see the different sales documents that you can create output conditions for.

Each submenu can be opened, and you'll see the various transactions for create, change, and display conditions for each document type.

As an example, to create an output condition for a delivery, follow the path LOGISTICS • SALES AND DISTRIBUTION • MASTER DATA • OUTPUT • SHIPPING • CREATE. When prompted, select Output Type LD00, which is the delivery note output. Now, click on the KEY COMBINATION button. A pop-up menu will appear offering the available key combinations for this output type. For our example, select the sales organization/document type.

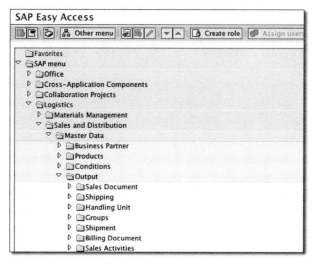

Figure B.1 Menu Path to Reach the Sales and Distribution Output Conditions

A *key combination* is the list of fields that are used to search and find a condition record. The more fields you select, the more flexibility you gain. It isn't the same to create a condition record that assigns an output to the whole sales organization as creating one that assigns it to a specific customer or even better to a customer within a specific distribution channel and division. This way you could have different outputs for the same customer in each division. In the selection screen for the output condition, as shown in Figure B.2, you need to select an output type and a key condition.

Figure B.2 Create Output – Condition Records: Shipping

In the next screen, you can enter the data that makes this condition record relevant for a delivery. In our case, we'll use sales organization 1000 and delivery type LF for a standard delivery order. The other fields you need to fill are listed in Table B.1.

Field	Description	Possible Values	
Function	The role the partner plays in the sales cycle, here: Ship-to	▶ AA	SP contract rel. ord
		▶ AB	Department resp.
		▶ AD	Additionals
		▶ AI	IS-PAM: cert. owner
		▶ AO	Author
		▶ AR	IS-PAM: Agency
		▶ AS	Applicant warranty
		▶ AU	Author
		▶ AW	SH contract rel. ord
		▶ AZ	A.payment recipient
		▶ BE	IS-PAM: Doc. receiv.
		▶ BP	Bill-to party
		▶ BU	Buyer
		▶ CA	Contract address
		▶ CE	IS-PAM: Chiffre rec.
		▶ CP	Contact persons
		▶ DC	PersResp for shippng
		▶ DE	IS-PAM: DU receiver
		▶ DK	IS-PAM: Acc.deb.rec.
		▶ DP	Delivering plant
		▶ DS	IS-PAM: DU sender
		▶ EA	EIC agent
		▶ EC	Receive.CD warehouse
		▶ ED	EDI mail recipient
		▶ EL	External warehouse
		▶ ER	Employee responsible
		▶ ET	Label service agent
		▶ EU	Enduser for F.Trade

Table B.1 Fields Relevant for a Delivery

Field	Description	Possible Values
		▶ FA Forwarding agent
		▶ FS Freight service agt
		▶ GS Goods supplier
		▶ HR Manufacturer
		▶ I1 IM: Applicant
		▶ I2 IM: Interested party
		▶ I3 IM:PersonResponsible
		▶ I4 IM: Approver 1
		▶ I5 IM: Approver 2
		▶ I6 IM: Approver 3
		▶ IP Invoice presented by
		▶ IS IS-PAM: Advertiser
		▶ IT Interested party
		▶ KB Credit rep.
		▶ KM Credit manager
		▶ KO Coordinator
		▶ KP Sls activity partner
		▶ KT IS-PAM: Competitor
		▶ KU Coordinator
		▶ L1 Originating attorney
		▶ L2 Billing attorney
		▶ L3 Managing attorney
		▶ L4 Matter coordinator
		▶ L5 Fee earner
		▶ L6 Risk manager
		▶ L7 Administrative asst
		▶ LS Logical system
		▶ MA Mail partner address
		▶ MB Notif. process
		▶ ME Buyer
		▶ MP Manufacturing plant
		▶ OA Ordering address
		▶ P1 Project manager

Table B.1 Fields Relevant for a Delivery (Cont.)

Field	Description	Possible Values
		▶ P2 Project controller
		▶ P3 Sales VP
		▶ PA Work center
		▶ PC PersClerk PCR
		▶ PE Cont.pers.fresh prod
		▶ PR Position responsible
		▶ PS Position
		▶ PY Payer
		▶ Q1 QtyCertRec/shpTo pt
		▶ Q2 QtyCertRec/soldTo pt
		▶ RA Addr.recursiveness
		▶ RC Personnel officer RC
		▶ SB Spec.stock partner
		▶ SC Suppler CD warehouse
		▶ SE Sales employee
		▶ SH Ship-to party
		▶ SO Customer type 4
		▶ SP Sold-to party
		▶ SR Mat.Safety sheet rec
		▶ TL Head of lading
		▶ TR Cleaning firm (T.)
		▶ TU Envelope serv. agent
		▶ TV Insurance (T.)
		▶ TZ Customs agent
		▶ VN Vendor
		▶ VU User responsible
		▶ VW Person responsible
		▶ WC Sales partners
		▶ Y1 Sales representative
		▶ YV Loadport
		▶ YW Disch.Port
		▶ YW Disch.Port
		▶ YX Location

Table B.1 Fields Relevant for a Delivery (Cont.)

Field	Description	Possible Values	
Partner	The number our customer's ship-to address has in the customer master. In our example, we can leave it empty because we're assigning the output to the whole sales organization.	Entries in vendor master	
Message Transmission Medium	The output mode the message will be sent to.	▶ 1	Print output
		▶ 2	Fax
		▶ 4	Telex
		▶ 5	External send
		▶ 6	EDI
		▶ 7	Simple mail
		▶ 8	Special function
		▶ 9	Events (SAP Business Workflow)
		▶ A	Distribution (ALE)
		▶ T	Tasks (SAP Business Workflow)
Dispatch Time	The moment when we want the output to be sent to the output medium.	▶ 1	Send with periodically scheduled job
		▶ 2	Send with job, with additional time specification
		▶ 3	Send with application own transaction
		▶ 4	Send immediately (when saving the application)

Table B.1 Fields Relevant for a Delivery (Cont.)

Field	Description	Possible Values
Language	The language you use to communicate with your client. You need to make sure that the message form is created in that specific language. Consult with your IT analyst to make sure you can send communications to your customer in the required language.	▶ AF Afrikaans ▶ AR Arabic ▶ BG Bulgarian ▶ CA Catalan ▶ CS Czech ▶ DA Danish ▶ DE German ▶ EL Greek ▶ EN English ▶ ES Spanish ▶ ET Estonian ▶ FI Finnish ▶ FR French ▶ HE Hebrew ▶ HR Croatian ▶ HU Hungarian ▶ ID Indonesian ▶ IS Icelandic ▶ IT Italian ▶ JA Japanese ▶ KO Korean ▶ LT Lithuanian ▶ LV Latvian ▶ MS Malaysian ▶ NL Dutch ▶ NO Norwegian ▶ PL Polish ▶ PT Portuguese ▶ RO Romanian ▶ RU Russian ▶ SH Serbian (Latin)

Table B.1 Fields Relevant for a Delivery (Cont.)

Field	Description	Possible Values
		▶ SK Slovakian
		▶ SL Slovenian
		▶ SR Serbian
		▶ SV Swedish
		▶ TH Thai
		▶ TR Turkish
		▶ UK Ukrainian
		▶ Z1 Customer reserve
		▶ ZF Chinese trad.
		▶ ZH Chinese

Table B.1 Fields Relevant for a Delivery (Cont.)

As you can see in Figure B.3, you can enter many delivery types for each sales organization.

Figure B.3 Condition Record Create Screen

From the Message Transmission Medium selection pop-up (Figure B.4), select option 1 (Print Output).

As shown in Figure B.5, there are different times when you can send the output to the printer or any other medium you select. This allows each business to execute the printing of documentation in different moments depending on their shipping process. In this example, select menu option 4 (when saving the application). This means that the moment that you save the delivery order, it will send out the delivery note to the printer. This might not always be very effective because you have yet to execute the picking, you haven't packed the goods, and some time will elapse from the moment you create the delivery until you're ready to dispatch the order.

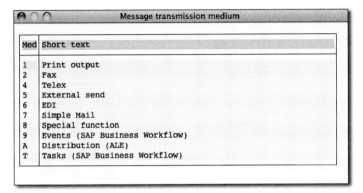

Figure B.4 Message Transmission Medium Selection

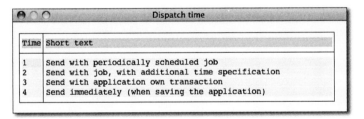

Figure B.5 Dispatch Time Selection

If, for example, you select option 3, then you can print the delivery note when you're actually ready for it. Or if you select option 1, then it will be picked up by a scheduled job and sent out at the same time with all other delivery notes.

Next, you have to select the line you just entered, and click on the COMMUNICATION button. This will take you to the screen shown in Figure B.6.

Output conditions   Edit   Goto   System   Help

Create Condition Records (Delivery note) : Communication

Variabler Key

Sales Org.	Delivery Type	Description
1000	LF	Delivery

Print output

Output Device	LP00	☑ Print immediately
Number of messages		☑ Release after output
Spool request name		
Suffix 1		
Suffix 2		
SAP cover page	Do Not Print	
Recipient		
Department		
Cover Page Text		
Authorization		
Storage Mode	1 Print only	

Print settings

Layout module	
Form	
SmartForm	

Figure B.6 Communication Screen

Here you have to select the printer where you want the output to be printed, as well as two other very important parameters:

▶ OUTPUT DEVICE: This is the name by which SAP ERP knows the printer. You can click on the match code button to see a list of the system printers.

▶ PRINT IMMEDIATELY: This option will send the output to the selected printer as soon as it's produced; otherwise, the system will create a spool request, and the output will sit on the printer's spool until it's manually sent to the printer.

▶ RELEASE AFTER OUTPUT: This option takes care of cleaning up the printer's spool by deleting the spool request as soon as the output is sent to the printer. If you want to keep a list of the messages you print for reconciliation or just to be able to print a copy later, leave this checkbox unselected. Keep in mind that you'll need to take care of cleaning the spool periodically.

Now you can save your condition record.

> **Note**
>
> It's common practice to create a system printer that will send the output to your local Windows printer. The standard system configuration delivers a printer named LOCL, which will print to whatever the default printer is in your PC. If you can't find this printer, ask your IT system analyst which printer you should use for this purpose.

Now that you know how to create a condition record, let's see how it appears in a delivery order.

B.2   Output Settings in Delivery Orders

To change a delivery, choose LOGISTICS • SALES AND DISTRIBUTION • SHIPPING AND TRANSPORTATION • OUTBOUND DELIVERY • CHANGE • SINGLE DOCUMENT, select an existing delivery, and press ⌑Enter⌑. To go to outputs, go to EXTRAS • DELIVERY OUTPUT • HEADER, as shown in Figure B.7.

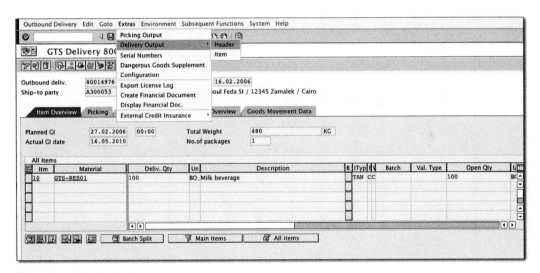

Figure B.7 View Outputs

In the header outputs screen, you'll see a list of the outputs that were generated for this delivery, as shown in Figure B.8. Each message has a traffic light status; when they are just generated and before they're actually output, the status is yellow. If the message is output correctly, the status changes to green. And if the output fails, then it becomes red.

Figure B.8 Each Message Has an Output Status

When you're expecting to see a message and you don't, or you see a message that you didn't expect to see, then you can use determination analysis. *Determination analysis* is an invaluable troubleshooting tool that displays all of the conditions that apply for the document and the values that they collect trying to fulfill the requirements (key combinations) for each.

To display the processing log, choose GoTo • Determination Analysis, as shown in Figure B.9.

In determination analysis, you can see how each condition was or wasn't fulfilled. This way, you can try to either make changes to the condition record or to some values within the document itself. Display the values of the key fields in a condition to know if it fulfills the requirements of the condition record, as shown in Figure B.10.

Figure B.9 Processing Log

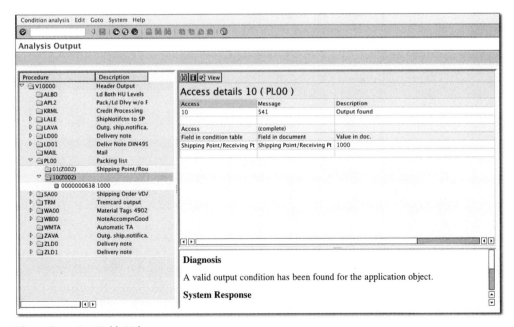

Figure B.10 Key Fields Values

When a message is being sent through transmission medium 6-EDI or A-ALE, you also need to maintain another type of record called a partner profile. The partner profile contains a list of all of the messages you exchange with a specific partner.

To display the partner profile, choose Logistics Execution • Internal Warehouse Processes • Communication with External Systems • ALE Administration • Run Time Settings • Partner Profiles. A partner profile (Figure B.11) has to be maintained for each partner, or customer, in this case.

Figure B.11 Partner Profile

C   Availability Check

In this appendix, we'll describe how the availability check process is used in SD. While you, as the end user, can't change the configuration settings without the help of an IT analyst, this section provides instruction to allow you to understand why products appear to be available or not available while processing sales documents.

Whenever you create a sales order, you should perform an availability check to make sure you have enough product on hand or that you'll have enough of it to provide for a customer on the requested delivery date.

> **Note**
>
> Not all materials require an availability check; it depends on what's defined on the material master and in the SALES GENERAL/PLANT tab, as shown in Figure C.1.

Figure C.1 Availability Check Settings in the Material Master

When your system is configured, you can specify all of the influencing elements that you're going to use during the availability check, which is illustrated in the example of configuration for the availability check using ATP in Figure C.2. From there, another important configuration setting specifies whether a schedule line category of the sales document will perform the availability check and transfer of requirements.

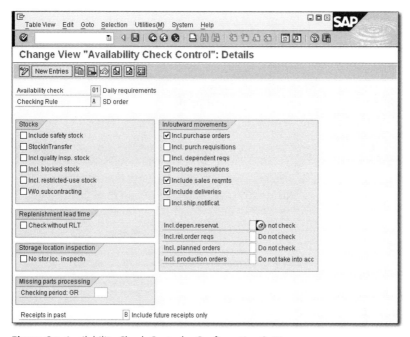

Figure C.2 Availability Check Control – Configuration Settings

In the example for the availability check control in Figure C.2, you define what types of stock (e.g., safety, stock in transfer or stock in quality inspection), what incoming stock (i.e., materials on pending purchase orders or production orders), and what outbound transactions (e.g., sales orders or reservations) are included in the availability check.

Returning to the discussion of the process, anytime you're creating a sales order and using materials where you could run into a potential stock shortage situation, you're making your SD requirements visible to procurement (see Figure C.3 demonstrating the transfer of requirements). This transfer of requirements can influence the availability check because your materials could potentially be provided by an internal production facility or external supplier. This could mean a seven-day delivery from the vendor.

Figure C.3 Requirements Transfer Mechanism

The other influencing factors that impact availability check results include loading time, transportation planning time (route stage duration), goods receipt processing time, picking time and packing time, and so on.

Taking all of this into account, the system must first carry out backward scheduling to establish your material availability date, as illustrated in Figure C.4. The formula for this is as follows:

Availability Date = Requested Delivery Date – Transportation Processing – Loading Time – Picking and Packing Time

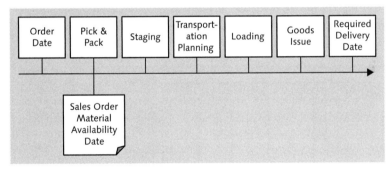

Figure C.4 Material Availability Date Calculation Routine

On the determined date, an availability check using ATP logic is carried out, where

ATP qty = [Total Warehouse Stock Qty + Planned Receipts Qty's (Incoming Stock)] – Planned Issues Qty's (Outgoing Stock)

To illustrate this, let's imagine a scenario of material not being available in full. During the order entry, the system proposes a new date for complete delivery (which you don't accept) and selects a partial delivery of what was available on hand at that time. This is shown by the two schedule lines created in an example captured in Figure C.5.

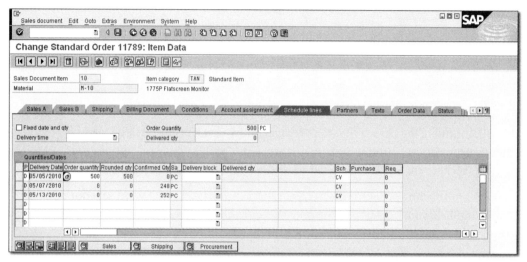

Figure C.5 Availability Check Resulting in Two Schedule Lines

You can always re-run the availability check from within the order by clicking on the AVAILABILITY CHECK icon 📊 or by pressing Ctrl + F5 . See Figure C.6 for reference. The choices you were originally presented with will appear again, and you can choose to process the complete delivery using the COMPLETE DELIVERY button, process the proposed delivery using available products on-hand by clicking the DELIVERY PROPOSAL button, or process delivery by clicking on CONTINUE with system-determined dates and other constraints and defaults from master data. You can also display the reports showing actual ATP quantities calculations and scope of check—displayed from configuration and other plants—which allows you to verify on the fly whether other locations have the stock available to fulfill your order requirements.

To simulate the results of the system availability check, you can also run Transaction CO09 (Availability Overview) or choose LOGISTICS • SALES AND DISTRIBUTION • SALES • ENVIRONMENT • AVAILABILITY OVERVIEW.

On the initial screen of the transaction, as shown in Figure C.7, you have to specify the material, plant, and checking rule, which is the configured set of rules we talked about initially.

Figure C.6 Availability Check Re-Run Screen

Figure C.7 Availability Check–Transaction CO09 – Initial Screen

Using the dropdown menu, select the type of checking rule you need to apply to your scenario (most likely, you'll be using either checking rule A – SD Orders or B – SD Deliveries). After you make your selection, press ⎡Enter⎤. On the following screen, you'll see a report showing the results of the simulated availability check, as shown in see Figure C.8.

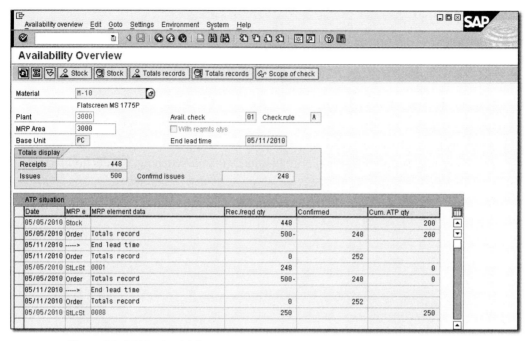

Figure C.8 CO09 – Availability Overview Screen

You can mold the displayed results to your liking by selecting different options and by clicking on available buttons such as STOCK, TOTAL RECORDS, and so on.

D   Global Available-to-Promise

This appendix is dedicated to Global Available-to-Promise (known as GATP or Global ATP). GATP is a component of the SAP APO (Advanced Planning and Optimization) application, which in turn is the heart of SAP Supply Chain Management (SCM). The use of SCM offers planning and optimization functionalities in different business processes. The modules of the SAO SCM component are Demand Planning, Supply Planning, Supply and Demand Matching, Production Planning Detailed Scheduling, Global Available-to-Promise, and Transportation Management. This appendix will not only introduce you to the GATP, but also will highlight the basics of ATP check methods, and explain the differences between SD ATP and Global ATP.

Global Available-to-Promise is an enhancement to the regular ATP functionality in ECC, primarily used in the Sales and Distribution component. In Appendix C, we discussed in detail what regular ATP means, and how sales documents perform the availability check and transfer of requirements in ECC. Our discussion also included the ATP formulas to calculate product availability. Many SAP clients use GATP as a way to improve the accuracy of product availability offered to their customers, especially during sales order processing inside of the Sales and Distribution component.

We'll first discuss how an organization benefits from Global ATP, see the task flow, and then discuss specific Global ATP/SD crossover functions.

D.1   What Global ATP Does for Your Company

Has your company experienced product availability over commitment? In reality, manufacturing companies often commit to their customers without knowing exactly whether the demand will be met. This is a common problem in global or international companies. GATP will give you the tools required to avoid over-commitments, and, because it has a global view, GATP will allow you to search in different locations or plants where the product inventory may be located. Instead of you or your team searching across multiple locations for a specific product, GATP will perform that task automatically for you. You'll benefit from a significant reduction in the amount of time invested in processing a sales order. GATP also provides extended visibility of your sales commitments in each of the ATP checks, allowing you to prioritize customers and realign availability commitments when required. This is commonly used during the end of the month or year, marketing campaigns, or rush sales, when inventory could be shuffled based on your customer's priorities.

In simple terms, GATP represents the search your company can provide to your customers for a requested product at the requested time and the required quantity. It can help to resolve the complexities that arise out of order-promising. Table D.1 shows the two main methods used, based on your system configuration, to check for availability among the plants and available locations. The proper selection of the ATP checks in your company is critical to providing your customers better availability accuracy, especially for your global customers. Even though a detailed discussion of each of the ATP methods is beyond the scope of this guide, it's important for you to become familiar with these terms and methods.

SCM-ATP	
ATP Framework	
Basic Methods	**Advanced Methods**
▶ Product availability check	▶ Combination of basic methods
▶ Product allocation	▶ Production (CTP or MATP)
▶ Check against forecast	▶ Rules-based ATP
	▶ Rules-based ATP and/or production

Table D.1 Availability Check Methods

Now let's find out how GATP checks SAP SCM for product availability.

D.2   Global ATP Task Flow

If you currently have the SAP SCM component or GATP installed in your system, you may wonder why you need to log into SAP several times: one into the ERP box and another for the SCM box. The answer is simple—SCM uses two different systems in the overall landscape; both are synchronized via the core interface

(CIF). Figure D.1 illustrates how SAP ERP Sales and Distribution connects to the SAP SCM execution box, and the SCM planning holds Global ATP, using CIF. While you create an SD sales order, GATP will use this structure to retrieve and check the availability to each of the products in the order.

Figure D.1 Sales and Distribution with SCM Execution and Planning

Master data, transactional data, and planning results are replicated using the CIF between SAP ERP and APO. However, master data is only transferred from SAP ERP to APO, and planning results are only transferred from APO into SAP ERP.

GATP provides you with several capabilities that can help your company respond to customer orders faster and in real time. In addition, you'll benefit from the following:

▶ **ATP based on rules**: Rules-based ATP allows you to determine availability based on different criteria according to your needs, and the verification of availability in alternative locations or plants.

▶ **Integration with other SAP components and applications:** GATP integrates internally with ECC components in addition to CRM.

▶ **Ability to perform checks on various SAP documents:** Including sales orders, deliveries, stock transfer, and replenishment, among others, conveyed mainly in the Sales and Distribution component.

- **Product allocation**: This will help you have tight control over products that are in short supply, and distribute them under various criteria that fit your needs.

- **Capable-to-promise**: CTP allows you to call production planning to produce ATP checks of remaining quantities, or explore external procurement sources.

- **Shipment and transportation scheduling**: Enables you to automatically perform checks based on the customer's required delivery date, backward scheduling to determine product availability date, and then forward scheduling to establish the committed date.

- **Backorder processing (BOP)**: Allows you to perform the order fulfillment based on priorities and business goals alignment. Backorder also helps reallocate inventory and ATP checks on customer orders, according to the current inventory situation and status.

Your customer will also benefit from the GATP, because it uses your customer's priorities to reorganize inventory commitments, realign orders, or perform reliable availability checks in real time, which will help avoid over-commitment.

In the following section, you'll learn how GATP is applicable to your daily activities, and overview some GATP flows and transactions.

D.3   Global ATP for Sales and Distribution

The main ATP run and checks are executed in the Sales and Distribution component inside SAP ERP. ATP checks inside the customer sales orders are performed using two main methods: basic and advanced ATP. We briefly discussed these in the previous section. Now, we'll address the specifics of how the basic method verifies the ATP. Figure D.2 shows us how the ATP flows from a sales customer order into GATP, and the checks that are performed to confirm quantities, either full or partial quantities, depending on the date and available product.

When GATP is active, sales orders move from ECC to APO, and each searches for stock availability. There are three possible outcomes of this search: a finding of full availability, partial availability, or no stock. These findings are based on defined rules. A production planned order can be created as well, and will update the delivery date in the sales order accordingly. In the next section, you'll learn how ATP and GATP compare, and the main differences between them.

Figure D.2 Order Processing in SD and APO Flow

D.3.1   Comparison between ATP and GATP

We've learned that the availability check needs to be comprehensive and accurate, in order to eliminate any impacts to your customers, including over-confirming. In Appendix C, you learned about the traditional ATP checks and how they're executed in the sales orders and deliveries. There's also an availability check at APO. You may wonder what the difference is between them, or if there is any advantage to using one or the other. Table D.2 compares ERP ATP and Global ATP. You may also notice that one of the most important differences between ATP and GATP is that only basic ATP methods are available in ATP, while GATP in SAP SCM enables you to view and have transparency across the full supply chain.

Requirements	ERP – ATP	Global ATP
Availability checks across locations	ATP checks are performed on a single location/product combination	Availability checks are performed across multiple locations
Product substitution	Product substitution is executed manually, especially during product shortages	Product substitution can be modeled during online availability check

Table D.2 Comparison Traditional ATP versus GATP

Requirements	ERP – ATP	Global ATP
Backorder processing (BOP)	Restricted backorder processing	Advanced backorder processing, allowing more flexibility, and sorting using BOP functionality
Production integration	Call of production is not possible	Call of production is possible
ATP verification to the lowest level of components	This feature is not offered	Checks run at multi-level ATP
ATP with reverse logistics and customer returns	This feature is not offered	ATP checks consider customer returns as planned receipts
Inventory verification and searching using different systems	This feature is not offered	ATP checks are performed in several OLTP systems
Fast ATP confirmation	ATP checks are performed using database tables or shared buffers	GATP uses LiveCache technology, which increases ATP confirmation response
Complex ATP verifications	You can only use one basic method	You can use a combination of basic methods
Integration with transportation	Transportation via Shipping and Delivery	GATP offers integration with transportation planning and vehicle scheduling modules to eliminate constraints

Table D.2 Comparison Traditional ATP versus GATP (Cont.)

You'll now learn in more detail how GATP is handled in SD processes, as well as the most commonly used GATP documents. You'll also see how the ATP checks are performed during a sales order in Global ATP.

D.3.2 Global ATP Documents

You can use any of the following documents for GATP. Table D.3 describes the most commonly used ones. However, the main use of Global ATP is during the availability check from the sales order in Sales and Distribution in ECC and CRM.

Document	Samples
SD documents	Sales orders or deliveries
Stock transfers	Stock transfer requisitions and in-plant stock transfer reservations
Component check	Production orders, planned orders, subcontract procurement
Inventory management	Goods issue, check MM, reservation

Table D.3 Commonly Used Documents in Global ATP

With the use of GATP, your customer satisfaction increases, mainly due to the reliable supplier confirmations made available to them. Internally, your logistics, including the logistics with the supply chain, will be improved using GATP. In summary, traditional ATP is recommended if your company operation is simplified, or the number of your locations is limited or highly controlled. This means that traditional ATP offers basic business requirements for ATP checks under a simplified network, while Global ATP provides you with the ability to model complex business variants and rules.

> **Note**
>
> ATP checks may not be appropriate for all industries. As an example, in consumer industries, companies prefer to wait until the delivery document is created for ATP checks, or rely on the production forecast. Make-to-order environments is another example where ATP checks may not be suitable, because the sales order triggers the production order. Your particular industry will dictate what type of ATP is more suitable.

D.3.3 Processing ATP Checks in the Sales Orders Document

The ECC ATP checks and formulas were addressed in Appendix C. You can find further information on how it works and which configuration controls ECC ATP checks in the same appendix. The key ECC ATP characteristics are depicted in Table D.2, and we could describe ECC ATP as a fixed and stable ATP check done based on the material master record.

GATP, just like ECC ATP, can have three main outputs—full confirmation, partial confirmation, or no confirmation. The first case is when ATP is fully confirmed. Figure D.3 illustrates the sales order when full ATP quantities are confirmed based on the customer's REQUIRED DELIVERY DATE. The item level quantity is confirmed, and nothing really happens. This is a similar behavior in both ECC ATP and GATP.

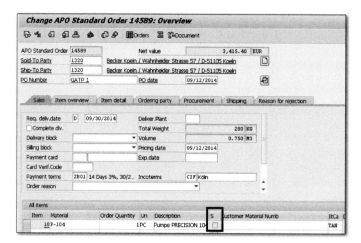

Figure D.3 Sales Order with Completed ATP Check at Requested Delivery Date

Similar to ECC ATP, GATP is controlled by the scenarios that have been configured based on your specific needs. The scope of the GATP check is set in the configuration, as shown in Figure D.4. You may not have access to how this set of configurations is performed, but the items included should be familiar as to what is to be checked or in scope while GATP runs, based on your specific needs and customer scenarios, or the OLTP systems to be used for verification.

The other possible outcomes are partial confirmation or no confirmation. In these situations, GATP has been unable to fully confirm the amount, or has only been able to partially do so. This is due to the activities GATP performed from the following configured scenarios based on your specific needs:

▶ Basic ATP in APO

▶ Rules-based ATP check (product substitution, location substitution, including calculation profile)

▶ Multi-level ATP check

▶ Product allocation check

▶ Capable-to-promise check

▶ Any combination of the above

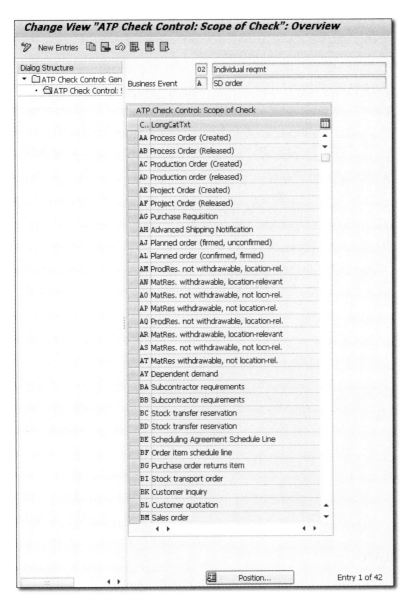

Figure D.4 GATP Scope of the Check Configuration

Each of the scenarios which have been configured for your particular needs will provide a slight variation on the GATP output for partial or no confirmation while processing the sales order. You may see one or more ATP screens to match your individual configuration and your specific GATP needs.

However, in the event of partial ATP confirmation, you'll be prompted for a decision as follows (see Figure D.5):

▶ ONE-TIME DELIVERY: Confirming the partial delivery and closing any future requirements or backorders.

▶ DELIVERY PROPOSAL: Confirming the partial amount based on the proposed date. The sales item remains open for future deliveries and backorders.

▶ ATP QUANTITIES: You'll be presented with an overview of the availability, including receipts, issues and confirmed issues, as well as stocks and simulated requirements.

▶ SCOPE OF CHECK: Display of the availability check and the checking rule, which includes a stock overview, in/outward movements, replenishment lead time, receipts in the past, and storage location inspection.

▶ OTHER PLANTS: You'll be presented with the list of relevant plants where the specific product can be located. Select one or more, or even all of them, and click on CHECK PLANT. You'll be presented with the plant, requirement quantity, requirement date and confirm/allocated quantity. Select an alternative plant accordingly. A new ATP check will be run based on the newly selected plant.

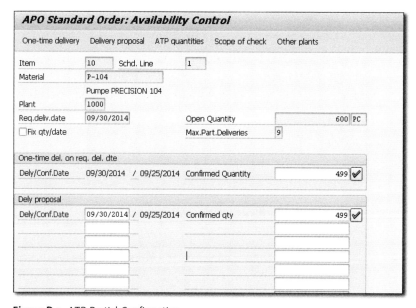

Figure D.5 ATP Partial Confirmation

This scenario is not unique. Depending on the steps followed in your specific checking process, based on the specific business needs and requirements of your own company, you may see different screens than the ones described here. Figure D.6 shows a typical output screen on a Global ATP check, where confirmation is not met at the component levels. Note the use of red, yellow, and green to indicate different confirmation statuses.

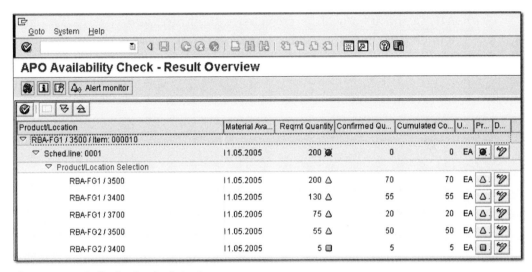

Figure D.6 APO Checks: Results Output

You'll receive other specific ATP outputs and screens in accordance with your configured scenarios. We recommend that you pay close attention to each screen, and get familiar with the possible combinations and outcomes in your company.

E   The Authors

Matt Chudy is an independent SAP Logistics consulting lead. He has more than 17 years of experience in SD, MM, and Logistics, spanning project administration, design, gap-analysis, testing, implementation, and supporting and training. He has been a strong team leader and covered several SAP project lifecycles. His specialties include Logistics Execution System, Transportation Management, Sales and Distribution, Inventory and Warehouse Management, Materials Management, and Production Planning. He currently lives in the greater Chicago area.

Luis Castedo is an independent systems and business consultant with more than 20 years of experience. For the past 15 years, he has been focused on SAP implementations. He has experience working with Fortune 500 companies and on multisite projects. He is a certified SAP MM consultant, and his specialties include Sales and Distribution, Materials Management, Inventory and Warehouse Management, Shipping, and Transportation. He currently lives in the Mexico City area.

Ricardo Lopez is a PMP project manager with SD certification by SAP America. He's a senior manager professional with a solid background coordinating and managing major OTC projects and devising plans and schedules. Ricardo possesses experience in directing worldwide SAP OTC implementations for a wide range of clients worldwide. Ricardo holds SD certified 4.x by SAP Americas with more than eighteen years of consulting experience across applications such as SAP Fiori, SD, FSCM/Biller Direct, and Credit and Dispute Management. He has participated in more than 18 full go-live cycles, and 20 template roll-outs around the globe. He currently lives in the New York City area.

Ricardo would like to thank the following people:

I dedicate this book to my family, especially my mother Eva, from whom I received all the strength I needed to face life, and who has always supported me. I owe it all to her. To my brothers and sisters, Rosaura, Salvador, and Alma Rosa; and my in-laws, nephews, and nieces, for always being the pillars of my life.

A special mention to Dr. Christian Huygen; without his contributions and support, this book would not have been written, and who represents a long-lasting love.

Index

Interested in reading more?

Please visit our website for all new
book and e-book releases from SAP PRESS.

www.sap-press.com